Medieval Culture and Society

Medieval Culture and Society

edited by DAVID HERLIHY

WAVELAND
PRESS, INC.
Prospect Heights, Illinois

For information about this book, write or call:
Waveland Press, Inc.
P.O. Box 400
Prospect Heights, Illinois 60070
(708) 634-0081

Cover Print: Catalogus Gloriae Mundi/New York Public Library
Picture Collection

Preface

лллллллллллллллллллллллллг

The brief bibliographies following each introductory section are meant to suggest to the reader books of broad scope which should be available in most libraries and which constitute, in the editor's opinion, worthwhile introductions to medieval social and cultural history. Some older works are included, but the editor has in the main limited the citations to recent publications. The existence of paperback editions has been noted.

The editor would like to thank his wife, who read the entire manuscript and made numerous suggestions for its improvement. He would also like to express his appreciation to the students he has taught who were members of the Integrated Liberal Studies Program at the University of Wisconsin. Many of the ideas expressed and the readings given in this book were first presented to them, in the freshman course called "Medieval and Renaissance Culture." Through their reactions and comments, the freshmen of "ILS" provided the principal inspiration for this book, and no little part of whatever insight and discernment it may contain.

Madison, Wisconsin
September, 1967

Contents

ᒻᒻᒻᒻᒻᒻᒻᒻᒻᒻᒻᒻᒻᒻᒻᒻᒻᒻᒻᒻᒻᒻᒻᒻᒻᒻᒻ

PART TWO: THE CENTRAL MIDDLE AGES,
CA. 1000–1350

PART THREE: THE LATE MIDDLE AGES, CA. 1350–1500

General Introduction

Essays on medieval civilization require at the outset some definition of that awkward and misleading term, "medieval." Perhaps they also require some apology for its use. For the modern scholarly understanding of the Middle Ages is now much different from the meaning given the concept at its birth. The authors of the notion of a "middle" age (and the creators of its venerable reputation for darkness) were the Italian humanists of the fourteenth and fifteenth centuries. Francesco Petrarch (1304–74), one of the first and greatest of their number, professed a stronger attachment and a closer spiritual kinship to the great classical writers than to his own medieval predecessors. The disdain he expressed for the allegedly idle speculations and bad Latin of the medieval authors soon became the fashionable slogan of the humanist movement. Apparently the first to use the precise words *media tempestas*, or Middle Age, was Giovanni Andrea, bishop of Aleria in Corsica, in a history of Latin poetry published by him in 1469.

Characteristically, the humanists looked upon the centuries separating their own age from the distant brilliance of the classical world as a forlorn and barren time, devoid of memorable cultural achievements. In this Middle Age, good manners and good letters had both sunk nearly out of sight in a sea of triumphant barbarism. Never the victims of false modesty, the humanists roundly congratulated themselves and their times for restoring the arts in which the classical world had excelled. Foremost among those arts were the mastery of good manners and the ability to produce, and to appreciate, good literature.

The modern view of the Middle Ages differs from this traditional concept on several fundamental counts. Confronting a now massive body of evidence, most modern scholars conclude that

Western society in this medieval period must be considered neither stagnant nor uncreative. So considerable were the changes experienced in those centuries that most historians even doubt whether they may appropriately be regarded as parts of a single historical epoch. Europe at about the year 500 pretty much resembled the grim world conjured up and condemned by the humanists. Its predominantly rural society lived a poor, uncouth and often violent life, and achieved little originality in its literature or thought. But Europe by the thirteenth century had attained a much higher level of civilization. It boasted great cities, thriving agriculture and trade, complex governmental and legal systems, crowded and creative universities and magnificent cathedrals. Its literature, philosophy and art may be fairly compared with the finest produced in any other century of Western history.

To do justice to the great and dramatic changes experienced by medieval society, to give recognition to this fundamental fact of growth, scholars today are prone to divide the single Middle Age of traditional historiography into separate epochs, each quite distinct from the others. The chronological division outlined and followed here, although one of many proposed, seems to be gaining considerable favor among historians. The centuries from the fall of the Roman empire in the West to about the year 1000, which may be simply called the "early Middle Ages," have a certain basic unity. These centuries constitute the true "Dark Ages," if any period of Western history really deserves that opprobrious title. They are dark for two reasons. Comparatively few documents have survived to illuminate them for us, and fewer still are the literary or artistic works produced in these times which could be considered major cultural monuments.

But the early Middle Ages still made fundamental contributions to the formation of the new Western civilization. The great theme of their history is the emergence of Europe, and the beginnings of a distinctively Western or European culture. There was no "Europe" in ancient times, in the sense of a traditional association of Western peoples, retaining their identity but sharing certain common cultural assumptions and ideals. This association of peoples, ultimately including Latins, Celts, Germans, Slavs and others, this true Europe of cultural history, was born in the early Middle Ages. It resulted from the divisions of the ancient Roman empire, the migrations of the barbarians, the conquests of the Franks, and the conversions of the Latin Christian Church. The first, truly Western culture was also a product of these centuries. It was based in large part upon a fusion of three prior cultural traditions. These were the classical civilization of the Roman empire, the religious heritage of Judeo-Christianity, and the popular or "vulgar" cultures of the Western peoples, including the barbarians. The early Middle Ages could claim few brilliant cultural accomplishments, but the period did create a stable social and cultural framework for Western civilization and pointed the way towards its later, great achievements.

The years from about 1000 to 1350 form the central or the high Middle Ages. This was the great creative period of medieval civilization. From about the year 1000, European peoples began to grow, in numbers, in territory, in wealth, skills and learning. Against the background of expanding frontiers, crusades, rising towns and a growing trade, medieval society also embarked upon a series of bold cultural innovations. New schools grew up in the cities, and universities developed out of many of them. The university in turn ranks as one of the Middle Ages' most influential institutional creations. Scholars within the schools created a novel and even audacious system of thought known as scholasticism. Medieval culture was enriched with the emergence of distinctive social and literary attitudes concerning women, love, chivalry and romance. For the first time, nearly all the major vernacular tongues of Europe could lay claim to masterpieces, and in all these languages, traditions of literary expression were established which have since remained lively and unbroken. "Modern" European literature, someone has remarked, begins in the twelfth century. Perhaps modern art does too. The art and architecture known as Romanesque which dates from this period is the first great artistic style properly indigenous to the West. It also marks the beginning of a rich tradition of artistic production which has similarly remained continuous to the present. Our modern civilization is in fact much closer in type as well as time to the society and culture of the high Middle Ages than it is to the world of the ancient Mediterranean. For this reason, some historians have dared to see in these transformations of the central Middle Ages a major turning point in Western history, marking the emergence of ideals, attitudes and traditions of behavior which have since remained a permanent part of our own "modern" civilization.

From the early fourteenth century, numerous catastrophes—plagues, famines, wars and social disturbances—struck the medieval world, and this somber experience introduces the third and final period of medieval history. This period is the late or closing Middle Ages (ca. 1350–1500). During these years of dislocations and disasters, medieval civilization changed in tone. A new extravagance and a corresponding lack of balance, restraint and plain good sense appeared in the traditional practices of chivalry and piety. In thought and religion, a new sceptical and critical spirit emerged. Many philosophers and theologians turned to a critical and partially destructive revaluation of older systems of thought and belief. Amid extravagance and criticism, the cultural unity and consensus of the early Middle Ages began to disintegrate. In the fourteenth and fifteenth centuries, the Western world was already moving towards that system of cultural pluralism which has characterized its civilization in the modern age.

In view of the great changes experienced by Western society between 500 and 1500, is there still sufficient reason for speaking of a "middle" age? There seems to be at least one justification for the continued use of the term: Europeans of the period did preserve a certain agreement and consensus, founded upon their allegiance to a single Church and a common ideal of Christendom. The end of that unity—and it was badly weakened well before the Reformation—marks the end of a properly "medieval" culture.

But the term should not suggest, as the humanists intended, that medieval culture is something foreign to our own. Many ideas and ideals of the Middle Ages have exerted a permanent influence upon the culture of the modern world and have been a permanent source of enrichment for it.

In this collection of sources concerned with medieval society and culture, we shall follow this tripartite division of medieval history. The documents assembled for each of these three periods are intended to serve two purposes. An initial selection will illustrate for each period its society and social milieu. The second group of documents will give examples of the chief forms of literary expression and illustrate some of the characteristic cultural attitudes of the age.

In surveying so lengthy a period, the editor is well aware that he has left poorly represented some centuries, some countries, and some types of medieval sources. But no group of selected readings can do justice to the enormous range and volume of the surviving documents of medieval civilization. Perhaps this anthology may at least stimulate in the reader a deeper appreciation for and wider interest in the rich and still living heritage of the medieval world. If it does, then it will have served its purpose.

RECOMMENDED READINGS

Frederick B. Artz, *The Mind of the Middle Ages* (3rd ed., New York: Knopf, 1962).

P. Boissonnade, *Life and Work in Medieval Europe (Fifth to Fifteenth Centuries)*, trans. with an Introduction by Eileen Power (New York: Knopf, 1927; Harper Torchbooks, 1964, TB 1141).

Frederick C. Copleston, *Medieval Philosophy* (London: Methuen, 1952; New York: Harper Torchbooks, 1961, TB 376).

C. G. Crump and E. F. Jacob, *The Legacy of the Middle Ages* (Oxford: Clarendon Press, 1926).

Étienne Gilson, *History of Christian Philosophy in the Middle Ages* (New York: Random House, 1955).

David Knowles, *The Evolution of Medieval Thought* (Baltimore: Helicon Press, 1962; New York: Random House, Vintage V 246).

Paul Lacroix, *France in the Middle Ages. Customs, Classes and Social Conditions* (New York: Ungar, 1963).

Gordon Leff, *Medieval Thought. St. Augustine to Ockham* (Chicago: Quadrangle Books, 1959; Baltimore: Penguin Books, A 424).

Sydney Painter, *Medieval Society* (Ithaca: Cornell University Press, 1951).

Eileen Power, *Medieval People* (10th ed., New York: Barnes and Noble, 1963; University Paperbacks UP 49).

F. J. E. Raby, *A History of Christian-Latin Poetry from the Beginnings to the Close of the Middle Ages* (2nd ed., Oxford: Clarendon Press, 1953).

F. J. E. Raby, *A History of Secular Latin Poetry in the Middle Ages* (Oxford: Clarendon Press, 1934).

H. O. Taylor, *The Medieval Mind* (4th ed., 2 vols., Cambridge: Harvard University Press, 1959).

Part One

The Early Middle Ages,

ca. 500–1000

Introduction

Lᒐᒐᒐ

While it still presents mysteries to historians, the crisis of ancient civilization must be ranked as one of the most radical breaks in the history of human cultural traditions. The character of the new medieval society, as it emerged from the debacle of the Roman empire, was strikingly different from that of its classical predecessor. The formation of this new society was accompanied by an equally profound revolution in values.

A. The formation
of early medieval society and culture

Many social and economic changes marked the transition from the ancient world to the Middle Ages. Slavery, which had been a mainstay of the ancient economy, faded in importance; agriculture came to depend upon the peasant family, settled upon its own farm, rather than upon the gangs of landless slaves who had tilled the great villas of the Roman empire. The active commerce of the ancient Mediterranean world also declined. Trade in the early Middle Ages, at least in the West, was anemic, markets weak and money rare. Communities consciously sought a high level of self-sufficiency, which would free them from a hazardous dependence on distant areas for their needs.

The one social change which best summarizes all these other transformations, and which also casts much light on the character of the new medieval culture, is probably this: the decline and near disappearance of the ancient city, and the emergence in the early Middle Ages of a predominantly, even overwhelmingly rural society.

In nearly all its aspects, ancient civilization reflected the strength and vigor of its urban life. The city was the economic hub of the surrounding region. Estates were run not with an eye to self-sufficiency, but in order to deliver agricultural produce to demanding urban markets. The cities in turn supplied their regions with manufactures and professional services. This lively exchange economy linked together not only city and countryside, but distant regions. The complex commercial economy helped support an equally complex society. The city was crowded with slaves, free artisans, merchants, lawyers and professional men, and civil administrators. It was a society marked by the presence of a strong middle class (in the sense of persons neither very rich nor very poor), but also by wide contrasts in wealth between the extremes of the social scale.

The group with the greatest social weight, the true backbone of ancient society, was made up of well-to-do landlords, who characteristically divided their time between their rural estates and their regional capitals. These were called the *decuriones* or *curiales*. They were distinguished both by their public spirit and their high level of education. They served in their cities as skilled and loyal administrators, often using their personal fortunes for the embellishment of their towns, for the erection of a new amphitheater or aqueduct. The central government at Rome was heavily dependent upon the allegiance and the services of such enlightened men. A great historian of the ancient world, M. I. Rostovtzeff, even described the Roman empire as a federation of city states, held together primarily by the mutual interests and loyalty of the landholding *curiales*.

These men also influenced the culture of the ancient world, particularly in its more literary and learned manifestations. They could read, and were often well-educated; they provided a discerning and appreciative audience for the philosophers and writers of antiquity.

The crisis of the ancient world was accompanied by, and to some measure rooted in, the disintegration of this curial class of public-spirited and educated landlords, and of the ancient city to which they helped give life. The chronology, as well as the causes, of this decline of the ancient city in the West is very obscure. Many historians date it from the fourth and fifth centuries, the period of the barbarian invasions of the empire. Still others believe that cities retained their importance until the seventh century. But there is no doubt concerning the direction of this social movement. By the time of the great Frankish king and emperor Charlemagne (768–814), European society had become predominantly rural in character. Cities, to be sure, did not entirely disappear; they continued to serve as residences for bishops and as fortresses for the defense of the surrounding peasant populations. But they were not important centers, either for the economy or the culture of Carolingian Europe.

The basic unit of Carolingian economic, social and political life had become the large estate, or manor. The manor was a tightly disciplined community of peasants, under the rule and authority of a lord or *seigneur*. Historians still cannot determine the exact importance of the manor relative to other forms of agricultural organization. Undoubtedly many peasants and lands escaped its meshes. But there seems little reason to doubt that the manor was a principal economic and administrative support for the Carolingian empire.

As a unit of economic production, the manor combined small-scale, peasant agriculture with extensive, plantation cultivation. It was physically divided into two parts. Numerous family farms, called most commonly *mansi*, took up a substantial portion of its area, often as much as one-half; the remaining land, worked directly for the lord, was the demesne or seigneurial reserve.

On these manors, landless slaves, who had principally staffed the villas of antiquity, were relatively insignificant. Most manorial inhabitants continued to be described by classical terminology, by such terms as *coloni* (free peasants settled on another's land) or *servi* (a word then drifting on the margins between its classical sense of "slave" and its new medieval meaning of "serf"). But even those technically slaves were usually settled with their families on their own farms. They could not leave the manor, but neither could their farms be taken from them. They had to meet a great variety of rents and charges, but their most important obligation was to devote a certain time, usually three days per week, to the cultivation of the lord's demesne.

The lord was political chief as well as economic boss of the manorial community. He judged the legal disputes of his dependents. He enjoyed certain "banal" rights; he might, for example, own the manor's only mill or wine press, or monopolize the sale of iron or salt. He collected the equivalent of taxes, and could demand special services such as the guarding or repair of the manor house or the conveying of messages. His dependents usually brought him yearly gifts—eggs in the spring or a capon in the fall—in recognition of his position as chief of the manorial community.

The burdens of the serfs were thus quite varied and heavy, but those same burdens were fixed by custom and could not be altered. The serfs enjoyed in turn the protection of the manor, and had an assured, if humble, station in life. Fixed to the soil, they at least knew that their sons would benefit from what improvements they made upon their farms.

In large measure, the contrast between ancient and early medieval culture reflects the differences between the city-dominated society of antiquity and the rural, manorial society of the new medieval world. The population of artisans, skilled businessmen and trained administrators which had filled the ancient cities had all but disappeared. Literacy by Carolingian times had largely become a monopoly of monks and clerics. Even the curial class of well-to-do landlords found no exact correspondent in the new aristocracy of the medieval world. That aristocracy, from which the manorial lords were recruited, consisted of great churchmen and warriors. The lay aristocrats, the knights and nobles, were principally occupied with war, and were trained from youth in the arts of mounted combat. They rarely or never went to school, and rarely if ever learned to read. They had little familiarity with or appreciation of literary or scholarly culture. This lack of a literate lay class helps explain the character, and also the poverty, of early medieval culture.

This emergence in the early Middle Ages of a predominantly rural society of lords and peasants did not mean that all contact with past cultural traditions was broken. Rather, medieval society was already combining elements from classical, Judeo-Christian and barbarian sources to form its own, new values and attitudes.

It remains to evaluate the contributions of each of these traditions to the rise of early medieval culture.

THE CLASSICAL CONTRIBUTION

It is hardly possible to do justice in a few words to the nature and importance of the classical heritage for the Middle Ages. One of the chief characteristics of classical civilization was exactly the extraordinary range and wealth of the ideas and values it nurtured. We can, however, attempt to summarize the classical contribution to medieval culture under two categories. Antiquity passed on to the Middle Ages certain ways of doing things. It also offered to the medieval world certain values—distinctive attitudes, opinions and judgments concerning the purpose of human life and the nature of human fulfillment.

Within this category of ways of doing things, we can list two great classical accomplishments, one touching upon society and the other upon thought. The ancient world developed remarkable skills in organizing human groups effectively. On the intellectual level, it also created vigorous habits and effective techniques of systematic thought.

The Romans were of course the great social organizers of antiquity, the masters of government and administration. Their skill is amply reflected in the growth and lengthy survival of their huge empire, and in their magnificent system of law. The Greeks, on the other hand, had been the leaders in the systematic application of reason to the problems presented by the world about them. However much their many philosophical schools differed, most agreed that the inquiring and reasoning intellect was a serviceable tool in dealing with reality.

Within our second category of values, ancient opinions concerning the meaning and purpose of human life may be grouped under the broad title "classical humanism." In spite of wide disagreements, most philosophical schools of antiquity shared certain basic assumptions. Most of them agreed that the good life or human fulfillment had to be achieved on this earth if it was to be achieved at all. They lacked faith in a world after death, where the defects of present existence might be corrected. Moreover, in seeking his destiny, man could use only what present nature had given him; he could not count on a "super-nature," on extraordinary interventions by divine power, to aid him in his present situation. While strains of pessimism were common in ancient philosophies, most of them held out an encouraging vision of the sufficiency and benevolence of nature. Through reason, through living in conformity with nature, the wise man could at least approach human fulfillment, even if ultimate satisfaction was denied him. This confidence in the possibility of human improvement through natural effort in this life is the essence of classical humanism.

With the triumph of Christianity, these different parts of the classical heritage encountered different fates. The classical traditions of effective social organization and systematic thought weakened in the new rural and barbarized social milieu, but they were not entirely lost. They survived, but in a quite distinctive context: in the service of the dominant institution of the new medieval world, the Christian Church. The Church, itself the child of ancient Mediterranean culture, was profoundly, even if perhaps unwillingly, influenced by its early surroundings. Inevitably, as it grew to become an institution more extensive even than the Roman empire, it adopted and adapted classical techniques of social organization and administration in solving its own complex governmental problems. The juridical character of the powers accorded bishops and the pope, the procedures of ecclesiastical courts, the quality of the new canon law, the organization of monasticism, all reflected the deep influence of Roman legal thinking and practices.

Moreover, Christian writers, and the tradition of Christian theology they developed, were instrumental in preserving at least in part classical rhetoric and logic—the fruits of the ordered intellect of antiquity. This use of classical rhetoric and philosophy in the elaboration of Christian theology was in part an unconscious and inevitable movement. The Christian fathers and writers were educated in the same schools as their pagan contemporaries, and were subject to the same intellectual formation. The Church in the Roman empire was so steeped in classical culture that it did not even consider it desirable or possible to establish a separate system of Christian schools.

Moreover, in spite of much hesitation, the Church eventually allowed its members to make full use of pagan works. In the figure used by St. Augustine, they were permitted to carry off the treasures of the Egyptians, to put them to the service of the new chosen people. There were several reasons for this fateful decision. Christians who wished to refute the attacks of pagans had to utilize, for effective apologetics, the same rhetoric and logic as their opponents. These skills were best learned through the close study of the great pagan authors. Many learned and liberal Christians were also willing to concede that pagan philosophies contained a grain of truth, although much inferior to their own revelation. But the decisive reason for studying the pagan classics was this: Christianity, like Judaism from which it sprang, was a "book" religion. Its theology was dependent upon the correct understanding of the written word. To know God's will as authoritatively revealed in the Bible required a command both of grammar and interpretation or exegesis. For both skills, the study of pagan texts was essential, even when the philosophy and morals they preached were repugnant to the Christian mind. In the service of Christian theology, classical traditions of rhetoric and reasoning were kept alive for the Middle Ages and for later renaissances.

Classical values, as distinct from classical ways of doing things, met a different fate in the early Middle Ages. The Christian religion implicitly rejected the humanist assumption that man's hope was confined to this world, and that only his natural powers could help him achieve the purposes of life. In the strong, "otherworldly" atmosphere of the early Middle Ages, humanistic values were out of favor. But they were never entirely out of mind, perhaps for the reason that the humanistic emphasis on the dignity of reason and the importance of present living had become too ingrained through the classical experience ever to be entirely suppressed.

The real if tenuous survival of humanistic ideas is illustrated by the great popularity in the Middle Ages of a work called the *Consolation of Philosophy*, written by the prominent Roman official Boethius, in 524 or 525. Boethius was then in prison awaiting execution, probably on a charge of treason to the Ostrogothic king of Italy, Theodoric. His work was thus a meditation on his own approaching death. Although he was a Christian, he mentioned in his work neither Christ nor the hope of heaven. While there is nothing anti-Christian in his book, he spoke of death as the pagans had taught him. In spite of the lack of a religious content, the *Consolation* remained one of the most widely read and admired books in the Middle Ages. It survived in hundreds of manuscripts, and King Alfred the Great of England prepared a translation of it into Anglo-Saxon. It continued to suggest to men, at least to the learned, that reason alone could be of value in the confrontation with human problems.

Moreover, the assumptions of classical humanism, while out of favor in the early Middle Ages, still found expression in numerous texts, which scholars routinely encountered as part of their education in grammar and rhetoric. The ideas of classical humanism were thus easily retrievable, and would be retrieved in future revivals of ancient thought.

THE CHRISTIAN CONTRIBUTION

The Christian Church, as we have mentioned, preserved in its government classical traditions of effective social organization, and in its theology, traditions of rhetoric, philosophy and orderly thought. For these reasons alone, it exerted a profound influence upon the medieval world. It also introduced new values into medieval life, which for long held a position of dominance.

Christianity rejected the humanist assumptions that nature was sufficient and benevolent, and that men must seek their destiny in accordance with it. In the Christian viewpoint, nature was defective and in some measure even evil. Through original sin, man had severely injured himself, and was encumbered with a strong penchant for sin. This was known as concupiscence. Through his own unaided powers, he could not hope to avoid sin, gain merit and win heaven. Even the world in which he lived had been thrown out of joint by his fall. He no longer enjoyed the pleasant paradise of Eden, with his wants supplied by a benign and bountiful nature. The world had become cruel to him, and he had to earn his bread through toil and sweat.

Although present nature and his own powers were defective, all hope was not abandoned. God had decided to intervene, to restore His damaged creation and give man another chance to gain salvation. First through the instrumentality of the Jewish people, then through Christ, then through the Christian Church, God was returning to His creation, in order, as it were, to re-create, to guide men through His grace along the ways of His providence.

The Christian thus confronted a world fashioned by a double action of God, by original creation and the nature it established, and by the special, supernatural interventions of grace. The world operated under two economies or managements, one of nature and the other of grace. To find the relationships and the balance between these two operations of God was and has remained perhaps the central problem of Christian theology. This dualistic view has also had a major influence in shaping the cultural attitudes of Christian peoples.

In the early Middle Ages, the God of grace virtually crowded from the scene the God of nature. Most writers of the age, predominantly monks by vocation, expressed indifference or disdain towards the visible world and this present life. For them, the source of order and meaning in the world was not the regular operations of nature, but the miraculous interventions of God. They looked forth on a cosmos troubled by a chaotic and malignant nature, but corrected and reorganized through grace. The extraordinary taste for the miraculous in medieval writings reflects this wish to organize experience around the interventions of grace and the theme of salvation. Early medieval culture, with nature and the present life given low prestige, thus assumes a pronounced ascetic, contemplative and other-worldly tone.

It should perhaps be added that this Christian dualism did not necessarily mean an ascetic rejection of the present world, a denial of its beauties and indifference to its problems. But it did breed an intense dissatisfaction with the present arrangements of life, and a conviction that God intended something better for men. Later in Western history, men would react to this dissatisfaction not by fleeing the world but by attempting to correct it, to bring it closer to what God's providence intended it to be. This is a foremost paradox of Judeo-Christian dualism: its ability to sustain, at different historical epochs, the indifference and inaction of the contemplative, and the passionate commitment of the social reorganizer and reformer.

THE BARBARIAN CONTRIBUTION

One other tradition profoundly influenced the formation of the new medieval civilization: the popular or "vulgar" culture of the people. We know little about the culture of the uneducated masses of the Roman empire. We may guess that it more nearly resembled the culture of the barbarian peoples than that of their own learned and wealthy masters. We are better informed concerning the customs of the barbarian peoples which were coming to form part of the new Europe—the Celts, Germans, Slavs and others. But even here, our knowledge is unfortunately defective. These barbarian societies were peasant or pastoral in character. Before their conversion to Christianity, they made no use of writing. Both their laws and literature had to be preserved by oral tradition. They were not written down until comparatively late dates, and then only under Christian influences.

There is, however, no doubt that the vulgar traditions of the people, both barbarians and Latins, substantially influenced the new medieval society, both in its institutions and in its culture.

The social institutions of the barbarian world reflected two peculiarities of the milieu in which they developed: frequent turbulence and violence, and the weak character of the barbarian kingship and state.

Most barbarian tribes did not even have kings before the period of invasions, and their notions of kingship and authority for long remained irresolute and vague. Without the protection of a strong king, the barbarian had to look to his family or clan to help him survive in his violent surroundings. The barbarian, ever in quest of help, also frequently formed with his fellows associations of mutual assistance. One such was the guild, an association of equals who gave their "brothers" aid in times of need. Unlike the guilds of the later Middle Ages, these barbarian associations had at first no connection with economic life, but were entirely fraternal and religious in character.

Another association of self-help was the *comitatus* or "following." The Roman historian Tacitus, writing in A.D. 98, has left a famous description of this influential institution among the Germans, but it was common to most barbarian societies. In it, young men attached themselves to the person of a senior warrior or chief, followed him to battle, fought for him and, if needed, died with him upon the field. Their chief in turn gave them a share of the booty taken, supported them at his table, and equipped them with arms. This relationship between warriors and chief provided one model for the mutual obligations of vassals and their lord under the later system of feudalism.

With personal security a supreme need, military values saturated barbarian culture. The freeman was first of all a fighter, and he was expected to show courage, generosity, loyalty to comrades and fidelity in service. Barbarian ideals undoubtedly lent to early medieval culture its pronounced military tone.

For the militant barbarians, the most prestigious social type was the hero. The hero fulfilled an essential function in barbarian society. With a weak king and no real state, the hero offered the community its principal hope for protection against the real and imagined enemies which threatened it. He was a savior, although, in keeping with a certain pessimistic cast to barbarian culture, often a doomed one. The Anglo-Saxon epic *Beowulf*, soon to be discussed, gives us perhaps our richest insight into the essential services the hero performed for the weakly organized barbarian society.

Barbarian religious attitudes were equally influential in shaping medieval culture. Barbarian paganism characteristically distinguished two sets of gods at work in the world. The high gods—Thor, Odin and their consorts, to use their Germanic names—reigned in heaven and took an occasional distant interest in the affairs of men. But much closer to human lives was a vast array of minor spirits, who inhabited groves, mountains, fields and streams. These spirits, sprites, leprechauns, might be benign or mischievous in character, but their relations with men could be controlled through spells, incantations, charms and other magical appeals. The barbarians introduced into the medieval world its strong taste for magic and superstition, which were foreign both to classical paganism and Mediterranean Christianity. Churchmen repeatedly condemned superstition, magic and witchcraft in the Middle Ages, but they continued to survive in the beliefs and practices of the people.

The barbarians also discerned in the surrounding world, especially in the forbidding depths of the forests and in the dark sea, horrid dragons and monsters. Nature, especially among the Germans, was taken as a hostile force, and this perhaps reflects the cruel environment of their northern homes.

Appropriating these elements from the past, early medieval society composed its new culture. We shall examine that culture in two of its principal manifestations: the largely Latin, largely monastic culture of the educated; and the vernacular traditions of the people.

B. Monastic culture

From the fall of the Roman empire until the eleventh century, medieval culture in its learned or scholarly forms was nearly a monopoly of Christian monks. An understanding of the spirit and character of Christian monasticism is therefore essential for an appreciation of medieval civilization during the age which some historians call the "Benedictine centuries."

This is not the place to recount in detail the origins and growth of monasticism within the Christian Church. We may only note that the monastic movement in its origins was both late and lay. The hostility and frequent persecutions of the imperial Roman government offered the first Christians ample opportunity for the practice of heroic virtue. The early Church was a bastion of asceticism and heroic sanctity, making much the same demands and offering the same rewards as the later monastic system. With the toleration of Christianity (313) and its establishment later in the century as the empire's official religion, the Church's membership grew rapidly, but its ascetic ardor cooled in comparable measure. Christians who wished to practice a sterner kind of faith took flight from the world, first as hermits living alone in the wilderness, then as "cenobitic" monks, who joined with one another in common communities.

Egypt was the great early center of monasticism, and among its "desert fathers" the first and most influential was St. Anthony (251–356). His life, written by St. Athanasius, was soon translated into Latin and other languages, and set a high ideal for the universal Christian Church. The West was soon producing its own great hermits, such as St. Martin of Tours (d. 397), who had been a soldier. According to a favorite medieval legend, Martin the soldier encountered one winter's day a beggar, who asked for his compassion. With nothing else to offer, Martin gave him half of his military cloak. That night in a dream, Christ appeared to thank him for it; he was wearing the cloak.

An early and strong center of Western monasticism was Ireland. The Irish had been converted to Christianity in the middle of the fifth century through St. Patrick, and their Church soon acquired a strong monastic organization. Irish monks, distinguished by their stern asceticism, roamed through the continent, converting pagans, founding monasteries, reviving learning, and reprimanding the wicked rulers of the day. They dominated Western piety and learning in the sixth and seventh centuries.

In spite of the early strength of Irish monasticism, the principal architect of the Latin monastic life, the man whose rule eventually became the common code of monks living in the West, was St. Benedict of Nursia (ca. 480–ca. 547). Benedict's career was typical of many of these monastic founders. Born in central Italy, the son of rich parents, he was educated at Rome but was soon appalled by its vices. He retreated to the wilderness, and acquired a widespread reputation for sanctity. First at Subiaco (ca. 500–29), then at Monte Cassino (529), he organized monastic communities, and for Monte Cassino he wrote his famous rule.

The great qualities of the Benedictine rule were its clarity and good sense. Benedict wanted his monastery to be a stable community; he invested the abbot with supreme authority and enjoined complete obedience on the brothers. But he also wished his abbot to make no decision without consultation. On important matters, he should seek out the counsel of the entire community, including its youngest members. On less weighty affairs, the advice of the older brothers would be sufficient. Benedict tried to anticipate all the practical and spiritual problems of monastic life, and to legislate concerning them. But he also left his rules flexible enough so that they could be adapted to varying conditions in different parts of Europe. It is not too much to say that his clear and wise rule still shows the inspiration of the Roman governmental genius.

Benedict was also prudent. He wanted all novices or new brothers to serve a trial period of one year before taking vows, so that they could judge the community and the community them. He thought of his monastery as a "school for the service of God," not a place for the performance of individual acts of extreme asceticism. The life of the monk was primarily devoted to the worship of God through the performance of the liturgical hours—regular prayer through the day and night which Benedict called the *opus Dei*, the work of God. All monks, except those exempted for reasons of health, were further expected to perform some manual labor. This obligation helped lend to physical labor a dignity which both the Romans and the barbarians had denied it. At all cost, idleness was to be avoided; it was, as Benedict put it, the "enemy of the soul."

We are here interested in the cultural implications of monasticism. The rule, surprisingly, says nothing about schools. But it implies throughout that the monk would be able to read. The preparation for the monastic life thus required for many an introduction to letters. The monasteries therefore established and maintained schools, for their own novices and even for boys not destined to be monks.

Education and meditation both further required that texts be available, and many monasteries therefore maintained writing offices or *scriptoria*, in which scribes carefully copied out the works of Christian and pagan antiquity. The great majority of texts which have survived from the ancient world have come down to us through copies made by monastic scribes in the early Middle Ages.

Finally, the education and edification of their fellows inspired monastic authors to produce a considerable body of original tracts. These monastic works constitute the core of the Latin literary heritage of the early Middle Ages.

The spirit of these writings eminently reflects the supreme values of the monastic life. The monk was an "impatient angel"; he wanted to live as he believed the angels lived, in the continuing praise of God and contemplation of His wonders. He sought to discern in all things the marvelous work of God, Who always had governed and still was governing the world and leading His people to salvation.

The most wonderful work of God was the Bible itself, and a substantial part of monastic writing is devoted to commentaries upon it. The monastic theology of the early Middle Ages was not, as later scholasticism, speculative or rigorously systematic in character. It was primarily interpretative or exegetical, content with exploring the meanings of the passages without seeking to construct elaborate theological systems from them.

Other works of God deserving attention were the lives of His saints. Hagiography, or the biography of a saint, was one of the most popular forms of monastic literature. The lives combined interesting and even exciting tales with edifying proofs of God's willingness to aid His loved ones. Many of these lives were completely fabricated (perhaps nothing was certainly known about the saint except his name and day of death), but many others are valuable historical sources, and all have great cultural interest.

Monastic scholars were equally interested in history. Both Christianity and Judaism are historically oriented religions. Both hold that history is the scene where God is realizing His plans for His people and the world. The monks therefore studied and preserved the accounts of the past, and carefully recorded the great and small events of their own times. The information they have left us is priceless. But their history again shows their characteristic conviction that the extraordinary interventions of grace, not so much the natural play of events, gave the events of past and present their real interest.

Monastic authors, fairly prolific in the production of educational manuals, theological commentaries, hagiographies and chronicles, were less given to "creative" writing, to producing works of pure imagination. They did, however, turn out a considerable volume of

The King's Library

poetry, written in a great variety of verse forms and meters. They utilized both the classical metrical schemes based on the quantity (long or short) of syllables, and the new meters based on accent. Many of their poetic efforts were in the nature of school exercises, and many of them are of unrelieved dullness. Only in dealing with religious subjects, and especially when intended for liturgical performance, do their poems and hymns tap the wells of authentic sentiment and achieve real quality.

Apart from the composers of hymns, perhaps the most gifted of the creative monastic authors of the early Middle Ages was a lady, Hrotswitha, who served as a nun in Gandersheim in Germany in the middle tenth century. She has left us, besides other, less appealing works, six short dramas, based on an imitation of Terence. They show a real dramatic flair. But such skill and such dramatic interests are otherwise nearly unknown within the monastic, literary tradition.

While not distinguished by great originality, monastic authors still made a major contribution to the growth of European culture. Under difficult circumstances, they kept alive a tradition of scholarship and learning. Their schools and *scriptoria* assured the survival of classical texts and, equally important, the skills to understand them. They retained or revived a knowledge of classical Latin grammar and spread its use through Europe. Through the flexible linguistic tool of medieval Latin, scholars of all nationalities in the West learned to communicate with one another. In real measure, the monks laid the foundations for the continuing cultural unity of western Europe.

C. Vernacular traditions

The learned monks, writing in Latin, still represent only one specialized part of early medieval culture. Alongside this monastic learning was the "vulgar" culture of the people, expressed in their spoken, vernacular languages. Most of their literature, orally expressed, has been lost to us, but some knowledge can be salvaged concerning its character.

All the modern vernacular languages of Europe make their literary debuts in the early or central Middle Ages, but they developed at much different rates and left behind them heritages of varying wealth.

The Romance languages were very slow to be written down in literary form. The Romance or vulgar Latin of the people was too

easily confused with the traditional, "correct" Latin of the learned.
It was long considered poor form to speak this vulgar Latin, and
poorer form to write it. Not until the revival of learning under
Charlemagne did scholars differentiate sharply between the Latin
of erudite discourse and the spoken Romance of the people. In
creating and defining medieval Latin as a distinct language of learning, the Carolingians simultaneously freed the Romance vernaculars to develop as independent languages. The first literary text in
Old French is an oath taken by the sons of Louis the Pious at Strassburg (842). But the great age of medieval Romance literature was
not to dawn until nearly 1100, and it tells us little about earlier,
vernacular culture.

The non-Romance vernaculars, which could not be confused
with Latin, were quicker in developing, but with certain exceptions. The Western Slavs (Slovaks, Czechs, Poles and others) were
late in acquiring a written vernacular literature. From 861, the two
brothers Cyril and Methodius began the conversion of the Slavs of
Moravia, and Cyril is credited with creating an alphabet for their
language. (The "Cyrillic" characters used today in Russian and
other languages of the Eastern and Southern Slavs are probably
later, simplified versions of his original alphabet.) A considerable
literature in Old Church Slavonic grew up, but its real centers were
eastern, in Macedonia, Bulgaria and Russia. A strong preference
for Latin in almost all literary texts long delayed the development
of a written vernacular literature among the Western Slavs.

Of the Celtic languages, the richest was Old Irish. Irish society
was marked by the high social position it accorded to the professional story-teller, the *fili*, and he in turn was expected to know
hundreds of tales, for the entertainment of the kings and people.
A large body of epics and sagas has survived, characteristically
written in prose with poetic interludes. The best of them is probably the *Táin*, which records an attempt at cattle rustling, and the
efforts of the hero Cúchulinn to prevent it. These stories are
marked by ingenuity of plot, by frequent magical interventions,
and by a broad humor—all of which do credit to the Irish imagination. Irish literature has also preserved short lyric poems, which
express an idyllic delight in the beauties of nature, much in contrast
to the somber attitudes of the Germanic tradition. Fragments of
Old Irish are certainly very old, reflecting Celtic life even before
the conversion to Christianity. The bulk of Old Irish writings,
however, has been preserved only in late copies, which present a

mixture of passages from different periods. We have no major
work of Irish literature which could be called entirely and authentically the product of the early Middle Ages.

Germanic or Teutonic languages were especially precocious in
developing, and have preserved our best sources for early medieval
vernacular culture.

Germanic languages are usually divided into four major families.
The first of them to appear in a written text was South-Germanic
or Gothic—the language of the first successful invaders of the
Roman empire. When the Visigoths were still settled beyond the
Danube, a Christian bishop named Ulfilas (ca. 311–83) preached
Christianity to them, and translated the Bible into Gothic. Fragments of this translation have survived, to give us our oldest literary
monument in a Germanic tongue. The Goths in the period of
migrations dispersed throughout the empire, and Ulfilas' Bible is
not only the oldest monument of Gothic, but very nearly the last
(we have besides it only an incomplete commentary on St. John's
Gospel, a fragment of a calendar, and two Latin charters with
interpolated Gothic sentences.) While the Gothic Bible is of great
philological interest, it gives only scant evidence on the character
of early Germanic culture.

A second group of Germanic languages is Central Germanic or
Old German, which is sometimes grouped with Frisian and Anglo-
Saxon as a West Germanic family. The first literary monuments
in Old German date from the Carolingian age, and their preserva-
tion is associated with the Carolingian revival of learning. Christian
missionaries, concerned with advancing their religion among the
unconverted Germans, found it expedient to preserve examples of
their language, or to translate Christian texts into it. Survivals,
however, remain sparse. One of the most interesting is the *Heliand*,
a religious poem of nearly six thousand lines recounting the life
of Christ. It contains a picturesque and revealing effort to make
Christian meekness palatable to the fierce Germans. Christ is presented much as a Germanic hero, with the apostles grouped around
him to form his *comitatus*.

A work of real merit is the short and incomplete poem, the
Hildebrandslied, or *Song of Hildebrand*. This is the oldest heroic
poem in any Germanic language. It tells of the encounter of a warrior father and his son on opposite sides of a field of battle. The
ending is lost, but the fragment succeeds in conveying the pathos
of the situation. However, the great age of medieval German litera-

ture does not begin until much later, after the late tenth century. The greatest medieval German poem, the *Niebelungenlied*, although it tells a story set in the early Middle Ages, was not written down in its present form until about 1200.

Comparably late in appearing as written literature was another family of Germanic languages, North Germanic or Old Norse. Christianity triumphed late in the northern countries, and was already an influence in northern life when the ancient epics and sagas were reduced to writing. Iceland, although newly settled by the Norse, was the great center of Old Norse literary culture. The great medieval masterpiece of the tongue was the prose *Edda*, a collection of tales and historical narratives put together in its present form by Snorri Sturlason about 1222.

Of all the Germanic languages, the richest in terms of age is Anglo-Saxon, or Old English. A considerable body of both prose and poetry has survived. Laws written in Anglo-Saxon have reached us from as early as the reign of Ethelbert of Kent (d. 616). In the ninth century, under King Alfred the Great (871–99), England experienced something of a vernacular renaissance. Alfred revised the laws and probably also supervised the first redaction of the *Anglo-Saxon Chronicle*, a prime source for the history of his kingdom. Alfred or his scholars also translated into Anglo-Saxon Boethius' *Consolation of Philosophy*, Gregory the Great's *Pastoral Care* and *Dialogues*, Orosius' *History against the Pagans*, and Bede's *Ecclesiastical History*.

Old English literature also possesses some examples of lyric poetry. They are not numerous; four manuscripts, copied shortly before or after the year 1000, contain nearly all the survivals. The names of three poets are known to us: Caedmon of Whitby, who according to Bede was the first to treat Christian themes in vernacular verse; Cynewulf, also known for his religious poetry; and Alfred himself, who translated Boethius into rough but charming verse.

The greatest masterpiece of Old English poetry is the epic poem *Beowulf*. It is the only complete heroic epic of early Germanic literature. The difficult problems concerning the circumstances of its composition are later discussed. We may, however, mention here that it possesses extraordinary interest as a document of early medieval vernacular, especially Germanic culture. Furthermore, apart from its documentary interest, it deserves to be considered a literary masterpiece in its own right—the oldest masterpiece in a European vernacular tongue.

These monuments of popular culture offer precious insights into the lives of the peoples of Europe in the early Middle Ages and the values they embraced. This same popular culture continued to act as a major influence in the further growth of medieval culture.

RECOMMENDED READINGS

Christopher Dawson, *The Making of Europe. An Introduction to the History of European Unity* (New York: Sheed and Ward, 1952; Cleveland: Meridian, M 35).

Gerhart Ladner, *The Idea of Reform. Its Impact on Christian Thought and Action in the Age of the Fathers* (Cambridge: Harvard University Press, 1959).

M. L. W. Laistner, *Thought and Letters in Western Europe, A.D. 500 to 900* (2nd ed., Ithaca, New York: Cornell University Press, 1957).

W. W. Lawrence, *Beowulf and the Epic Tradition* (Cambridge: Harvard University Press, 1928).

Jean Leclercq, *The Love of Learning and the Desire for God. A Study of Monastic Culture*, trans. C. Misrahi (New York: Fordham University Press, 1961; New American Library, Mentor MT 432).

E. K. Rand, *Founders of the Middle Ages* (Cambridge: Harvard University Press, 1928; New York: Dover T 369).

H. O. Taylor, *The Classical Heritage of the Middle Ages* (New York: Macmillan Co., 1901; Harper Torchbooks, 1958, TB 1117).

J. M. Wallace-Hadrill, *The Barbarian West: The Early Middle Ages, A.D. 400–1000* (London: Hutchinson, 1962; New York: Harper Torchbooks, 1962, TB 1061).

I. Early medieval society

1. Tacitus' description of Germanic culture

The richest of all ancient sources concerning the Germans is the *Germania*, written by the Roman historian Tacitus in A.D. 98. Although the author himself apparently never visited Germany, many Roman soldiers, administrators and merchants were personally familiar with the region and with the tribes which inhabited it. German captives and slaves were also common at Rome. Through interviewing such persons, Tacitus had ample opportunity to learn about Germanic society. Writing for Romans, he tended to emphasize those qualities of barbarian culture which differed from their own civilization (and which, incidentally, were to be of major influence in shaping the new medieval society). He thus stressed the predominantly rural tone of barbarian life (amounting even to an aversion for cities), the weakness of their kings, the role of kinship ties and of institutions of self-help such as the *comitatus*, and the importance of military virtues among them.

The following selection from the *Germania* gives in their entirety the first twenty-seven chapters, in which Tacitus speaks of the general characteristics of Germanic culture. The translation, slightly modified, is taken from "Germany," trans. Arthur C. Howland, *Translations and Reprints from the Original Sources of European History*, VI, No. 3 (Philadelphia: Department of History of the University of Pennsylvania, 1900), 4–16.

1. Germany proper is separated from the Gauls, the Rhaetians and the Pannonians by the Rhine and the Danube, from the Sarmatians and Dacians partly by the mountains, partly by their mutual fears. The ocean washes its other boundaries, forming deep bays and embracing large islands where various tribes and their kings have become known to us through the disclosures of recent war. The Rhine takes its rise in the steep and inaccessible fastnesses of the

Rhaetian Alps, and, bending slightly to the west, flows into the northern ocean. The Danube, pouring down from the gently sloping ridge of Mount Abnoba, passes the borders of many nations, and finally forces its way through six outlets into the Black Sea; a seventh channel is swallowed up by the marshes.

2. I should say that the Germans themselves were an indigenous people, without any subsequent mixture of blood through immigration or friendly intercourse; for in ancient times it was by sea and not by land that those who wished to change their homes wandered, and the ocean, hostile, as it were, and of boundless extent on the further side, is rarely traversed by ships from our part of the world. And not to mention the danger of the terrible and unknown sea, who indeed would leave Asia or Africa or Italy to seek Germany with its wild scenery, its harsh climate, its sullen manners and aspect, unless, indeed, it were his native country? They tell in their ancient songs, the only kind of tradition and history that they have, how Tuisto, a god sprung from the earth, and his son Mannus were the originators and founders of their race. Mannus is supposed to have had three sons from whose names those nearest the ocean are called Ingaevones, those in the middle country, Hermiones, and the others, Istaevones. Certain people assert with the freedom permitted in discussing ancient times that there were many descendants of the god, and many tribal names, such as Marsi, Gambrivii, Suebi, Vandilii, and that these were their true and ancient names. But the name Germany, they say, is modern and of recent application, since those who first crossed the Rhine and expelled the Gauls, and who are now called Tungri, were then named Germans; thus what had been a tribal, not a national name, spread little by little, so that later they all adopted the newly-coined appellation that was first employed by the conquerors to inspire fear and called themselves Germans.

3. They say that Hercules himself once visited them, and when about to go into battle they sing of him as the first of all heroes. They have also certain songs, by the intonation of which (*barditus*, as it is called) they excite their courage, while they divine the fortune of the coming battle from the sound itself. They inspire or feel terror according to the character of the cheering, though what harmony there is in the shouting is one of valor rather than of voices. The effect they particularly strive for is that of a harsh noise, a wild and confused roar, which they attain by putting

their shields to their mouths so that the reverberation swells their deep, full voices. Ulysses, too, is thought by some to have reached this ocean in those long and fabulous wanderings of his, and to have been cast upon the shores of Germany. They say he built and named Asciburgium, a town on the banks of the Rhine still inhabited; nay even that an altar consecrated by him and inscribed with the name of his father Laertes has been found at the same place, and that certain monuments and tombs with Greek letters on them still exist within the confines of Germany and Rhaetia. I have no mind to argue either for or against the truth of these statements; let each one believe or reject them as he feels inclined.

4. I myself subscribe to the opinion of those who hold that the German tribes have never been contaminated by intermarriage with other nations, but have remained peculiar and unmixed and wholly unlike other people. Hence the bodily type is the same among them all, notwithstanding the extent of their population. They all have fierce blue eyes, reddish hair and large bodies fit only for sudden exertion; they do not submit patiently to work and effort and cannot endure thirst and heat at all, though cold and hunger they are accustomed to because of their climate.

5. In general the country, though varying here and there in appearance, is covered over with wild forests or filthy swamps, being more humid on the side of Gaul but bleaker toward Noricum and Pannonia. It is suitable enough for grain but does not permit the cultivation of fruit trees; and though rich in flocks and herds these are for the most part small, the cattle not even possessing their natural beauty nor spreading horns. The people take pride in possessing a large number of animals, these being their sole and most cherished wealth. Whether it was in mercy or wrath that the gods denied them silver and gold, I know not. Yet I would not affirm that no vein of German soil produces silver or gold; for who has examined? They do not care for their possession and use as much as might be expected. There are to be seen among them vessels of silver that have been presented as gifts to their ambassadors and chiefs, but they are held in no more esteem than vessels of earthenware; however those nearest to us prize gold and silver because of its use in trade, and they recognize certain of our coins as valuable and choose those. The people of the interior practice barter and exchange of commodities in accordance with the simple and ancient custom. They like the old and well known coins, those with milled edges bearing the stamp of a two-horse chariot.

They are more anxious also for silver coins than for gold, not because of any special liking, but because a number of silver coins is more convenient in purchasing cheap and common articles.

6. Not even iron is abundant, as is shown by the character of their weapons. Some few use swords or long spears, but usually they carry javelins, called in their language *framea*, tipped with a short narrow piece of iron but so sharp and so easy to handle that as occasion demands they employ the same weapon for fighting at close range or at a distance. A horseman is content with a shield and a javelin, but the footmen, either nude or lightly clad in a small cloak, rain missiles, each man having many and hurling them to a great distance. There is no particular adornment to their weapons except that their shields are distinguished by the most carefully chosen colors. A few wear cuirasses, but hardly any have helmets of metal or leather. Their horses are noted neither for their beauty nor their speed, nor are they trained to perform evolutions as with us. They move straight ahead or make a single turn to the right, the wheel being executed with such perfect alignment that no man drops behind the one next to him. One would say that on the whole their chief strength lies in their infantry. A picked body of these are chosen from among all the youth and placed in advance of the line where they fight mixed with the horsemen, since their swiftness makes them fully equal to engaging in a cavalry contest. Their number is fixed; there are a hundred from each canton, and from this circumstance they take their name among their own people, so that what was at first a number is now become an appellation of honor. The main body of troops is drawn up in wedge-shaped formation. To yield ground, provided you press forward subsequently, is considered a mark of prudence rather than a sign of cowardice. They carry off the bodies of the fallen even where they are not victorious. It is the greatest ignominy to have left one's shield on the field, and it is unlawful for a man so disgraced to be present at the sacred rites or to enter the assembly; so that many after escaping from battle have ended their shame with the halter.

7. They choose their kings on account of their ancestry, their generals for their valor. The kings do not have free and unlimited power and the generals lead by example rather than command, winning great admiration if they are energetic and fight in plain sight in front of the line. But no one is allowed to put a culprit to death or to imprison him, or even to beat him with stripes

except the priests, and then not by way of a punishment or at the command of the general but as though ordered by the god who they believe aids them in their fighting. Certain figures and images taken from their sacred groves they carry into battle, but their greatest incitement to courage is that a division of horse or foot is not made up by chance or by accidental association but is formed of families and clans; and their dear ones are close at hand so that the wailings of the women and the crying of the children can be heard during the battle. These are for each warrior the most sacred witnesses of his bravery, these his dearest applauders. They carry their wounds to their mothers and their wives, nor do the latter fear to count their number and examine them while they bring them food and urge them to deeds of valor.

8. It is related how on certain occasions their forces already turned to flight and retreating have been rallied by the women who implored them by their prayers and bared their breasts to their weapons, signifying thus the captivity close awaiting them, which is feared far more intensely on account of their women than for themselves; to such an extent indeed that those states are more firmly bound in treaty among whose hostages maidens of noble family are also required. Further, they believe that the sex has a certain sanctity and prophetic gift, and they neither despise their counsels nor disregard their answers. We ourselves in the reign of the divine Vespasian saw Valaeda, who was considered for a long time by many as a sort of divinity; and formerly also Albruna and many others were venerated, though not out of servility nor as though they were deified mortals.

9. Among the gods they worship Mercury most of all, to whom it is lawful to offer human sacrifices also on stated days. Hercules and Mars they placate by the sacrifice of worthy animals. Some of the Suebi sacrifice to Isis. The reason for this foreign rite and its origin I have not discovered, except that the image fashioned like a galley shows that the cult has been introduced from abroad. On the other hand they hold it to be inconsistent with the sublimity of the celestials to confine the gods in walls made by hands, or to liken them to the form of any human countenance. They consecrate woods and sacred groves to them and give the names of the deities to that hidden mystery which they perceive by faith alone.

10. They pay as much attention as any people to augury and lots. The method of casting lots is uniform. They cut off a branch from a fruit-bearing tree and divide it into small wands marked with

certain characters. These they throw at random on a white cloth. Then the priest of the tribe, if it is a matter concerning the community, or the father of the family in case it is a private affair, calling on the gods and keeping his eyes raised toward the sky, takes up three of the lots, one at a time, and then interprets their meaning according to the markings before mentioned. If they have proven unfavorable there can be no further consultation that day concerning that particular matter; but if they are favorable, the confirmation of auspices is further demanded. Even the practice of divination from the notes and flight of birds is known; but it is peculiar to this people to seek omens and warnings from horses also. These sacred animals are white and never defiled by labor, being kept at public expense in the holy groves and woods. They are yoked to the sacred chariot by the priest and the king or chief of the tribe, who accompany them and take note of their neighing and snorting. In no other kind of divination is there greater confidence placed either by the common people or by the nobles; for the priests are considered merely the servants of the gods, but the horses are thought to be acquainted with their counsels. They have another sort of divination whereby they seek to know the result of serious wars. They secure in any way possible a captive from the hostile tribe and set him to fight with a warrior chosen from their own people, each using the weapons of his own country. The victory of the one or the other is accepted as an indication of the result of the war.

11. Concerning minor matters the chiefs deliberate, but in important affairs all the people are consulted, although the subjects referred to the common people for judgment are discussed beforehand by the chiefs. Unless some sudden and unexpected event calls them together they assemble on fixed days either at the new moon or the full moon, for they think these the most auspicious times to begin their undertakings. They do not reckon time by the number of days, as we do, but by the number of nights. So run their appointments, their contracts; the night introduces the day, so to speak. A disadvantage arises from their regard for liberty in that they do not come together at once as if commanded to attend, but two or three days are wasted by their delay in assembling. When the crowd is sufficient they take their places fully armed. Silence is proclaimed by the priests, who have on these occasions the right to keep order. Then the king or a chief addresses them, each being heard according to his age, noble blood, reputa-

tion in warfare and eloquence, though more because he has the power to persuade than the right to command. If an opinion is displeasing they reject it by shouting; if they agree to it they clash their spears. The most complimentary form of assent is that which is expressed by means of their weapons.

12. It is also allowable in the assembly to bring up accusations and to prosecute capital offenses. Penalties are varied to suit the crime. Traitors and deserters are hung to trees. Shirkers and cowards and those guilty of infamous crimes are cast into the mire of swamps with a hurdle placed over their heads. This difference of penalty looks to the distinction that crime should be punished publicly while infamy should be hidden out of sight. Lighter offences also are punished according to their degree, the guilty parties being fined a certain number of horses or cattle. A part of the fine goes to the king or the tribe, part to the injured party or his relatives. In these same assemblies are chosen the magistrates who decide suits in the cantons and villages. Each one has the assistance of a hundred associates as advisers and with power to decide.

13. They undertake no business whatever either of a public or a private character save they be armed. But it is not customary for any one to assume arms until the tribe has recognized his competence to use them. Then in a full assembly some one of the chiefs or the father or relatives of the youth invest him with the shield and spear. This is the sign that the lad has reached the age of manhood; this is his first honor. Before this he was only a member of a household, hereafter he is a member of the tribe. Distinguished rank or the great services of their parents secure even for mere striplings the claim to be ranked as chiefs. They attach themselves to certain more experienced chiefs of approved merit; nor are they ashamed to be looked upon as belonging to their retinues [*comitatus*]. This order of companions even has different ranks, assigned by the judgment of its leader. There is great rivalry among these companions as to who shall rank first with the chief, and among the chiefs as to who shall have the most and the bravest followers. It is an honor and a source of strength always to be surrounded by a great band of chosen youths, for they are an ornament in peace, a defence in war. It brings reputation and glory to a leader not only in his own tribe but also among the neighboring peoples if his following is superior in numbers and courage; for he is

courted by embassies and honored by gifts, and often his very fame decides the issue of wars.

14. When they go into battle it is a disgrace for the chief to be outdone in deeds of valor and for the followers not to match the courage of their chief. Furthermore, for any one of the followers to have survived his chief and come unharmed out of a battle is life-long infamy and reproach. It is an accordance with their most sacred oath of allegiance to defend and protect him and to ascribe their bravest deeds to his renown. The chief fights for victory; the men of his retinue, for their chief. If the tribe to which they belong sinks into the lethargy of long peace and quiet, many of the noble youths voluntarily seek other tribes that are still carrying on war, because a quiet life is irksome to the Germans and they gain renown more readily in tne midst of perils, while a large following is not to be provided for except by violence and war. For they look to the liberality of their chief for their war-horse and their deadly and victorious spear; the feasts and entertainments, however, furnished them on a homely but liberal scale, fall to their lot as mere pay. The means for this bounty are acquired through war and plunder. Nor could you persuade them to till the soil and await the yearly produce so easily as you could induce them to stir up an enemy and earn glorious wounds. Rather, they even think it tame and stupid to acquire by their sweat what they can purchase by their blood.

15. In the intervals of peace they spend little time in hunting but much in idleness, given over to sleep and eating; all the bravest and most warlike do nothing, while the hearth and home and the care of the fields are given over to the women, the old men and the various infirm members of the family. The masters lie buried in sloth by that strange contradiction of nature that causes the same men to love indolence and hate peace. It is customary for the several tribesmen to present voluntary offerings of cattle and grain to the chiefs which, though accepted as gifts of honor, also supply their wants. They are particularly delighted in the gifts of neighboring tribes, not only those sent by individuals, but those presented by states as such—choice horses, massive arms, embossed plates and armlets. We have now taught them to accept money also.

16. It is well known that none of the German tribes live in cities, nor even permit their dwellings to be closely joined to each other. They live separated and in various places, as a spring or a meadow

or a grove strikes their fancy. They lay out their villages not as with us in connected or closely-joined houses, but each one surrounds his dwelling with an open space, either as a protection against conflagration or because of their ignorance of the art of building. They do not even make use of rough stones or tiles. They use for all purposes undressed timber, giving no beauty or comfort. Some parts they plaster carefully with earth of such purity and brilliancy as to form a substitute for painting and design in color. They are accustomed also to dig out subterranean caves which they cover over with great heaps of manure as a refuge against the cold and a place for storing grain, for retreats of this sort render the extreme cold of their winters bearable and, whenever an enemy has come upon them, though he lays waste the open country he is either ignorant of what is hidden underground or else it escapes him for the very reason that it has to be searched for.

17. Generally, their only clothing is a cloak fastened with a clasp, or if they haven't that, with a thorn; this being their only garment, they pass whole days about the hearth or near a fire. The richest of them are distinguished by wearing a tunic, not flowing as is the case among the Sarmatians and Parthians, but close-fitting and showing the shape of their limbs. There are those, also, who wear the skins of wild beasts, those nearest the Roman border in a careless manner, but those further back more elegantly, as those do who have no better clothing obtained by commerce. They select certain animals, and stripping off their hides sew on them patches of spotted skins taken from those strange beasts that the distant ocean and the unknown sea bring forth. The women wear the same sort of dress as the men except that they wrap themselves in linen garments which they adorn with purple stripes and do not lengthen out the upper part of the tunic into sleeves, but leave the arms bare the whole length. The upper part of their breasts is also exposed. However, their marriage code is strict, and in no other part of their manners are they to be praised more than in this. For almost alone among barbarian peoples they are content with one wife each, excepting those few who because of their high position rather than out of lust enter into more than one marriage engagement.

18. The wife does not bring a dowry to the husband, but the husband to the wife. The parents and relatives are present at the ceremony and examine and accept the presents—gifts not suited

to female luxury nor such as a young bride would deck herself
with, but oxen, a horse and bridle and a shield together with a
spear and sword. In consideration of these offerings the wife is
accepted, and she in her turn brings her husband a gift of weapons.
This they consider as the strongest bond, these as their mystic
rites, their gods of marriage. Lest the woman should think herself
excluded from aspiring to share in heroic deeds and in the dangers
of war, she is admonished by the very initiatory ceremonies of
matrimony that she is becoming the partner of her husband's labors
and dangers, destined to suffer and to dare with him alike in peace
and in war. The yoke of oxen, the caparisoned horse, the gift of
arms, give this warning. So must she live, so must she die. What
things she receives she must hand down to her children worthy
and untarnished and such that future daughters-in-law may receive
them and pass them on to her grandchildren.

19. Thus they live in well-protected virtue, uncorrupted by the
allurements of shows or the enticement of banquets. Men and
women alike know not the secrecy of correspondence. Though
the race is so numerous, adultery is very rare, its punishment being
immediate and inflicted by the injured husband. He cuts off the
woman's hair in the presence of her kinsfolk, drives her naked
from his house and flogs her through the whole village. Indeed, the
loss of chastity meets with no indulgence; neither beauty, youth
nor wealth can procure the guilty woman a husband, for no one
there laughs at vice, nor is corrupting and being corrupted spoken
of as the way of the world. Those tribes do better still where
only the virgins marry and where the hope and aspiration of
married life is done with once for all. They accept one husband,
just as they have one body and one life, that they may have no
thought beyond this, no further desire; that their love may be
as it were not for the married state, but for the husband. To limit
the number of children or to put any of the later children to death
is considered a crime, and with them good customs are of more
avail than good laws elsewhere.

20. In every household the children grow up naked and unkempt
into that lusty frame and those sturdy limbs that we admire. Each
mother nurses her own children; they are not handed over to
servants and paid nurses. The lord and the slave are in no way to
be distinguished by the delicacy of their bringing up. They live
among the same flocks, they lie on the same ground, until age
separates them and valor distinguishes the free born. The young

men marry late and their vigor is thereby unimpaired. Nor is the marriage of girls hastened. They have the same youthful vigor, the same stature as the young men. Thus well-matched and strong when they marry, the children reproduce the robustness of their parents. An uncle shows the same regard for his sister's children as does their own father. Some tribes consider this relationship more sacred and binding than any other, and in taking hostages lay special stress upon it on the ground that they secure thus a stronger hold on the mind and a wider pledge for the family. A man's heirs and successors, however, are his own children, and no wills are made. If there are no children the next heirs are the brothers, then come the paternal and maternal uncles. The more relatives a man has and the greater the number of his connections, the more honored is his old age. Childlessness has no advantages. 21. A German is required to adopt not only the feuds of his father or of a relative, but also their friendships, though the enmities are not irreconcilable. For even homicide is expiated by the payment of a certain number of cattle, and the whole family accepts the satisfaction, a useful practice as regards the state because feuds are more dangerous where there is no strong legal control.

No other race indulges more freely in entertainments and hospitality. It is considered a crime to turn any mortal man away from one's door. According to his means each one receives those who come with a well-furnished table. When his food has been all eaten up, he who had lately been the host becomes the guide and companion of his guest to the next house, which they enter uninvited. There is no distinction among guests; they are all received with like consideration. No one makes any difference between friend and stranger so far as concerns the rights of hospitality. If the guest on going away asks for any gift, it is customary to grant it to him, and the host on his side feels the same freedom from constraint in making a request. They take great pleasure in presents, but they do not reckon them as favors nor do they put themselves under obligations in accepting them. 22. As soon as they awake from sleep, which they prolong till late in the day, they bathe, usually in warm water as their winter lasts a great part of the year. After the bath they take food, each sitting in a separate seat and having a table to himself. Then they proceed to their business or not less often to feasts, fully armed. It is no disgrace to spend the whole day and night in drinking.

Quarreling is frequent enough as is natural among drunken men, though their disputes are rarely settled by mere wrangling, but oftener by bloodshed and wounds. Yet it is at their feasts that they consult about reconciling enemies, forming family alliances, electing chiefs, and even regarding war and peace, as they think that at no other time is the mind more open to fair judgment or more inflamed to mighty deeds. A race without natural or acquired cunning still continues to disclose the secret thoughts of the heart in the freedom of festivity. Therefore at such a time the minds of all are free and unconstrained. On the next day the matter is reconsidered and a particular advantage is secured on each occasion. They take counsel when they are unable to practice deception; they decide when they cannot be misled.

23. A liquor for drinking bearing a certain resemblance to wine is made by the process of fermentation from barley or other grain. Those next to the border also buy wine. Their food is of a simple kind, wild fruit, fresh game or curdled milk. They satisfy their hunger without elaborate preparation and without the use of condiments. In the matter of thirst they do not use the same temperance. If you should indulge their love of drink by furnishing them as much as they wanted, they might be conquered more easily by their vices than by arms.

24. As to games, but one and the same kind is seen in all their gatherings. Naked youths who make profession of this exhibition leap and dance among swords and spears that threaten their lives. Constant practice has given them skill, skill has given them grace. Still they do not indulge in this pastime with a view to profit. The pleasure of the spectators is the reward for their recklessness, however daring. They indulge in games of chance, strange as it may seem, even when sober, as one of their serious occupations, with such great recklessness in their gains and losses that when everything else is gone they stake their liberty and their own persons on the last and decisive throw. The loser goes into voluntary slavery. Though he may be the younger and the stronger of the two, he suffers himself to be bound and led away. Such is their stubbornness in a bad practice. They themselves call it honor. They sell slaves of this description to others that they may not feel the shame of such a success.

25. But they do not employ slaves as we do with distinct functions prescribed throughout the establishment. Each has his own domicile

and rules his own house. The lord exacts a certain amount of grain or cloth or a certain number of cattle as in the case of a tenant and this is the extent of his servitude. Other duties, those of the household, are performed by the lord's wife and children. To beat a slave or to punish him with chains and task work is rare. They occasionally kill one, not in the severity of discipline but impetuously and in sudden wrath as they would kill an enemy, except that the deed goes without punishment. Freedmen do not rank much above slaves; they are not of much account in the household and never in the state, except only in those tribes that are ruled by kings. For there they are elevated above the free born and the nobles. The inferior position of the freedman elsewhere is the mark of the free state.

26. To trade with capital and to let it out at interest is unknown, and so it is ignorance rather than legal prohibition that protects them. Land is held by the villages as communities according to the number of cultivators, and is then divided among the freemen according to their rank. The extent of their territories renders this partition easy. They cultivate fresh fields every year and there is still land to spare. They do not plant orchards nor lay off meadow-lands nor irrigate gardens so as to require of the soil more than it would naturally bring forth of its own richness and extent. Grain is the only tribute exacted from their land, whence they do not divide the year into as many seasons as we do. The terms winter, spring and summer have a meaning with them, but the name and blessings of autumn are unknown.

27. There is no pomp in the celebration of their funerals. The only custom they observe is that the bodies of illustrious men should be burned with certain kinds of wood. They do not heap garments and perfumes upon the funeral pile. In every case a man's arms are burned with him, and sometimes his horse also. They believe that stately monuments and sculptured columns oppress the dead with their weight; the green sod alone covers their graves. Their tears and lamentations are quickly laid aside; sadness and grief linger long. It is fitting for women to mourn, for men to remember.

Such are the facts I have obtained in general concerning the origin and customs of the Germans as a whole. Now I will mention the institutions and rites of the separate tribes in so far as they differ from one another, and speak of the nations that have wandered over into Gaul.

[In the concluding part of the *Germania*, chapters 28 to 46, Tacitus goes on to describe the names and locations of more than fifty Germanic tribes.]

⌐⌐⌐⌐⌐⌐⌐⌐⌐⌐⌐⌐⌐⌐⌐⌐⌐⌐⌐⌐⌐

2. Martin of Braga, *On the Correction of Peasants*

One of the great gaps in our knowledge of early medieval society is the "vulgar" culture—the customs, attitudes and values—of the uneducated and illiterate peasant masses. One precious source which casts some light on the beliefs of the rural population is a sermon written by a Spanish bishop and saint, Martin of Braga, who lived from ca. 510/20 to 579. It is called *De correctione rusticorum*, and warns the peasants against such pagan practices as calling days of the week after pagan gods, or beginning the year on January 1. It illustrates the strong persistence of pagan attitudes and practices well into the Middle Ages.

The Latin text of the *De correctione* is published in *Martini episcopi bracarensis opera omnia*, ed. C. W. Barlow (New Haven: Yale University Press for the American Academy in Rome, 1950), pp. 159–203. The translation here given is by D. Herlihy.

H ERE begins the letter of the saint and bishop Martin to Bishop Polemius, on the correction of peasants.

Bishop Martin to the most blessed lord and brother in Christ Bishop Polemius, whom I miss sorely.

1. I have received the letter of your holy charity, in which you write to me that I should send to you some things written on the origin of idols and on their crimes, a few words on a large subject, for the chastisement of peasants who, still restrained by the former superstition of the pagans, pay more honor to demons than to God. But since it is necessary to provide, as a kind of appetizer, some little information on the reason for their existence from the beginning of the world, I have had to treat the gigantic forest of past times and deeds in abbreviated speech of slight weight, and to prepare food for the rustics in rustic language. And therefore, with God aiding you, this shall be the beginning of your sermon.

2. We wish, dearly beloved sons, to announce to you in the name of the Lord things which either you have not heard at all or perhaps, having heard them, you have consigned them to oblivion. Therefore we beseech your charity to listen attentively to these things which are said for your salvation. There is indeed much detail laid out through Holy Scriptures, but in order that you may retain at least a little in memory, we give you few words on many things.

3. When in the beginning God made heaven and earth, he created in that heavenly abode spiritual creatures, that is, angels, who would stand in his sight and praise him. Of these, one was an archangel who had been made the first among all the angels. He saw himself shining in such glory, that he did not give honor to God his creator, but said he was equal to him. For this pride he was cast down from that heavenly habitation in the air which is under heaven. Many other angels who supported him fell with him. And he, who had been an archangel before, lost the light of his glory and became a dark and horrible devil. Likewise those other angels who agreed with him had been cast down with him from heaven. Having lost their splendor, they became demons. However, the remaining angels who were subject to God, continued in splendid glory in the sight of God. And they are called the holy angels. Those who with their prince Satan were cast down for their pride are called the fugitive angels and demons.

4. After this angelic ruin it pleased God to form man from the slime of the earth. He placed him in Paradise, and said to him that, if he obeyed the command of the Lord, he would attain without death that heavenly place whence those fugitive angels fell. If, however, he should disobey the command of God, he would die the death. The devil saw that man had been made for this reason, that he might succeed in his place in the kingdom of God, whence he himself had fallen. Moved by envy, he persuaded man that he should break the commands of God. For this offense man was thrown down from Paradise into the exile of this world, where he suffers many labors and pains.

5. The first man was called Adam, and his wife, whom God created from his flesh, was called Eve. From these two the entire race of men is descended. Men, forgetting God their creator and committing many crimes, provoked God to wrath. For this reason God sent a flood and destroyed all men, saving one just man, by the name of Noe, whom he preserved with his sons in order to

restore the human race. From the first man Adam to the flood there passed 2242 years.

6. After the flood the human race was again restored through the three sons of Noe, who had been saved with their wives. When the growing multitude began to fill the earth, men again forgot God the creator of the world. They began to worship creatures, ignoring God. Some adored the sun, others the moon or the stars, others fire, others deep seas or streams of water. They believed not that all these things had been made by God for the use of men, but that they were gods arisen from themselves.

7. Then the devil with his ministers the demons, who were cast down from heaven, saw that ignorant men, ignoring God their creator, were erring through creatures. They began to show themselves to men in diverse forms, to speak with them and to ask of them, that they offer sacrifices to them in the high mountains or in thick forests and that they worship them as God. They took for themselves the names of wicked men, who had led their lives in all crimes and impieties. Thus, one said he was Jupiter, who had been a magician and who was unchaste in so many adulteries that he took as wife his own sister, who was called Juno. He corrupted his own daughters Minerva and Venus, and basely debauched his nieces and all his relatives. Another called himself Mars; he was a perpetrator of arguments and discord. Still another demon called himself Mercury, and he was the crafty inventor of all theft and fraud. Avaricious men sacrificed to him as to the god of profit; they did this by throwing stones together into piles of rocks at crossroads. Another demon took for himself the name of Saturn, who lived in all cruelty and even ate the sons born to him. Another demon also pretended to be Venus, who was a woman prostitute. She played the prostitute not only with countless adulterers, but also with her own father Jupiter and with her own brother Mars.

8. Behold what sort of people these wretched men were at that time, whom ignorant peasants through their delusions most wickedly honored. Their names the demons assumed for themselves, so that men should honor them as gods and offer sacrifices to them and imitate the deeds of those whose names they invoke. The demons also persuaded them to make temples for them and to place there pictures and statues of reprobate men and set up altars to them. On the altars they spilt in their honor the blood not only of animals but also of men. Moreover, many demons from among those who were expelled from heaven presided over

the sea or rivers or streams or forests. Men, ignoring God, worship
these also as gods and sacrifice to them. And in the sea they call
one Neptune, and in rivers Lamias, in streams Nymphs, in the
forests Dianas. All these beings are wicked demons and bad spirits,
who injure and vex unfaithful men, who do not know how to
protect themselves with the sign of the cross. However, they
injure them not without the permission of God, because they have
angered God and do not believe with their whole heart in the faith
of Christ. But they are so much without faith that they give the
names of the demons to individual days, and they name a day
of Mars and of Mercury and of Jupiter and of Venus and of
Saturn. These created no day but were wicked men and criminals
among the race of the Greeks.

9. However, God Almighty, when he made heaven and earth,
himself then created light, which was turned seven times according to the division of his works. On the first revolution, God made
light, which was called the day; on the second, the firmament of
heaven was made; on the third, the land was divided from the sea;
on the fourth, the sun and moon and stars were made; on the fifth,
the quadrupeds and flying things and swimming things; on the
sixth, man was formed; however, on the seventh day, as the whole
world and its ornament were completed, God called for a rest. One
light, therefore, which was first made among the works of God,
which was revolved seven times according to the different works
of God, was called a week. What folly is it, therefore, that a man
baptized in the faith of Christ should not observe the Lord's day,
in which Christ rose, and should say that he honors the day of
Jupiter and Mercury and Venus and Saturn, who have no day, but
were adulterers and magicians and evil men and died badly in their
provinces. But, as we have stated, under the form of these names,
stupid men give worship and honor to demons.

10. Likewise this error holds ignorant and rustic men, that they
think that January 1 is the beginning of the year. This is altogether most false. For, as Sacred Scripture says, the beginning
of the year was established on March 25 at the time of the
equinox. For thus is it written: *and God divided the light from the
darkness* (Genesis 1:4). For all right division has equality, as on
March 25 the day has the same length of hours as the night. And
therefore it is false that the beginning of the year is on January 1.

11. What should be said in sorrow concerning this most stupid
error: they observe days of moths and mice and, if it is allowed

to say it, a Christian man venerates mice and moths in place of God? If the protection of a cupboard or casket did not keep bread or cloth away from these pests, they would by no means spare whatever they might find, in spite of the feasts in their honor. However, the miserable man makes these prognostications without cause; as if, should he be sated and happy with all things in the beginning of the year, thus it will be with him throughout the year. All these auguries of the pagans are interpreted according to the inventions of the demons. But woe to that man who may not have had a merciful God and who may not have received from him satiety of bread and security of life! Behold, you perform these vain superstitions either secretly or openly, and never refrain from these sacrifices of the demons. And why do they not grant to you that you are always full and secure and happy? Why, when God is angry, do not the empty sacrifices defend you from the locust, the mouse and from the many other tribulations, which an angry God sends upon you?

12. Do you not fully understand that the demons are deceiving you in these your views which you hold vainly, and that they deceive you in the auguries which you attend so frequently. For as the most wise Solomon said: *divinations and omens are vanities* (Eccl. 34:5); and the more a man has fear of these things, so much the more is his heart deceived. *Set not thy heart upon them, for dreams have deceived many* (ibid. 34:6–7). Behold, Sacred Scripture says this, and it is most certain. As long as demons persuade unhappy men through the voices of birds, until they lose even the faith of Christ through silly and empty things, they themselves will encounter the destruction of their own death without warning. God has not ordered man to know future things. He has ordered him to live always in his fear, and to seek from him guidance and aid in his life. It is God's alone to know something before it happens. Demons, however, deceive men with diverse arguments, until they lead them to offend God and they drag their souls with them into hell. From the beginning they have done this out of envy, lest man should enter the kingdom of heaven, from which they were thrown out.

13. For this reason, when God saw that miserable men were so deceived by the devil and his bad angels that, forgetting their creator, they adored demons for God, he sent his Son, that is wisdom and his word, to lead them back from the error of the devil to the worship of the true God. Because the divinity of the

Son of God could not be seen by men, he took on human flesh from the womb of the Virgin Mary, conceived not by marriage with a man, but by the Holy Spirit. The Son of God was born, therefore, into human flesh, invisible God concealed within but on the outside a visible man. He preached to men and taught them to escape from the power of the devil, leaving behind idols and evil works, and to return to the worship of their creator. After he taught, he wished to die for the human race. He suffered death voluntarily, under no compulsion. He was crucified by the Jews under the judge Pontius Pilate, who, a native of the province of Pontus, at that time ruled the province of Syria. Taken down from the cross, he was placed in a sepulcher; the third day he rose again alive from the dead, and for forty days lived with his twelve disciples. In order to show them that his true flesh had been resurrected, he ate after the resurrection before his disciples. After forty days had passed, he ordered his disciples to proclaim to all nations the resurrection of the Son of God. They should baptize them in the name of the Father and of the Son and of the Holy Spirit in remission of their sins, and they should teach those who were baptized to abandon evil works, that is, idols, murders, thefts, perjury, and fornication. They should not do to others what they did not want done to themselves. After he commanded these things, he ascended into heaven in the sight of these disciples. There he sits at the right hand of the Father, from whence at the end of this world he shall come with that flesh which he took with himself into heaven.

14. When the end of this world shall come, all nations and every man who took their origin from these first men, that is, from Adam and Eve—all shall rise, both the good and the evil. All shall come before the judgment seat of Christ. Those who were in their lives faithful and good are then separated from the evil. They enter into the kingdom of God with the holy angels. Their souls shall be with their flesh in eternal rest, never again to die. There shall be for them neither labor nor pain nor sorrow nor hunger nor thirst nor heat nor cold nor darkness nor night. Forever happy, satisfied, they shall be like to the angels of God in splendor and glory, for they merited to enter into the place whence the devil with his like-minded angels fell. There all who have been faithful to God shall remain for eternity. But those who have not believed or were not baptized or, if they might have been baptized, returned after their baptism to idols and murders or adulteries or perjuries and

other evils and died without penance—all who may be found such are damned with the devil and with all the demons whom they worshipped and whose work they did. They are sent into eternal fire with their flesh in hell. There unquenchable fire burns forever, and the flesh already received from the resurrection is tortured forever, groaning. The flesh wishes again to die, so that it may not feel the pains, but it is not allowed to die, so that it may bear eternal tortures. Behold, this says the law, this say the prophets, these things the gospel of Christ, these things the Apostle, these things the entire Holy Scripture attests. We saw these things simply to you now, a few things out of many. Yours it is from now on, dearly beloved sons, to remember the things which we have said. By doing good, hope for future rest in the kingdom of God, or (God forbid!) by doing evil, expect perpetual fire to come in hell. For both eternal life and eternal death are placed in the decision of man. Whatever each one chooses for himself, this he shall have.

15. You therefore, faithful people, who have come to Christ's baptism in the name of the Father and of the Son and of the Holy Spirit, consider what sort of agreement you made with God in that baptism. For when you individually gave your name at the baptismal font, as, for example, Peter or John or any name, you were asked this by the priest: "How are you called?" You answered, if you were already able to answer or, at any rate, he answered who made faith for you, "He is called John." The priest then asked: "John, do you renounce the devil and his angels, his worship and his idols, his thefts and frauds, fornications and his drunkenness, and all his evil works?" You answered: "I do renounce." After this renunciation of the devil you were asked again by the priest: "Do you believe in God the Father Almighty?" You answered: "I do believe." "And in Jesus Christ His only Son, God and our lord, who was born of the Holy Spirit from the Virgin Mary, suffered under Pontius Pilate, was crucified and was buried; he descended into hell, the third day he rose again from the dead; he ascended into heaven; he sits at the right hand of the Father, from whence he shall come to judge the living and the dead. Do you believe?" And you answered: "I do believe." And again you were asked: "Do you believe in the Holy Spirit, the holy Catholic Church, the remission of all sins, the resurrection of the flesh, and life everlasting?" And you answered: "I do believe." Behold, therefore, and consider what agreement you made with God in baptism.

You promised to renounce the devil and his angels and all his
evil works, and you confessed that you believed in the Father and
the Son and the Holy Spirit and that you hoped for the resurrection of the flesh in the end of the world and life everlasting.
16. Behold by what sort of promise and confession you are bound
before God! And how is it that some of you, who renounced the
devil and his angels and his worship and his evil works, now again
return to the worship of the devil? For to light candles before
rocks and trees and streams and at crossroads—is this anything else
but the worship of the devil? To observe divinations and auguries
and days of the idols—is this anything else but the worship of the
devil? To observe "vulcanalia" and the kalends [feasts at the first
day of the months], to decorate tables and place wreaths and
watch your step, to place fruit and pour wine into a fire on the
trunk of a tree, to place bread upon the stream—is this anything
else but the worship of the devil? For women at their looms to call
on Minerva; to observe for marriages the day of Venus; to pay
attention as to what day to begin a journey—is this anything else
but the worship of the devil? To cast spells over herbs for the
purpose of evil, to call upon the names of demons in casting spells
—is this anything else but the worship of the devil? Many other
things are done which are too numerous to mention! Behold, you
do all these things after renouncing the devil, after baptism. You
return to the worship of demons and to the wicked works of
idols. You break your faith and violate the agreement which you
made with God. You put aside the sign of the cross, which you
received in baptism, and you pay attention to other signs of the
devil in little birds and sneezings and through many other things.
How does a divination not injure me or any right Christian? Because, where the sign of the cross precedes, the sign of the devil is
nothing. Why does it injure you? Because you scorn the sign of
the cross, and you fear that which you yourselves imagine is in the
sign. Likewise you put aside holy incantations. These are the
creed which you accepted at baptism, which is "I believe in God
the Father Almighty," and the Lord's prayer, which is "Our
Father who art in heaven." You keep diabolical incantations and
songs. Therefore, whosoever scorns the sign of the cross of Christ
and takes other signs, loses the sign of the cross which he received
in baptism. Similarly he who holds other incantations invented by
magicians and criminals, loses the incantation of the holy creed
and of the Lord's prayer, which he received in the faith of Christ.

He treads upon the faith of Christ, because both God and the devil cannot be at once adored.

17. If therefore you recognize, dearly beloved sons, all these things which we have said, if anyone knows that he himself has done these things after having received baptism and that he has broken the faith of Christ, let him not despair of himself nor should he say in his heart: "Because I have done so many evil things after baptism, perhaps God will not forgive me my sins." Do not doubt the mercy of God. Only make in your heart an agreement with God, that you will no more honor the worship of demons, nor adore anything else but the God of heaven, nor commit murder, nor adultery nor fornication, nor rob nor perjure. And when you promise this to God with your whole heart and commit these sins no more, faithfully hope for pardon from God, because God says through prophetic scripture: *In whatever day the wicked should forget his iniquities and do justice, I will not remember all his iniquities* (Ezech. 18: 21-22). For God awaits the penance of the sinner. This however is true penitence, that a man should do no more the evils that he has done, but that he should seek indulgence for past sins, and should not care for the future lest he return again to them, but on the other hand, he should in particular do good works. He should show mercy to the starving pauper, refresh the tired stranger, and should do to another whatever he wishes done to him by another. And what he does not wish done to him, let him not do this to another, because in this word the commandments of God are fulfilled.

18. We therefore ask you, dearly beloved brothers and sons, that you hold in mind these commands, which God has deigned to give to you through us, though we are humble and lowly. Think how you can save your souls. You should consider not only this present life and the passing utility of this world, but you should especially remember that which you promised to believe in the creed, that is, the resurrection of the flesh and life eternal. If therefore you have believed and now believe that there will be a resurrection of the flesh and life eternal in the kingdom of heaven among the angels of God, as we have said to you above, think about this as much as possible, and not just about the misery of this world. Prepare your way in good works. Frequently visit the church to pray to God or the places of the saints. Do not scorn the Lord's day, which is called the Lord's for this reason, that the Son of God, our Lord Jesus Christ, on that day rose from the dead, but keep it with

reverence. Do not do servile work, that is, in the field, meadow, vineyard or whatever is heavy, except only as much as pertains to the needs of restoring the body through cooking food and the necessity of a long journey. It is licit to travel to nearby places on the Lord's day, not however for evil purposes but rather for good reasons, that is, to visit holy places or to visit a brother or a friend; to console the sick; to give counsel to the troubled; or to bring help for a good cause. It is fitting for a Christian man to venerate the Lord's day in such a manner. For it is sufficiently evil and base that those who are pagans and ignore the Christian faith, worshipping the idols of demons, honor the day of Jupiter or some other demon and refrain from work, although it is certain that the demons neither created a day nor have one. And we, who adore the true God and believe that the Son of God rose from the dead, do not venerate at all the day of his resurrection, that is, the Lord's day. Do not therefore do injury to the Lord's resurrection, but honor it and keep it with reverence for our hope which we have in it. For as our Lord Jesus Christ, Son of God, who is our head, on the third day rose again from the dead, so also we, who are his members, hope ourselves to rise in our flesh at the end of the world, so that everyone shall receive either eternal rest or eternal punishment, as he chose in his body in this world.

19. Behold, in this sermon, with the testimony of God and the holy angels who heard us, we have paid to your charity our debt and we have lent you the coin of the Lord, as we were commanded. Yours it is now to think and to see to it that everyone shall return as much as he received with interest, when the Lord comes in the day of judgment. We invoke the mercy of the Lord, that he may guard you from all evil and make you worthy companions of the holy angels in his kingdom, with the help of him who lives and reigns forever and ever. Amen.

3. The Carolingian capitulary, *De Villis*

Sometime probably shortly before the year 800, an unknown Frankish ruler issued a set of regulations concerning the management of royal estates or manors. Frankish laws and administrative directives were known as capitularies, for the reason that they were divided into *capitula* or chapters. This capitulary *De Villis* ("Concerning Estates") has been the source of lengthy scholarly arguments concerning its authorship and the circumstances of its composition. Most historians now believe that Charlemagne himself issued it, and that he wanted it applied over a wide area of his empire, probably excluding only Italy.

The capitulary contains detailed instructions to the stewards, who are called literally "judges," concerning their responsibilities. The range of those responsibilities—economic, judicial, administrative, military—illustrates quite well the spectrum of services the manor performed for the Carolingian state. It also gives a good if somewhat disorganized view of the obligations of the manorial serfs. We can thus learn from it how a large part, if not the larger part, of Europeans lived in the eighth and ninth centuries.

The following translation is based upon the Latin text given in the *Capitularia regum Francorum*, ed. A. Boretius and V. Krause, I (Monumenta Germaniae Historica, Legum Sectio II, 1), pp. 83–91. The translation is by D. Herlihy.

1. We wish that our estates, which we have established to serve our needs, shall serve entirely for our benefit and not for that of other men.

2. That the people on our estates be well taken care of, and that they be reduced to poverty by no one.

3. That the stewards do not dare to enlist our people in their own service. They should not force them to perform agricultural labors, to cut wood or to do other work for them. Nor should the stewards accept any gifts from them, neither a horse nor an ox nor cow nor pig nor sheep nor piglet nor lamb nor anything else, excepting bottles of wine, garden produce, fruits, chickens and eggs.

4. If any of our people commit against our interests the crime of robbery or other offense, let him make good the damage, and further, let him be punished by whipping in satisfaction of the law, except in cases of murder and arson, for which fines may be collected. The stewards should strive to render to other men the justice which they may deserve, according to the law. Our people, as we have said, instead of paying fines, are to be whipped. Freemen, however, who reside on our properties and estates, should strive to make good whatever injuries they may commit according

to their law. Whatever they give in fines, whether in cattle or other payments, should be collected for our use.

5. Whenever our stewards are to see that our work is performed —sowing, plowing, harvesting, cutting of hay or gathering of grapes—let each of them at the proper time and place supervise and give directions how the work is to be done, so that it may be done well. If the steward is not within his district and cannot come to a particular place, let him send a good messenger from among our people or another reliable man, in order to supervise our affairs and conduct them to a good end. The steward should diligently see to it that he sends a faithful man to take care of this matter.

6. We wish that our stewards pay a full tenth of all produce to the churches which are on our property, and do not let our tenth be given to the church of another [lord], unless in places where this is an ancient custom. Other clerics should not hold these churches, but only our own or those from our people or from our chapel.

7. That every steward should perform his full service as he has been directed. And if necessity requires that he should serve additional time, he should determine whether he should increase the [day] service or the night service.

8. That our stewards take care of our vineyards which are in their territory, and make sure that they are worked well. Let them place the wine in good containers and let them diligently see to it that nothing is lost in shipping it. Let them acquire through purchase special kinds of wine, in order to send it to the royal estates. And when more of this wine has been purchased than is needed for the provisioning of our estates, they should inform us of this, so that we may command whatever may be our will. They should have vine slips from our vineyards sent for our use. The rents from our estates which are paid in wine are to be stored in our cellars.

9. We wish that every steward keep in his territory measures of *modia, sextaria,* containers of eight *sextaria,* and baskets, of the same type as we have in our palace.

10. That our mayors, foresters, stablemen, cellarers, deans, toll collectors and other servants do regular services and pay pigs for their farms [*mansi*]. In place of manual labor let them perform their offices well. And whatever mayor may have a benefice, let him send a substitute, who may perform for him the manual labor and other service.

11. That no steward take lodging for himself or for his dogs from our men or from those living outside our estates.

12. That no steward should commend [with a benefice] any hostage on our estates.

13. That the stewards should take good care of our stallions and not allow them to remain too long in one place, lest the pasturage be damaged. And if a stallion should be unhealthy or old so as to be likely to die soon, they should inform us of this at the proper time, before the season comes when they are to be placed with the mares.

14. That they should watch our mares well, and segregate the colts at the proper time. And if the fillies should increase in number, they should be separated so as to form a new herd by themselves.

15. Let them have our foals sent to our winter palace at the feast of St. Martin [November 11].

16. We wish that whatever we or the queen should command to any steward, or whatever our servants, the seneschal or the butler, should order, the stewards in our name or that of the queen, they should perform as was told them. Whoever should fail to do so through negligence, let him abstain from drink from the time he has been told until he appears in our presence or that of the queen and requests pardon from us. And if the steward was in the army or on guard duty or on a mission or elsewhere, and ordered his subordinates to perform something and they did not do so, then they should come on foot to the palace. They should abstain from drink and meat while they give the reasons why they were negligent. Then they should accept their punishment, either in whipping or however else it may please us or the queen.

17. The steward should appoint as many men as there are estates in his territory, to keep bees for our needs.

18. At our mills the stewards should keep chickens and geese according to the quality of the mill and as many more as can be maintained.

19. The stewards should keep in the barns of our principal estates no fewer than 100 chickens and 30 geese; on smaller farms let them have no fewer than 50 chickens and 12 geese.

20. Every steward should always send the produce [of the fowls] to our court abundantly throughout the year, except when they make visits three or four or more times.

21. Every steward should keep fish ponds on our estates where they were in the past. He should enlarge them if possible. And if they were not there in times past but can now be made, let them be made.

22. Those who hold our vineyards should keep for our use no fewer than three or four crowns of grapes.

23. The stewards should maintain in each of our estates cow barns, pig pens, folds for sheep and goats, as many as possible. No estate should be without them. Moreover, let them have cows delivered by our serfs in fulfillment of their service, so that our cow barns or plow teams are not diminished by service on our demesne. Let them also obtain, in order to supply meat, lame but healthy oxen and cows, horses which are not mangy, or other healthy beasts. As we have said, our cow barns or plow teams should not be diminished for this.

24. Every steward should see to it that whatever is provided for our table be good and of highest quality, and that whatever they deliver has been prepared carefully and cleanly. And whenever someone serves at our table, he should receive for his service two meals of wheat every day. The other provisions, whether in flour or in meat, should similarly be of good quality.

25. The stewards should report on the first of September whether or not there is pasturage for the hogs.

26. Mayors should not administer a territory which is too large for them to ride through and inspect in a single day.

27. Our manor houses should have continuous watch fires and guards so that they may be secure. When our *missi* or a legation come to or from the palace, they should not take lodging in the royal manor houses, unless by our special permission or that of the queen. The count in his district or those men who have been traditionally accustomed to care for the *missi* or legations should continue to provide pack horses in the usual fashion and all things needed by them. Thus they may journey to and from our palace with ease and dignity.

28. We wish that every year, on Palm Sunday in Lent, which is called "Hosanna Sunday," the stewards should deliver to us at our command the monetary part of our revenue, after we find out for the present year how great our revenue is.

29. Every steward should see to it that those of our men who wish to plead cases are not required to come into our presence to plead. He should not through negligence allow those days to be lost which the man should serve. If our serf should have to seek justice outside our estates, his master should expend every effort to gain justice for him. If the serf is unable to obtain justice in a particular locale, the master should not allow our serf to suffer for this,

but through himself or his messenger he should inform us of this.
30. We wish that our stewards separate from the entire revenue that which is needed in our service. Similarly, let them take out supplies needed to fill the carts sent into the army, both those of householders and those of shepherds. And let them know how much they send for this purpose.

31. That they should similarly deduct each year what is to be given to the household servants or to the women working in the women's quarters. Let them give it fully at the proper time and let them inform us how they have done so and from where it was taken.

32. That every steward should see to it that he always has good seed of highest quality, by purchase or otherwise.

33. After all these parts of our revenue have been allocated or sown or consumed, whatever is left from the produce should be kept in expectation of our order, so that it may be sold or stored according to our command.

34. Whatever is made by hand should be closely supervised with all diligence, so that they are made or prepared with the maximum cleanliness: that is, lard, smoked meat, sausage, newly salted meat, wine, vinegar, mulberry wine, boiled wine, garn, mustard, cheese, butter, malt, beer, mead, honey, wax, and flour.

35. We wish that tallow be made from fat sheep and also from pigs. Furthermore, let them keep in each estate no less than two fattened oxen, whether to be fattened there or to be delivered to us.

36. That our woods and forests be well protected. And where there is room for clearing, let the stewards clear it, and they should not allow fields to become overgrown with woods. And where woods should be, they should not allow them to be excessively stripped and damaged. Let them guard well our wild beasts within the forests. Similarly, let them take care of our falcons and hawks for our use, and collect our rents diligently. If our stewards or mayors or their men let their hogs forage in our forest for fattening, let them be the first to pay a tenth, in order to set a good example, so that in the future other men will pay their tenth fully.

37. That our stewards maintain our fields and cultivated lands well, and let them guard our meadows in season.

38. That they should always keep fat geese and chickens for our needs, when they ought to provide them for us or deliver them to us.

39. Let them receive the chickens and eggs which serfs or residents

of farms return every year; when they are not needed, they should sell them.

40. Let every steward always keep for the sake of ornament on every estate swans, peacocks, pheasants, ducks, pigeons, partridges and turtledoves.

41. Let the buildings within our manors and the fences about them be well cared for, and let stables, kitchens, bakeries or wine presses be carefully constructed, so that our servants can perform their tasks properly and cleanly.

42. Let every estate have within its hall beds, mattresses, pillows, bed linens, table cloths, seat covers, vessels of bronze, lead, iron and wood, andirons, chains, pot hangers, planes, axes, hatchets, knives and all sorts of tools, so that it will not be necessary to seek them elsewhere or to borrow them. Let the stewards also have the responsibility of seeing to it that the iron tools which they provide for the army are good and that when they are returned they are sent to the manor hall.

43. To the workshop of the women they should provide material to work at suitable times, as has been commanded: that is, linen, wool, woad, red dye, madder, carding implements, combs, soap, oil, containers, and other small things which are needed there.

44. Concerning Lenten food, let two-thirds be sent every year for our use, in vegetables, fish or cheese, butter, honey, mustard, vinegar, millet, panic, dry or green herbs, roots, turnips and wax or soap or other small items. Let them inform us by letter what is left over. They should by no means fail to do this, as they have in the past, because through those two parts we wish to learn about the third part which remains.

45. That every steward should have in his territory good artisans: that is, smiths, blacksmiths, gold- and silversmiths, tailors, turners, carpenters, shield makers, fishermen, falconers (that is, those who look after the birds), soap makers, brewers (that is, those who know how to make beer or cider, perry or other liquid fit to drink), bakers who can make bread for our need, net makers who know how to make nets for hunting, fishing or fowling, and other servants. It would be too long to name them all.

46. That the stewards should take good care of our woods, which the people call *brogilos* [walled parks], and let them always repair them in good time, and not delay until it should be necessary to rebuild them entirely. Let them take similar care of every building.

47. That our hunters and falconers and other servants, who serve us zealously in the palace, should receive help in our villages, as we or the queen may command through our letters, when we send them forth for any errand, or when the seneschal and butler should command them to do anything on our behalf.

48. The wine presses on our estates should be kept ready for use, and let the stewards take care that no one dare crush our grape harvest with his feet, but everything should be clean and orderly.

49. That our women's workshops be well arranged, that is, their houses, heated rooms, and living rooms. Let them have good fences throughout and strong doors, in order that they may perform our work well.

50. That every steward should determine how many horses should remain in one stable and how many grooms should stay with the horses. And those grooms who are freemen and have benefices for their service should support themselves by their benefices; freemen too, who have farms [*mansas*] on our public property which feed them. Whoever does not have this, should be given support from the demesne.

51. Every steward should take care lest wicked men conceal our seed under the ground or elsewhere. This makes our harvest grow sparser. Similarly, they should beware of other wicked deeds, to make sure that they never happen.

52. We wish that serfs on the public lands or our own serfs or freemen who are settled on our properties or estates give full and complete justice, whatever is fitting, to men [from other estates].

53. That every steward should see to it that the men of their territory in no wise become thiefs or criminals.

54. That every steward should see to it that our people work well at their tasks and do not go about wasting time at markets.

55. We wish that the stewards write in one document whatever income they have been given or provided or received in our service, and in another whatever they have spent. They should inform us by letter what is left over.

56. That every steward in his territory hold frequent hearings, dispense justice and see to it that our people live law-abiding lives.

57. If any of our serfs should wish to inform us of anything which is to our interest concerning his master, he should not be prevented from coming to us. And if the steward knows that those under his charge wish to come to the palace to complain against him, then the steward should deliver to us at the palace arguments against

them, why their complaint should not cause resentment in our ears. And thus we wish to know, whether the subordinates are coming from necessity or under pretense.

58. When our puppies are given to stewards to be raised, the steward should feed them at his own expense or commend them to his subordinates, that is, the mayors, deans or cellarers, in order that they should feed them from their own property, unless by our own order or that of the queen they are to be raised on our estate. Then the steward should send a man to feed them, and should set aside that from which they are to be fed. It will not be necessary for the man to go daily to the kennels.

59. Every steward, during the time that he is on service, should give each day three pounds of wax, and eight *sextaria* of soap. Furthermore, at the feast of St. Andrew [November 30], he should give six pounds of wax, wherever we may be with our people. He should give the same in mid-Lent.

60. Mayors should never be chosen from powerful men, but from those of moderate station who are faithful.

61. During the time the steward performs his service, he should have his malt delivered to the palace. Similarly, let masters come who know how to make good beer there.

62. That every steward should make known to us yearly on Christmas, with everything arranged in the proper order, what we have received by way of income, so that we may learn what and how much we possess of all things; what land our plowmen work with their cattle; what holdings they ought to plow; what taxes, rents, judgment costs, fees, fines for taking animals in our forests without our permission, and payments for other reasons; what income from mills, forests, fields, bridges or ships; what payments from freemen and from hundreds who serve our fisc; what revenues from markets, vineyards and those who pay in wine; what revenue from hay, wood, torches, planks or other lumber; what from wastelands, vegetables, millet and panic, wool, linen or hemp, fruits of trees, large or small nuts and graftings of various trees, gardens, turnips, fish ponds, skins, furs, horns, honey and wax; what from mulberry wine, cooked wine, mead and vinegar; what from beer, new and old wine, new and old grain, chickens, eggs and geese; what from fishermen, smiths, shield makers or tailors; what from kneading troughs, boxes or cases; what from turners or saddlers; what from forges and mines, that is, iron diggings or other

lead diggings; what from persons liable to tribute payments; what from colts and fillies.

63. Concerning the above mentioned things, it should not disturb our stewards if we make inquiry, for we wish that they in like fashion require all these things from their subordinates without causing resentment. And all things whatsoever that a man ought to have in his house or estates, our stewards should have on our estates.

64. That our carts which go to the army, that is, the war carts, be well constructed, and that their coverings be well made of skins. They should be so sewn together that, if it is necessary to cross water, they can go across the rivers with their provisions inside and no water can enter. It should be possible to cross, as we have said, with our provisions protected. We wish that flour be placed in each cart at our expense, that is, twelve *modia* of farina. In those carts which carry wine let them put twelve *modia* according to our measurement. And let them supply for each cart a shield, lance, quiver and bow.

65. That the fish from our ponds be sold and others put in their place, so that there will always be a supply of fish. However, when we do not visit the estates, then they should be sold and the stewards should make profit from them to our advantage.

66. Let the stewards give us an accounting of the male and female goats and of their horns and skins; and let them bring to us yearly newly salted meat of fat goats.

67. Concerning deserted farms and newly acquired slaves, the stewards should inform us if they have any surplus [of slaves] and cannot find a place for them.

68. We wish that all stewards have always ready good barrels bound with iron, which they can send to the army and to the palace. They should not make containers of skins.

69. They should at all times keep us informed concerning wolves, how many each one has caught, and they should send us the skins. In May, they should hunt wolf cubs and catch them, both with poison and with hooks, as well as with traps and dogs.

70. We wish that they should have in the garden all kinds of plants: that is, lily, roses, fenugreek, costmary, sage, rue, southernwood, cucumbers, pumpkins, gourd, pea, cumin, rosemary, caraway, chick-pea, squill, gladiola, estragon, anise, colosynth, heliotrope, spicknel, seseli, lettuce, spider's foot, rocket salad, garden

cress, burdock, penny royal, hemlock, parsley, celery, lovage, juniper, dill, sweet-fennel, endive, dittany, white mustard, summer savory, water mint, garden mint, wild mint, tansy, catnip, centaury, garden poppy, beets, hazelwort, marshmallows, hollyhock, mallows, carrots, parsnip, garden-orach, amaranth, kohlrabi, cabbages, onions, chives, leeks, radishes, shallots, cibols, garlic, madder, teasel, broad beans, large peas, Moorish peas, chervil, capers, clary. And the gardener should have Jove's beard [house-leek] growing on his house.

Concerning trees we wish that they have apple, pear, plum, sorb, medlar, chestnut and peach trees of different kinds; quince, hazel, almond, mulberry, laurel, pine, fig nut, and cherry trees of different kinds.

The names of apple trees are *gozmaringa, geroldinga, crevedella, spirauca*, sweet, bitter, those which keep well and those to be eaten at once, and early apples. They shall have three or four kinds of pears, those which keep well, sweet, cooking and late pears.

⎍⎍⎍⎍⎍⎍⎍⎍⎍⎍⎍⎍⎍⎍⎍⎍⎍⎍⎍⎍⎍⎍⎍⎍⎍⎍⎍⎍

4. The inventory of a Carolingian manor

The capitulary *De Villis* may present a slightly idealized picture of Carolingian manorial organization; it tells us only what the king wanted, not necessarily what he received. But we also possess several surveys or inventories of established manors, in which the extent and quality of lands and the obligations of serfs were carefully entered. By far the richest of these is the "Polyptych" or survey of the estates of the great abbey of Saint-Germain des Prés near Paris. It was drawn up probably between 806 and 829 when the Abbot Irminon ruled the monastery.

The following selection gives the survey of one of the smaller estates of Saint-Germain, that of Neuillay or Neuilly, which one scholar, A. Longnon, identifies with Neuillay-les-Bois in Berry. The "bunuarium" used to measure land seems to have been equivalent to about 3.16 acres, and the arpent was one-tenth its size. It does not seem possible to determine even approximately the capacity of the "modius," the measure of cereals.

Even on this small estate, the cultivators show considerable contrasts in their legal status. The "coloni," who were technically free-men though still bound to the soil, had the lightest obligations. The "servi" or slaves had the heaviest. The "lidi" or half-free were some-where in between. The lidi may have been originally barbarian colo-nists or even prisoners of war settled upon the land to aid in its cultiva-tion.

The Latin text is given in the *Polyptyque de l'abbaye de Saint-Germain des Prés*, ed. A. Longnon (Paris: H. Champion, 1886), pp. 158–61. The translation is by D. Herlihy.

THERE is in Neuillay a seigneurial manor amply equipped with other buildings. There are on the estate 10 fields, which are 40 bunuaria in size and which can be sown with 200 modia of oats. There are 9 arpents of meadow, from which 10 loads of hay can be harvested. There is a forest there; it is estimated to be 3 leagues long and 1 league wide. In it 800 pigs can find forage.

1. Electeus a slave and his wife a colona, by the name of Landina. They are dependents of Saint-Germain. They live in Neuillay. He holds half a farm, which has in arable land 6 bunuaria, in meadow one-half an arpent. He plows in the winter field 4 perches and in the spring field 13. He carts manure to the lord's field, and per-forms no other services nor pays anything in addition, for the service that he provides.

2. Abrahil a slave and his wife, a lida, by the name of Berthildis. They are dependents of Saint-Germain. These are their children: Abram, Avremarus, and Bertrada. And Ceslinus a lidus and his wife a lida, named Leutberga. These are their children: Leutgardis, and Ingohildis. And Godalbertus a lidus. These are their children: Gedalcaus, Celsovildis and Bladovildis. These three [families] live in Neuillay. They hold a farm, which has in arable land 15 bunuaria and in meadow 4 arpents. They do carting to Anjou, and in the month of May to Paris. They pay for the army tax 2 muttons, 8 chickens, 30 eggs, 100 planks and as many shingles, 12 staves, 6 hoops and 12 torches. They bring 2 loads of wood to Sutré. They inclose, in the lord's court, 4 perches with a palisade, in the meadow 4 perches with a fence, and at the harvest as much as is necessary. They plow in the winter field 8 perches and in the spring field 26 perches. Along with their corvées and labor services, they cart manure into the lord's field. Each pays a head tax of 4 pennies.

3. Gislevertus a slave and his wife a lida, by name Gotberga. These
are their children: Ragno, Gausbertus, Gaujoinus, and Gautlindis.
And Sinopus a slave and his wife a slave, by name Frolaica. These
are their children: Siclandus, Frothardus, Marellus, Adaluildis and
Frotlildis. And Ansegudis a slave. These are their children:
Ingalbertus, Frobertus, Frotlaicus, and Frotberga. These three
[families] live in Neuillay. They hold one farm, which has in
arable land 26 bunuaria, and in meadow 8 arpents. They pay as
the above.
4. Maurifius a lidus and his wife a colona, by name Ermengardis.
Ermengildis is their child. And Guadulfus a lidus and his wife a
lida, by name Celsa. Gaudildis is their child. These two [families]
live in Neuillay. They hold one farm, having in arable land 28
bunuaria and in meadow 4 arpents. They pay as the above.
5. Ragenardus a slave and his wife a colona, by name Dagena.
Ragenaus is their son. And Gausboldus a slave and his wife a lida,
by name Faregildis. These two [families] live in Neuillay. They
hold one farm, which has in arable land 11 bunuaria and in meadow
4 arpents. They perform services as the above.
6. Feremundus a slave and his wife a colona, by name Creada.
And Feroardus a slave and his wife a lida, by name Adalgardis.
Illegardis is their daughter. And Foroenus a slave. And Adalgrimus
a slave. These four [families] live in Neuillay. They hold one
farm, which has in arable land 8 bunuaria and in meadow 4 arpents.
They perform services as the above.
7. Gautmarus a slave and his wife a lida, by name Sigalsis. These
are their children: Siclevoldus and Sicleardus. He lives in Neuillay.
He holds a fourth part of a farm, which has in arable land 1 and
one-half bunuaria and in meadow 1 arpent. He pays the fourth part
of a full farm.
8. Hildeboldus a slave and his wife a lida, by name Bertenildis.
These are their children: Aldedramnus, Adalbertus, Hildegaudus,
Trutgaudus, Bernardus, Bertramnus, Hildoinus, Halderudis and
Martinga. And Haldemarus a slave and his wife a colona, by name
Morberga. These are their children: Martinus, Siclehildis and
Bernegildis. These two live in Neuillay. They hold one-half a
farm, having in land 6 bunuaria and in meadow one-half arpent.
They pay half the obligation of an entire farm.
9. Bertlinus a lidus and his wife a colona, by name Lantsida. These
are their children: Creatus, Martinus and Lantbertus. He lives in
Neuillay. He holds a quarter part of a whole farm, which has in

arable land 3 bunuaria, and in meadow 2 arpents. He does service. He must pay a quarter part of an entire farm, but for this obligation he looks after the pigs.

10. There are in Neuillay 6 and one-half inhabited farms, and one-half is not occupied. They are distributed among 16 families. They pay to the army tax 12 muttons; in head tax, 5 shillings and 4 pennies; 48 chickens, 160 eggs, 600 planks and as many shingles, 54 staves and as many hoops, and 72 torches. They make 2 cartings for wine, and during May 2 and one-half cartings, and give half an ox.

11. These are the slaves: Electus, Gislevertus, Sinopus, Ragenardus, Gausboldus, Feremundus, Gedalbertus, Faroardus, Abrahil, Faroinus, Adalgrimus, Gautmarus, and Hildevoldus. They pay torches and do portage.

12. These are the lidi: Maurifius, Gaudulfus, Bertlinus, Ceslinus, and Gedalbertus.

13. These are the women slaves: Frotlina, Ansegundis, Alda and Framberta. They feed chickens and make cloth, if wool is given to them.

14. These are the women lidae: Berthildis, Leutberga, Gotberga, Celsa, Faregildis, Sigalsis and Bertenildis. They pay 4 pennies in tax.

15. Ragenardus holds of the seigneurial property 1 bunuaria. Gislevertus keeps on his farm 2 geese.

II. *The Latin culture of the early Middle Ages*

ⴰⴰⴰⴰⴰⴰⴰⴰⴰⴰⴰⴰⴰⴰⴰⴰⴰⴰⴰⴰⴰⴰⴰ

5. The monastic virtues, according to St. Benedict

The best introduction to the practice and spirit of medieval monasticism remains the Rule of St. Benedict, which was written probably around the year 540. In most of the rule, Benedict deals with practical matters concerning the organization of the monastery, authority of the abbot, responsibilities of the brothers, and routines of daily living. In Chapters 4 through 7, however, he speaks of the virtues to be cultivated by the monks, and especially stresses the achievement of humility. Throughout the Middle Ages and, of course, even in the present, these words have taught monks the purpose of their calling.

The translation is taken from the Latin text given in the *Regula*, ed. Rudolphus Hanslik, Corpus Scriptorum Ecclesiasticorum Latinorum, 75 (Vienna: Hoelder, Pichler, Tempsky, 1960), pp. 29-52. The translation is by D. Herlihy.

IV. *What are the instruments of good works*

FIRST of all, to love the Lord God with the whole heart, the whole soul, and all strength.

Then, to love one's neighbor as oneself.

Then, not to kill.

Not to commit adultery.

Not to steal.

Not to lust.

Not to bear false witness.

To honor all men.

Not to do to another what one would not have done to oneself.

To deny oneself, in order to follow Christ.

To discipline the body.

Not to embrace pleasures.

To love fasting.

To refresh the poor.

To clothe the naked.

To visit the sick.

To bury the dead.

To aid those in tribulation.

To console the sorrowing.

To become a stranger to the doings of the world.

To value nothing more than the love of Christ.

Not to lose one's temper.

Not to remain in anger.

Not to harbor deceit in the heart.

Not to make a false peace.

Not to become remiss in charity.

Not to swear, lest one be perjured.

To speak the truth with heart and mouth.

Not to return evil for evil.

Not to do injury, but patiently to suffer injuries done to one.

To love one's enemies.

Not to curse in return those who curse us, but rather to bless them.

To suffer persecution for justice's sake.

Not to be proud.

Not to be a drunkard.

Not to be a glutton.

Not to be slothful.

Not to be lazy.

Not to complain.

Not to calumniate.

To place one's trust in God.

To attribute what one finds good in oneself to God, not to oneself.

To recognize, on the other hand, that evil is done by us, and we should impute it to ourselves.

To fear the day of judgment.

To be terrified of hell.

To long for eternal life with all spiritual desire.

To keep the vision of death daily before one's eyes.

To guard the actions of one's life at every hour.

To recognize that God knows all things in all places.

When evil thoughts enter the mind, to shatter them at once within Christ, and to reveal them to one's spiritual father.

To guard one's tongue from wicked or depraved speech.

Not to love to talk a great deal.

Not to pronounce idle or frivolous words.

Not to love frequent and loud laughter.

To listen willingly to sacred readings.

To give oneself frequently to prayer.

To confess daily, in prayer to God, one's past transgressions with tears and sighs.

Henceforth to avoid those transgressions.

Not to give in to the desires of the flesh.

To hate one's own will.

To obey the commands of the abbot in all things, even if he himself should do otherwise (God forbid!). Be mindful of the Lord's command: *All things, therefore, that they command you, observe and do. But do not act according to their works* (Matt. 23.3).

Do not wish to be called a holy man before you are holy, but first be holy, so that it may be said of you in truth.

To fulfill each day God's commands in one's actions.

To love chastity.

To hate no one.

Not to bear secret grudges.

Not to be envious.

Not to love strife.

To flee arrogance.

To honor elders.

To love the young.

To pray for enemies in the love of Christ.

To make peace with an adversary before the sunset.

Never to despair of God's mercy.

See, these are the instruments and tools of the spiritual profession. When we shall have made use of them continuously day and night and returned them on the day of judgment, the Lord will give to us the wages that he promised. *Eye has not seen or ear heard, nor has it entered into the heart of man, what things God has prepared for those who love him* (I Cor. 3.9).

The workshop, where we diligently utilize all these tools, is the cloister of the monastery and its stable congregation.

v. *Concerning obedience*

The first step of humility is attained by unhesitating obedience. This is fitting to those who believe, whether through the holy service which they have professed or through fear of hell or through desiring the glory of eternal life, that nothing is dearer than Christ. Such monks do not know how to allow delay in fulfilling whatever a superior has commanded them. They act as if they were ordered by God. The Lord said concerning them: *At the hearing of the ear he has obeyed me* (Ps. 17.45). And he also said to the teachers, *He who hears you, hears me* (Luke 10.16).

Monks such as these leave at once their own affairs and abandon their own will. With hands unoccupied, they give up their unfinished work. With the prompt tread of obedience they follow in deeds the command of the superior. It is as if in one moment the command of the master and the completed work of the disciple are both of them rapidly executed together, with speed brought by the fear of God, by persons urged forward by the desire of attaining eternal life. Thus, they choose the narrow way, of which the Lord said: *Narrow is the way which leads to life* (Matt. 8.14). Living not for their own will, not the slaves of their own desires and pleasures, but walking under another's judgment and authority, living in monasteries, they wish the abbot to hold command over them. Without doubt such disciples fulfill the words of the Lord, when he said: *I came not to do my own will, but the will of him who sent me* (John 5.30).

This obedience will be both acceptable to God and pleasing to men, if what is ordered is accomplished not in fear, or slowly or reluctantly with grumblings and complaint. Obedience which is given to elders is shown to God. For he has said: *He who hears you, hears me* (Luke 10.16). The disciples should also obey with a good spirit, because *God loves a cheerful giver* (2 Cor. 9.7). For if the disciple obeys with a bad spirit, if he should murmur not only in mouth, but also in his heart, even if he fulfills the command, it will not be accepted by God, who sees his complaining heart. For such an act he attains no grace; rather does he incur the penalty of murmurers, if he does not correct his ways with penance.

vi. *On silence*

Let us do what the Prophet says: *I have said, I will keep my ways, that I offend not with my tongue. I have been watchful over my mouth: I held my peace and humbled myself and was silent from speaking even good things* (Ps. 38.2–3). Here the Prophet shows this: if we ought at times in observing silence to refrain even from good speech, how much the more, under penalty of sin, ought we to desist from wicked talk.

Even in regard to good and devout discourse, a source of edification, permission to speak should rarely be given, even to perfect disciples, because of the importance of silence. Thus it is written: *In much speaking, you shall not escape sin* (Prov. 10.9), and elsewhere, *Death and life are in the power of the tongue* (Prov. 18.21). The master indeed should speak and teach, but the disciple should be silent and listen. If anything is to be asked of the prior, let it be done with all humility and with reverent submission.

Vulgarities, however, idle words and those which provoke to laughter, we completely exclude in all places, and we do not allow the disciple to open his mouth for such speech.

VII. *On humility*

Brethren, divine Scripture cries out to us, saying: *Everyone who exalts himself shall be humbled, and he who humbles himself shall be exalted* (Luke 14.11). When it says these words, it instructs us that every kind of exaltation of self is a type of pride. The Prophet warns us against this, saying: *Lord, my heart is not exalted, neither are my eyes lifted up; neither have I walked in great things, nor in wonders above myself* (Ps. 130.1). And why? *If I did not think humbly, but exalted my soul: as a child weaned from his mother, so will you regard my soul* (Ps. 130.2).

Therefore, brethren, if we wish to attain the highest summit of humility and to arrive quickly at that heavenly glorification, which one attains through the humiliation of the present life, we must build by our upward-moving deeds a ladder, such as was seen by Jacob in his dream, on which there appeared to him angels climbing and descending. Without doubt that going down and up should be interpreted by us in no other fashion, but that we lower ourselves through exalting ourselves, and we climb upwards through humility. For the ladder we build is our life in this world, which, if we act with humble heart, the Lord will lift up to heaven. We may call our body and soul the sides of that ladder. In them, our divine vocation has set the various levels of humility and discipline which are to be mounted.

The first step of humility is attained, if the monk always places the fear of God before his eyes, and never allows himself to forget it. Such a man is always mindful of all which God has commanded. He turns over continuously in his mind that those who defy God are burned in hell for their sins, and that life eternal has been prepared for those who fear the Lord. He guards himself every hour from sins and vices, whether of thought, tongue, hands, feet or self-will, and from the desires of the flesh. He knows God watches man from heaven always and in every hour, that his deeds done everywhere are viewed in the divine sight and reported every hour by the angels. The Prophet proves this to us, when he shows us that God is always present in our thoughts, stating: *God searches the hearts and reins* (Ps. 7.10). And again: *The Lord knows the thoughts of men* (Ps. 93.11). And again he says: *You have understood my thoughts afar off* (Ps. 138.3). And, *The thought of man shall confess you* (Ps. 75.11). In order therefore to stand guard against one's own wicked thoughts, the faithful monk will repeat continuously in his heart: *But I shall be blameless before him, if I shall keep me from iniquity* (Ps. 17.24).

We are forbidden to do our own will, since Scripture says to us: *Leave your own will and desire* (Eccl. 18.30). And again: *We beg of God in prayer that his will may be done in us* (Matt. 6.10).

We are therefore rightly taught not to do our own will, since we take heed of that which Scripture says: *There are ways which to men seem right, the end whereof plunges even into the deep pit of hell* (Prov. 16.25). And again, when we fear what is said concerning the negligent: *They are corrupted, and are made abominable in their pleasures* (Ps. 52.2).

But in regard to the desires of the flesh, we ought to believe that we are ever in God's presence, as the Prophet says to the Lord: *O Lord, all my desire is before you* (Ps. 37.10).

If then *the eyes of the Lord look upon the good and the evil* (Ps. 13.2) and *the Lord looks down from heaven upon the children of men to see if there be one who understands and seeks God* (Ps. 13.3), and if the accomplishments of our actions are daily reported, day and night, to the Lord by the angels set over us, we must be on our guard every hour, brethren. This for the reason that God may not find us, as the Prophet says, *inclined to evil and become unprofitable servants* (Ps. 49.21). Even though he spare us this time, because he is loving and waits for us to better our ways, beware lest he say to us in the future: *These things you have done, and I held my peace* (Ps. 49.21).

The second step of humility is attained when the monk, no longer loving his own will, takes no delight in following his own desires, but rather executes in his actions those words of the Lord:

I came not to do my own will, but the will of him who sent me (John 6.38). Scripture also says: pleasure brings punishment, but necessity merits a crown.

The third step of humility is attained when, for the love of God, the monk submits himself in all obedience to his superior, imitating the Lord, of whom the Apostle said: *He was made obedient even unto death* (Phil. 2.8).

The fourth step of humility is attained by virtue of that same obedience, if a monk even in hard and contrary things, even amid unprovoked injuries, accepts the suffering silently and in good spirit. And in bearing them he does not grow weary or retreat, as the Scripture says: *He that perseveres to the end shall be saved* (Matt. 24.13), and again: *Let your heart be comforted, and expect the Lord* (Ps. 26.14). And showing that the faithful man ought to bear for the Lord's sake all possible difficulties, the Psalmist says through the mouth of sufferers: *For you we suffer death all the day long: we are esteemed as sheep for the slaughter* (Ps. 49.21). Later, secure in the hope of divine reward, they rejoice, saying: *But in all things we overcome by the help of him who has loved us* (Rom. 8.37). Also, in another place, the Scripture says: *You have proved us, O Lord; you have tried us, as silver is tried, with fire. You have brought us into the snare; you have laid tribulations upon our backs* (Ps. 65.10–11). And in order to show us that we should be subject to a prior, he continues, saying: *You have placed men over our heads* (Ps. 65.12). Moreover, those who, struck on one cheek, turn the other; who to one taking away their coat give their cloak also; who when forced to carry a burden one mile go along two; who with the apostle Paul put up with false brethren and those who curse them—these too fulfill the command of the Lord, with their patience amid adversities and injuries.

The fifth step of humility is attained if a monk does not conceal but humbly confesses to his abbot all the wicked thoughts which enter his heart, and the wicked things he has secretly committed. In this respect, Scripture exhorts us, saying: *Reveal your ways to the Lord and hope in him* (Ps. 36.5). And again it says: *Confess to the Lord, because he is good, because his mercy endures forever* (Ps. 105.1). And the prophet also says: *I have made known to you my offense, and my injustices I have not hidden. I have said, I will declare openly against myself my injustices to the Lord; and you have pardoned the wickedness of my heart* (Ps. 31.5).

The sixth step of humility is attained, if a monk is content with things lowly and mean, and if he considers himself a poor and undeserving workman, in regard to those things which have been enjoined upon him. He says of himself, with the Prophet: *I have been brought to nothing, and knew it not. I have become as a beast before you, and I am always with you* (Ps. 72.22–23).

The seventh step of humility is attained if the monk not only proclaims with his tongue that he is lower and more worthless than anyone, but also believes this in his heart. Such a man, humiliating himself, says with the Prophet: *I am a worm and no man, the reproach of men and the outcast of the people* (Ps. 21.7). *I have been exalted and am humbled and confounded* (Ps. 87.16). And again: *It is good for me that you have humbled me that I may learn your commandments* (Ps. 118.7).

The eighth step of humility is attained, if the monk does nothing, saving what is urged upon him by the common rule of the monastery and the example of his elders.

The ninth step of humility is attained, if the monk restrains his tongue from speaking and maintains silence, not speaking until a question is put to him. Scripture shows that: *In much speaking you shall not escape sin* (Prov. 10.9), and *A talkative man shall not be directed upon the earth* (Ps. 139.12).

The tenth step of humility is attained, if he is not quick and ready to laugh, as it is written: *The fool lifts his voice in laughter* (Eccl. 21.23).

The eleventh step of humility is attained, if, when the monk speaks, he speaks softly and without laughter, humbly, gravely, and uses few and sensible words, and is not loud in his voice. For it is written: *A wise man is known by a few words* (Ps. 118.107).

The twelfth step of humility is attained if the monk not only in his heart but with his whole body is a lesson in humility to those who see him. We mean: in the performance of the liturgy [*in opere Dei*] at church, in the monastery, in the garden, on the road, in the field or anywhere. Whether sitting, walking or standing he should lower his head, and keep his eyes cast downward. Every hour, thinking himself guilty of his sins, he should imagine himself brought before the awesome judgment of God. He should continuously say in his heart, with the publican in the Gospel, with his eyes cast upon the earth: *Lord, I a sinner am not worthy to lift my eyes to heaven* (Luke 18.13); and also with the Prophet: *I am bowed down and humbled on every side* (Ps. 69.2).

When all these steps of humility have been mounted, the monk shall soon attain to that love of God which, being perfect, casts out fear. Through this love, all that he had hitherto observed not without fear, he shall begin to keep with no labor, naturally out of habit, no longer from fear of hell, but for the love of Christ, by the accustomed enjoyment of virtues. All this the Lord shall deign to show in his servant, now pure of defects and sins, through the instrumentality of the Holy Spirit.

6. Biblical exegesis, according to Gregory the Great

Pope Gregory the Great (590–604) is traditionally considered the last of the four Latin fathers of the Church (the first three are Jerome, Ambrose and Augustine). The son of a Roman official, Gregory as a layman had served in the civil administration of Rome, eventually filling its highest office, that of prefect. He then sought to retire into a monastery, but was summoned back into the world to aid in the government of the Roman church. As deacon, he administered the church's extensive properties, and led an embassy to Constantinople to negotiate with the Eastern emperor. Elected pope in 590, he took an active interest in the feeding and defense of Rome, and through negotiations tried to ward off the threat mounted against the city by the Lombards. He warmly supported Benedictine monasticism, and in 597 sent Augustine and a company of monks to begin the conversion of the English people. The vigorous leadership he exerted in both secular and spiritual affairs makes him the dominant figure among the popes of the early Middle Ages.

Gregory's writings are not as intellectually sophisticated as those of the other Latin fathers, but they enjoyed a great and lasting popularity. In his *Pastoral Care*, he instructed priests on the duties of their ministry, composing a kind of Benedictine rule for the secular clergy (i.e. those living in the world). In his *Dialogues*, he recounted the lives of the holy men of Italy, including St. Benedict (see following section). He also wrote an extensive commentary on the Book of Job, called the *Moralia in Job*.

In a dedicatory letter prefixed to the *Moralia*, Gergory explained his methods of Biblical interpretation. He distinguished three kinds of meaning which could be sought and, on occasion, had to be sought from Scripture. These were the literal, the allegorical and the moral.

(Other commentators looked also for a fourth level of meaning in the text, the "anagogical," which meant the mystical or prophetic.) Gregory was indebted for his methods primarily to St. Augustine and, beyond him, to the great Greek theologian and exegete Origen. But he brought a considerable imagination to his search for allegorical associations, and his *Moralia* was intensively studied in the Middle Ages as something of a model of the genre.

The followng selection contains Chapters 3 and 4 of the dedicatory letter to the *Moralia in Job*. The Latin text may be found in the *Patrologia Latina*, ed. J. P. Migne (Paris, 1849), LXXV, cols. 509–16. The translation is by D. Herlihy.

3. Let it be known that we survey some passages with a literal interpretation. Other passages we examine by means of allegory in a figurative interpretation. Still others we study through the exclusive use of moral comparisons. Finally, some passages we investigate with greater care through the combined use of all three ways. Thus, we first lay a foundation of literal meaning. Then, through the figurative sense, we raise the structure of the mind into a citadel of faith. Finally, through the moral interpretation, we clothe our building with an additional shading.

For surely, what else are the words of truth if not nourishments to refresh the spirit? By interpreting these words in many various ways, we offer a meal to the palate [of the reader]. Thus, we avoid tiring the taste of the invited reader, who is, as it were, our fellow guest at dinner. When he sees many servings offered him, he may take what he considers the more appetizing. Sometimes we neglect to expound literally the clear passages, lest we come too slowly to those which are obscure. Sometimes even, they cannot be understood in a literal meaning, because their sense, superficially considered, engenders error rather than enlightenment among readers. Consider, for example, the words [of Job]: *under him they stoop that bear up the world* (9.13). Who does not know that this great man never believed in the empty tales of the poets? He never thought that the weight of the world is borne up by the exertions of a giant. Job says elsewhere amid his troubles: *so that my soul rather chooseth hanging, and my bones death* (8.15). What person, knowing the truth, would believe that a man of such renown, who, it is certain, received from the Eternal Judge rewards for the virtue of patience, had decided under his blows to end his life by hanging? Sometimes even, if they should be taken in the literal sense, the passages are literally contradictory. Thus, Job says: *Let the day perish wherein I was born, and the night in which it was said: A man child is conceived* (3.3). And a little later he adds: *Let darkness cover it, and let it be wrapped up in bitterness* (3.5). In cursing the same night he adds: *Let that night be solitary* (3.7). Certainly, the day of his birth cannot still be in existence, since time is passing. By what manner, therefore, does he want it wrapped up in darkness? Once having passed, it was no longer in existence. Even if it existed in nature, it could hardly feel bitterness. It is therefore certain, that it was by no means the sensible day, which Job wished stricken with bitterness. And if the night of his conception had passed away in union with other nights, how could he wish it to be solitary? Just as it could not be fixed apart from the flow of time, so it could not be separated from its connection with other nights.

He further said: *How long wilt thou not spare me, nor suffer me to swallow down my spittle* (7.19)? But he said a little before: *The things which before my soul would not touch, now through anguish are my meats* (6.7). Who does not know that it is easier to swallow spittle than meat? It is very difficult to see how a man who announces that he is taking meat at the same time denies that he is able to swallow spittle. And he says again: *I have sinned. What shall I do to thee, O keeper of men* (7.20)? He also says clearly: *thou wilt consume me for the sins of my youth* (13.26). But he adds in another response: *my heart doth not reprehend me in all my life* (27.6). How can it be that his heart has not reproached him, since he publicly states that he sinned? For guilty deeds and an unreproaching heart never go together. When passages taken literally do not agree, they show that something different is to be sought in them. It is as if they are saying: "since you discern that in our superficial sense we lose all meaning, seek rather the meaning within us which may be found logical and consistent."

4. Sometimes, however, if one neglects to accept the literal meaning, he hides the light of truth offered to him. While he seeks laboriously to find in the passages some other profound meaning, he loses that which can be apprehended without difficulty on the surface. For the holy man said: *If I have denied to the poor what they desired, and have made the eyes of the widow wait; if I have eaten my morsel alone, and the fatherless hath not eaten thereof; if I have despised him that was perishing for want of clothing, and the poor man that had no covering; if his sides have not blessed me, and if he were not warmed with the fleece of my sheep* (31.16–20). If we

force these words violently under an allegorical interpretation, we devoid all his charitable deeds of meaning. For just as the divine word exercises the learned with its mysteries, so it frequently cheers the simple with its clarity. In its obvious sense, it has food to nourish little ones. In its secret meaning, it can command the admiration of the most learned minds. It is, if I may say so, almost like a river, both shallow and deep, in which a lamb may walk and an elephant swim. According as the context of each passage requires, I carefully change the order of interpretation. So much the better does one find the sense of the divine word, the more he varies the kinds of interpretation, according to need.

7. The founding of Monte Cassino, according to Gregory the Great

The *Dialogues* of Pope Gregory the Great, which were written in 594, recount the lives of the holy men of Italy, and are an excellent example of hagiographical literature and miracle stories, which enjoyed so great a popularity in the early Middle Ages.

The *Dialogues*, in four books, are cast in the form of a conversation between Gregory and a young man named Peter. The second book deals with the life of St. Benedict, who had died probably in 547, nearly fifty years before Gregory composed it. In spite of its late date, it is, apart from the Rule itself, our principal source concerning the career of the great legislator of Latin monasticism.

The following selection takes up the story of Benedict's life at about the year 520. Benedict, who had been living as a hermit in a cave at Subiaco in central Italy, had attracted a fair number of disciples through his reputation for sanctity. He organized them into twelve small communities, but the hostility of a local priest convinced him that he should move elsewhere. He selected Monte Cassino in the Campania for his new home. The monastery he founded there has since been regarded as the motherhouse of the Benedictine order.

The translation is adapted from an English version of the *Dialogues* published at Paris in 1609 and reedited in *The Dialogues of Saint Gregory surnamed the Great, translated into our English Tongue by P. W. and printed at Paris in 1609*. Reedited with an introduction and notes by Edmund G. Gardner (London: Philip Lee Warner, 1911),

pp. 65–101. Spellings, names, punctuation and some phrases have been
modernized, and the chapter headings of the original omitted. Some
corrections have also been made in the interest of greater accuracy,
by comparisons with the Latin text published in *Gregorii Magni Dia-
logi,* ed. U. Moricca (Rome: Tipografia del Senato, 1924).

8. *Gregory:* The foresaid monasteries were zealous in the love of
our Lord Jesus Christ, and their fame spread far and near. Many
persons abandoned the secular life, and subdued the passions of
their soul under the light yoke of our Savior. Then (as the manner
of wicked people is, to envy at that virtue which they themselves
do not wish to follow) one Florentius, priest of a near-by church,
and grandfather to Florentius our subdeacon, possessed with diabolical malice, began to envy the holy man's virtues, to criticize his
manner of living, and to prevent as many as he could from going
to visit him. But then he saw that he could not hinder his virtuous
activities but that, on the contrary, the fame of his holy life increased and many daily, upon the very report of his sanctity, betook themselves to a better state of life. Burning more and more
with the coals of envy, he became far worse. Though he did not
desire to imitate his commendable life, yet he wanted to have the
reputation of his virtuous way of living. In conclusion, so much
did malicious envy blind him, and so far did he wade in that sin,
that he poisoned a loaf, and sent it to the servant of almighty God,
as if it were a holy present. The man of God received it with great
thanks, yet was not ignorant of that which was hidden within. At
dinner time, a crow daily used to come to him from the next wood,
and took bread from his hands. Coming that day after his manner,
the man of God threw him the loaf which the priest had sent him,
giving him this command: "In the name of Jesus Christ our Lord,
take up that loaf, and leave it in some such place where no man
may find it." Then the crow, opening his mouth, and lifting up
his wings, began to hop up and down about the loaf, and after his
manner to cry out, as though he would have said that he was willing to obey, and yet could not do what he was commanded. The
man of God again and again bade him, saying: "Take it up without
fear, and throw it where no man may find it." At length, with
much ado, the crow took it up, and flew away. After three hours,
having dispatched the loaf, he returned back again, and received his
usual allowance from the man of God.

But the venerable father, perceiving the priest so wickedly bent against his life, was far more sorry for him than grieved for himself. Florentius, seeing that he could not kill the body of the master, now labored at destroying the souls of his disciples. For that purpose he sent into the yard of the abbey before their eyes seven naked young women. There they joined hands, played and danced a long time before them, to the end that, by this means, they might inflame their minds to sinful lust. The holy man beheld this damnable sight out of his cell, and feared the danger which thereby might ensue to his younger monks. Considering that all this was done only for the persecuting of himself, he gave in to the man's envy. Therefore, after he had appointed governors for those abbeys and oratories which he had built there, and left some under their charge, he himself, in the company of a few monks, removed to another place. Thus the man of God, with humility, gave place to the other's malice. But yet almighty God of justice did severely punish his wickedness. For when the foresaid priest, being in his chamber, learned of the departure of holy Benedict, and was very glad of that news, behold (the whole house besides continuing safe and sound) that chamber alone in which he was, fell down, and so killed him. The holy man's disciple Maurus learned of the strange accident, and straightways sent him word, as he was as yet scarce ten miles off. He wanted him to return again, because the priest that persecuted him was slain. When Benedict heard this, he was exceedingly sorrowful, and lamented much, both because his enemy died in such a fashion, and also because one of his monks rejoiced at it. Therefore he gave him penance, for the reason that sending such news, he presumed to rejoice at his enemy's death.

Peter: The things you report are strange, and much to be wondered at. For in making the rock to yield forth water, I see Moses. In the iron, which came from the bottom of the lake, I behold Heliseus. In the walking of Maurus upon the water, I perceive Peter. In the obedience of the crow, I contemplate Helias. And in lamenting the death of his enemy, I recognized David. Therefore, in my opinion, this one man was full of the spirit of all good men.

Gregory: The man of God, Benedict, had the spirit of the one true God, who, by the grace of our redemption, has filled the hearts of his elect servants. Of him, St. John says: *He was the true light, which doth lighten every man coming into this world* (John 1.9). Of him, again, we find it written: *Of his fullness we have all received* (John 1.16). For God's holy servants might receive virtues of our Lord, but to bestow them upon others they could not. Therefore it was he who gave the signs of miracles to his servants, and who promised to give the sign of Jonas to his enemies. He deigned to die in the sight of the proud, and to rise again before the eyes of the humble, to the end that the proud might behold what they contemned, and the humble see that which they ought to worship and love. By reason of this mystery it comes to pass that, whereas the proud cast their eyes upon the contempt of his death, the humble, to the contrary, lay hold of the glory of his power and might, against death.

Peter: To what places, I implore you, after this, did the holy man go? Did he afterwards in them work any miracles, or no?

Gregory: The holy man, changing his place, did not for all that change his enemy. For afterwards he endured so much the more grievous battles, to the extent that he now had the master of all wickedness fighting openly against him. For the town, which is called Cassino, stands upon the side of a high mountain, which contains, as it were in the lap thereof, the foresaid town, and beyond it so rises in height the space of three miles, that its top seems to touch the very heavens. In this place there was an ancient chapel in which the foolish and simple country people, according to the custom of the old pagans, worshipped the god Apollo. Round about it likewise upon all sides, there were woods for the service of the devils, in which, even to that very time, the mad multitude of infidels offered most wicked sacrifice. The man of God coming thither, beat in pieces the idol, overthrew the altar, set fire on the woods, and in the temple of Apollo he built the oratory of St. Martin. Where the altar of the same Apollo was, he made an oratory of St. John. By his continual preaching, he brought the people dwelling in those parts to embrace the faith of Christ. The old enemy of mankind, not taking this in good part, did not now stealthily or in a dream, but in open sight present himself to the eyes of that holy father. With great outcries he complained that he had suffered violence. The monks heard the noise which he made, but they could not see the devil himself. As the venerable father told them, he appeared visibly to him most dark and wrathful, as though, with his fiery mouth and flaming eyes, he would have torn him in pieces. The monks did hear what the devil said to him. For first he would call him by his name. Because the man of God elected not to answer him, then he would fall cursing and railing at him. What he cried out, calling him "Blessed Benedict," and yet found that he gave him no answer, straightways he would change his tune, and say: "Cursed Benedict, and not blessed. What have you to do with me? And why do you so persecute me?" Thus, new battles of the old enemy against the servant of God are to be looked for. Against him he willingly made war but, against his will, he gave him occasion of many notable victories.

9. Upon a certain day, when the monks were building up the cells of the same abbey, there lay a stone which they meant to employ about that business. When two or three were not able to remove it, they called for more help, but all in vain. It remained so immovable as though it had grown into the very earth. From this they plainly perceived that the devil himself was sitting upon it, since so many men's hands could not so much as once move it. Therefore, finding that their own labors could do nothing, they sent for the man of God, to help them with his prayers against the devil, who hindered the removing of that stone. The holy man came, and after some praying, he gave it his blessing. Then they carried it away so quickly, as though it had been of no weight at all.

10. Then the man of God thought it good that they should at once before his departure dig up the ground in the same place. With this accomplished, and a deep hole made, the monks found there an idol of brass. The idol was by chance thrown into the kitchen. Suddenly they beheld fire come from it, which to all their sight seemed to set the whole kitchen on fire. To quench it, the monks cast on water, and made such a noise that the man of God, hearing it, came to see what the matter was. He beheld no fire at all, which they said that they did, and he bowed down his head forthwith to his prayers. Then he perceived that they were deluded with fantastical fire. He therefore bade them bless their eyes, that they might behold the kitchen safe and sound, and not those fantastical flames, which the devil had falsely devised.

11. Again, as the monks were making a certain wall somewhat higher, because that was necessary, the man of God in the meantime was in his cell at his prayers. The old enemy appeared to him in an insulting manner, telling him that he was now going to his monks, who were working. Of this, the man of God, in all haste, gave them warning, wishing them to look to themselves, because the devil was at that time coming among them. The message was scarcely delivered, when the wicked spirit overthrew the new wall which they were building. With the fall he slew a little young child, a monk, who was the son of a certain courtier. At this pitiful

accident, all were very sorry and exceedingly grieved, not so much for the loss of the wall, as for the death of their brother. In all haste they sent this grave news to the venerable man Benedict. He commanded them to bring to him the young boy, mangled and maimed as he was. This they did, but yet they could not carry him any otherwise than in a sack. For the stones of the wall had not only broken his limbs, but also his very bones. When he was brought in that manner to the man of God, he bade them lay him in his cell, and in that place upon which he used to pray. Then, putting them all forth, he shut the door, and fell more earnestly to his prayers than he did at other times. O admirable miracle! For the very same hour he made him sound, and as lively as ever he was before. He sent him again to his former work, that he also might help the monks to finish that wall. The old serpent thought he could have mocked Benedict concerning this boy's death!

Among other miracles which the man of God did, he began also to be famous for the spirit of prophecy, as to foretell what was to happen, and to relate to them who were present such things as were done in their absence.

12. The order of his abbey was, that when the monks went abroad (to deliver any message), never to eat or drink anything out of their cloister. This was diligently observed, according to the prescription of their rule. Upon a certain day, some of the monks went forth upon such business. Being obligated in dispatching it to tarry somewhat long abroad, it happened that they stayed at the house of a religious woman. There they ate and refreshed themselves. It was late before they came back to the abbey. They went as the manner was, and asked their father's blessing. He demanded of them, where they had eaten. They said nowhere. "Why do you," he said, "tell an untruth? For did you not go into such a woman's house? And eat such and such kind of meat, and drink so many cups?" When they heard him so recount in particular, both where they had stayed, what kind of meat they had eaten, and how often they had drunk, and perceived well that he knew all whatsoever they had done, they fell down trembling at his feet, and confessed that they had done wickedly. He straightways pardoned them for that fault, persuading himself that they would not any more in his absence presume to do any such thing, seeing they now perceived that he was present with them in spirit.

13. A brother of Valentinian the monk, of whom I made mention before, was a layman, but devout and religious. He used every year

to travel from his own house to the abbey, to visit his natural brother as well as to seek the prayers of God's servant. His manner was not to eat anything at all that day before he came there. After he had been a while upon his journey, he lighted into the company of another, who carried meat with him to eat on the way. After the day was well spent, he spoke to him in this manner. "Come brother," he said, "let us refresh ourselves, lest we faint on our journey." He answered him: "God forbid, for I shall not eat by any means, seeing that I am now going to the venerable father Benedict, and my custom is to fast until I see him." The other, upon this answer, said no more for the space of a hour. But afterward, having traveled a little farther, again he urged him to eat something. Yet then likewise he utterly refused, because he meant to go through fasting as he was. His companion was content, and so went forward with him, without taking anything himself. But when they had now gone very far, and were well wearied with long traveling, at length they came to a meadow. There they found a fountain, and all such other pleasant things as can refresh men's bodies. Then his companion said to him again, "Behold, here is water, a green meadow, and a very sweet place, in which we may refresh ourselves and rest a little, that we may be the better able to finish the rest of our journey." These kind words bewitched his ears, and the pleasant place flattered his eyes. He was content to yield to the suggestion, and so they took to eating the meat together. Coming afterward in the evening to the abbey, they brought him to the venerable father Benedict. He asked his blessing. Then the holy man held up against him what he had done on the way, speaking to him in this manner: "How did it happen, brother," he said, "that the devil talking to you, by means of your companion, could not at the first nor second time persuade you? But yet he did at the third, and made you do what best pleased him?" The good man, hearing these words, fell down at his feet, confessing the fault of his frailty. He was grieved, and so much the more ashamed of his sin, because he perceived that though he was absent, he yet offended in the sight of that venerable father.

Peter: I see well that the holy man had in his soul the spirit of Heliseus, who was present with a disciple who was far from him.

Gregory: You must, good Peter, for a little while be silent, that you may know matters yet far more important.

14. In the time of the Goths, Totila their king learned that the holy man had the spirit of prophecy. As he was going towards his

monastery, he remained in a place somewhat far off, and beforehand sent the father word of his coming. Answer was returned to
him, that he might come at his pleasure. The king, as he was a man
wickedly disposed, thought he would try whether the man of God
was a prophet, as it was reported, or no. He had a certain man of
his guard named Riggo. He had his own shoes placed upon him,
and had him dressed with his other princely robes, commanding
him to go as if it were himself to the man of God. To give the
better color to this device, he sent three to attend him, who especially were always with the king, to wit, Vultericus, Rudericus and
Blindinus. He charged them that in the presence of the servant of
God, they should be close to him, and behave themselves in such
fashion as though he had in fact been King Totila. They should
diligently do for him all other services, to the end that both by
such dutiful kind of behavior, and also by his purple robes, he
might in truth be taken for the king himself. Riggo, furnished with
that brave apparel, and accompanied with many courtiers, came towards the abbey. The man of God was then sitting a little way off.
When Riggo had come so near that he could well understand what
the man of God said, he spoke thus, in the hearing of them all:
"Take off, my good son, take off that apparel. That which you are
wearing is not your own." Riggo, hearing this, fell straightways
down to the ground. He was very much afraid, for presuming to
have mocked so worthy a man. All his attendants and servants fell
down likewise to the earth. After they rose up again, they dared
not approach any nearer to his presence. Returning back to their
king, they told him with fear how quickly they were discovered.
15. Then Totila himself in person went to the man of God. Seeing
him sitting afar off, he dared not come near, but fell down to the
ground. The holy man, speaking to him two or three times, desired him to rise, and at length came to him, and with his own hands
lifted him up from the earth, where he lay prostrate. Then, entering into talk, he reprehended him for his wicked deeds, and in a
few words told him all which would befall him, saying: "You
daily commit much wickedness, and have done many great sins.
Now at length give up your sinful life. Into the city of Rome shall
you enter, and over the sea shall you pass. Nine years shall you
reign, and in the tenth you shall leave this mortal life." The king,
hearing these things, was sorely afraid. Asking the holy man to
commend him to God in his prayers, he departed. From that time
forward he was not at all so cruel as he had been before. Not long

after he went to Rome, sailed over into Sicily, and, in the tenth year of his reign, he lost his kingdom together with his life.

The bishop of Camisina also used to visit the servant of God. The holy man dearly loved him for his virtuous life. The bishop, therefore, talking with him of King Totila, of his taking of Rome, and the destruction of the city, said: "This city will be so spoiled and ruined by him, that it will never be more inhabited." The man of God answered him: "Rome," he said, "shall not be utterly destroyed by strangers. But it shall be so shaken with tempests, lightnings, whirlwinds, and earthquakes, that it will fall to decay of itself." The mysteries of this prophecy we now behold as clear as the day. For we see before our eyes in this very city, the walls shaken by storms, houses ruined, churches overthrown, and buildings rotten with old age daily collapsing. It is true that Honoratus, who told me of this prophecy, says that he heard it not from Benedict's own mouth, but learned of it from other monks, who did hear it themselves.

16. At the same time a certain clergyman, who served in the church of Aquino, was possessed by the devil. The venerable man Constantius, bishop of the city, sent him to many places of holy martyrs for help. But God's holy martyrs would not deliver him, to the end that the world might know what great grace was in the servant of God, Benedict. At length he was brought to him. Benedict, praying for help to Jesus Christ our Lord, at once cast the old enemy out of the possessed man's body. He gave him this charge: "Go your way, and henceforth do not eat meat. Do not presume to enter into holy orders. If ever you shall attempt any such thing, the devil again will have power over you."

The man departed safe and sound. Because punishment fresh in memory tends to terrify the mind, he observed for a time what the man of God had given him in commandment. But after many years, when all his elders were dead, and he saw men younger than himself preferred to holy orders, he neglected the words of the man of God, as though forgotten through length of time. He took upon him holy orders. Thereupon straightways the devil that before had left him entered again, and never ceased tormenting him, until he had separated his soul from his body.

Peter: This holy man, as I perceive, did know the secret counsel of God. For he saw that this clergyman was delivered to the power of the devil, to the end that he should not presume to enter into holy orders.

Gregory: Why should he not know the secrets of God, as he kept the commandments of God. The Scripture says: *He that cleaveth unto our Lord, is one spirit with him* (1 Cor. 6. 17).

Peter: If he that cleaves to our Lord is one spirit with our Lord, what is the meaning of that which the Apostle says: *Who knoweth the sense of our Lord, or who hath been his counselor* (Rom. 11.34)? For it does not seem consistent that he, who is united in one spirit with the Lord, should be ignorant of his thoughts.

Gregory: Holy men, who are one with our Lord, are not ignorant of his thoughts. For the same Apostle says: *For what man knoweth those things which belong to man, but the spirit of man which is in him? Even so, the things which belong to God, no man knoweth, but the spirit of God* (1 Cor. 2.9–11). And to show also that he knew such things as belong to God, he adds straight after: *But we have not received the spirit of this world, but the spirit which is of God.* And for this reason, he says again: *that eye hath not seen, nor ear heard, nor hath it entered into the heart of man, the things which God hath prepared for them that love him, but God hath revealed to us by his spirit.*

Peter: If then the mysteries of God were revealed to the same Apostle by the spirit of God, why did he then, in treating this question, first set down these words: *O the depth of the riches of the wisdom and knowledge of God: how incomprehensible are his judgments, and his ways undiscoverable* (Rom. 11.33)? And again, while I am thus speaking of this matter, another question comes to my mind. For the prophet David said to our Lord: *With my lips have I uttered all the judgments of thy mouth* (Ps. 118.13). Since it is less a thing to know than to utter, what is the reason that St. Paul affirms that the judgments of God are incomprehensible, and yet David says that he did not only know them, but also with his lips pronounced them?

Gregory: To both these questions I have already briefly answered, when I said that holy men, in that they are one with our Lord, are not ignorant of the thoughts of our Lord. For all such, as do devoutly follow our Lord, are also by devotion one with our Lord. Yet for all this, in that they are laden with the burden of their corruptible flesh, they are not with God. And so in that they are joined with him, they know the secret judgments of God, and in that they are separated from God, they know them not. For seeing they do not as yet perfectly penetrate his secret mysteries, they give testimony that his judgments are incomprehensible. But those who do adhere to him with their soul, and cleaving to the sayings of the Holy Scripture, or to secret revelations, acknowledge what they receive—such persons both know these things and do utter them. For those judgments which God conceals they know not, and those which he utters they know. Therefore, when the prophet David had said *I have with my lips uttered all the judgments* (Ps. 118.13), he adds immediately, *of thy mouth*, as though he would plainly say: "Those judgments I may both know and utter, which I knew you spoke, for those things which you did not speak, without all question you have concealed from our knowledge." Thus, the sayings of David and St. Paul agree together. For the judgments of God are incomprehensible, and yet those which he himself with his own mouth deigned to speak are uttered with men's tongues. Thus, men may come to a knowledge of them, and being revealed, they may be uttered, and by no means can they be kept secret.

Peter: Now I see the answer to my question. But I pray you to proceed, if anything yet remains to be told of his virtue and miracles.

17. *Gregory:* A certain noble man called Theoprobus was by the good counsel of holy Benedict converted. Because of his virtue and merit of life, he was very close and friendly with him. One day this man, coming into his cell, found him weeping very bitterly. Having waited a good while, and yet not seeing him cease to weep (for the man of God did not usually weep in his prayers, but was rather sad), he asked the cause of his great sorrow. He answered him at once, saying: "All this abbey which I have built, and all such things as I have made ready for my brethren, are by the judgment of almighty God delivered to the pagans, to be pillaged and overthrown. Scarcely could I obtain of God to have their lives spared, who should then live in it." His words Theoprobus then heard, but we see them to be proved most true. We know that that very abbey is now suppressed by the Lombards. For not long since, in the night time, when the monks were asleep, they entered in, and pillaged all things. But not one man could they capture there. And so almighty God fulfilled what he promised to his faithful servant. For though he gave them the house and all the goods, he yet preserved their lives. In this I see that Benedict resembled St. Paul. Although Paul's ship lost all the goods, yet, for his consolation, he had the lives of all who were in his company saved for him, so that no man was cast away.

18. Upon a certain time, Exhilaratus our monk, a lay brother, whom you know, was sent by his master to the monastery of the man of God, to carry to him two wooden bottles, commonly called flagons, full of wine. As he was going on the way, he hid one of them in a bush for himself, and presented the other to venerable Benedict. He took it very thankfully and, when the man was going away, he gave him this warning: "Take heed, my son," he said, "that you do not drink from that flagon which you have hidden in the bush. But first be careful to tilt it down, and you shall find what is within it." The poor man, thus pitifully confounded by the man of God, went his way. Coming back to the place where the flagon was hidden, he wished to try the truth of what was told him. As he was tilting it down, a snake at once leaped forth. Then Exhilaratus, perceiving what had gotten into the wine, began to be afraid of that wickedness which he had committed.

19. Not far from his abbey there was a village, in which many men had been converted by the sermons of Benedict from idolatry to the true faith of Christ. Certain nuns also were there in the same town. To them he often sent some of his monks to preach to them, for the good of their souls. One day, a monk who was sent, after he had ended his exhortation, took by the entreaty of the nuns certain small napkins, and hid them for his own use under his habit. Upon his return to the abbey, the man of God very sharply rebuked him, saying: "How did it happen, brother, that sin has entered under your habit?" At these words the monk was much amazed, for he had quite forgotten what he had put there. He therefore did not know any cause why he should deserve that rebuke. Thereupon the holy man spoke to him in plain terms, and said: "Was not I present when you took the handkerchiefs of the nuns, and put them under your habit for your own private use?" The monk, hearing this, fell down at his feet, and was sorry that he had behaved himself so improperly. He drew forth those handkerchiefs from under his habit and threw them all away.

20. Once, while the venerable father was at supper, one of his monks, who was the son of a great man, held the candle. As he was standing there, and the other was eating, he began to entertain proud thoughts in his mind, and to speak thus within himself: "Who is he, that I thus serve at supper, and hold the candle for him? And who am I, that I should do him any such service?" With that thought, the holy man at once turned to him, and with severe rebuke spoke thus to him: "Cross your heart, brother, for what

is it that you say? Cross your heart." Immediately, he called another of the monks, and bade him take the candle out of his hands. He commanded the other to cease serving, and to repose himself. When he was asked by the monks, what it was that he thought, he told them how inwardly he swelled with pride, and what he spoke against the man of God secretly in his own heart. Then they all saw very well that nothing could be hidden from venerable Benedict, seeing that the very sound of men's inward thoughts came to his ears.

21. At another time, there was a great famine in the same country of Campania, so that all kinds of people tasted of the misery. All the wheat of Benedict's monastery was spent, and likewise all the bread, so that there remained no more than five loaves for dinner. The venerable man, seeing the monks sad, both rebuked them modestly for their downcast spirits, and comforted them with this promise: "Why," he said, "are you so grieved in your minds for lack of bread? Indeed, today there is some scarcity, but tomorrow you shall have plenty." And so it happened, for the next day two hundred bushels of flour were found in sacks before his cell door, which almighty God sent them. But by whom, or what means, that is unknown to this very day. When the monks saw this miracle, they gave thanks to God, and by this they learned that, during scarcities, they should not have any doubt of plenty.

Peter: Tell me, I pray you, whether this servant of God had always the spirit of prophecy, when it pleased himself or only at certain times?

Gregory: The spirit of prophecy does not always illuminate the minds of the prophets. As it is written of the Holy Ghost that *he breatheth where he will* (John 3.8), so we are also to know that he breathes likewise for whatever cause, and whenever he pleases. And thus it happened, that when King David asked Nathan whether he might build a temple for the honor of God, the prophet Nathan gave his consent, and yet afterward utterly forbade it. Likewise, when Heliseus saw the woman weeping and did not know the cause, he said to his servant who was troubling her: *Let her alone, for her soul is in grief, and God hath concealed it from me, and hath not told me* (4 Kings 4.27). Almighty God does this out of his great goodness. For giving at some times the spirit of prophecy, and at other times withdrawing it, he both lifts up the prophets' minds on high, and yet preserves them in humility. Thus, by the gift of the Spirit, they may know what they are by God's grace,

and at other times, destitute of the same Spirit, they may understand what they are of themselves.

Peter: There is very great reason for what you say. But, I pray
you, let me hear more of the venerable Benedict, if there is anything else that comes to your remembrance.

22. *Gregory:* At another time he was asked by a certain virtuous
man to build an abbey for his monks upon his property, not far
from the city of Taracina. The holy man was content, and appointed an abbot and prior, with different monks under them.
When they were departing, he promised that, upon such a day,
he would come and show them in what place the oratory should
be made, and where the refectory should stand, and all the other
necessary rooms. Taking his blessing, they went their way. For
the day appointed, which they greatly expected, they made all
such things ready as were necessary to entertain him, and those
who might come in his company. But the very night before, the
man of God appeared to the abbot and the prior in their sleep, and
described in detail to them where each place and office was to be
built. When they were both risen, they compared together what
each of them had seen in their sleep. But yet not giving full credit
to that vision, they awaited the man of God himself in person,
according to his promise. When they saw that he was not coming,
they came back to him very sorrowfully, saying: "We expected,
father, that you should have come according to promise, and told
us where each place should have been built. This you did not do."
He answered them: "Why do you say so, good brethren? Did I
not come as I promised you?" When they asked at what time it
was: "Why," he said, "did I not appear to each of you in your
sleep, and appoint how and where every place was to be built?
Go your way, and according to that vision which you then saw,
build up the abbey." They much marveled at this word, and going
back, they had it built in such a fashion as they had been taught
by him through revelation.

Peter: I would gladly learn by what means that could be done,
that is, that he should go so far to tell them something in their
sleep, which they should both hear and know by vision.

Gregory: Why do you, Peter, seek out and doubt, in what
manner this thing was done? For it is certain that the soul is of a
more noble nature than the body. By authority of Scripture we
know that the prophet Habacuc was carried from Judea and was
suddenly set in Chaldea, with that dinner by which the prophet

Daniel was refreshed; and presently afterwards he was brought back to Judea. If then Habacuc could in a moment with his body go so far and carry provision for another man's dinner, what marvel is it, if the holy father Benedict obtained grace to go in spirit and to inform the souls of his brethren who were asleep, concerning such things as were necessary? As Habacuc went bodily with bodily food, so Benedict went spiritually about the dispatch of spiritual business.

Peter: I confess that your words have satisfied my doubtful mind. But I would like to know what manner of man he was in his ordinary talk and conversation.

23. *Gregory:* His common talk, Peter, was usually full of virtue. For his heart conversed so above in heaven, that no vain words could proceed from his mouth. If at any time he spoke anything, yet not as one that determined what was best to be done, but only in a threatening manner, his speech in that case was so effectual and forcible, as though he had not doubtfully or uncertainly, but assuredly pronounced and given sentence. For not far from his abbey there lived two nuns in a place by themselves, born of noble parents. A good religious man served them for the dispatch of their outward business. But as nobility of family breeds in some ignobility of mind, and makes them show less humility in conversation, because they remember still what superiority they had above others, even so it was with these nuns. For they had not yet learned to temper their tongues, and to subdue them with the bridle of their habit. They often by their indiscreet speech provoked the foresaid religious man to anger. He bore with them a long time, and at length complained to the man of God. He told him with what reproachful words they addressed him. Thereupon he sent them this message immediately: "Amend your tongues, otherwise I do excommunicate you." He did not then actually pronounce this sentence of excommunication, but only threatened it if they did not amend themselves. But they, for all this, changed their habits not at all. Not long after, both departed this life, and were buried in the church. When solemn mass was celebrated in the same church, the deacon, according to custom, said with a loud voice: "If there be any here who do not communicate, let them depart." Their old nurse, who used to give to our Lord an offering for them, at that time saw them rise out of their graves and leave the church. Having seen that many times, at those words of the deacon, they left the church and could not tarry within, she re-

membered what message the man of God sent them while they were yet alive. For he told them that he did deprive them of the communion, unless tney amended their tongues and habits. Then with great sorrow, the whole matter was told to the man of God. He at once with his own hands gave an oblation, saying: "Go your ways, and have this offered to our Lord for them, and they shall not remain any longer excommunicate." When this oblation was offered for them, and the deacon, as he used to, crying out that such as did not communicate should depart, they were not seen any more to go out of the church. Thereby it was certain that, since they did not depart with those who did not communicate, that they had received the communion of our Lord by the hands of his servant.

Peter: It is very strange what you report. How could he, though a venerable and most holy man, while still living in mortal body, absolve those souls which stood now before the invisible judgment of God?

Gregory: Was he not still mortal, Peter, who heard from our Savior: *Whatsoever thou shalt bind upon earth, it shall be bound also in heaven; and whatsoever thou shalt loose on earth, shall be loosed also in the heavens* (Matt. 16.19)? His place of binding and loosing is held at this time by those who by faith and virtuous life are governing the Church. To bestow such power upon earthly men, the Creator of heaven and earth descended from heaven to earth. God, who for man's sake was made flesh, deigned to bestow upon him that flesh might judge of spiritual things. From this our weakness rose up above itself; from this the strength of God was weakened under itself.

Peter: Your words do yield a very good reason for the power of his miracles.

24. *Gregory:* Upon a certain day, a young boy who was a monk, loving his parents more than reason allowed, went from the abbey to their house, without requesting the father's blessing beforehand. On the same day that he came home to them, he departed this life. And being buried, his body, the next day after, was found cast out of the grave. They again had it placed within, and again, the day following, they found it as before. Then in great haste they went to the man of God, fell down at his feet, and with many tears beseeched him to show his favor to him who was dead. The man of God with his own hands gave to them the holy communion of our Lord's body, saying: "Go, and with great reverence lay

this our Lord's body upon his breast, and so bury him." When they had done this, the dead corpse after that remained quietly in the grave. By this you perceive, Peter, what merit he possessed with our Lord Jesus Christ, seeing that the earth would not accept the body of one who departed this world out of Benedict's favor.

Peter: I perceive it very well, and wonderfully admire it.

25. *Gregory:* There was a certain monk who was so inconstant and fickle of mind, that he wished to abandon the abbey. For this fault, the man of God daily rebuked him, and often times gave him good admonitions. But yet, for all this, he would by no means stay among them, and therefore he pleaded continually that he might be discharged. The venerable man at one time, wearied with his requests, in anger bade him depart. He was no sooner out of the abbey gate, but he found a dragon in the way awaiting him with open mouth. As it was about to devour him, he began in great fear and trembling to cry out aloud, saying: "Help, help! This dragon will eat me up." At this noise the monks ran out. They saw no dragon, but finding him there shaking and trembling, they brought him back again to the abbey. He immediately promised that he would never more forsake the monastery, and so ever after he continued in his profession. For by the prayers of the holy man, he saw the dragon coming against him, whom before, when he saw it not, he willingly followed.

26. But I must not here pass over with silence that which I heard from the honorable man, Anthony. He said that his father's servant was so pitifully punished with a leprosy, that all his hair fell off, his body swelled, and filthy corruption openly came forth. He was sent by his father to the man of God, who quickly restored him to his former health.

27. Nor is that to be omitted, which one of his disciples called Peregrinus used to tell. Upon a certain day, an honest man, who was in debt, found no other means to help himself, but thought it best to acquaint the man of God with his need. Thereupon he came to the abbey, and finding the servant of almighty God, told him how he was troubled by his creditor for twelve shillings which he owed him. The venerable man said to him that he did not himself have so much money. Yet giving him comforting words, he said: "Go your way, and after two days come to me again, for I cannot help you at present." In these two days, after his manner, he gave himself to prayer. When upon the third day the poor man came back, thirteen shillings were suddenly found upon the

chest of the abbey, which was full of wheat. The man of God had them given to him who needed but twelve, both to pay his debt, and also to defray his own expenses. But now I shall return to speak of such things as I learned from the mouth of his own disciples, who were mentioned before in the beginning of this book. A certain man had an enemy who did notably spite and malign him. His damnable hatred proceeded so far that he poisoned his drink. Although it did not kill him, yet it changed his skin in such a fashion that it was of many colors, as though he had been infected with a leprosy. But the man of God restored him to his former health. For as soon as he touched him, immediately all that variety of colors departed from his body.

28. At that time there was a great famine in Campania. The man of God gave away all the wealth of the abbey to poor people, so that in the cellar there was nothing left but a little oil in a glass. A certain subdeacon called Agapitus came to him, insistently asking that he would bestow a little oil upon him. Our Lord's servant, who was resolved to give away all upon earth, that he might find all in heaven, commanded that oil to be given him. The monk who kept the cellar heard what the father commanded, but he did not perform it. When Benedict inquired not long after whether he had given that which he wanted, the monk told him that he had not, adding that if he had given it away there would be nothing left for the convent. Then in anger he commanded others to take that glass with the oil, and to throw it out the window, to the end that nothing might remain in the abbey contrary to obedience. The monks did so, and threw it out a window. Under the window there was a steep cliff, full of rough and craggy stones. The glass landed upon them, but yet remained for all that as sound as though it had never been thrown out at all. Neither the glass was broken nor any of the oil shed. Then the man of God commanded that it be taken up again and, whole as it was, be given to him who asked for it. In the presence of the other brethren he reprimanded the disobedient monk, both for his infidelity, and also for his proud mind.

29. After this rebuke, he fell to praying with the rest of his brethren. In the place where they were there stood an empty barrel with a cover upon it. As the holy man continued in his prayers, the oil within so increased that it lifted up the cover, which at length fell off. The oil, which was now higher than the mouth of the barrel, began to run over upon the pavement.

As soon as the servant of God, Benedict, saw this, immediately he ceased his prayers, and the oil likewise ceased to overflow the barrel. Then he again admonished that mistrusting and disobedient monk, that he would learn to have faith and humility. He, upon so wholesome an admonition, was ashamed, because the venerable father had by miracle shown the power of almighty God, as before he told him when he had first rebuked him. Thus, there was no cause why any should afterward doubt his promise, since at one and the same time, in place of a small glass almost empty which he gave away, he bestowed upon them a whole barrel full of oil. 30. One time, he was going to the oratory of St. John, which is on top of the mountain. The old enemy of mankind upon a mule, like a physician, met him, carrying in his hand a horn and a mortar. When he demanded where he was going, he replied: "To your monks, to give them some medicine." The venerable father went forward to his prayers. When he had done, he returned in all haste. But the wicked spirit found an old monk drawing water. He entered into him, and immediately cast him upon the ground and grievously tormented him. The man of God, coming from his prayers and seeing him in such pitiful condition, gave him only a little blow with his hand. At the same instant he cast out that cruel devil, so that he dared not any more presume to return.

Peter: I would gladly know, whether he always worked such notable miracles by prayer. Or else did he sometimes do them only at his will and pleasure?

Gregory: Those who are the devout servants of God, when necessity requires, commonly work miracles in both manner of ways. Sometimes they effect wonderful things by their prayers, and sometimes only by their power and authority. St. John says: *So many as received him, he gave them power to be made the sons of God* (John 1.12). What marvel is it, if they who by power are the sons of God are able by power to do wonderful things? That they work miracles in both ways we learn from St. Peter. He by his prayers raised up Tabitha, and by his sharp reprimand sentenced Ananias and Sapphira to death for their lying. For we do not read that he prayed at all at their death, but only rebuked them for that sin which they had committed. It is therefore certain that sometimes they do these things by power, and sometimes by prayer. By severely rebuking Ananias and Sapphira, St. Peter deprived them of life, and by prayer restored Tabitha to life. For proof of this, I shall now tell you of two miracles, which the faithful servant of God, Benedict, did, in which it shall appear most plainly that he wrought the one by that power which God gave him, and obtained the other by virtue of his prayers.

31. There was a certain Goth called Zalla, an Arian heretic. In the time of King Totila, he persecuted religious men of the Catholic Church with such monstrous cruelty that whatever priest or monk came into his presence never departed alive. On a certain day, this man, intent upon rapine and pillage, pitifully tortured a poor countryman, to make him confess where his money and wealth were. Overcome with extremity of pain, he said that he had committed all his property to the custody of Benedict, the servant of God. This he did, to the end that his tormentor, believing his words, might at least for a while pause from his horrible cruelty. Hearing this, Zalla tortured him no longer. But binding his arms fast with strong cords, he drove him before his horse, to bring him to this Benedict, who, as he said, had his wealth in keeping. The country fellow, thus pinioned and running before him, led him to the holy man's abbey. There he found him sitting before the gate, reading a book. Then turning back to Zalla who came raging after, he said: "This is father Benedict, of whom I told you." He looked upon him in a great fury, and thought to deal as terribly with him as he had with others. He cried out aloud to him, saying: "Get up, get up, and give me quickly such wealth as you have of this man's in keeping." The man of God, hearing such a noise, immediately lifted up his eyes from reading, and beheld both him and the country fellow. Turning his eyes to his cords, very strangly they fell from his arms, and that so quickly as no man even in haste could have undone them. Zalla, seeing him so wonderfully and quickly freed, fell down trembling. He prostrated himself upon the earth, bowed down his cruel and stiff neck to the holy man's feet, and with humility commended himself to his prayers. But the venerable man for all this did not rise from his reading. Calling for some of his monks, he commanded them to take him in, and to give him some food. When he was brought back again, he gave him a good lesson, admonishing him not to use any more such rigor and cruel dealing. His proud mind was thus humbled. He went away, but after that did not dare demand anything of the country fellow, whom the man of God, not with hands, but only with his eyes, had loosed from his cords. This is what I told you, Peter. Those who in a more familiar fashion serve God sometimes work miracles by certain power and authority bestowed upon

them. For sitting still, he appeased the fury of that cruel Goth and untied with his eyes those knots and cords which pinioned the innocent man's arms. He thus plainly showed by the quickness of the miracle that he had received power to work all that which he did. And now I shall likewise tell you of another miracle, which by prayer he obtained at God's hands.

32. One day when he had gone out with his monks to work in the field, a countryman, carrying the corpse of his dead son, came to the gate of the abbey, lamenting the loss of his child. He inquired for holy Benedict, and they told him that he was abroad with his monks in the field. He laid the dead body down at the gate, and with great sorrow of soul ran in haste to seek out the venerable father. At the same time, the man of God was returning homeward from work with his monks. As soon as the man saw Benedict, he began to cry out: "Give me my son, give me my son!" The man of God, amazed at these words, stood still, and said: "What, have I taken away your son?" "No, no," said the sorrowful father, "but he is dead. Come for Christ Jesus' sake and restore him to life." The servant of God, hearing him speak in that manner, and seeing that his monks were compassionately begging for the poor man's request, said with great sorrow of mind: "Away, my good brethren, away. Such miracles are not for us to work, but for the blessed apostles. Why will you lay such a burden upon me, as my weakness cannot bear?" But the poor man, pressed by excessive grief, would not give up his petition, but swore that he would never depart, unless he raised up his son. "Where is he, then?" said God's servant. He answered that his body lay at the gate of the abbey. When the man of God came to that place with his monks, he knelt down and lay upon the body of the little child. Rising, he held up his hands towards heaven, and said: "Look not, O Lord, upon my sins, but upon the faith of this man, who asks to have his son raised to life. Restore that soul to the body, which you have taken away." He had scarcely spoken these words, when behold, the soul came back again. At this the child's body began to tremble in such fashion that all who were present saw it pant and shake in a strange manner. Then he took it by the hand and gave it to his father, but alive and in health. It is certain, Peter, that this miracle was not in his own power. Prostrate upon the ground, he had so earnestly prayed for it.

Peter: What you said before is most true. What you affirmed in words, you have now verified by examples and works. But tell me,

I beseech you, whether holy men can do all the things they please, and obtain at God's hands whatsoever they desire.

33. *Gregory:* What man is there, Peter, in this world, who is in greater favor with God than was St. Paul? Yet he three times asked our Lord to be delivered from the prick of the flesh, and did not obtain his petition. Concerning this point, I should also tell you how there was one thing which the venerable father Benedict wanted to do, and yet could not. For his sister called Scholastica, dedicated from her infancy to our Lord, used to come once a year to visit her brother. In meeting her the man of God went not far from the gate, to a place belonging to the abbey, there to entertain her. One time as she was coming there according to her custom, her venerable brother with his monks went to meet her. There they spent the whole day in the praises of God and spiritual talk. When it was almost night they ate together. As they were yet sitting at the table, talking of devout matters, darkness came on. The holy nun his sister entreated him to stay there all night, that they might spend it in discoursing of the joys of heaven. But by no persuasion would he agree to that, saying that he might not by any means tarry all night out of his abbey. At that time, the sky was so clear that no cloud was to be seen. The nun, receiving this refusal of her brother, joined her hands together and laid them upon the table. Bowing down her head upon them, she made her prayers to almighty God. As she was lifting her head from the table, there fell suddenly such a tempest of lightning and thundering, and such abundance of rain, that neither venerable Benedict, nor his monks who were with him, could put their heads out of doors. For the holy nun, resting her head upon her hands, had poured forth such a flood of tears upon the table, that she brought a watery sky to the clear air. Thus, after the end of her devotions, that storm of rain followed. Her prayer and the rain so met together that as she lifted up her head from the table, the thunder began. In one and the same instant, she lifted up her head and brought down the rain. The man of God saw that he could not by reason of such thunder and lightning and great abundance of rain return to his abbey. He grew severe and complained to his sister, saying: "God forgive you, what have you done?" She answered him: "I asked you to stay, and you would not listen to me. I have asked our good Lord, and he has deigned to grant my petition. Therefore, if you can now depart, in God's name return to your monastery, and leave me here alone." But

the good father was not able to go forth. He tarried there against his will, where willingly before he would not stay. In that manner they watched all night, and with spiritual and heavenly talk mutually comforted one another. Therefore, by this we see, as I said before, that he would have wanted this one thing, and yet he could not obtain it. For if we consider the venerable man's mind, there is no question but that he would have wanted the same fair weather to continue as it was when he set forth. But he found that a miracle had thwarted his desire, which, by the power of almighty God, a woman's prayers had wrought. It is not surprising that a woman, who had not seen her brother for a long time, might do more at that time than he could. According to the saying of St. John, *God is charity* (1 John 4.8), and therefore it was right that she who loved more did more.

Peter: I confess that I am wonderfully pleased with what you tell me.

34. *Gregory:* The next day the venerable woman returned to her nunnery, and the man of God to his abbey. Three days later, standing in his cell, and lifting up his eyes to heaven, he beheld the soul of his sister (which had departed from her body) ascend in the likeness of a dove into heaven. Rejoicing much to see her great glory, he gave thanks to almighty God with hymns and lauds. He imparted the news of this her death to his monks. He also presently sent them to bring her corpse to his abbey, to have it buried in that grave which he had provided for himself. By this means it happened that, as their souls were always one in God while they lived, so their bodies continued together after their death.

35. At another time, Servandus, the deacon, and abbot of that monastery which in times past was founded by the noble man Liberius in the country of Campania, used ordinarily to come and visit the man of God. The reason why he came so often was that he too was a man full of heavenly doctrine. They two had together frequent spiritual conferences, to the end that, although they could not perfectly feed upon the celestial food of heaven, yet, by means of such sweet discourses, they might at least, with longing and fervent desire, taste of those joys and divine delights. When it was time to retire, the venerable father rested in the top of a tower. At its foot Servandus the deacon was lodged. One pair of stairs went to them both. Before the tower there was a certain large room in which the disciples of both lay. The man of God, Benedict, being

diligent in watching, rose up early before the time of matins, while his monks were yet at rest. He came to the window of his chamber, where he offered up his prayers to almighty God. Standing there, all of a sudden in the dead of night, as he looked forth, he saw a light which banished away the darkness of the night. It glittered with such brightness, that the light which shone in the midst of darkness was far clearer than the light of the day. With this sight a marvelous and strange thing followed. As he himself afterwards reported, the whole world was gathered as it were together under one beam of the sun and was presented before his eyes. While the venerable father stood attentively watching the brightness of that glittering light, he saw the soul of Germanus, bishop of Capua, carried up by angels in a fiery globe into heaven. Then, wishing to have some witness of so notable a miracle, he called with a very loud voice Servandus the deacon two or three times by his name. Servandus, troubled at such an unusual crying out of the man of God, went up in all haste. Looking forth, he saw nothing else but a little remnant of the light. As he was wondering at so great a miracle, the man of God told him all in order what he had seen. Sending at once to the town of Cassino, he commanded the religious man Theoprobus to dispatch someone that night to the city of Capua, to learn what had become of Germanus their bishop. This was done, and the messenger found that the reverend prelate had departed this life. Inquiring with interest concerning the time, he understood that he died at that very instant, in which the man of God beheld him ascending up to heaven.

Peter: A strange thing and very much to be admired. But since you say that the whole world, as it were under one sunbeam, was presented before his eyes, I must confess that in myself I never had experience of any such thing. I thus cannot conceive by what means the whole world can be seen by any one man.

Gregory: Be certain, Peter, of that which I tell you. I mean that all creatures are as it were nothing to that soul which beholds the Creator. For though it see but a glimpse of that light which is in the Creator, yet very small do all things seem that are created. By means of that supernatural light, the capacity of the inner soul is enlarged. It is so extended in God, that it is far above the world. Yes, and the soul of him who sees in this manner is also above itself. For being swept up in the light of God, it is inwardly in itself enlarged above itself. When it is so exalted and looks downward, then it sees how little all things are. It could not see this before in its former baseness. The man of God, therefore, who saw the fiery globe, and the angels returning to heaven, doubtlessly could see those things only in the light of God. What marvel, then, if he saw the world gathered together before him? Swept up in the light of his soul, he was at that time out of the world. Although we say that the world was gathered together before his eyes, heaven and earth were not compressed into any less room than they are of themselves. But the soul of the viewer was more enlarged. Swept up in God, it might without difficulty see that which is under God. Therefore, in that light which appeared to his outward eyes, the inner light which was in his soul carried the mind of the viewer to heavenly things, and showed him how small all earthly things were.

Peter: I perceive now that it was to my greater profit that I did not understand you before. By reason of my slow capacity, you have given so notable an explanation. But now, because you have made me thoroughly to understand these things, I beseech you to continue on your former narration.

36. *Gregory:* I want, Peter, to tell you many things of this venerable father. But I omit some things on purpose, because I am hastening to treat also the acts of other holy men. But I would have you know that the man of God, along with so many miracles, for which he was so famous in the world, was also sufficiently learned in divinity. For he wrote a rule for his monks, both excellent for its discretion and also eloquent for its style. If anyone is curious to know more about his life and character, he may through the institution of that rule understand all his manner of life and discipline. For the holy man could not otherwise teach than he himself lived.

37. The same year in which he departed this life, he told the day of his holy death to his monks. Some of them lived daily with him, and some dwelt far off. He wanted those who were present to keep it secret, and told those who were absent by what sign they would know that he was dead. Six days before he left this world, he gave orders to have his sepulcher opened. Immediately falling into a fever, he began with burning heat to grow faint. As the sickness daily increased, upon the sixth day he commanded his monks to carry him into the oratory. There he armed himself by receiving the body and blood of our Savior Christ. Having his weak body supported between the hands of his disciples, he stood with his own arms lifted up to heaven. As he was in that manner

praying, he gave up the ghost. On this day, two monks, one in his cell and the other at a great distance, had one and the same vision concerning him. They saw that the entire way from the holy man's cell, towards the east even up to heaven, was hung and adorned with tapestries, and shining with an infinite number of lamps. At the top of the way stood a man, reverently attired. He asked if they knew who passed on that way. They answered him that they did not know. Then he spoke thus to them: "This is the way," he said "by which the beloved servant of God Benedict is going up to heaven." By this means, as his monks who were present knew of the death of the holy man, so likewise they who were absent learned of the same thing, by the sign which he foretold them. He was buried in the oratory of St. John the Baptist which he himself had built, when he overthrew the altar of Apollo. 38. So too in that cave in which he first dwelled, even to this time he works miracles for those who ask with faith. The incident which I mean now to tell you happened only recently. A certain woman went mad. She so much lost the use of reason that she walked up and down, day and night, in mountains and valleys, in woods and fields, and rested only in that place where extreme weariness forced her to stay. One day it so happened that although she wandered aimlessly, yet she did not miss the right way. For she came to the cave of the blessed man Benedict. Not knowing anything, she went in, and rested there that night. Rising up in the morning, she departed as sound in sense and well in her wits, as though she had never been distracted in her whole life. So she remained always after, even to her dying day.

Peter: What is the reason that in the patronage of martyrs we oftentimes find that they do not confer so great benefits by their bodies as they do by other of their relics? Why do they work greater miracles in places where they themselves are not present?

Gregory: Where the holy martyrs lie in their bodies, there is no doubt, Peter, but that they are able to work many miracles. Yes, and they also do infinite labor, for those who seek them with a pure mind. But simple people might have some doubt whether they are present and whether they do hear their prayers in those places where their bodies are not. It is therefore necessary that they should show greater miracles in those places where weak souls may most doubt of their presence. But he whose mind is fixed in God, has so much the greater merit of his faith, in that he both knows that they are not resting there in body, and yet they are present to hear our prayers. Therefore our Savior himself, to increase the faith of his disciples, said: *If I do not depart, the Comforter will not come unto you* (John 16.7). It is certain that the comforting Spirit always proceeds from the Father and the Son. Why then does the Son say that he will depart that the Comforter may come, who never is absent from the Son? Because the disciples, seeing our Lord in the flesh, always desired to see him with their corporal eyes, very well did he say to them: *Unless I do go away, the Comforter will not come.* It was as if he had plainly told them: "If I do not withdraw my body, I cannot let you understand what the love of the spirit is. Unless you cease to love my carnal presence, you will never learn true spiritual love for me."

Peter: What you say pleases me very well.

Gregory: Let us now for a while cease our discourse. Thus, if we intend to go through the miracles of other saints, we may through silence be the better able to perform it.

The End of the Second Book

ШГILILILILILILILILILILILILIL

8. Clovis and the vase of Soissons, according to Gregory of Tours

Gregory, bishop of Tours, who lived from 538 to 594, was born in Auvergne in southern France, the offspring of a patrician family which had for several generations given prelates to the Church. He became bishop of Tours in 573, and played a role of some prominence in the tangled politics of the Merovingian kingdom. As an author, he is best known for his *History of the Franks* in ten books, which went from the beginning of the world to 591. He also wrote a commentary on the Psalms, eight books on miracles, and a handbook on how to tell time by the stars (*De cursibus ecclesiasticis*). His *History* is composed in an odd kind of Latin that treats classical case endings with seeming whimsy. (He explains in his Preface that he wrote in such a fashion because liberal culture was "perishing" in Gaul.) But for all its lack of polish, Gregory's *History of the Franks* deserves to be ranked with Bede's *Ecclesiastical History of the English People* as one of the most valuable and interesting products of early medieval historiography.

The selection given here, from the second book of the *History*, relates an incident of the reign of Clovis (481–511), first of the Merovingian kings to emerge fully into the light of history and the real founder of the Frankish monarchy. The story of the vase of Soissons illustrates the weak juridical character of Germanic kingship (even a common freeman could defy royal wishes), and the element of violence upon which power in barbarian society ultimately rested.

The translation is taken from Gregory of Tours, *History of the Franks*, trans. Ernest Brehaut (New York: Columbia University Press, 1916), pp. 36–38.

27. After these events Childeric died and Clovis his son reigned in his stead. In the fifth year of his reign Siagrius, king of the Romans, son of Egidius, had his seat in the city of Soissons which Egidius, who has been mentioned before, once held. And Clovis came against him with Ragnachar, his kinsman, because he used to possess the kingdom, and demanded that they make ready a battle-field. And Siagrius did not delay nor was he afraid to resist. And so they fought against each other and Siagrius, seeing his army crushed, turned his back and fled swiftly to king Alaric at Toulouse. And Clovis sent to Alaric to send him back, otherwise he was to know that Clovis would make war on him for his refusal. And Alaric was afraid that he would incur the anger of the Franks on account of Siagrius, seeing it is the fashion of the Goths to be terrified, and he surrendered him in chains to Clovis' envoys. And Clovis took him and gave orders to put him under guard, and when he had got his kingdom he directed that he be executed secretly. At that time many churches were despoiled by Clovis' army, since he was as yet involved in heathen error. Now the army had taken from a certain church a vase of wonderful size and beauty, along with the remainder of the utensils for the service of the church. And the bishop of the church sent messengers to the king asking that the vase at least be returned, if he could not get back any more of the sacred dishes. On hearing this the king said to the messenger: "Follow us as far as Soissons, because all that has been taken is to be divided there and when the lot assigns me that dish I will do what the father asks." Then when he came to Soissons and all the booty was set in their midst, the king said: "I ask of you, brave warriors, not to refuse to grant me in addition to my share, yonder dish," that is, he was speaking of the vase just mentioned. In answer to the speech of the king those of more sense replied: "Glorious king, all that we see is yours,

and we ourselves are subject to your rule. Now do what seems well pleasing to you; for no one is able to resist your power." When they said this a foolish, envious and excitable fellow lifted his battle-ax and struck the vase, and cried in a loud voice: "You shall get nothing here except what the lot fairly bestows on you." At this all were stupefied, but the king endured the insult with the gentleness of patience, and taking the vase he handed it over to the messenger of the Church, nursing the wound deep in his heart. And at the end of the year he ordered the whole army to come with their equipment of armor, to show the brightness of their arms on the field of March. And when he was reviewing them all carefully, he came to the man who struck the vase, and said to him: "No one has brought armor so carelessly kept as you; for neither your spear nor sword nor ax is in serviceable condition." And seizing his ax he cast it to the earth, and when the other had bent over somewhat to pick it up, the king raised his hands and drove his own ax into the man's head. "This," said he, "is what you did at Soissons to the vase." Upon the death of this man, he ordered the rest to depart, raising great dread of himself by this action. He made many wars and gained many victories.

9. The Synod of Whitby, according to Bede the Venerable

The foremost monastic historian of the early Middle Ages, and perhaps also the foremost monastic scholar, was the Englishman Bede the Venerable (672/73–735). From the age of seven, Bede lived, studied and prayed at the double monastery of Jarrow and Wearmouth in Northumbria. (See below, Section 10, for Bede's own brief account of his life, which contains nearly everything that we know about him.)

Bede's greatest work was his *Ecclesiastical History of the English People*, which was finished in 731. In it, he sought to recount the history of the English from earliest times until the present. As is characteristic of monastic historiography, Bede took as the chief theme of his work the conversion of the English to Christianity, and the history of the Christian Church among them. He thus gives great attention to the religious attitudes of the English kings, and lovingly describes the careers and accomplishments of English saints. He clearly believed that miracles, by which God proclaimed the virtues of his holy men, were to be expected in this life, and he describes many of them.

At the same time, Bede shows the influence of classical literature and, even more deeply, classical habits of mind. His Latin grammar is impeccable, and his style is direct, simple and graceful. The *Ecclesiastical History* is a model of late Latin literature. Moreover, he pursued his work in an orderly and even systematic fashion. He made strenuous efforts to gain the best information available. He made use of written records (even including papal letters in his history) and took the trouble to interview living witnesses to the events he was describing. While he had no difficulty accepting miraculous occurrences, he still felt that they should be investigated. He included in his history only those for which he felt there was respectable testimony. The discipline of his method, the clarity of his argument, and the beauty of his style show that the classical heritage could still live within the framework of monastic culture.

The following selection from the *Ecclesiastical History* describes the Synod of Whitby (663/64), a climactic event in the history of the early English Church. Meeting under the auspices of King Oswiu of Northumbria, the Synod was to decide whether the young English Church should follow the practices and discipline of the insular Celts (especially the Irish) or those of the continent and Rome. The chief specific issue was the proper method of calculating the date of Easter. But in deciding this, the Synod was also determining the cultural tone and orientation of English Christianity. The Synod heard the arguments of both sides, but opted in favor of continental Roman practices.

As the following passage shows, Bede himself strongly believed that England's orientation to the continent was a victory not only for Christian unity, but also for Christian learning. The decision resulted in close cultural ties between England and the continent in the subsequent two centuries. English scholars gained the benefit of continental learning, and proved to be able students. By the eighth century, English scholarship was the best in Latin Europe, and Bede himself was its finest product.

The following selection gives in its entirety Chapter 25 of Book III, from the *Ecclesiastical History* (*Baedae, Opera Historica*, trans. J. E. King, based on the version of Thomas Stapleton, 1565 [Loeb Classical Library, London-New York, 1930]).

How the controversy about the time
of Easter was moved against those who
had come from Scotland [664].

In the meanwhile, after the Bishop Aidan was taken from this life, Finan in his room had received the degree of bishop, being ordained and sent of the Scots: who in the isle of Lindisfarne made a church meet for a bishop's see; the which nevertheless after the manner of the Scots he builded not of stone but all of sawed oaken timber and thatched it with reed, and afterwards the most reverend Archbishop Theodore dedicated it in the honor of the blessed apostle Peter. But the bishop of the selfsame place, Eadbert, took off the reeds and set to cover it all with plates of lead, that is to say, both the roof and also the walls thereof themselves.

About this time there was raised a hot and constant disputation touching the observance of Easter, they who had come from Kent or from France affirming that the Scots kept the Easter Lord's day contrary to the accustomed manner of the universal Church. Among these there was a very earnest defender of the true Easter, one named Ronan, a Scot born but yet instructed fully in the rule of ecclesiastical truth in the parts of France and Italy; who coupling and disputing with Finan set many aright or inflamed them to a more careful inquiry of the truth: yet was he able in no way to correct Finan; nay, rather he exasperated him by his reproof, being a man of hasty nature, and made him an open adversary of the truth. On the other hand James, once deacon (as we have shown before) of the venerable Archbishop Paulinus, with all whom he was able to instruct in the better way, observed the true and Catholic Easter. Eanfled also, the queen, with her train observed after the same manner as she had seen it practiced in Kent, having with her a priest of Catholic observation out of Kent, by name Romanus: whereby, as is said, it happened sometimes in those days that in one year Easter was kept twice, and when the king was breaking his fast and solemnizing the Lord's Easter, then the queen and her company continued yet the fast and kept the day of palms. Yet this diversity of keeping Easter, as long as Aidan lived, was borne in patience of all men, who had come to know very well, that though he was not able to celebrate Easter contrary to the custom of those who had sent him, yet he set himself diligently to perform works of faith, mercy, and love according to the manner customable with all holy men: upon which consideration he was deservedly beloved of all men, even of those which varied from him about Easter: and was held in reverence not only of the common sort but also of the bishops themselves, Honorius of the men of Kent and Felix of the East English.

But after the death of Finan which came after Aidan, when Colman succeeded to the bishopric, who also himself was sent from Scotland, there arose a sharper disputation about the observance of Easter as well as upon other rules of ecclesiastical life: by occasion whereof this inquiry rightly stirred the minds and hearts of many from fear, lest, having gained the name of Christians, they did run or had run in vain. The dispute reached too to the ears of the princes themselves, to wit of King Oswy and his son Alchfrid; of whom Oswy, being brought up and baptized of the Scots and right skillful also in their tongue, thought nothing better than the manner which they had taught. In his turn Alchfrid, having for his teacher in Christian instruction Wilfrid, a man of great learning (for he had both traveled to Rome on his first visit for the sake of ecclesiastical teaching and spent a long time at Lyons with Dalfinus, archbishop of France, of whom also he had taken the crown of ecclesiastical tonsure), knew that Wilfrid's teaching was rightly to be chosen rather than all the traditions of the Scots: wherefore also he had granted him a monastery of forty households in the place which is called Inhrypum; which place indeed a little before he had given to those which followed the Scots, to have in possession for a monastery. But because afterwards, when choice was offered to them, they preferred to depart and yield up the place rather than to change their accustomed manner, it was given by the prince to him whose life and teaching he held to be worthy thereof. About that time Agilbert, bishop of the West Saxons, of whom we have made mention before, a friend of King Alchfrid and of Wilfrid the abbot, had come to the province of Northumberland and was staying with them for a space; who also at the request of Alchfrid made Wilfrid a priest in his monastery aforesaid. Now Agilbert had with him a priest named Agatho. The question therefore concerning Easter and the tonsure and other ecclesiastical matters being there raised, it was agreed on both sides that in the monastery called Strenaeshalc (which is by interpretation Lighthouse Bay, over which Hild, a woman vowed to God, was abbess), a Synod should be kept for the deciding of this

question. And thither came both the kings, namely, the father and
the son; the bishops, Colman with his clergy of Scotland, and
Agilbert with Agatho and Wilfrid, priests. On the part of these last
were James and Romanus: Hild the abbess with her company were
of the Scottish part, whereon also was the venerable Bishop Cedd
long since ordained of the Scots, as we have shown before, who in
that assembly came forward also as a most watchful interpreter
on both sides.

And first King Oswy said beforehand by way of preparation
that it behoved those who were united in serving God to keep one
rule of living and not to vary in celebrating the heavenly sacraments, who looked all for one kingdom in the heavens; but rather
they should search out what was the truer tradition and this should
be followed uniformly of everyone: and first he commanded his
Bishop Colman to declare what his observation was, and from
whence he drew the source thereof and whom he followed therein.
Then Colman saith: "The Easter which I am accustomed to
observe I have received of my elders of whom I was sent hither
bishop, and this all our fathers, men beloved of God, are known
to have solemnized after the same manner. And this observation,
that none may think it a light matter or to be rejected, is the selfsame which the blessed evangelist John, the disciple whom the
Lord specially loved, kept, as we read, with all the churches over
the which he was head." And when he spake these and such like
words the king commanded also Agilbert to declare before them
all the manner of his observation, whence it was that it had beginning and by what authority he followed it. Agilbert answered:
"Let, I beseech you, my scholar, the priest Wilfrid, speak herein
for me, for we both, along with all the other followers after the
ecclesiastical tradition, who sit here, are of one mind; beside, he
can better and more clearly express our opinion in the very tongue
of the English, than I am able to do, using an interpreter." Then
Wilfrid, the king commanding him to speak, thus began: "The
Easter which we follow we have seen to be kept by all at Rome
where the blessed apostles Peter and Paul lived, taught, suffered
and were buried: this manner we have noted to be practiced of
all in Italy, and in France, countries which we have passed through
in pursuit of knowledge or desire to pray: this manner we have
found to be performed in Africa, Asia, Egypt, Greece and all the
world (wherever the Church of Christ hath been spread, throughout different nations and tongues), after one order of time and

that without variableness: apart only from these men and them that are partakers of their obstinacy, the Redshanks I mean and the Britons, with whom, being natives of the two farthermost islands of the Ocean sea, and yet not the whole of them neither, these men with fond endeavor do contend against the whole world." To whom so speaking Colman replied: "I marvel wherefore you be ready to term our endeavor fond, wherein we follow the example of so excellent an Apostle who was worthy to lean upon the Lord's breast; seeing that all the world accounteth him to have lived most wisely." Whereat Wilfrid saith: "God forbid we should charge John with fondness for keeping the decrees of the Mosaic law literally, according as the Church followed yet in many things the Jewish manner, and the apostles had not power upon the sudden to renounce all observance of the law ordained of God (in the way that all that come to the faith must of necessity abandon idols invented of devils), lest forsooth they might cause offense to those Jews which lived among the Gentiles. For in the like consideration Paul did circumcise Timothy, offered sacrifices in the temple, shaved his head at Corinth with Aquila and Priscilla: truly to no other intent but that the Jews might not be offended. Upon this consideration James said unto the same Paul: 'Thou seest, brother, how many thousands of Jews there are which believe; and they are all zealous of the law.' Notwithstanding, the light of the Gospel now shining throughout the world, it is neither necessary, no, nor lawful for believers to be circumcised or to offer up to God sacrifices of the flesh of beasts. And so John, according to the custom of the law, in the 14th day of the first month at evening began to celebrate the Paschal Festival, not regarding whether it fell out the Sabbath day or any other day of the week. But in truth Peter preaching at Rome, remembering that the Lord rose again from the dead the first day after the Sabbath and gave therewith the hope of Resurrection to the world, understood that Easter must be kept in such sort that, according to the custom and commandments of the Law, he ever looked (even as John did) for the rising of the moon at evening in the 14th day of his age, in the first month: and at the rising thereof, if Sunday (which then was called the first day after the Sabbath) was to come on the morrow, he began on that very evening to observe the Lord's Pasch, as we too are wont to do today. But if the Sunday were not to come the next morrow after the 14th day of the change of the moon, but the 16th or 17th or any other day of the moon until the one-and-twentieth, he tarried for that Sunday, and the Sabbath before, upon the evening, he began the most holy solemnity of Easter; and so it came to pass that the Easter Sunday was kept only between the 15th day of the change of the moon until the one-and-twentieth and no day else. Neither doth this tradition of the Gospel and of the apostles break the Law but rather fulfill it, for in the Law it is commanded that the Passover should be solemnized from the evening of the 14th day of the change of the moon of the first month until the one-and-twentieth day of the same moon at evening: to the following of which observation all the successors of blessed John in Asia after his death and all the Church throughout the world were converted. And it was by the Nicene Council not newly decreed but confirmed (as the ecclesiastical history witnesseth), that this is the true Easter, this only is to be celebrated by believing men. Whereby it is clear, my lord Colman, that you neither follow the example of John (as you suppose), neither of Peter, whose tradition you wittingly withstand, nor do you agree with the Law nor the Gospel in the observation of your Easter. For John observing the Paschal time according to the decrees of the Mosaic law had no regard to the first day after the Sabbath; and this you do not follow, who keep Easter only on the first day after the Sabbath. Peter celebrated the Lord's Easter day from the 15th day of the change of the moon until the one-and-twentieth day; which you follow not, which keep the Lord's Easter day from the 14th day of the moon until the 20th: so that oftentimes you begin Easter in the 13th day of the change of moon at evening, of which neither hath the Law made any mention, neither did the Lord, the maker and giver of the Gospel, on that day, but on the 14th, eat either the old Passover in the evening, or hand down the sacraments of the New Testament to be celebrated of the Church in commemoration of his passion. Likewise the one-and-twentieth day of the moon, which the Law expressly commanded for celebration, you do utterly exclude from the celebrating of your Easter: and thus, as I said, in the observation of the highest festival you agree neither with John, nor Peter, nor the Law, nor the Gospel."

To this Colman replied and said: "How think ye? Did Anatolius, a holy man and much commended in the ecclesiastical history before of you alleged, think contrary to the Law and the Gospel, writing that Easter ought to be celebrated from the 14th unto the 20th day of the moon? Is it to be believed that our most reverend father Columba and his successors, men beloved of God, who after the same manner kept their Easter, thought or acted contrary to the divine pages? Seeing there were very many among them, to whose holiness witness was borne by heavenly signs and miracles of mighty works wrought by them: and as I doubt not but they were holy men, so I cease not myself ever to follow their life, manners and trade of discipline."

"In good sooth," saith Wilfrid thereupon, "it is well known that Anatolius was a right holy man, very well learned and worthy of much praise; but what have ye to do with him, seeing ye keep not his rulings neither? For Anatolius in his Easter, following assuredly the rule of truth, accounted the compass of nineteen years, which you are either ignorant of or if ye know it, yet though it be close kept by the whole Church of Christ, ye set light by it. He reckoned the 14th day of the moon to fall on the Lord's Easter in such a way that he allowed that same day at evening to be the 15th of the change, after the manner of the Egyptians. He also assigned the 20th day to the Lord's Easter in such a way that he held it for the one-and-twentieth when the sun had set. Which his rule and distinction, that ye be ignorant of is manifest by this, that some time ye keep your Easter clean before the full of the moon, that is upon the 13th day of the change. Moreover, as touching your father Columba and those which followed him, whose holiness ye claim to copy and whose rule and commandments ye say that ye follow, as the which have been confirmed by heavenly signs, to this I could have answered, that in the day of Judgment when many say unto the Lord that they have prophesied and cast out devils and done many wonderful works in His name, the Lord will answer that He never knew them. But God forbid that I should say this of your fathers: for it is much more righteous to think well of such as we know not than to think evil. Wherefore also I deny not that they were servants of God and beloved of God, as they which loved God, though in rude simplicity, yet with a godly intention. Neither do I think that the manner of their observation of Easter is much prejudicial against them, as long as none had come to show them the decrees of more perfect practice, the which they should follow: of whom I verily believe that had any Catholic reckoner then come unto them, they would have followed his admonitions in the same manner in which they are shown to have followed those commands of God which they knew and had learned. But as for thee and thy companions, if hearing the decrees of the apostolic see, nay, rather of the universal Church and these confirmed by Holy Writ, you scorn to follow them, you sin herein undoubtedly. For though thy fathers were holy men, is yet their fewness proceeding from one corner of the uttermost island of the earth to be put above the universal Church of Christ dispersed throughout the world? And if he your father Columba (yea, and our father if he was Christ's) was holy and mighty in works, can he by any means be chosen above the most blessed chief of the apostles, to whom our Lord said: "Thou art Peter, and upon this rock I will build my church, and the gates of hell shall not prevail against it, and I will give unto thee the keys of the kingdom of heaven"?

When Wilfrid thus concluded the king said: "Were these things, Colman, indeed spoken to that Peter of our Lord?" And the bishop said: "They were indeed, my lord king." Whereat the king saith: "Can you bring forward any so special authority given your Columba?" Whereon the bishop said: "No." Again the king said: "Whether do ye both agree in this without any question, that these words were principally spoken unto Peter, and that unto him the keys of the kingdom of heaven were given of the Lord?" They answered: "Yea, certainly." Whereon the king thus concluded and said: "And I say unto you that I will not gainsay such a porter as this is; but as I know and have power, I covet in all points to obey his ordinances; lest it may be, when I come to the doors of the kingdom of heaven, I find none to open unto me, having his displeasure who is proved to hold the keys thereof."

When the king so spake, all that sat or stood by, the greater along with them of mean degree, gave their consent thereto; and abandoning their former imperfect usage hastened to change over to those things which they had learned to be better.

10. The bibliography of Bede the Venerable

Besides his justly famous *Ecclesiastical History*, Bede composed numerous other works—grammatical manuals, treatises on the calendar and on such scientific subjects as geography and weather, works of history and hagiography and, most numerous of all, Biblical commentaries. These works enjoyed a wide circulation and exerted great influence both in England and on the continent.

In the closing pages of the *Ecclesiastical History*, Bede gave the following account of his education and the books that he wrote during his productive life. The bibliography of this monastic prince of scholars permits the modern student to discern the range and nature of the intellectual interests characteristic of the monastic culture of the early Middle Ages.

The selection is taken from the last half of Chapter 24, Book V. (*Baedae, Opera Historica*, trans. J. E. King, based on the version of Thomas Stapleton, 1565 [Loeb Classical Library, London-New York, 1930]).

This much concerning the ecclesiastical history of Britain, and especially of the English nation (so far as I could learn either from the writings of the ancients, or by tradition of my elders, or by my own knowledge), has by the Lord's help been brought into order by me, Bede, the servant of Christ and priest of the monastery of the blessed apostles Peter and Paul, which is at Wearmouth and Jarrow.

Who being born in the territory of the same monastery, when I was seven years of age, was delivered up by the hands of my kinsfolk to be brought up of the most reverend Abbot Benedict, and afterward of Ceolfrid; and from that time spending all the days of my life in the mansion of the same monastery, I have applied all my diligence to the study of the Scriptures; and observing the regular discipline and keeping the daily service of singing in the church, I have taken delight always either to learn, or to teach, or to write.

Further, in the nineteenth year of my life I was made deacon; in my thirtieth year I took the degree of the priesthood, both which orders I received by the hand of the most reverend Bishop John, at the commandment of Ceolfrid my abbot.

And from the time that I took the priesthood until the fifty-ninth year of my age, I have employed myself upon holy Scripture, for my own need and that of my brethren, briefly to note and gather from what the venerable fathers have written, and in addition thereto to expound after the manner of their meaning and interpretation these following works:

On the beginning of Genesis as far as the birth of Isaac and the casting forth of Ishmael, four books.

Of the tabernacle and its vessels, and of the vestments of the priests, three books.

On the first part of Samuel, that is to say, as far as the death of Saul, three books.

Of the building of the temple, of allegorical exposition, as also the rest, two books.

Likewise on the book of Kings, thirty questions.

On the Proverbs of Solomon, three books.

On the Song of Songs, seven books.

On Isaiah, Daniel, the twelve prophets, and part of Jeremiah, divisions of chapters drawn from the treatise of the blessed Jerome.

On Ezra and Nehemiah, three books.

On the Song of Habakkuk, one book.

On the book of the blessed father Tobias, one book of allegorical exposition concerning Christ and his Church.

Likewise chapters of readings on the Pentateuch of Moses, Joshua and Judges.

On the books of Kings and Chronicles.

On the book of the blessed father Job.

On the Proverbs, Ecclesiastes, and the Song of Songs.

On the Prophet Isaiah, also Ezra and and Nehemiah.

On the Gospel of Mark, four books.

On the Gospel of Luke, six books.

Of Homilies on the Gospels, two books.

On the Apostle whatsoever I have found expounded in the writings of St. Augustine, hath all been by me diligently written down in order.

On the Acts of the Apostles, two books.

On the Seven Catholic Epistles, one book on each Epistle.

On the Revelation of St. John, three books.

Likewise Chapters of readings on all the New Testament, except only the Gospel.

Likewise a book of Epistles to divers persons: whereof one is of the six ages of the world: one of the halting-places of the children of Israel, one of the words of Isaiah: "And they shall be shut up in the prison, and after many days they shall be visited"; one of the reason of Leap Year; one of the Equinox, after Anatolius.

Likewise of the histories of the Saints; a book of the life and passion of St. Felix, confessor, hath been by me translated into prose after the work in meter of Paulinus.

The Book of the life and passion of St. Anastasius, which was ill translated from the Greek, and worse amended by some unskillful person, I have corrected to the sense as well as I was able.

I have written first in heroic verse, and afterwards also in prose the Life of the Holy Father Cuthbert, monk as well as bishop.

The History of the abbots of this monastery, wherein I with joy do serve the divine goodness, to wit of Benedict, Ceolfrid, and Huetbert, in two books.

The Ecclesiastical History of our island and nation, in five books.

The Martyrology of the birth days of the holy martyrs, in which I have with all diligence endeavored to set down all those whom I could find, not only on what day, but also by what manner of contest, and under whom as judge they overcame the world.

A Book of Hymns in divers sorts of meter or rhythm.

A Book of Epigrams in heroic or elegiac verse.

Of the Nature of things and of the Times, one book apiece.

Likewise of the Times another greater book.

A Book of Orthography divided in the order of the alphabet.

Also a book of the Art of Poetry; and added thereto another book of Figures and Tropes, that is to say, figures and modes of speech in which the holy Scriptures are veiled.

And I beseech Thee, merciful Jesus, that to whom thou hast of thy goodness given sweetly to drink in the words of the knowledge of thee, thou wilt also vouchsafe in thy loving-kindness that he may one day come to thee, the fountain of all wisdom, and stand forever before thy face.

ⅬⅬⅬⅬⅬⅬⅬⅬⅬⅬⅬⅬⅬⅬⅬⅬⅬⅬⅬⅬⅬⅼ

11. Latin poems

The great majority of Latin poems written in the early Middle Ages were school exercises, verbally dexterous but dead to sentiment. There are, however, certain notable exceptions. The first poem given here is the well-known hymn, *Veni Creator Spiritus*, attributed to Hrabanus Maurus, abbot of Fulda (ca. 776–856), who for his scholarly attain-

ments was known as the "teacher of Germany." It is traditionally
considered one of the seven great hymns of the medieval Church. The
second selection, the *O Roma Nobilis*, or "A Song for Sts. Peter and
Paul's Day," was written probably at Verona by an unknown author
in the tenth century. It was a favorite of pilgrims, who sang it as they
approached the eternal city.

The translation of the *Veni Creator Spiritus*, by John Dryden, is
taken from *Great Hymns of the Middle Ages*, ed. Eveline W. Brainerd
(New York: Century Co., 1909), pp. 36–38. The Latin text of the *O
Roma Nobilis* may be found in Charles H. Beeson, *A Primer of Medieval Latin* (New York: Scott, Foresman, 1925), p. 340. Its translation
here is by D. Herlihy.

Veni Creator Spiritus

Veni creator, Spiritus
Mentes tuorum visita,
Imple superna gratia
Quae tu creasti pectora.

Creator Spirit, by whose aid
The world's foundations first were laid,
Come visit every pious mind;
Come pour Thy joys on human-kind;
From sin and sorrow set us free,
And make Thy temples worthy be.

O Source of uncreated light,
The Father's promised Paraclete!
Thrice holy fount, thrice holy fire,
Our hearts with heavenly love inspire;
Come, and Thy sacred unction bring
To sanctify us, while we sing.

Plenteous of grace, descend from high,
Rich in Thy sevenfold energy!
Thou strength of His Almighty hand,
Whose power does heaven and earth command;
Proceeding Spirit, our defence,
Who dost the gift of tongues dispense,
And crown'st Thy gift with eloquence.

Refine and purge our earthly parts;
But, oh, inflame and fire our hearts!
Our frailties help, our vice control,

Submit the senses to the soul;
And when rebellious they are grown,
Then lay Thy hand, and hold them down.

Chase from our minds the infernal foe,
And peace, the fruit of love, bestow;
And lest our feet should step astray,
Protect and guide us in the way.

Make us eternal truths receive,
And practice all that we believe:
Give us Thyself, that we may see
The Father, and the Son, by Thee.
Immortal honor, endless fame,
Attend the Almighty Father's name:

The Savior Son be glorified
Who for lost man's redemption died:
And equal adoration be,
Eternal Paraclete, to Thee.
                    [Trans. John Dryden]

O Roma Nobilis

O Roma nobilis	*orbis et domina,*
Cunctarum urbium	*excellentissima,*
Roseo martyrum	*sanguine rubea,*
Albis et virginum	*liliis candida;*
Salutem dicimus	*tibi per omnia,*
Te benedicimus:	*salve per saecula.*

O noble Rome	the world's sovereign mistress,
Among all cities	the most excelling,
Glowing red	with the rose blood of martyrs,
Glowing white	with the lilies of virgins,
Greetings we give you,	blessings we bear you,
Prosper, we say	for ever and ever.

Peter the mighty	heavenly porter,
Hear without waiting	the prayers of your suppliants,
Since you are the judge	of tribes twelve in number,
Mercifully judge,	show us your kindness,
To those who address you,	now at this moment
Bear to us aid,	in your compassion.

O Paul, receive	these our entreaties
You by your zeal	confounded philosophers,
Now made a steward	in the King's palace,
Bear to us servings	of heavenly favor,
Grant, that the wisdom	which came to fill you
Fill us in turn,	brought by your teachings.

เนนนนนนนนนนนนนนนนนนนนร

12. The *Dulcitius* of Hrotswitha of Gandersheim

Monastic education was founded upon a close imitation of classical models, but rarely did this scholastic approach produce works of true literary merit. A notable exception was the literary efforts of a tenth-century German nun. This was Hrotswitha of Gandersheim (she herself interpreted her name as meaning "strong voice"), who lived from about 935 to not long after 973. Her life approximately coincided with the reigns of Emperors Otto I and II, who ruled from 936 to 983. These emperors tried to advance the study of letters, and were, incidentally, patrons of Hrotswitha's own convent at Gandersheim. She is herself one of the principal figures of what is sometimes called, rather euphemistically, the Ottonian renaissance.

Hrotswitha does manifest a remarkable erudition, especially for a woman. She composed eight narrative poems on conventional religious themes, and versified chronicles on the foundation of her own convent and on the deeds of Otto I. Her most remarkable works are six Latin dramas, written in prose and loosely modeled after the Roman comical dramatist Terence. They were probably intended for performance, or at least reading, within the convent, but we know nothing as to how they were produced.

As Hrotswitha explained it, her purpose was to put into the service of God the arts and skills which seemed to be monopolized by those serving the devil. The plays are largely concerned with the tribulations and triumphs of Christian maidens, and the dauntless defense of their chastity against pagan lechery. Both plots and characters are drawn from traditional saints' lives and legends, but the lady dramatist does succeed in imparting to them considerable life. Her dialogue is spirited and witty, and the plot moves rapidly to a happy ending, usually the martyrdom or death of the maidens.

Hrotswitha's importance derives partially from the fact that her works are the sole link between the classical drama and the miracle plays of the late Middle Ages. Her dramas are of considerable merit in their own right, and deserve to be ranked among the more admirable products of monastic education.

The *Dulcitius* given here is based upon an ancient legend of the martyrdom of the three maidens Agape, Chionia and Irene. The translation, by D. Herlihy, is based upon the Latin text in *Die Werke der Hrotsvitha*, ed. K. A. Barack (Nuremberg: Bauer and Raspe, 1858), pp. 175–89.

*T*he *argument of* Dulcitius: *The passion of the holy virgins Agape, Chionia and Irene, whom Dulcitius the governor secretly approached under cover of darkness, yearning to satiate himself with their embraces. But as soon as he entered he was struck in the mind. He embraced and kissed jars and pots as if they were the virgins. Meanwhile his face and garments were infested with a repulsive blackness. Finally, he delivered the virgins to be punished at the command of Count Sisinnius. He was also tricked in marvelous ways, but did order Agape and Chionia to be burned, and Irene to be shot with arrows.*

[Cast:] Diocletian, Agape, Chionia, Irene, Dulcitius, Soldiers, [Sisinnius], [his wife and servants], Guards.

[*Scene 1*]

DIOCLETIAN: The brilliance of your family, your free birth, the serenity of your beauty demand that you be joined in marriage to the leading men in the palace. We would command that this be done, if you deny Christ and offer sacrifice to our gods.

AGAPE: You may relax, and don't trouble yourself with the preparation of our weddings. We can never be compelled to deny that name which should be confessed, or to lose our virginity.

DIOCLETIAN: What does this mean? What foolishness has seized you?

AGAPE: What sign of foolishness have you discerned in us?

DIOCLETIAN: One conspicuous and great.

AGAPE: Where is it found?

DIOCLETIAN: In this principally, that you have abandoned the observance of the old religion, and you are following the pointless novelty of Christian superstition.

AGAPE: Take care lest you offend the dignity of God almighty. Danger!

DIOCLETIAN: To whom?

AGAPE: To you and the commonwealth you rule.

DIOCLETIAN: She's raving. Take her away.

CHIONIA: My sister is not raving, but she has justly reproached you for your stupidity.

DIOCLETIAN: This one acts still more wildly, like a drunken woman. Let her also be removed from our sight. We'll talk with the third girl.

IRENE: Will you approve of a third rebel, one who opposes you in her spirit?

DIOCLETIAN: Irene, you are younger in years, why not be greater in dignity?

IRENE: Show me, I ask, how to do so?

DIOCLETIAN: Bow your head to the gods, and be to your sisters an example of reform, and their means of liberation.

IRENE: Let those sully themselves with idols—those who wish to incur the wrath of the High Thunderer. I shall not dishonor my head, anointed with royal unction, by lowering it to the feet of images.

DIOCLETIAN: The worship of the gods does not bring indignity, but rather honor.

IRENE: And what disgrace is more shameful, and what shame greater, than to worship slaves as if they were lords?

DIOCLETIAN: I don't ask you to worship slaves, but the gods of lords and rulers.

IRENE: But isn't he a slave of some man, who is purchased at a price from an artisan, just like one at the slave mart?

DIOCLETIAN: This one's boldness at speech shall be removed by tortures.

IRENE: This we desire, this we embrace, that we should be mangled by tortures for the love of Christ!

DIOCLETIAN: These disrespectful girls, disobeying our decrees, shall be bound in chains, and kept in the dirt of prison, awaiting the inquest of Dulcitius the governor.

[*Scene 2*]

DULCITIUS: Bring them forth, soldiers. Bring forth the girls whom you hold in prison.

SOLDIERS: Here they are, the ones you summoned,

DULCITIUS: My! What beautiful, what attractive, what wonderful young things!

SOLDIERS: They're really lovely.

DULCITIUS: I am captivated by their beauty.

SOLDIERS: It's not surprising.

DULCITIUS: I am burning to win them for my love.

SOLDIERS: We doubt that you'll accomplish it.

DULCITIUS: Why not?

SOLDIERS: Because they are firm in the faith.

DULCITIUS: What if I tempt them with favors?

SOLDIERS: They scorn them.

DULCITIUS: What if I terrorize them with tortures?

SOLDIERS: They hardly care.

DULCITIUS: Then what should be done?

SOLDIERS: Think about it.

DULCITIUS: Put them under guard, in the inner chamber of the shop. The place where, in the anteroom, the servants keep their containers.

SOLDIERS: Why there?

DULCITIUS: So that I can see them every so often.

SOLDIERS: As you command.

[Scene 3]

DULCITIUS: And what are the prisoners doing this evening?

SOLDIERS: They spend the time singing hymns.

DULCITIUS: Let's go nearer.

SOLDIERS: We can hear the sound of the musical voices from afar.

DULCITIUS: Watch outside with the lanterns. I am going to enter and take my fill of the embraces I want.

SOLDIERS: Go inside. We'll wait for you.

AGAPE: What's making the noise outside.

IRENE: Unhappy Dulcitius is coming in.

CHIONIA: May God protect us!

AGAPE: Amen.

CHIONIA: What is the meaning of that clattering of jars, pots and pans?

IRENE: I'll see. Come, please, look through the slits!

AGAPE: What is it?

IRENE: Look, that stupid man has gone out of his mind. He thinks that he is hugging us in his arms.

AGAPE: What is he doing?

IRENE: Now he fondles the jars on his soft lap, now he embraces the pots and pans, and gives them gentle kisses.

CHIONIA: How funny!

IRENE: His face, hands and clothing are now becoming dirtied and befouled. The blackness which is coming over him makes him look like an Ethiopian.

AGAPE: It's only fitting that a man possessed by the devil in his heart should look that way in his body.

IRENE: Look, he's getting ready to go. Let's wait and see what the soldiers waiting outside will do when he comes out.

SOLDIERS: Who is this satanic creature coming out? Or rather, is it the devil himself? We'd better run.

DULCITIUS: Soldiers, where are you fleeing? Stop, wait, take me with the lanterns to bed.

SOLDIERS: The voice is that of our master, but he looks like the devil. We'd better not stay here, or delay our flight. The apparition means to do us harm.

DULCITIUS: I shall go to the palace, and make known to the princes the sad state of spirit I am suffering.

[*Scene 4*]

DULCITIUS: Guards, take me into the palace, for I have a secret for the emperor.

GUARDS: What is this vile and repulsive monster, covered with torn and black rags? Let's punch him with our fists, and throw him down the staircase, lest he be given free access to the palace.

DULCITIUS: Misery! Misery! What is happening? Am I not dressed in the most splendid garments, am I not brilliant from head to toe? But whoever sees me, shows disgust as if he were looking at a horrible monster. I shall return to my wife, and learn from her what has happened to me. Look, she is coming out with her hair disheveled, and the entire household follows in tears.

WIFE: Alas, alas, my lord Dulcitius. What are you suffering? Are you out of your head? You have become a joke to the despicable Christians.

DULCITIUS: Now I realize, that I have been made a mockery by the sorcery of those girls.

WIFE: This greatly disturbs me, and this especially saddens me that you did not know what you were suffering.

DULCITIUS: I command that those mischievous girls be brought forward. Let them be stripped of their clothing, and displayed publicly in the nude. That way they in turn may learn what our jokes can accomplish.

SOLDIERS: We struggle in vain, we work uselessly. See, the clothing sticks to their virginal bodies like skin. And that one, the governor, who directed us to strip the girls, remains seated, and no one can arouse him from sleep. Let us go to the emperor and reveal to him the things which have happened.

[Scene 5]

DIOCLETIAN: I am much disheartened, to hear that Dulcitius has been now mocked, now reproached, now accused. But lest those vile young ladies boast that they can make fun of our gods and their worshippers with impunity, I shall send Count Sisinnius to extract vengeance.

[Scene 6]

SISINNIUS: Soldiers, where are the mischievous girls who are to be tortured?

SOLDIERS: They are being punished in prison.

SISINNIUS: Leave Irene, and bring the others forth.

SOLDIERS: Why do you spare one?

SISINNIUS: I have mercy on her tender years. Perhaps she will more easily change her mind, if she is not terrorized by the presence of her sisters.

SOLDIERS: Very good. They are here, the ones you summoned.

SISINNIUS: Give consent, Agape and Chionia, to my advice.

AGAPE: And if we do?

SISINNIUS: Make libations to the gods.

CHIONIA: We shall without ceasing pour forth the sacrifice of praise to the true and eternal Father, his coeternal Son, and the Holy Paraclete of both.

SISINNIUS: I cannot persuade you to do this, but I can force you by punishments.

AGAPE: You shall not force us. We shall never sacrifice to demons.

SISINNIUS: Put away this hardness of heart, and sacrifice. If you do not, I shall have you killed, according to the command of Emperor Diocletian.

CHIONIA: It is fitting that in killing us you obey the commands of your emperor, whose decrees you know that we scorn. But if you delay by sparing us, it is just that you be killed.

SISINNIUS: Don't wait, soldiers! Don't wait to seize these blasphemous women, and cast them alive into the fire.

SOLDIERS: Let us hurry to build the pyre, and throw them into the raging flames, where we shall put an end to their insults.

AGAPE: Is not this unusual power from you, O Lord, that the fire forgets the force of its nature in obeying you. But we are weary of delays. We therefore ask you, to loosen the moorings of our souls so that, with the death of our bodies, our spirits may in your presence make praises in the sky.

SOLDIERS: What an unheard-of, astounding miracle! Look, the souls have left the bodies, and no marks of injury can be found. Neither the hair nor the garments have been scorched by the fire, let alone the bodies.

SISINNIUS: Bring forth Irene.

SOLDIERS: Here she is.

SISINNIUS: Take heed, Irene, at the death of your sisters, and be careful lest you also perish as did they.

IRENE: I wish to follow their example in dying, so that I may deserve to rejoice forever with them.

SISINNIUS: Give in, give in to my advice.

IRENE: I shall hardly give in to one recommending crime.

SISINNIUS: If you do not give in, I shall not grant you a quick death, but I will delay it, and for days add new tortures.

IRENE: The more cruelly I am tortured, the more gloriously I shall be exalted.

SISINNIUS: Aren't you afraid of tortures? I shall do something else which you shall find terrifying.

IRENE: Whatever you inflict against me, I shall escape with the help of Christ.

SISINNIUS: I shall have you brought to a house of prostitution, and your body basely fouled.

IRENE: It is better that the body be soiled by some injuries than that the soul be polluted by idols.

SISINNIUS: If you become a partner of prostitutes, you can no longer as a fallen woman be considered a member of the company of virgins.

IRENE: Pleasure brings punishment, but constraint earns a crown. Something cannot be considered a crime to which the mind has not assented.

SISINNIUS: I spared her in vain; in vain I had mercy upon her tender years.

SOLDIERS: We knew that she could never be bent to the worship of the gods, nor could she ever be broken by terror.

SISINNIUS: I shall spare her no longer.

SOLDIERS: Right.

SISINNIUS: Seize her without mercy, drag her roughly and take her to the house of prostitution without honor.

IRENE: They shall not take me.

SISINNIUS: Who is there to prevent them?

IRENE: He who governs the world by his providence.

SISINNIUS: Let's try him.

IRENE: As quickly as possible.

SISINNIUS: You are not frightened, soldiers, by the false prophecies of this blasphemous girl?

SOLDIERS: We are not frightened but we are trying to obey your commands.

[*Scene* 7]

SISINNIUS: Who are these men, who are coming towards us? How similar they are to the soldiers, to whom we delivered Irene. They are the soldiers! Why have you returned so soon? Where are you going so breathlessly?

SOLDIERS: We are looking for you.

SISINNIUS: Where is the girl whom you took away?

SOLDIERS: On the ridge of the mountain.

SISINNIUS: What mountain?

SOLDIERS: That one near by.

SISINNIUS: O, you insane and stupid men, you are incapable of all reason!

SOLDIERS: Why do you berate us? Why do you threaten us in voice and expression?

SISINNIUS: May the gods destroy you!

SOLDIERS: What have we done to you? What injuries have we caused you? What of your commands have we not obeyed?

SISINNIUS: Didn't I tell you to take that rebel against the gods to a house of shame?

SOLDIERS: You commanded, and we were making an effort to obey your orders. But two unknown young men overtook us. They said they were your messengers, sent with this command: we were to take Irene to the peak of the mountain.

SISINNIUS: I knew nothing of them.

SOLDIERS: We saw them.

SISINNIUS: What were they like?

SOLDIERS: They were dressed in splendid robes, and were rather dignified in countenance.

SISINNIUS: Did you follow them?

SOLDIERS: We did.

SISINNIUS: What did they do?

SOLDIERS: They placed themselves on Irene's right and left sides, and they led us here, so that you would know the outcome.

SISINNIUS: The only thing left to do is to get on my horse and follow them. I shall find out who they are, who have so freely tricked us.

[*Scene 8*]

SISINNIUS: Alas, I don't know what I am doing. I am cast down by the sorceries of Christians. Look, I go around the mountain and, though I sometimes find the trail, I can neither take the way up, nor go down the way I came.

SOLDIERS: We are all of us tricked in remarkable fashion, and we are getting tired with a great weariness. If you permit the mad person to live any longer, you shall destroy yourself and us.

SISINNIUS: Whoever is with me, strenuously draw the bow, shoot the arrow, and pierce this sorceress.

SOLDIERS: It is as it should be.

IRENE: Unhappy man! Blush, Sisinnius, blush. Mourn the fact that you have been shamefully conquered. You were unable to overcome the childhood of a tender young girl without the use of arms.

SISINNIUS: Whatever shameful happens, I shall bear it lightly, for I don't doubt that you shall die.

IRENE: From this comes a deed of greatest joy for me, but for you of greatest sorrow. For the cruelty of your wickedness, you shall be condemned to hell. But I shall receive the palm of martyrdom and the crown of virginity. For I shall enter the heavenly bridal chamber of the Eternal King, to Whom is honor and glory forever.

III. *The vernacular culture of the early Middle Ages*

⊔⎍⊔⎍⊔⎍⊔⎍⊔⎍⊔⎍⊔⎍⊔⎍⊔⎍⊔⎍⊔⎍⊔⎍⊔⎍⊔⎍⊔⎍⊔⎍⊔

13. The *Song of Hildebrand*

The fragment known as the *Song of Hildebrand* (*Hildebrandslied*) is the oldest surviving example of heroic poetry in a Germanic tongue. Its language is Old High German, and it was written down by two monks at Fulda at about 800, on the bindings of a Latin manuscript since destroyed. Charlemagne, according to his biographer Einhard, liked to have recited to him the "old rude songs" of the Franks, and ordered them written down so that they could be preserved. Unfortunately none of these copies has survived. This *Song of Hildebrand* is the only surviving example of the kind of poetry that once delighted the great Frankish emperor.

The *Song* tells of the confrontation on opposite sides of a field of battle of Hildebrand and his son Hadubrand. They had been separated for many years, and the young warrior refuses to believe that the old Hun who faces him is really his father. The ending is lost, and scholars have speculated upon its character. The likely assumption is that the poem ended in tragedy.

The translation is taken from Francis A. Wood, *The Hildebrandslied* (Chicago: University of Chicago Press, 1914), pp. 4–7.

I heard this tale   [of hap and harm],
That two warriors wielded   their weapons amain,
Hildebrand and Hadubrand,   between two hosts.
The father and son   fastened their armor,
Buckled their harness,   belted their swords on
Over coat of mail   as to combat they rode.
Hildebrand spake then,   the hoary-hair'd warrior,
More wise in life's wisdom: he warily asked,
And few were his words,   who his father was

In the folk of the foemen.   "[Thy friends would I know,
And kindly tell me]   what kin thou dost claim.
If thou namest but one,   I shall know then the others:
The kin of this kingdom   are couth to me all."

Hadubrand answer'd,   Hildebrand's son:
"This lore I learned   from long ago,
From the wise and old   who were of yore,
That Hildebrand hight my father: my name is Hadubrand.
Off to the east he wander'd,   the anger of Ottokar fleeing,
Marching away with Dietrich,   and many a man went with him.
He left in the land   a little one lorn,
A babe at the breast   in the bower of the bride,
Bereft of his rights: thus he rode to the east
But later Dietrich   lost my father
And lived henceforth   a lonely man.
For the foe of Ottokar,   so fierce and keen,
Was the dearest of thanes   to Dietrich his lord.
He was fain to fight   where the fray was thick:
Known was his bravery   among bold warriors.
I can not believe   that he lives longer."

"I swear by the God   who sways the heavens
That the bonds of blood   forbid our strife."
Then he unclaspt from his arm   the clinging gold,
Which was wrought of coin   that the king had given,
The lord of the Huns: "With love I give it."
But Hadubrand answer'd,   Hildebrand's son:
"With the tip of the spear   one takes the gift
From the sharpened edge   of the foeman's shaft.
Thou thinkest, old Hun,   thy thoughts are deep,
Thou speakest alluring words,   with the spear it would like
      thee to wound me.
With untruth art thou come to old age,   for trickery clings
      to thee ever.
It was said to me   by seafarers
Coming west over the wave   that war slew him.
Dead is Hildebrand,   Heribrand's son."

"Great Weirdwielder,   woe worth the day!
For sixty winters   and summers I wander'd
Battling with foemen   where blows keen fell.

From the scarpèd wall   unscathed I came.
Now the son of my loins   with the sword will hew me;
He will deal me death   or I dash him to earth.
But now canst thou strike,   if strong be thine arm,
Canst win the harness   from so hoary a man,
And strip the spoils   from the stricken foe."

Hadubrand answer'd,   Hildebrand's son:
"Full well I hold,   from thy harness rich,
That thou comest hither   from a kindly lord,
In whose kingdom thou wast not   a wandering wretch."
"The heart of a coward   would the Hun now have
Who would shrink from a foe   so fain to fight,
To struggle together.   Let each now strive
To see whether today   he must bite the dust
Or may bear from the field   the byrnies of both."

Then first they hurled   the hurtling spears
In sharpest showers   that shook the shields.
Then they clasht with their brands,   the battleboards bursting,
And hewed with might   the white linden
Till they shivered the shields   with shattering strokes,
As they wielded their weapons . . .

⎍⎍⎍⎍⎍⎍⎍⎍⎍⎍⎍⎍⎍⎍⎍⎍⎍⎍⎍⎍

14. Anglo-Saxon lyric poetry

Lyric poetry in Anglo-Saxon or Old English has not survived in any
abundance (most of it is preserved in only four manuscripts). But it
does contain works of real power. Two Old English poems are given
here. The first of these, Caedmon's poem in celebration of God's creation, may be mediocre in quality, but it is memorable for the reason
that it is the oldest datable poem in the English language. According
to Bede (*Ecclesiastical History*, IV, 24), Caedmon was a herdsman
of Northumbria. He knew nothing of poetry, and when at feasts the
harp was passed to him to take his turn in singing, he had to leave the
company. One night, when he had left a feast and was guarding cattle
in a stable, a stranger appeared to him, and asked him to sing about the

beginning of created things. He suddenly and, he thought, miraculously found himself able to do so.

Caedmon began to compose between 658 and 680, and Bede believed that he was unequaled for the beauty of his songs. The first of his poems on the creation was given a Latin paraphrase by Bede himself and entered into his *History*. The Anglo-Saxon original was copied into a manuscript of the *History* only a few years after Bede's death in 735. There is no reason to doubt its authenticity.

The *Dream of the Rood* deserves to be considered one of the loveliest Christian religious poems in any language. In the poet's dream, the rood or cross speaks to him, recounting in restrained but moving language how it was taken from the forest, used for Christ's death, and then venerated as a symbol of salvation.

Like poetry in the other Germanic languages, Anglo-Saxon poems are based not upon regular rhythm or rime, but upon alliteration. Each line is broken into two relatively equal halves by a pause or caesura. The number of syllables in each half-line may vary, but both will usually contain two stresses. One or both of the stressed syllables of the first half-line will alliterate with the first stress of the second half-line. The rules were quite complex, but they did allow considerable flexibility to a gifted poet.

The translations of these two poems are taken from A. S. Cook and C. B. Tinker, *Select Translations from Old English Poetry* (Boston: Ginn and Co. 1902), pp. 76 and 93–99.

Caedmon's Hymn

Now must we hymn the Master of heaven,
The might of the Maker, the deeds of the Father,
The thought of His heart. He, Lord everlasting,
Established of old the source of all wonders:
Creator all-holy, He hung the bright heaven,
A roof high upreared, o'er the children of men;
The King of mankind then created for mortals
The world in its beauty, the earth spread beneath them,
He, Lord everlasting, omnipotent God.

[Trans. Albert S. Cook]

The Dream of the Rood

Hark! of a matchless vision would I speak,
Which once I dreamed at midnight, when mankind
At rest were dwelling. Then methought I saw
A wondrous cross extending up on high,

With light encircled, tree of trees most bright.
That beacon all was overlaid with gold;
And near the earth stood precious stones ablaze,
While five more sparkled on the shoulder-beam.
Gazing on it were angels of the Lord,
From their first being's dawn all beautiful.
No cross was that of wickedness and shame,
But holy spirits, men on earth, and all
The glorious creation on it gazed.
  Sublime the tree victorious; while I,
Stained with iniquity, was galled with sins.
There, clothed as with a garment, I beheld
That tree of glory shining joyfully,
Adorned with gold, enriched with precious stones,
Which covered worthily the Ruler's cross.
However, through the gold I could perceive
That wretched ones had battled there of old;
For on the right side once it had been bleeding.
Then all my spirit was with sorrow stirred;
Fearful was I before that radiant sight.
There I beheld that beacon, quick to change,
Alter in vesture and in coloring;
Now dewed with moisture, soiled with streaming blood,
And now with gold and glittering gems adorned.
  A long time lying there I sadly looked
Upon the Savior's cross, until I heard
Resounding thence a voice. That wood divine
Then spake these words:
                        "It was long, long ago—
Yet I recall—when, at the forest's edge,
I was hewn down, and from my stem removed.
Resistless were the foes that seized me there,
They fashioned for themselves a spectacle,
Commanded me to bear their criminals;
And on men's shoulders carried me away
Until they set me down upon a hill,
And stayed me fast; mine enemies indeed!
  "Then I beheld the Master of mankind
Approach with lordly courage as if he
Would mount upon me, and I dared not bow
Nor break, opposing the command of God,

Although I saw earth tremble; all my foes
I might have beaten down, yet I stood fast.
"Then the young Hero laid his garments by,
He that was God almighty, strong and brave;
And boldly in the sight of all he mounted
The lofty cross, for he would free mankind.
Then, as the Man divine clasped me, I shook;
Yet dared I not bow to the earth nor fall
Upon the ground, but I must needs stand fast.
"A cross upraised, I lifted a great King,
Lifted the Lord of heaven; and dared not bow.
"They pierced me with dark nails, and visible
Upon me still are scars, wide wounds of malice,
Yet might I injure none among them all.
They mocked us both together; then was I
All wet with blood, which streamed from this Man's side
When he at length had breathed his spirit out.
"Many a vile deed I suffered on that mount;
The God of hosts I saw harshly outstretched,
And darkness hid the body of the King,
With clouds enshrouded its effulgent light;
Forth went a shadow, black beneath the clouds;
And all creation wept, lamented long—
Their King had fallen, Christ was on the cross.
"Yet eagerly some hastened from afar
To him who was their Prince; all this I saw.
Ah, then with sorrow was I deeply stirred;
Yet to the hand of men I bowed me down,
Humbly, with ardent zeal. They took him then,
Lifted from his dire pain almighty God.
The warriors left me standing, swathed in blood,
And with sharp arrows wounded sore was I.
Him they laid gently down, weary of limb,
And stood beside his body at the head,
Gazing upon the Lord of heaven; while he
Rested a while, with his great labor spent.
Then in the slayers' sight men there began
To build a sepulcher, from marble hewn;
And laid therein the Lord of victories.
A song of sorrow then for him they sang,
The desolate at eventide, when they,

O'erwearied, would depart from their great King.
And so companionless he rested.
                              "We,
After the warriors' cry uprose, yet stood
A long while there, on our foundations dripping.
The corpse, fair dwelling of the soul, grew cold.
   "Then one began to fell us to the earth—
A fearful fate! and in the entombing mold
Deep buried us. Yet, undismayed, for me
The friends and followers of the Lord made search—
And when from out the earth they lifted me,
With silver they adorned me, and with gold.
   "Now mayest thou know, O hero mine, beloved!
Unutterable sorrows I endured,
Base felons' work. But now hath come the time
When, far and wide, men on the earth, and all
The glorious universe doth honor me,
And to this beacon bow themselves in prayer.
On me a while suffered the Son of God;
Therefore now full of majesty I tower
High under heaven; and I have power to heal
All those who do me reverence.
                              "Of old
Was I a punishment, the cruelest,
The most abhorred by men, ere I for man
Had opened the true way of life. Lo, then
The Prince of glory, Guardian of heaven,
Above all other trees exalted me,
As he, almighty God, in sight of men
His mother honored, blessèd among women,
Mary herself.
                 "Now, hero mine, beloved,
I bid thee tell this vision unto men,
Reveal with words that 'tis the glory-tree
On which almighty God suffered for sin,
The many sins of man, and Adam's deeds
Done long ago. There once he tasted death;
But afterwards the Lord from death arose
By his own mighty power, a help for men.
To heaven he then ascended, whence shall come
Once more upon the earth to seek mankind

At the last judgment day, the Lord himself,
Almighty God, surrounded by his angels.
And there shall he, who hath the power of doom,
Adjudge to everyone the just reward
Which he on earth, in this short life, hath earned.
Then unabashed and bold can no one be
Before the word which he, the Ruler, speaks:
'Where is the man,' he asks the multitude,
'Who for the Lord would taste of bitter death
As he himself once did upon the cross?'
Then are they fearful, little can devise
What they shall say to Christ. But need is none
That any at that time should be afraid
Who beareth in his heart this sacred sign;
For through the cross alone must every soul
Seek out the kingdom from the earthly way,
Who hopes hereafter with the King to dwell."

   Happy in mind I prayed then to the rood
With great devotion, where I was alone
Without companionship; my soul within
Was quickened to depart, so many years
Of utter weariness had I delayed.
And now my life's great happiness is this,
That to the cross victorious I may come
Alone, above the wont of other men,
To worship worthily. Desire for this
Is great within my heart, and all my help
Must reach me from the rood. Of powerful friends
Not many do I own on earth, for hence
Have they departed, from the world's delights;
They followed after him, their glorious King,
And with the Father now in heaven they live,
Dwelling in bliss. Each day I longing ask:
"When will the cross of Christ, which formerly
I here on earth beheld, call me away
From this my transient life, and bring me hence
To all delight, the joyous harmonies
Of heaven, where sit at feast the folk of God,
And gladness knows no end—so placing me
Where with the saints in glory I may dwell,

Enjoying greatly their glad minstrelsy?"
Be gracious unto me, O Lord, who once
For sins of men suffered upon the cross.
He freed us, gave us life, and home in heaven.

Hope was restored with blessedness and joy
To those who had erewhile endured the fire.
Triumphant in this journey was the Son,
Mighty and prosperous, when he advanced
Into God's kingdom with a multitude,
A host of souls; when to his angels came
The almighty Master for their joy, to those
The holy ones in heaven, who from the first
Had dwelt in glory; when their Ruler came,
Almighty God, into his fatherland.

[Trans. LaMotte Iddings]

15. Beowulf

Beowulf is the only complete heroic epic in Old English (or, for that
matter, in any Old Germanic tongue), and is a work of nearly un-
rivaled interest for an understanding of the vernacular culture of the
early Middle Ages.

In spite of decades of intensive scholarly research, much obscurity
surrounds *Beowulf's* origins. It has survived in only a single manuscript, which on paleographic grounds may be dated to about the year
1000. The author is unknown. He was certainly a Christian, although
Christian elements in the poem are rather superficial. He seems to
have been a learned man (some vague reminiscences of Vergil have
been detected), and was therefore perhaps a monk. While he wrote in
the West-Saxon dialect, peculiarities of his usage suggest that he was a
Northumbrian, or was working with Northumbrian materials.

The date of his life has long perplexed scholars, and no consensus
exists among them. *Beowulf* alludes to events mentioned by Gregory
of Tours in the sixth century, but all scholars agree that the poem
could not have been written down until Christianity was well estab-

lished in England, that is, not until after 650. Probably a majority of
Anglo-Saxon philologists would place the composition of the poem
between 650 and 750, arguing that its language is distinctly archaic.
Historians, in the main, seem to favor a later date. The poem has this
salient peculiarity. Written in Old English, it never mentions the
English. It is wholly concerned with incidents in Scandinavian history
or legends. This has suggested to many scholars that the poem could
only be the product of a period when England and Scandinavia were
closely associated, perhaps during the Viking migrations of the ninth
and tenth centuries. Some historians have even proposed the reign of
Canute (1017–35), when England, Denmark and Norway were parts
of a single northern kingdom under Danish rule. While recognizing the
difficulties of the problem, the present editor believes that the arguments for a later date are the more cogent; he would favor the tenth
century as the most likely period for the poem's composition. Even
if late in origin, *Beowulf* certainly includes much earlier materials.

The poem consists of 3182 lines, and is written in the characteristic
alliterative verse of Old English. Each line is divided into two halves
by a pause or caesura; each half-line usually contains two stresses, and
stressed syllables usually begin with the same alliterating consonant or
vowel.

The story itself divides into three major parts, each concerned with
the hero's struggle against three separate monsters. In the first part,
Hrothgar, king of the Danes, has built "the greatest banquet hall ever
known," called Herot. But a monster named Grendel, apparently a
giant in human form, begins to attack the hall at night and repeatedly
carries off human victims. The Danes can do nothing, and for twelve
years Herot lies deserted. But in the far-off land of the Geats, the
hero Beowulf hears of Hrothgar's plight, and comes with fourteen
companions to aid him. They feast in the great hall; at night the Danes
withdraw, leaving Beowulf and his Geats alone. The monster breaks
into Herot and kills one of the hero's companions. But Beowulf, the
strongest man alive, grapples with Grendel, and tears off an arm. The
monster, mortally wounded, drags himself away, to die in his mother's
lair under the sea.

The second part of the epic tells of Beowulf's battle with Grendel's
mother. Angered by the death of her son, she invades the great hall and
kills a Danish noble (Beowulf and his companions were sleeping elsewhere). The hero goes to the shores of the sea, plunges under the
water, finds the monster's lair, and kills it after a ferocious struggle.

In the third part, Beowulf returns home, and tells the story of his
adventures to Higlac, king of the Geats. After Higlac and his son
die, Beowulf himself becomes king, and rules peacefully over his people for fifty years. Then a sleeping dragon, guarding a treasure, is

aroused and angered when a cup is stolen from his hoard. He ravages the land and burns the royal hall. The aged king determines to fight him in single combat. With twelve companions to witness the battle, he approaches the dragon's den. The fight begins, and only one of his men, Wiglaf, stays with his king. With Wiglaf's help, he kills the dragon, but suffers a mortal wound. In dying, he asks that his ashes be enshrined in a great mound on the headlands facing the sea, so that sailors could see it from afar and be guided by it.

Beowulf presents an excellent picture of the place and importance of the hero in Germanic society. That society, to begin with, was set within a cruel and hostile environment, the abode of dreadful monsters, who envied men their music, songs, gold and measure of happiness. The poet makes effective use of light imagery in contrasting the happy fellowship of men with the gloomy exterior forces which threaten it. Polished armor, shimmering ringlets of iron and, above all, burnished gold are the marks of human society. Herot is a hall shining with gold, and gold, the reward of heroes, symbolizes the highest human attainments. The mark of the outer world, on the other hand, is darkness. Grendel is an obscure figure; his very shape is uncertain. He comes at night, and his home is the dark sea.

The worlds of men and of monsters are poised in a precarious balance. In building his great hall Herot, King Hrothgar had encroached upon the domain of darkness and challenged its power. Grendel came out of the gloom to claim revenge and win back the hall. In the war against him, the king can do nothing. This failure to cope with Grendel well illustrates the weak power and low prestige held by kings in Germanic society. The one means of vanquishing the monster is the hero. He thus makes an essential contribution to the survival and welfare of the people and is in fact their only hope.

Beowulf himself, even as an aged king, cannot rely upon the apparatus of an organized state. To fight the dragon, he thinks only in terms of single combat, even though he knows that death will be his fate.

The hero is essential for society, but he seems also to be doomed. There is an unmistakable note of pessimistic fatalism in Beowulf. We are given to know that not only is Beowulf marked for death, but also his entire people, the Geats, are destined for ultimate destruction. The hero must still keep to his work, even with assured knowledge of his own demise, and even while recognizing the final futility of his efforts. This heroic fatalism is what gives Beowulf his noble stature, and the poem its powerful impact.

The following translation, which gives the third part of the poem in its entirety, is taken from Beowulf, trans. Burton Raffel (New York and Toronto: New American Library, Mentor Classic, 1963), pp. 91–121. The editor is grateful for permission to reprint the passage here.

Afterwards, in the time when Higlac was dead   2200
And Herdred, his son, who'd ruled the Geats
After his father, had followed him into darkness—
Killed in battle with the Swedes, who smashed
His shield, cut through the soldiers surrounding
Their king—then, when Higd's one son   2205
Was gone, Beowulf ruled in Geatland,
Took the throne he'd refused, once,
And held it long and well. He was old
With years and wisdom, fifty winters
A king, when a dragon awoke from its darkness   2210
And dreams and brought terror to his people. The beast
Had slept in a huge stone tower, with a hidden
Path beneath; a man stumbled on
The entrance, went in, discovered the ancient
Treasure, the pagan jewels and gold   2215
The dragon had been guarding, and dazzled and greedy
Stole a gem-studded cup, and fled.
But now the dragon hid nothing, neither
The theft nor itself; it swept through the darkness,
And all Geatland knew its anger.   2220

32

But the thief had not come to steal; he stole,
And roused the dragon, not from desire
But need. He was someone's slave, had been beaten
By his masters, had run from all men's sight,
But with no place to hide; then he found the hidden   2225
Path, and used it. And once inside,
Seeing the sleeping beast, staring as it
Yawned and stretched, not wanting to wake it,
Terror-struck, he turned and ran for his life,
Taking the jeweled cup.   2230

That tower
Was heaped high with hidden treasure, stored there
Years before by the last survivor
Of a noble race, ancient riches
Left in the darkness as the end of a dynasty   2235
Came. Death had taken them, one
By one, and the warrior who watched over all

That remained mourned their fate, expecting,
Soon, the same for himself, knowing
The gold and jewels he had guarded so long   2240
Could not bring him pleasure much longer. He brought
The precious cups, the armor and the ancient
Swords, to a stone tower built
Near the sea, below a cliff, a sealed
Fortress with no windows, no doors, waves   2245
In front of it, rocks behind. Then he spoke:
    "Take these treasures, earth, now that no one
Living can enjoy them. They were yours, in the beginning;
Allow them to return. War and terror
Have swept away my people, shut   2250
Their eyes to delight and to living, closed
The door to all gladness. No one is left
To lift these swords, polish these jeweled
Cups: no one leads, no one follows. These hammered
Helmets, worked with gold, will tarnish   2255
And crack; the hands that should clean and polish them
Are still forever. And these mail shirts, worn
In battle, once, while swords crashed
And blades bit into shields and men,
Will rust away like the warriors who owned them.   2260
None of these treasures will travel to distant
Lands, following their lords. The harp's
Bright song, the hawk crossing through the hall
On its swift wings, the stallion tramping
In the courtyard—all gone, creatures of every   2265
Kind, and their masters, hurled to the grave!"
    And so he spoke, sadly, of those
Long dead, and lived from day to day,
Joyless, until, at last, death touched
His heart and took him too. And a stalker   2270
In the night, a flaming dragon, found
The treasure unguarded; he whom men fear
Came flying through the darkness, wrapped in fire,
Seeking caves and stone-split ruins
But finding gold. Then it stayed, buried   2275
Itself with heathen silver and jewels
It could neither use nor ever abandon.
    So mankind's enemy, the mighty beast,

Slept in those stone walls for hundreds
Of years; a runaway slave roused it,   2280
Stole a jeweled cup and bought
His master's forgiveness, begged for mercy
And was pardoned when his delighted lord took the present
He bore, turned it in his hand and stared
At the ancient carvings. The cup brought peace   2285
To a slave, pleased his master, but stirred
A dragon's anger. It turned, hunting
The thief's tracks, and found them, saw
Where its visitor had come and gone. He'd survived,
Had come close enough to touch its scaly   2290
Head and yet lived, as it lifted its cavernous
Jaws, through the grace of almighty God
And a pair of quiet, quick-moving feet.
The dragon followed his steps, anxious
To find the man who had robbed it of silver   2295
And sleep; it circled around and around
The tower, determined to catch him, but could not,
He had run too fast, the wilderness was empty.
The beast went back to its treasure, planning
A bloody revenge, and found what was missing,   2300
Saw what thieving hands had stolen.
Then it crouched on the stones, counting off
The hours till the Almighty's candle went out,
And evening came, and wild with anger
It could fly burning across the land, killing   2305
And destroying with its breath. Then the sun was gone,
And its heart was glad: glowing with rage
It left the tower, impatient to repay
Its enemies. The people suffered, everyone
Lived in terror, but when Beowulf had learned   2310
Of their trouble his fate was worse, and came quickly.

33

Vomiting fire and smoke, the dragon
Burned down their homes. They watched in horror
As the flames rose up: the angry monster
Meant to leave nothing alive. And the signs   2315
Of its anger flickered and glowed in the darkness,
Visible for miles, tokens of its hate

And its cruelty, spread like a warning to the Geats
Who had broken its rest. Then it hurried back
To its tower, to its hidden treasure, before dawn   2320
Could come. It had wrapped its flames around
The Geats; now it trusted in stone
Walls, and its strength, to protect it. But they would not.
  Then they came to Beowulf, their king, and announced
That his hall, his throne, the best of buildings,   2325
Had melted away in the dragon's burning
Breath. Their words brought misery, Beowulf's
Sorrow beat at his heart: he accused
Himself of breaking God's law, of bringing
The Almighty's anger down on his people.   2330
Reproach pounded in his breast, gloomy
And dark, and the world seemed a different place.
But the hall was gone, the dragon's molten
Breath had licked across it, burned it
To ashes, near the shore it had guarded. The Geats   2335
Deserved revenge; Beowulf, their leader
And lord, began to plan it, ordered
A battle-shield shaped of iron, knowing that
Wood would be useless, that no linden shield
Could help him, protect him, in the flaming heat   2340
Of the beast's breath. That noble prince
Would end his days on earth, soon,
Would leave this brief life, but would take the dragon
With him, tear it from the heaped-up treasure
It had guarded so long. And he'd go to it alone,   2345
Scorning to lead soldiers against such
An enemy: he saw nothing to fear, thought nothing
Of the beast's claws, or wings, or flaming
Jaws—he had fought, before, against worse
Odds, had survived, been victorious, in harsher   2350
Battles, beginning in Herot, Hrothgar's
Unlucky hall. He'd killed Grendel
And his mother, swept that murdering tribe
Away. And he'd fought in Higlac's war
With the Frisians, fought at his lord's side   2355
Till a sword reached out and drank Higlac's
Blood, till a blade swung in the rush
Of battle killed the Geats' great king.

Then Beowulf escaped, broke through Frisian
Shields and swam to freeedom, saving   2360
Thirty sets of armor from the scavenging
Franks, river people who robbed
The dead as they floated by. Beowulf
Offered them only his sword, ended
So many jackal lives that the few   2365
Who were able skulked silently home, glad
To leave him. So Beowulf swam sadly back
To Geatland, almost the only survivor
Of a foolish war. Higlac's widow
Brought him the crown, offered him the kingdom,   2370
Not trusting Herdred, her son and Higlac's,
To beat off foreign invaders. But Beowulf
Refused to rule when his lord's own son
Was alive, and the leaderless Geats could choose
A rightful king. He gave Herdred   2375
All his support, offering an open
Heart where Higlac's young son could see
Wisdom he still lacked himself: warmth
And good will were what Beowulf brought his new king.
    But Swedish exiles came, seeking   2380
Protection; they were rebels against Onela,
Healfdane's son-in-law and the best ring-giver
His people had ever known. And Onela
Came too, a mighty king, marched
On Geatland with a huge army; Herdred   2385
Had given his word and now he gave
His life, shielding the Swedish strangers.
Onela wanted nothing more:
When Herdred had fallen that famous warrior
Went back to Sweden, let Beowulf rule!   2390

34
But Beowulf remembered how his king had been killed.
As soon as he could he lent the last
Of the Swedish rebels soldiers and gold,
Helped him to a bitter battle across
The wide sea, where victory, and revenge, and the Swedish   2395
Throne were won, and Onela was slain.
    So Edgetho's son survived, no matter

What dangers he met, what battles he fought,
Brave and forever triumphant, till the day
Fate sent him to the dragon and sent him death.   2400
A dozen warriors walked with their angry
King, when he was brought to the beast; Beowulf
Knew, by then, what had woken the monster,
And enraged it. The cup had come to him, traveled
From dragon to slave, to master, to king,   2405
And the slave was their guide, had begun the Geats'
Affliction, and now, afraid of both beast
And men, was forced to lead them to the monster's
Hidden home. He showed them the huge
Stones, set deep in the ground, with the sea   2410
Beating on the rocks close by. Beowulf
Stared, listening to stories of the gold
And riches heaped inside. Hidden,
But wakeful, now, the dragon waited,
Ready to greet him. Gold and hammered   2415
Armor have been buried in pleasanter places!
   The battle-brave king rested on the shore,
While his soldiers wished him well, urged him
On. But Beowulf's heart was heavy:
His soul sensed how close fate   2420
Had come, felt something, not fear but knowledge
Of old age. His armor was strong, but his arm
Hung like his heart. Body and soul
Might part, here; his blood might be spilled,
His spirit torn from his flesh. Then he spoke: 2425
   "My early days were full of war,
And I survived it all; I can remember everything.
I was seven years old when Hrethel opened
His home and his heart for me, when my king and lord
Took me from my father and kept me, taught me,   2430
Gave me gold and pleasure, glad that I sat
At his knee. And he never loved me less
Than any of his sons—Herbald, the oldest
Of all, or Hathcyn, or Higlac, my lord.
Herbald died a horrible death,   2435
Killed while hunting: Hathcyn, his brother,
Stretched his horn-tipped bow, sent
An arrow flying, but missed his mark

And hit Herbald instead, found him
With a bloody point and pierced him through.   2440
The crime was great, the guilt was plain,
But nothing could be done, no vengeance, no death
To repay that death, no punishment, nothing.
   "So with the graybeard whose son sins
Against the king, and is hanged: he stands   2445
Watching his child swing on the gallows,
Lamenting, helpless, while his flesh and blood
Hangs for the raven to pluck. He can raise
His voice in sorrow, but revenge is impossible.
And every morning he remembers how his son   2450
Died, and despairs; no son to come
Matters, no future heir, to a father
Forced to live through such misery. The place
Where his son once dwelled, before death compelled him
To journey away, is a windy wasteland,   2455
Empty, cheerless; the childless father
Shudders, seeing it. So riders and ridden
Sleep in the ground; pleasure is gone,
The harp is silent, and hope is forgotten.

                            35
   "And then, crying his sorrow, he crawls   2460
To his bed: the world, and his home, hurt him
With their emptiness. And so it seemed to Hrethel,
When Herbald was dead, and his heart swelled
With grief. The murderer lived; he felt
No love for him, now, but nothing could help,   2465
Word nor hand nor sharp-honed blade,
War nor hate, battle or blood
Or law. The pain could find no relief,
He could only live with it, or leave grief and life
Together. When he'd gone to his grave Hathcyn   2470
And Higlac, his sons, inherited everything.
   "And then there was war between Geats and Swedes,
Bitter battles carried across
The broad sea, when the mighty Hrethel slept
And Ongentho's sons thought Sweden could safely   2475
Attack, saw no use to pretending friendship
But raided and burned, and near old Rennsburg

Slaughtered Geats with their thieving swords.
My people repaid them, death for death,
Battle for battle, though one of the brothers   2480
Bought that revenge with his life—Hathcyn,
King of the Geats, killed by a Swedish
Sword. But when dawn came the slayer
Was slain, and Higlac's soldiers avenged
Everything with the edge of their blades. Efor   2485
Caught the Swedish king, cracked
His helmet, split his skull, dropped him,
Pale and bleeding, to the ground, then put him
To death with a swift stroke, shouting
His joy.   2490
            "The gifts that Higlac gave me,
And the land, I earned with my sword, as fate
Allowed: he never needed Danes
Or Goths or Swedes, soldiers and allies
Bought with gold, bribed to his side.   2495
My sword was better, and always his.
In every battle my place was in front;
Alone, and so it shall be forever,
As long as this sword lasts, serves me
In the future as it has served me before. So   2500
I killed Dagref, the Frank, who brought death
To Higlac, and who looted his corpse: Higd's
Necklace, Welthow's treasure, never
Came to Dagref's king. The thief
Fell in battle, but not on my blade.   2505
He was brave and strong, but I swept him in my arms,
Ground him against me till his bones broke,
Till his blood burst out. And now I shall fight
For this treasure, fight with both hand and sword."
            And Beowulf uttered his final boast: 2510
    "I've never known fear; as a youth I fought
In endless battles. I am old, now,
But I will fight again, seek fame still,
If the dragon hiding in his tower dares
To face me."   2515
                  Then he said farewell to his followers,
Each in his turn, for the last time:
    "I'd use no sword, no weapon, if this beast

Could be killed without it, crushed to death
Like Grendel, gripped in my hands and torn   2520
Limb from limb. But his breath will be burning
Hot, poison will pour from his tongue.
I feel no shame, with shield and sword
And armor, against this monster: when he comes to me
I mean to stand, not run from his shooting   2525
Flames, stand till fate decides
Which of us wins. My heart is firm,
My hands calm: I need no hot
Words. Wait for me close by, my friends.
We shall see, soon, who will survive   2530
This bloody battle, stand when the fighting
Is done. No one else could do
What I mean to, here, no man but me
Could hope to defeat this monster. No one
Could try. And this dragon's treasure, his gold   2535
And everything hidden in that tower, will be mine
Or war will sweep me to a bitter death!"
    Then Beowulf rose, still brave, still strong,
And with his shield at his side, and a mail shirt on his breast,
Strode calmly, confidently, toward the tower, under   2540
The rocky cliffs: no coward could have walked there!
And then he who'd endured dozens of desperate
Battles, who'd stood boldly while swords and shields
Clashed, the best of kings, saw
Huge stone arches and felt the heat   2545
Of the dragon's breath, flooding down
Through the hidden entrance, too hot for anyone
To stand, a streaming current of fire
And smoke that blocked all passage. And the Geats'
Lord and leader, angry, lowered   2550
His sword and roared out a battle cry,
A call so loud and clear that it reached through
The hoary rock, hung in the dragon's
Ear. The beast rose, angry,
Knowing a man had come—and then nothing   2555
But war could have followed. Its breath came first,
A steaming cloud pouring from the stone,
Then the earth itself shook. Beowulf
Swung his shield into place, held it

In front of him, facing the entrance. The dragon   2560
Coiled and uncoiled, its heart urging it
Into battle. Beowulf's ancient sword
Was waiting, unsheathed, his sharp and gleaming
Blade. The beast came closer; both of them
Were ready, each set on slaughter. The Geats'   2565
Great prince stood firm, unmoving, prepared
Behind his high shield, waiting in his shining
Armor. The monster came quickly toward him,
Pouring out fire and smoke, hurrying
To its fate. Flames beat at the iron   2570
Shield, and for a time it held, protected
Beowulf as he'd planned; then it began to melt,
And for the first time in his life that famous prince
Fought with fate against him, with glory
Denied him. He knew it, but he raised his sword   2575
And struck at the dragon's scaly hide.
The ancient blade broke, bit into
The monster's skin, drew blood, but cracked
And failed him before it went deep enough, helped him
Less than he needed. The dragon leaped   2580
With pain, thrashed and beat at him, spouting
Murderous flames, spreading them everywhere.
And the Geats' ring-giver did not boast of glorious
Victories in other wars: his weapon
Had failed him, deserted him, now when he needed it   2585
Most, that excellent sword. Edgetho's
Famous son stared at death,
Unwilling to leave this world, to exchange it
For a dwelling in some distant place—a journey
Into darkness that all men must make, as death   2590
Ends their few brief hours on earth.
    Quickly, the dragon came at him, encouraged
As Beowulf fell back; its breath flared,
And he suffered, wrapped around in swirling
Flames—a king, before, but now   2595
A beaten warrior. None of his comrades
Came to him, helped him, his brave and noble
Followers; they ran for their lives, fled
Deep in a wood. And only one of them

Remained, stood there, miserable, remembering,   2600
As a good man must, what kinship should mean.

36

His name was Wiglaf, he was Wexstan's son
And a good soldier; his family had been Swedish,
Once. Watching Beowulf, he could see
How his king was suffering, burning. Remembering   2605
Everything his lord and cousin had given him,
Armor and gold and the great estates
Wexstan's family enjoyed, Wiglaf's
Mind was made up; he raised his yellow
Shield and drew his sword—an ancient   2610
Weapon that had once belonged to Onela's
Nephew, and that Wexstan had won, killing
The prince when he fled from Sweden, sought safety
With Herdred, and found death. And Wiglaf's father
Had carried the dead man's armor, and his sword,   2615
To Onela, and the king had said nothing, only
Given him armor and sword and all,
Everything his rebel nephew had owned
And lost when he left this life. And Wexstan
Had kept those shining gifts, held them   2620
For years, waiting for his son to use them,
Wear them as honorably and well as once
His father had done; then Wexstan died
And Wiglaf was his heir, inherited treasures
And weapons and land. He'd never won   2625
That armor, fought with that sword, until Beowulf
Called him to his side, led him into war.
But his soul did not melt, his sword was strong;
The dragon discovered his courage, and his weapon,
When the rush of battle brought them together.   2630
    And Wiglaf, his heart heavy, uttered
The kind of words his comrades deserved:
    "I remember how we sat in the mead-hall, drinking
And boasting of how brave we'd be when Beowulf
Needed us, he who gave us these swords   2635
And armor: all of us swore to repay him,
When the time came, kindness for kindness

—With our lives, if he needed them. He allowed us to join him,
Chose us from all his great army, thinking
Our boasting words had some weight, believing   2640
Our promises, trusting our swords. He took us
For soldiers, for men. He meant to kill
This monster himself, our mighty king,
Fight this battle alone and unaided,
As in the days when his strength and daring dazzled   2645
Men's eyes. But those days are over and gone
And now our lord must lean on younger
Arms. And we must go to him, while angry
Flames burn at his flesh, help
Our glorious king! By almighty God,   2650
I'd rather burn myself than see
Flames swirling around my lord.
And who are we to carry home
Our shields before we've slain his enemy
And ours, to run back to our homes with Beowulf   2655
So hard-pressed here? I swear that nothing
He ever did deserved an end
Like this, dying miserably and alone,
Butchered by this savage beast: we swore
That these swords and armor were each for us all!"   2660
    Then he ran to his king, crying encouragement
As he dove through the dragon's deadly fumes:
    "Belovèd Beowulf, remember how you boasted,
Once, that nothing in the world would ever
Destroy your fame: fight to keep it,   2665
Now, be strong and brave, my noble
King, protecting life and fame
Together. My sword will fight at your side!"
    The dragon heard him, the man-hating monster,
And was angry; shining with surging flames   2670
It came for him, anxious to return his visit.
Waves of fire swept at his shield
And the edge began to burn. His mail shirt
Could not help him, but before his hands dropped
The blazing wood Wiglaf jumped   2675
Behind Beowulf's shield; his own was burned
To ashes. Then the famous old hero, remembering
Days of glory, lifted what was left

Of Nagling, his ancient sword, and swung it
With all his strength, smashed the gray   2680
Blade into the beast's head. But then Nagling
Broke to pieces, as iron always
Had in Beowulf's hands. His arms
Were too strong, the hardest blade could not help him,
The most wonderfully worked. He carried them to war   2685
But fate had decreed that the Geats' great king
Would be no better for any weapon.
    Then the monster charged again, vomiting
Fire, wild with pain, rushed out
Fierce and dreadful, its fear forgotten.   2690
Watching for its chance it drove its tusks
Into Beowulf's neck; he staggered, the blood
Came flooding forth, fell like rain.

                                37
    And then when Beowulf needed him most
Wiglaf showed his courage, his strength   2695
And skill, and the boldness he was born with. Ignoring
The dragon's head, he helped his lord
By striking lower down. The sword
Sank in; his hand was burned, but the shining
Blade had done its work, the dragon's   2700
Belching flames began to flicker
And die away. And Beowulf drew
His battle-sharp dagger: the blood-stained old king
Still knew what he was doing. Quickly, he cut
The beast in half, slit it apart.   2705
It fell, their courage had killed it, two noble
Cousins had joined in the dragon's death.
Yet what they did all men must do
When the time comes! But the triumph was the last
Beowulf would ever earn, the end   2710
Of greatness and life together. The wound
In his neck began to swell and grow;
He could feel something stirring, burning
In his veins, a stinging venom, and knew
The beast's fangs had left it. He fumbled   2715
Along the wall, found a slab
Of stone, and dropped down; above him he saw

Huge stone arches and heavy posts,
Holding up the roof of that giant hall.
Then Wiglaf's gentle hands bathed   2720
The blood-stained prince, his glorious lord,
Weary of war, and loosened his helmet.
  Beowulf spoke, in spite of the swollen,
Livid wound, knowing he'd unwound
His string of days on earth, seen   2725
As much as God would grant him; all worldly
Pleasure was gone, as life would go,
Soon:
     "I'd leave my armor to my son,
Now, if God had given me an heir,   2730
A child born of my body, his life
Created from mine. I've worn this crown
For fifty winters: no neighboring people
Have tried to threaten the Geats, sent soldiers
Against us or talked of terror. My days   2735
Have gone by as fate willed, waiting
For its word to be spoken, ruling as well
As I knew how, swearing no unholy oaths,
Seeking no lying wars. I can leave
This life happy; I can die, here,   2740
Knowing the Lord of all life has never
Watched me wash my sword in blood
Born of my own family. Belovèd
Wiglaf, go, quickly, find
The dragon's treasure: we've taken its life,   2745
But its gold is ours, too. Hurry,
Bring me ancient silver, precious
Jewels, shining armor and gems,
Before I die. Death will be softer,
Leaving life and this people I've ruled   2750
So long, if I look at this last of all prizes."

38

  Then Wexstan's son went in, as quickly
As he could, did as the dying Beowulf
Asked, entered the inner darkness
Of the tower, went with his mail shirt and his sword.   2755
Flushed with victory he groped his way,

A brave young warrior, and suddenly saw
Piles of gleaming gold, precious
Gems, scattered on the floor, cups
And bracelets, rusty old helmets, beautifully   2760
Made but rotting with no hands to rub
And polish them. They lay where the dragon left them;
It had flown in the darkness, once, before fighting
Its final battle. (So gold can easily
Triumph, defeat the strongest of men,   2765
No matter how deep it is hidden!) And he saw,
Hanging high above, a golden
Banner, woven by the best of weavers
And beautiful. And over everything he saw
A strange light, shining everywhere,   2770
On walls and floor and treasure. Nothing
Moved, no other monsters appeared;
He took what he wanted, all the treasures
That pleased his eye, heavy plates
And golden cups and the glorious banner,   2775
Loaded his arms with all they could hold.
Beowulf's dagger, his iron blade,
Had finished the fire-spitting terror
That once protected tower and treasures
Alike; the gray-bearded lord of the Geats   2780
Had ended those flying, burning raids
Forever.
          Then Wiglaf went back, anxious
To return while Beowulf was alive, to bring him
Treasure they'd won together. He ran,   2785
Hoping his wounded king, weak
And dying, had not left the world too soon.
Then he brought their treasure to Beowulf, and found
His famous king bloody, gasping
For breath. But Wiglaf sprinkled water   2790
Over his lord, until the words
Deep in his breast broke through and were heard.
Beholding the treasure he spoke, haltingly:
    "For this, this gold, these jewels, I thank
Our Father in Heaven, Ruler of the Earth—   2795
For all of this, that His grace has given me,
Allowed me to bring to my people while breath

Still came to my lips. I sold my life
For this treasure, and I sold it well. Take
What I leave, Wiglaf, lead my people,   2800
Help them; my time is gone. Have
The brave Geats build me a tomb,
When the funeral flames have burned me, and build it
Here, at the water's edge, high
On this spit of land, so sailors can see   2805
This tower, and remember my name, and call it
Beowulf's tower, and boats in the darkness
And mist, crossing the sea, will know it."
    Then that brave king gave the golden
Necklace from around his throat to Wiglaf,   2810
Gave him his gold-covered helmet, and his rings,
And his mail shirt, and ordered him to use them well:
    "You're the last of all our far-flung family.
Fate has swept our race away,
Taken warriors in their strength and led them   2815
To the death that was waiting. And now I follow them."
    The old man's mouth was silent, spoke
No more, had said as much as it could;
He would sleep in the fire, soon. His soul
Left his flesh, flew to glory.   2820

                        39
    And then Wiglaf was left, a young warrior
Sadly watching his belovèd king,
Seeing him stretched on the ground, left guarding
A torn and bloody corpse. But Beowulf's
Killer was dead, too, the coiled   2825
Dragon, cut in half, cold
And motionless: men, and their swords, had swept it
From the earth, left it lying in front of
Its tower, won its treasure when it fell
Crashing to the ground, cut it apart   2830
With their hammered blades, driven them deep in
Its belly. It would never fly through the night,
Glowing in the dark sky, glorying
In its riches, burning and raiding; two warriors
Had shown it their strength, slain it with their swords. 2835
Not many men, no matter how strong,

No matter how daring, how bold, had done
As well, rushing at its venomous fangs,
Or even quietly entering its tower,
Intending to steal but finding the treasure's   2840
Guardian awake, watching and ready
To greet them. Beowulf had gotten its gold,
Bought it with blood; dragon and king
Had ended each other's days on earth.
   And when the battle was over Beowulf's followers   2845
Came out of the wood, cowards and traitors,
Knowing the dragon was dead. Afraid,
While it spit its fires, to fight in their lord's
Defense, to throw their javelins and spears,
They came like shamefaced jackals, their shields   2850
In their hands, to the place where the prince lay dead,
And waited for Wiglaf to speak. He was sitting
Near Beowulf's body, wearily sprinkling
Water in the dead man's face, trying
To stir him. He could not. No one could have kept   2855
Life in their lord's body, or turned
Aside the Lord's will: world
And men and all move as He orders,
And always have, and always will.
   Then Wiglaf turned and angrily told them   2860
What men without courage must hear.
Wexstan's brave son stared at the traitors,
His heart sorrowful, and said what he had to:
   "I say what anyone who speaks the truth
Must say. Your lord gave you gifts,   2865
Swords and the armor you stand in now;
You sat on the mead-hall benches, prince
And followers, and he gave you, with open hands,
Helmets and mail shirts, hunted across
The world for the best of weapons. War   2870
Came and you ran like cowards, dropped
Your swords as soon as the danger was real.
Should Beowulf have boasted of your help, rejoiced
In your loyal strength? With God's good grace
He helped himself, swung his sword   2875
Alone, won his own revenge.
The help I gave him was nothing, but all

I was able to give; I went to him, knowing
That nothing but Beowulf's strength could save us,
And my sword was lucky, found some vital   2880
Place and bled the burning flames
Away. Too few of his warriors remembered
To come, when our lord faced death, alone.
And now the giving of swords, of golden
Rings and rich estates, is over,   2885
Ended for you and everyone who shares
Your blood: when the brave Geats hear
How you bolted and ran none of your race
Will have anything left but their lives. And death
Would be better for them all, and for you, than the kind   2890
Of life you can lead, branded with disgrace!"

40

Then Wiglaf ordered a messenger to ride
Across the cliff, to the Geats who'd waited
The morning away, sadly wondering
If their belovèd king would return, or be killed,   2895
A troop of soldiers sitting in silence
And hoping for the best. Whipping his horse
The herald came to them; they crowded around,
And he told them everything, present and past:
"Our lord is dead, leader of this people.   2900
The dragon killed him, but the beast is dead,
Too, cut in half by a dagger;
Beowulf's enemy sleeps in its blood.
No sword could pierce its skin, wound
That monster. Wiglaf is sitting in mourning,   2905
Close to Beowulf's body, Wexstan's
Weary son, silent and sad,
Keeping watch for our king, there
Where Beowulf and the beast that killed him lie dead.
"And this people can expect fighting, once   2910
The Franks, and the Frisians, have heard that our king
Lies dead. The news will spread quickly.
Higlac began our bitter quarrel
With the Franks, raiding along their river
Rhine with ships and soldiers, until   2915
They attacked him with a huge army, and Higlac

Was killed, the king and many of our men,
Mailed warriors defeated in war,
Beaten by numbers. He brought no treasure
To the mead-hall, after that battle. And ever   2920
After we knew no friendship with the Franks.
"Nor can we expect peace from the Swedes.
Everyone knows how their old king,
Ongentho, killed Hathcyn, caught him
Near a wood when our young lord went   2925
To war too soon, dared too much.
The wise old Swede, always terrible
In war, allowed the Geats to land
And begin to loot, then broke them with a lightning
Attack, taking back treasure and his kidnaped   2930
Queen, and taking our king's life.
And then he followed his beaten enemies,
Drove them in front of Swedish swords
Until darkness dropped, and weary, lordless,
They could hide in the wood. But he waited, Ongentho   2935
With his mass of soldiers, circled around
The Geats who'd survived, who'd escaped him, calling
Threats and boasts at that wretched band
The whole night through. In the morning he'd hang
A few, he promised, to amuse the birds,   2940
Then slaughter the rest. But the sun rose
To the sound of Higlac's horns and trumpets,
Light and that battle cry coming together
And turning sadhearted Geats into soldiers.
Higlac had followed his people, and found them.   2945

41

"Then blood was everywhere, two bands of Geats
Falling on the Swedes, men fighting
On all sides, butchering each other.
Sadly, Ongentho ordered his soldiers
Back, to the high ground where he'd built   2950
A fortress; he'd heard of Higlac, knew
His boldness and strength. Out in the open
He could never resist such a soldier, defend
Hard-won treasure, Swedish wives
And children, against the Geats' new king.   2955

Brave but wise, he fled, sought safety
Behind earthen walls. Eagerly, the Geats
Followed, sweeping across the field,
Smashing through the walls, waving Higlac's
Banners as they came. Then the gray-haired old king   2960
Was brought to bay, bright sword-blades
Forcing the lord of the Swedes to take
Judgment at Efor's hands. Efor's
Brother, Wulf, raised his weapon
First, swung it angrily at the fierce   2965
Old king, cracked his helmet; blood
Seeped through his hair. But the brave old Swede
Felt no fear: he quickly returned
A better blow than he'd gotten, faced
Toward Wulf and struck him savagely. And Efor's   2970
Bold brother was staggered, half raised his sword
But only dropped it to the ground. Ongentho's
Blade had cut through his helmet, his head
Spouted blood, and slowly he fell.
The wound was deep, but death was not due   2975
So soon; fate let him recover, live
On. But Efor, his brave brother,
Seeing Wulf fall, came forward with his broad-bladed
Sword, hammered by giants, and swung it
So hard that Ongentho's shield shattered   2980
And he sank to the earth, his life ended.
Then, with the battlefield theirs, the Geats
Rushed to Wulf's side, raised him up
And bound his wound. Wulf's brother
Stripped the old Swede, took   2985
His iron mail shirt, his hilted sword
And his helmet, and all his ancient war-gear,
And brought them to Higlac, his new lord.
The king welcomed him, warmly thanked him
For his gifts and promised, there where everyone   2990
Could hear, that as soon as he sat in his mead-hall
Again Efor and Wulf would have treasure
Heaped in their battle-hard hands; he'd repay them
Their bravery with wealth, give them gold
And lands and silver rings, rich rewards for the glorious   2995

Deeds they'd done with their swords. The Geats agreed. And to
    prove
Efor's grace in his eyes, Higlac
Swore he'd give him his only daughter.
    "These are the quarrels, the hatreds, the feuds,
That will bring us battles, force us into war   3000
With the Swedes, as soon as they've learned how our lord
Is dead, know that the Geats are leaderless,
Have lost the best of kings, Beowulf—
He who held our enemies away,
Kept land and treasure intact, who saved   3005
Hrothgar and the Danes—he who lived
All his long life bravely. Then let us
Go to him, hurry to our glorious lord,
Behold him lifeless, and quickly carry him
To the flames. The fire must melt more   3010
Than his bones, more than his share of treasure:
Give it all of this golden pile,
This terrible, uncounted heap of cups
And rings, bought with his blood. Burn it
To ashes, to nothingness. No one living   3015
Should enjoy these jewels; no beautiful women
Wear them, gleaming and golden, from their necks,
But walk, instead, sad and alone
In a hundred foreign lands, their laughter
Gone forever, as Beowulf's has gone,   3020
His pleasure and his joy. Spears shall be lifted,
Many cold mornings, lifted and thrown,
And warriors shall waken to no harp's bright call
But the croak of the dark-black raven, ready
To welcome the dead, anxious to tell   3025
The eagle how he stuffed his craw with corpses,
Filled his belly even faster than the wolves."
    And so the messenger spoke, a brave
Man on an ugly errand, telling
Only the truth. Then the warriors rose,   3030
Walked slowly down from the cliff, stared
At those wonderful sights, stood weeping as they saw
Beowulf dead on the sand, their bold
Ring-giver resting in his last bed;

He'd reached the end of his days, their mighty   3035
War-king, the great lord of the Geats,
Gone to a glorious death. But they saw
The dragon first, stretched in front
Of its tower, a strange, scaly beast
Gleaming a dozen colors dulled and   3040
Scorched in its own heat. From end
To end fifty feet, it had flown
In the silent darkness, a swift traveler
Tasting the air, then gliding down
To its den. Death held it in his hands;   3045
It would guard no caves, no towers, keep
No treasures like the cups, the precious plates
Spread where it lay, silver and brass
Encrusted and rotting, eaten away
As though buried in the earth for a thousand winters.   3050
And all this ancient hoard, huge
And golden, was wound around with a spell:
No man could enter the tower, open
Hidden doors, unless the Lord
Of Victories, He who watches over men,   3055
Almighty God Himself, was moved
To let him enter, and him alone.

42

    Hiding that treasure deep in its tower,
As the dragon had done, broke God's law
And brought it no good. Guarding its stolen   3060
Wealth it killed Wiglaf's king,
But was punished with death. Who knows when princes
And their soldiers, the bravest and strongest of men,
Are destined to die, their time ended,
Their homes, their halls empty and still?   3065
So Beowulf sought out the dragon, dared it
Into battle, but could never know what God
Had decreed, or that death would come to him, or why.
So the spell was solemnly laid, by men
Long dead; it was meant to last till the day   3070
Of judgment. Whoever stole their jewels,
Their gold, would be cursed with the flames of hell,
Heaped high with sin and guilt, if greed

Was what brought him: God alone could break
Their magic, open His grace to man.   3075
    Then Wiglaf spoke, Wexstan's son:
    "How often an entire country suffers
On one man's account! That time has come to us:
We tried to counsel our belovèd king,
Our shield and protection, show him danger,   3080
Urge him to leave the dragon in the dark
Tower it had lain in so long, live there
Till the end of the world. Fate, and his will,
Were too strong. Everyone knows the treasure
His life bought: but Beowulf was worth   3085
More than this gold, and the gift is a harsh one.
I've seen it all, been in the tower
Where the jewels and armor were hidden, allowed
To behold them once war and its terror were done.
I gathered them up, gold and silver,   3090
Filled my arms as full as I could
And quickly carried them back to my king.
He lay right here, still alive,
Still sure in mind and tongue. He spoke
Sadly, said I should greet you, asked   3095
That after you'd burned his body you bring
His ashes here, make this the tallest
Of towers and his tomb—as great and lasting
As his fame, when Beowulf himself walked
The earth and no man living could match him.   3100
Come, let us enter the tower, see
The dragon's marvelous treasure one
Last time: I'll lead the way, take you
Close to that heap of curious jewels,
And rings, and gold. Let the pyre be ready   3105
And high: as soon as we've seen the dragon's
Hoard we will carry our belovèd king,
Our leader and lord, where he'll lie forever
In God's keeping."
                    Then Wiglaf commanded   3110
The wealthiest Geats, brave warriors
And owners of land, leaders of his people,
To bring wood for Beowulf's funeral:
    "Now the fire must feed on his body,

Flames grow heavy and black with him   3115
Who endured arrows falling in iron
Showers, feathered shafts, barbed
And sharp, shot through linden shields,
Storms of eager arrowheads dropping."
 And Wextan's wise son took seven   3120
Of the noblest Geats, led them together
Down the tunnel, deep into the dragon's
Tower; the one in front had a torch,
Held it high in his hands. The best
Of Beowulf's followers entered behind   3125
That gleaming flame: seeing gold
And silver rotting on the ground, with no one
To guard it, the Geats were not troubled with scruples
Or fears, but quickly gathered up
Treasure and carried it out of the tower.   3130
And they rolled the dragon down to the cliff
And dropped it over, let the ocean take it,
The tide sweep it away. Then silver
And gold and precious jewels were put
On a wagon, with Beowulf's body, and brought   3135
Down the jutting sand, where the pyre waited.

                          43
 A huge heap of wood was ready,
Hung around with helmets, and battle
Shields, and shining mail shirts, all
As Beowulf had asked. The bearers brought   3140
Their belovèd lord, their glorious king,
And weeping laid him high on the wood.
Then the warriors began to kindle that greatest
Of funeral fires; smoke rose
Above the flames, black and thick,   3145
And while the wind blew and the fire
Roared they wept, and Beowulf's body
Crumbled and was gone. The Geats stayed,
Moaning their sorrow, lamenting their lord:
A gnarled old woman, hair wound   3150
Tight and gray on her head, groaned
A song of misery, of infinite sadness
And days of mourning, of fear and sorrow

To come, slaughter and terror and captivity.
And Heaven swallowed the billowing smoke.   3155
    Then the Geats built the tower, as Beowulf
Had asked, strong and tall, so sailors
Could find it from far and wide; working
For ten long days they made his monument,
Sealed his ashes in walls as straight   3160
And high as wise and willing hands
Could raise them. And the riches he and Wiglaf
Had won from the dragon, rings, necklaces,
Ancient, hammered armor—all
The treasures they'd taken were left there, too,   3165
Silver and jewels buried in the sandy
Ground, back in the earth, again
And forever hidden and useless to men.
And then twelve of the bravest Geats
Rode their horses around the tower,   3170
Telling their sorrow, telling stories
Of their dead king and his greatness, his glory,
Praising him for heroic deeds, for a life
As noble as his name. So should all men
Raise up words for their lords, warm   3175
With love, when their shield and protector leaves
His body behind, sends his soul
On high. And so Beowulf's followers
Rode, mourning their belovèd leader,
Crying that no better king had ever   3180
Lived, no prince so mild, no man
So open to his people, so deserving of praise.

Part Two

The Central Middle Ages,

ca. 1000–1350

Introduction

⌐⌐⌐⌐⌐⌐⌐⌐⌐⌐⌐⌐⌐⌐⌐⌐⌐⌐⌐⌐⌐⌐⌐⌐

From about the year 1000, profound changes become evident on virtually all levels of medieval social and cultural life. These changes make of the central Middle Ages (ca. 1000–1350) certainly the most vigorous, and probably also the most creative period of medieval history.

A. Countryside and city

One of the forces active in transforming European society in the central Middle Ages was a sizeable growth in population. We are not sure when exactly this considerable population expansion began, but it seems to have been well under way by the eleventh century. We are not even sure when exactly it ended; population size had probably stabilized well before it was drastically cut back by the Black Death of 1348. Perhaps it had reached its medieval peak even before 1300. It is, however, certain that Europe by the late thirteenth century had become a remarkably crowded (perhaps even overcrowded) continent.

With a population surging upward at home, Europeans from the eleventh century were vigorously and, on the whole, successfully pushing beyond virtually all the land frontiers they confronted. The crusades, launched by Pope Urban II in 1095, are the most famous example of Western expansion in the central Middle Ages. But they were probably not the most significant. In the same period, German colonists were penetrating beyond the Elbe in a movement known as the "push to the east" (*Drang nach Osten*). By 1350, they had tripled the area of German settlement over what it had been in Carolingian times. In the Iberian peninsula, the *reconquista* or reconquest, led by the northern Christian states, exerted a strong and ultimately irrepressible pressure against the Moorish frontier. From the early eleventh century, in another manifestation of Europe's aggressive vitality, Norman soldiers of fortune were driving the Byzantines and Muslims from southern Italy and Sicily and bringing these lands into the Latin-Christian cultural sphere. At the same time, fleets from the mercantile cities of Italy were sweeping Saracen power from the waters of the western Mediterranean and restoring its islands to Latin rule.

Within Europe, an internal frontier of equal importance developed. Colonists energetically attacked the extensive forests which still covered much of the European north. By ca. 1300, these "great clearances" (*grands défrichements*) had won for the plow a larger area of France than is cultivated today. In other places (as, for example, in the Low Countries or the fen regions of eastern England), settlers were pushing back the sea or draining marshes, in order to gain still wider fields to plant.

Population growth, vigorous external expansion and internal colonization, inevitably had a profound impact upon Europe's social institutions and practices.

Within the countryside, perhaps the most fundamental social change was the gradual erosion of serfdom, and the parallel breakdown of the isolation and self-sufficiency of the medieval manor. With a growing population and an abundance of labor, it was no longer necessary to bind men tightly to the soil. With beckoning frontiers so accessible, it was difficult anyway to hold men on the land against their wills. Serfdom had also imposed traditional restrictions concerning the use of the land and froze the levels of rent. Even the lord could not unilaterally change the immemorial customs of the manor. Landlords who wished to reorganize their properties in the interest of higher returns had first to free the serfs if they wished to free the land. Already by the twelfth century, the manor was losing in importance to other, more flexible forms of agricultural exploitation.

The chronology of peasant emancipation differs widely in the various parts of Europe, although in all areas a similar trend is noticeable. In France, Italy, western Germany and Spain, serfdom had ceased to weigh upon the majority of the rural population probably by 1200. England, on the other hand, was rather exceptional. In the thirteenth century, it seems even to have experienced a "manorial reaction." In order to supply cereals to the new and demanding urban markets of the north, English lords revitalized and strengthened the traditional system of manorial agriculture and the labor obligation upon which it depended. In thirteenth-century England, serfdom enjoyed an Indian summer. But its demise was only delayed, not avoided, and in England too serfdom was in manifest decline not long after 1300.

With the emancipation of the serfs, lords largely abandoned the direct cultivation of their own demesnes. They preferred to lease out their properties, often for high rents, to peasant cultivators, who were in turn free to farm the land pretty much as they saw fit. The nobles of Europe were thus gradually transformed from a class of direct cultivators to one of rentiers.

The widespread decline of serfdom and manorial agriculture freed not only the serfs, but their former masters too. The lords were no longer needed to supervise plantings or plowings, or to watch the stewards charged with such duties. They could now more freely spend extended time away from home. They could travel widely over Europe, and join pilgrimages and crusades to distant shores. Perhaps most important of all, they could gather with their peers at certain favored centers or courts. For the first time, a vigorous court life sprang to life in the West, and with it came a new, rich, lay culture and literature.

Southern France in the twelfth century was particularly renowned for the elegance and sophistication of its noble courts. Most famous of them was probably that of the counts of Aquitaine at Poitiers. Among the notables who reflected its influence was Eleanor of Aquitaine, the wife first of Louis VII of France and then of Henry II of England. At court, the nobleman learned the new forms of "courteous" deportment. He was educated to the new, chivalrous attitudes concerning war, women and love, and helped form the audience for new types of literary expression. It would be hard to exaggerate the importance of courtly society in the development of the European vernacular literatures.

One other segment of European society directly benefited from the new freedom and mobility of the population: the towns. If the nobles of southern France liked to gather at the courts of great princes, their Italian counterparts rather preferred the city. Italian landlords and rentiers took to spending a good part of the year in the country's many towns, and their presence added substantially to the remarkable economic and political strength of the Italian communes.

Along with the appearance of feudal courts, this revitalization of urban life ranks as the great social novelty of the central Middle Ages. Historians have long argued futilely about the exact social origins of the European bourgeoisie. They have disputed whether the urban population was principally recruited from merchants or landlords, rich men or poor. Today, most historians prudently consider that towns were socially complex from their births. Their growth primarily reflects the new mobility, energy and enterprise of medieval society.

Paralleling this rise of towns, and lending it added thrust, was the development of new forms of economic endeavor. In Carolingian times, Europe's commerce had remained sluggish and anemic. From the eleventh century, Latin merchants came to manifest a hitherto unaccustomed vitality, as if to compensate for centuries of past lethargy. In Europe's south, Italians were the leaders in building new trade routes across the Mediterranean to Africa and to the Levant. At the same time, they were passing over the Alps, in a successful search for customers and partners. From about 1100 to 1300, the great fairs of the French province of Champagne served as the entrepôt where the wool cloth and raw materials of the north were exchanged for the luxuries of the Mediterranean. In the north, Frisian, Norse, Flemish, later German and English traders were similarly throwing lines of exchange across the Baltic and North Seas, linking England, Flanders, Scandinavia, Germany and Russia in a tight, lively and profitable trading area.

Large-scale manufacture in the cities was not much behind large-scale trade in developing, and was greatly stimulated by it. The greatest of all medieval industries was the manufacture of woolen cloth. The oldest centers of this important industry were the towns of Flanders, where a tradition of wool manufacture had existed apparently since Roman times. At the height of its prosperity in the thirteenth century, the Flemish industry was a true pioneer of capitalist business and industrial organization. It brought its raw materials from distant suppliers, and its finished products reached still more distant markets. It employed large quantities of capital, and supported a large and often restless body of laborers. But it was not for long unique in Europe. By the late thirteenth century, the wool industry in Italian cities rivaled it in size, and probably surpassed it in the sophistication of its business and marketing techniques.

By the thirteenth century, European society had undergone a remarkable transformation since Carolingian times. No longer overwhelmingly rural in character, no longer differentiated almost exclusively into peasants, warriors and clergy, no longer poor, the new European society had reached unprecedented levels of size, mobility, wealth and complexity. Besides peasants, priests and warriors, it now counted in its numbers merchants and artisans (even a nascent urban proletariat), and strong professional classes of lawyers, administrators and scholars.

It is not too much to say that the great social experience of the central Middle Ages was growth, and a vigorous exploration of new avenues of social endeavor in almost all areas of life. This sense of movement and taste of success encouraged a willingness to experiment in cultural fields too, and nourished a reassuring confidence that discoveries could be made.

B. *Schools and scholasticism*

One field of medieval culture which was quickly and decisively touched by the new social changes was education. Up until the late eleventh century, the monastery, usually rural in location, had dominated medieval education. But it had worked under several handicaps, which help explain the modest originality of early medieval thought. The humility and personal self-effacement expected of the monks were not likely to inspire a spirit of bold inquiry among them, nor did strict monastic discipline leave much room for the expression of daring ideas. The contemplative and mystical inclinations of the monks were also infertile ground for the development of a taste for and a tradition of hard, methodical analysis. Moreover, the isolation of the monasteries, staffed by men professionally committed to flee the world, made communications difficult, and upon good communications the dynamics of scholarly dialogue always depend.

From the eleventh century, a new kind of school replaced the monastic as the most influential educational institution of the medieval world. This was the bishop's school. It was of course located in the city. Bishops had always been responsible for the education of their clergy and were supposed to maintain schools, but their efforts tended to be ineffective (or at least scarcely visible) amid the economically and culturally starved cities of the early Middle Ages. On the other hand, the bishop's school was the direct beneficiary of the new size, movement, wealth and vitality of urban society after the eleventh century.

The bishop's school was distinctly more favorable than the monastery to the pursuit of creative scholarship. It was not isolated in the countryside, nor ascetic in character, nor did the scant discipline it maintained weigh heavily upon scholarly freedom. Both teachers and students were initially subject to a minimum of obligations. Both roamed at will from school to school in search of the best ideas, companions, teachers, or the most liberal atmosphere.

During the twelfth century, the schools in northern France acquired a particular reputation for scholarship. Chartres, for example, became the center for the study of Platonic philosophy (or what little was then known of it) and of rhetoric and *belles-lettres*. Paris acquired the highest prestige for logical and philosophical learning, which was won for it largely through the brilliance of Peter Abelard (1079–1142), of whom more will presently be said.

The medieval university in the north of Europe developed directly out of the bishop's school. The word *universitas* was a common medieval term for "guild." The university was exactly a guild of masters, organized like every other guild for two purposes: the defense and advancement of the art, and the training of young people to assure its survival over generations.

The stimuli which gave rise to such a guild organization among teachers were undoubtedly many, but one issue had a particular importance. This was the right of conferring the *licentia docendi*, or the "license to teach." In the course of the twelfth century, the bishop's school had found it necessary to impose some restriction upon the right of lecturing, in order to protect students from incompetent or unorthodox teachers. A man aspiring to be a master had first to offer proof of learning and accomplishment, and if judged competent was granted permission to lecture publicly. This *licentia docendi* was in fact the first academic degree, and was for long the only one. It was initially awarded by the chancellor, the bishop's secretary. However, the established masters felt that they, or their guild, rather than a non-academic episcopal official, should have the right of judging the qualifications of prospective teachers. They struggled to win that right for themselves, with eventual success. The masters of the school at Paris probably had gained this prerogative by 1200 (at least they then had a functioning guild, making Paris the oldest university in the north). We know that they certainly had it by 1231; it is mentioned in the great papal privilege of that date, the bull *Parens Scientiarum*, which was granted to the university of masters at Paris.

University origins in southern Europe were somewhat different. The academic strengths of the south were not logic and theology, but medicine and law. These were traditionally taught in professional schools, of which little is really known for the early medieval period. About the time that guilds of masters were gaining control of the bishop's school in the north, these professional schools were likewise falling under the authority of guilds. At the oldest of the southern universities, Bologna in Italy, and at others too, the dominant guild was made up of students rather than masters. The guild of students regulated the curriculum, the content of courses, and even the fees to be charged. While differing in origins, universities in both north and south were largely self-governing institutions, with power exercised by established or prospective masters.

For the first time in its history, Western society possessed in the university an institution which existed exclusively for the purpose of advancing learning and assuring its survival over generations. Understandably, its appearance brought a new dynamism into the intellectual life of the West.

The rise of the universities parallels an equally important social change: the emergence of a class of professional scholars. The first students, the "wandering scholars" or *clerici vagantes*, enjoyed, even among contemporaries, a reputation for boisterous living. A body of their student songs has survived, known as Goliardic poems, and these show that many scholars were indeed deeply interested in wine, women and song. But the charm and gaiety of their spirit should not obscure the uniqueness of the medieval university population. It was a true intelligentsia, the first intelligentsia in European history, and its influence on cultural development was thereafter profound.

Within the framework of the new schools, there also appeared a new style and system of thought, traditionally known as scholasticism.

Scholasticism, in its broadest sense, means the teaching characteristic of the medieval schools. In its narrower, and more usual meaning, it refers to the content of learning specifically characteristic of the bishop's school from about 1100, and then of the university which succeeded it.

The great intellectual interest of monastic scholarship in the early Middle Ages had been the proper understanding of Sacred Scripture through exegesis. Scholasticism, on the other hand, went much beyond textual interpretation. The basis of its method was "dialectic," which means the art or science of determining the logical relations of propositions within a discourse. Taking propositions initially from Christian dogma, then also from natural philosophy as expounded by Aristotle, the scholastics were committed to examining what if any logical ties connected them. They thus hoped to make of Christian theology a logically coherent and consistent system of thought. They ultimately sought to achieve a total synthesis of theology and natural philosophy, which would mirror the whole of intelligible reality.

The first thinker to manifest these new intellectual interests was St. Anselm of Canterbury (1033–1109). His own career excellently illustrates the mobility and action characteristic of the age. A north Italian by birth, he became successively abbot of Bec in Normandy (from 1078) and archbishop of the primal see of England (from 1093). He played a prominent role in the ecclesiastical and secular politics of the day.

His intellectual interests were no less enterprising. In his work known as the *Proslogium*, Anselm tried to prove without question the existence of God. He approached the problem in a novel manner; he set out to show that there was a necessary, logical connection between the traditional, Judeo-Christian concept of what God was, and the equally traditional affirmation that he was. Men thought of God as a perfect being, or, as Anselm put it, a being than which nothing greater can be conceived. But such a being, he argued, must have existence. If it did not, then a still greater being could be conceived which did exist. But this would be contrary to the original premise, that God, and only God, was the being than which nothing greater can be conceived. To avoid this logical contradiction, men must accept that the God they conceive of as a perfect being must also possess the perfection of existence.

This reasoning has since been called the "ontological" argument for the existence of God; the term "ontological" means that it is based on the "being" or character of concepts, rather than on direct experience.

In his *Cur Deus Homo* ("Why God Became Man"), Anselm attempted with still greater boldness to show the logical relationships linking three fundamental Christian beliefs: the infinite nature of God, the fact of original sin, and the incarnation of Christ. Anselm argued that the degree of an offense was measured by the dignity of the one offended. Original sin was therefore an act of infinite evil, as it offended God himself. But the worth of an apology or act of atonement was measured by the dignity of the one conferring the apology. Man, therefore, while capable of a sin of infinite magnitude, could not as a finite creature offer equal atonement. Only a man of infinite worth could do this, i.e. a man who was also God. If God wished to save man, argued Anselm, the only suitable way for him to do so was to allow his son to become one of them, to offer atonement for the human race.

Anselm defined his method as "faith seeking to understand" (*fides quaerens intellectum*). He stayed within the realm of dogma, and he never questioned its truth. But his search for logical connections and consistency (i.e. his search for the reasons why something was true, for *intellectus*) still had sensational implications. It implied that unaided human reason could explore the logical and metaphysical laws within which even God operated. Men could hope to understand in some measure the ways of God, and even in some measure rethink his thoughts.

This assumption that God acted in ways consistent with human logic struck many contemporaries (including the great Cistercian saint, Bernard of Clairvaux) as dangerously arrogant. To say that God acted with logical consistency seemed to impinge upon his sovereign freedom, and to claim that men could understand the suitability of even some of his actions was to cater to human pride. There is little doubt that the early scholastics did manifest an extraordinary intellectual boldness, and a courage to match.

Ranking with Anselm as the founder of scholasticism was Peter Abelard (1079–1142). Abelard, a brash young man from Brittany, established the reputation of the school of Paris by his logical powers and brilliant teaching. To show the necessity of dialectic he wrote a work called *Sic et Non* ("Yes and No"), the first version of which appeared probably in 1122. By later revisions, the work eventually came to include 158 theological questions ("Is God the author of evil, or no?" "Has God free will, or no?"). In response to these questions, Abelard lined up citations from the Bible and the fathers of the Church, some responding "yes" and some "no," in apparent flat contradiction with each other. The clear implication was that one either reconciled the discrepancies through dialectic, or conceded that the faith was a tissue of contradictions. Abelard's *Sic et Non* also helped define the scholastic method. Scholars after him continued to pose formal questions and continued to cite conflicting authorities. They then went on, as Abelard did not, to respond to the question and explain away the contradictions. *Sic et Non* thus showed the utility and even the necessity of dialectical reasoning within theology, and helped build a model for its systematic application.

This birth of dialectic forms part of the intellectual movement now usually called the "renaissance of the twelfth century." Until as late as 1200, the prestige of dialectic in the schools was rivaled by that of literary and rhetorical studies and by the cultivation of good writing. Chartres was the great center of these literary arts. But by the end of the century, dialectic was carrying the day, and went on to dominate the intellectual interests of the new universities. One reason for this was the new availability of the complete works of Aristotle. By the late twelfth century, scholars in Spain and elsewhere were busy translating Aristotle's metaphysical works from the Arabic into Latin. By the thirteenth century, translations were being made directly from the Greek. The Aristotelian *corpus* for the first time confronted Western scholars with an example of a thoroughly systematic and rationalistic natural philosophy. Aristotelian logic and philosophy seemed to offer a sure, scientific way to the truth, and the method claimed the enthusiastic allegiance of the brightest scholastic minds. The study and appreciation of *belles-lettres* faded from the medieval schools, and were not to be revived until the humanist movement of the fourteenth century.

The newly recovered Aristotle, and perhaps even more the rationalizing, confident spirit of the age which found him attractive, seriously challenged the hitherto dominant attitudes of medieval intellectual culture. Aristotle, to begin with, stressed the rational composition of the world, and the ability of human reason to know its order. He also stressed an empirical approach to reality. There was nothing in the intellect which was not first in the senses, and sensible nature was not therefore a cloud obscuring man's vision or

a temptation ensnaring him with its beauties. It was the one, perhaps the only road to truth. Nature, rationally constructed, was
also authoritative. All beings, including man, tended towards their
natural ends; human appetites were therefore good, as they were implanted by nature to assure the fulfillment of its design. Rather than
a defective if not an evil guide to life, nature was in fact the measure by which all things in this world should be judged. Aristotelian
rationalism and naturalism seemed antithetical to the traditional
Christian assumptions concerning the weakness of human faculties,
the inadequacies of nature, and the necessity of revelation and
grace.

The reconciliation of Aristotle, and the viewpoint he represented, with long-accepted cultural and religious attitudes was the
great philosophical problem of the thirteenth century. The great
figure in this work was Thomas Aquinas (ca. 1227–74). The son
of a nobleman of southern Italy, Thomas was destined by his family to become a monk, but he was attracted to the new Dominican
order. He studied at Cologne and Paris, and began to lecture at the
University of Paris in 1257. In a relatively short life, he produced
works of prodigious size and intellectual density, and touched upon
a wide variety of subjects of interest to Christian thought. His
greatest work, an attempt at a systematic examination (introduction, he called it modestly) of and to Christian theology was his
Summa Theologica. Although left unfinished at his death, it still
represents the greatest single achievement of medieval scholastic
thought.

Aquinas presents a fascinating example of the scholastic, syn-
thesizing mind at its most resourceful. Rarely does he accuse prior
philosophers of error, even those who take positions apparently
contradictory to his own. By drawing subtle and perceptive distinctions, he rather seeks to take from them the element of accu-
rate insight which he feels that they must possess, to illuminate
further the truth as he sees it. Through dialectic, he sought to
reconcile not only philosophical and theological propositions, but
entire viewpoints; specifically the Aristotelian emphasis on the
power of reason and the goodness of nature, with the Christian
emphasis on the need for a special divine intervention through
grace. It may also be said that Aquinas was seeking to reconcile
and thus to save two cultural experiences—the sense of human
helplessness, which was the inheritance of the troubled period of
the declining Roman empire; and the new confidence in human

power, which accompanied the vigorous growth of European society in the central Middle Ages. Thomas constantly reiterates the theme that reason is powerful but not powerful enough, that nature is good but not good enough. Both can take man far, but God has made it posible for him, through revelation and redemption, to go farther still.

C. *The literature of feudal society*

Modern literature, it may justly be argued, begins in the period of the central Middle Ages. Before 1000, literary survivals are sporadic and discontinuous, and a major family of European tongues —the Romance languages—is hardly represented at all by literary texts. From the late eleventh century, on the other hand, literary production in most European languages becomes abundant and thereafter nearly uninterrupted. The richest of the medieval literary languages are probably the Romance tongues, especially the two great dialects of France, the *langue d'oïl* spoken in the regions north of the Loire river, and the *langue d'oc* of the south. But all the vernaculars enter upon a great creative age after 1100. Only English, after a rich Anglo-Saxon period, was delayed in its development by the Norman conquest of 1066 and by the French, aristocratic culture it imposed upon the land.

Moreover, the same period witnesses the formation of a new literary style or tradition which has exerted a lasting influence in Western letters. If the great heritage of antiquity was the classical spirit, the central Middle Ages brought to life the equally influential traditions of romance.

This vernacular upsurge was initially associated with the lay aristocracy of medieval society, the warrior class of nobles and knights. European nobles from the eleventh century were touched with a passion for movement, which carried Western knights on pilgrimages and crusades to regions well beyond Europe's own frontiers. The nobility was also marked by a tendency, evident at an especially early date in southern France, to congregate in courts. The experiences of both the war camp and the court deeply influenced the earliest literature of feudal society.

We shall discuss that literature under three principal categories: the heroic epic, the lyric poetry of the troubadours, and the courtly romance.

The literature of the war camp is best represented by the heroic epic. The epic was one of the most popular forms of vernacular literature. The oldest and best of these epics is the *Song of Roland.* It was written in the language of the north of France probably in the last quarter of the eleventh century. It was thus nearly contemporary with the First Crusade, and authentically reflects its militant spirit. *Roland* is also the first representative of an extremely abundant tradition. The surviving number of heroic epics (or *chansons de geste*) written in French between the late eleventh and early fourteenth centuries falls somewhere between 80 and 100, and they include certainly over one million lines.

The second major genre of feudal literature appears at nearly the same time, but reflects a much different social milieu. This was the lyric poetry of the troubadours, who sang in the language of "oc." Of some 400 troubadours from whom works have survived, the earliest known is William IX, duke of Aquitaine, who lived from 1071 to 1127.

Troubadour lyric poetry reflected the life not of the battle camp, but the *mores* of the courts of southern France, where women had come to acquire a position of extraordinary influence. They had become what they were long to remain in many Western societies: the true arbiters of polite manners and acceptable morals. Troubadour poetry, influenced by the new courtly refinements, is therefore the first "courtly" literature.

The favorite theme of the troubadours was love, and they handled love in a manner unprecedented in the Western tradition. To the troubadours, love was something much more than a pleasant diversion or a way to sensuous gratification. It was a redemptive power. Love saved its devotee from an initial despondency (the lover was always suffering at the beginning of his courtship), took him through hope, and, if his lady was favorable, rewarded him with unequaled joy. Not only the lover but nature around him was transformed by this power; the world became decked in unending spring, the earthly equivalent of the Christian heaven.

The novelty of this interpretation of the redemptive powers of love is so striking that historians have devised numerous theories to explain it. Some see it as a foreign import, perhaps from the Islamic world, where a similar poetry seems to have been cultivated. Others consider it a reflection of the peculiar social importance gained by women in the noble class of southern France. Still others regard it as a Christian heresy, or at least a parody of Christian mysticism. It has also been called a parody of the feudal relationship between

lord and vassal (the lady is constantly addressed in terms appropriate to a feudal lord).

While much mystery surrounds its origins, there is no doubt
about its impact on both manners and literature. Troubadour lyric
poetry, in its praises of women and of love, established the great
clichés of the Western love tradition. All the literatures of western
Europe developed a love poetry comparable in attitude and style
to that of the troubadours. Their counterparts in northern France,
where love poetry became exceedingly popular after 1150, were
the trouvères. Before 1200, in German lands, the Minnesinger, or
poet of love, was similarly emulating the troubadour adoration of
love and women. Of these, the greatest lyric poet, hardly in fact to
be equaled as a master of verse in the entire history of German literature, was Walther von der Vogelweide (d. 1228).

Troubadour conventions also influenced Italian literature, which
was considerably less precocious than the French. Italian lyric
poets were being patronized in the south-Italian court of Frederick
II Hohenstaufen (1198–1250). In the last decades of the century, a
group of Tuscan poets, with Dante at their center, were experimenting with a new style of love poetry, called the "sweet new
style" (*dolce stil nuovo*). They tried to bring authentic sentiment
into their poems, and to avoid the more stilted conventions of the
early troubadour poetry, but their work remains very much within
the tradition of courtly love.

The third important genre of the literature of feudal society was
later than these first two in developing, and was in many ways a
combination of them both. This was the courtly romance, which
might be written in either prose or poetry. Northern France and
Germany have left us our richest heritage of these colorful narratives. Stories were drawn from a wide variety of sources. The
romance of *Aucassin and Nicolete*, written about 1200 partly in
verse and partly in prose and unique for that reason, has been
traced back to Arabic sources. *Tristan and Iseult*, perhaps the most
poignant of the medieval love stories, is clearly beholden to Celtic
folklore.

These abundant stories tended to divide according to their material into three groups or cycles. There was a cycle of Charlemagne, of Alexander the Great, but richest of all were the stories
dealing with the sixth-century British king Arthur and his company of knights. Arthur was undoubtedly a historical figure, but

the Arthur of these romances is fashioned very much after the
ideals of twelfth-century chivalry.

The exact origins of this enormously wealthy collection of stories centering on Arthur's court are still very obscure, and it is hard
to judge the relative contributions made by folklore, by learned
ecclesiastical scholars, or by imaginative writers working with little
more than a few traditional names. Arthur is mentioned sporadi-
cally in early medieval histories, but the basis of his fame was the
publication about 1137 of the *Histories of the Kings of Britain*, by
Geoffrey of Monmouth. Geoffrey devoted five books to Arthur,
and has given us our oldest abundant collection of stories concerning him.

From 1150, medieval romancers were turning out narratives in
great volume. Chrétien de Troyes was probably the most gifted of
the French authors, and is famed for his exquisitely contrived narratives inspired by Arthurian legends. In German, Gottfried von
Strassburg produced probably the most effective version of the
popular romance, *Tristan and Iseult*. Another popular theme was
the quest for the grail, a sacred amulet, perhaps the chalice used by
Christ at the Last Supper. Only a perfect knight could find it, and
perfection was judged by numerous, exotic tests. Wolfram von
Eschenbach's *Parzifal*, written in German, is probably the most
polished version of the grail legend.

The great contribution of courtly literature was its introduction
of attitudes, ideas and values which have since remained the basis
of the romantic tradition. The romantic characteristics of this literature are its love of the distant and the mysterious, its delight in
magic, the favor it shows to characters with extravagant attributes
of strength, virtue or beauty. More fundamentally, this literature
stressed the supreme importance of emotion and sentiment in human life. The way to an understanding of the world, to happiness
itself, was not through the intellect, but through feeling, sentiment
and love. The courtly lover, in his journey from despondency to
joy, went through a kind of sentimental education, an emotional
ascension, which equipped his soul with powers to discern harmony
and taste joy. This idea that the heart too has its truth, and that
man is wise to pursue it, is at the foundation of the romantic tradition. While the scholastics were helping form the Western intellect, the troubadours and romancers were simultaneously educating
Western sentiments.

D. *The literature of the towns*

Historians of medieval culture have traditionally distinguished feudal literature (i.e. works intended for a noble audience) from that devised for the entertainment of a wider social group, including especially the new urban classes. In the first category are placed the heroic epics, and the courtly lyrics and romances; in the second, the *fabliaux* and fables, notably the stories dealing with Reynard the Fox.

Today the tendency is to recognize that medieval literature cannot be classified too rigorously along social or class lines. Both courtly and bourgeois literature often make use of the same material. Town literature sometimes even parodies courtly themes, and this assumes that the audience would be familiar with them.

While it would be wrong to imply that medieval literature developed in categories rigidly defined by social classes and completely isolated from each other, it still remains permissible to describe certain genres as primarily appealing to an urban audience, and reflective of its taste.

The *fabliaux*, one of the most important of these genres, means "little fables." More exactly, they were short stories, written in French in eight-syllabled, rimed couplets. The great age for their composition extended from the late twelfth to the middle fourteenth century. According to the perhaps too strict standards of a modern scholar (Per Nykrog), there are 160 stories which may be accurately called *fabliaux*.

The *fabliaux* differ from the courtly romances on several counts. Rather than dwelling on distant and exotic events, they treat of people and scenes familiar from daily life. They thus introduce a new note of social realism into medieval literature. Their plots are frequently racy, not to say obscene. They share nothing of the idealism of the courtly romance. They are vicious in their characterization of women, who are presented as quarrelsome, greedy, lecherous and faithless. They also hurl shafts at the clergy and the monks, venal officials and ignorant peasants. They are little concerned with character analysis or development. Their mark is fast narrative action, and their tone is almost always humorous.

The distinctive feature of the *fabliaux* is that they represent probably the first literary genre intended not to teach, improve or inspire, but simply to entertain. They are a literature of pure diversion.

Similar to the *fabliaux* in spirit were the fables, after the manner of Aesop. The most abundant of fables were those recounting the adventures of Reynard the Fox, the *Roman de Renart*. Composed chiefly between the late twelfth and thirteenth centuries, these stories reached a huge volume of about 30,000 verses. The oldest tales were entertaining accounts of the repeated triumphs of sly wit (Reynard) over such characteristics as unthinking force (Isegrim the wolf) or pompous dullness (Noble the lion). By the late thirteenth century, the stories came to mask considerable social satire and criticism, and their moralizing tone compromised somewhat their popularity. Still, the appeal of these tales is shown by the fact that the proper name Reynard has become the modern French word for fox (*renard*).

E. Religious literature

A deep religious feeling permeated all classes of medieval society, and literature dealing with religious themes enjoyed a continuing popularity.

Saints' lives and miracle stories retained their appeal, and provided a religious counterpoise to the secular and ribald *fabliaux*. The most important collection of saints' lives was put together by the archbishop of Genoa, Iacobus de Voraggine, sometime between 1258 and 1270. This was the *Legenda Aurea*, or *Golden Legend*, an anthology of 180 brief lives of the saints. It remained a medieval best-seller, and grew over the years, eventually including some four hundred tales. Translated into English by William Caxton in 1483, it was one of the first books to be printed in the English language.

The *Golden Legend* seems clearly intended for a primarily urban and lay audience. Monastic saints are comparatively few, and the saintly figures are in the main spirited young ladies, brave young men, or wise bishops, living under the temptations or persecutions of the Roman empire. Miracles are common and colorful, and seem consciously designed to be entertaining and exciting as well as edifying. These stories have been called a Christian *Arabian Nights*.

Medieval religious literature also reflects the changing character and style of Christian piety. Simultaneously as the troubadours were exploring the emotional content of profane love, religious thinkers and artists were bringing a more pronounced sentimental and emotional element into the practice of religion. This is reflected in

the remarkable growth of devotion to the Virgin Mary. All the
major Gothic cathedrals built after 1150 are named in her honor.
A rich body of stories grew up around her, similar in spirit to the
Golden Legend, which celebrated her motherly concern for sinners
and her gracious intercessions.

Perhaps the major figure in this new sentimental approach to
religion was a man who styled himself God's troubadour: Giovanni Bernadone, or Francis of Assisi (1181/82–1226). He was
the son of a rich merchant of Assisi in central Italy (he acquired the
name "Francis," or the "French one," as his father was away trading in France at his birth). A sensitive young man, familiar with
the troubadours (his mother may have been French), he set out
early in life to find for himself that great troubadour ideal: perfect
joy. He tried the satisfactions available in the city to a rich man's
son, but was disappointed in them. He became a knight, but here
too joy eluded him. Finally, he turned to religion. He abandoned
all his possessions, in order, as he put it, to take up the courtship of
Lady Poverty. But he brought a new spirit into this act of traditional asceticism. Rather than rejecting nature as a deception and
a snare, he composed canticles or songs to its creatures, praised
their loveliness and celebrated God's wonderful handiwork in
them. He preached to the birds and persuaded a wolf, who had
been terrorizing the small town of Gubbio, to reform his ways, out
of love of God.

One of the great cultural novelties of the central Middle Ages
is the rehabilitation of nature, the rediscovery of its dignity and
beauty. This spirit finds nowhere a more charming expression than
with Francis. He further maintained that the fruits of true religion
were not sorrow and grim resignation, but abounding joy. The
rewards which the troubadours located in the love of women,
Francis found in the love of God.

Franciscan piety evoked an extraordinary response in the thirteenth century. The mendicant or begging order he founded
spread with an extraordinary rapidity, and soon became the largest
in the Church. His delight in creation affected the visual arts. The
Florentine painter Giotto (1266–1337), who among other works
painted Francis' life, manifested a spirit which is unmistakably
Franciscan. His own effort at visual accuracy makes him the first
major figure of Italian, properly Renaissance art.

Francis' influence on literature was similarly pervasive. Two
great hymns of the thirteenth century, the *Dies Irae* by an un-

known author, and the *Stabat Mater* by the Franciscan Thomas of Celano, reflect the new Franciscan sentiment. He also inspired a collection of legends concerning him, the *Fioretti* or *Little Flowers*. They seem to have been put together in their present form about 1330, by a Franciscan living in the Marches of Ancona in central Italy. They remain today probably the best introduction to the religion and the spirit of Francis, greatest of the medieval saints.

The most important of all the religious works of the central Middle Ages is the *Divine Comedy* of Dante Alighieri (1265–1321). Dante was in several ways the representative and the beneficiary of the enriched culture of the central Middle Ages. He was born in 1265 at Florence, which was then on its way to becoming one of Europe's biggest towns, a capital of large-scale banking and high finance. Little is known about his education. He undoubtedly attended the grammar schools which were numerous in the Italian cities, and apparently also heard lectures on philosophy and theology at the city's many religious houses. What is certain is that Dante, although a layman and not a university graduate, acquired an enormous erudition. He was knowledgeable in most of the major branches of medieval learning, and his *Comedy* is one of literature's most erudite poems.

His experience of town life and his own active participation in the politics of his city seem to have convinced him that abstract or speculative learning was wasted if it did not offer a guide to men in their practical affairs, if it did not direct them in their earthly behavior. As he explained in a letter written to Can Grande della Scala, tyrant of Verona and his own patron, his *Comedy* was an exercise not in speculative but in practical wisdom; it was intended to "remove those who are living in this life from the state of wretchedness, and to lead them to the state of blessedness."

Before writing the *Comedy*, Dante produced several works, which may be viewed as preparatory exercises for his masterpiece. In 1295, he wrote his *Vita Nuova*, or *New Life*. This was an extended commentary on thirty-one love poems or *canzoni* written in honor of the Lady Beatrice. It is invaluable for the biographical information concerning his youth and encounter with Beatrice. These *canzoni* include some of the most graceful in the Italian language. They are among the best examples of the Tuscan type of love poetry known as the "sweet new style," or *dolce stil nuovo*. In 1305–08, in his Latin tract *De vulgari eloquentia* ("On Vulgar

Eloquence"), he defended the dignity of the vernacular, and maintained that it could be used for the most exalted forms of literary expression. Another tract, of uncertain date, was a defense, on largely Aristotelian principles, of the Holy Roman Empire, and a rebuttal of papal claims to authority over it. This was called the *De monarchia*. The *Convivio*, or "Banquet," written between 1305 and 1308 but left unfinished, was, like the *Vita Nuova*, a commentary on his sonnets and the philosophical assumptions behind them.

The *Comedy* itself was written between 1313 and 1321. Like all great works of literature, it has several dimensions of meaning. It was reflective of Dante's own life. As a young man (he says he was only nine years old), he met and fell in love with Beatrice, then only eight. She is usually identified as Beatrice Portinari, from a prominent Florentine family. She later married Simone de' Bardi, and died in 1290. While he could have seen her no more than a few times, his love for her illuminated his young years and gave him that sense of harmony and joy which, as the troubadours had taught him, were the expected rewards of love. But troubles then shattered his idyllic world. For political reasons, Dante was exiled from his native Florence in 1302, and he never returned. He died in 1321, and his body is buried at Ravenna. While experiencing the personal disaster of his exile, he was a close witness of the troubles disturbing the Italy of his day. Wars among the towns and unrest within them were nearly continuous. The great universal powers of Church and Empire seemed powerless to advance the high ideals of peace and unity which they were supposed to serve. Dante had reason for bitterness and disillusionment.

The *Comedy* may be considered a reflection upon the poet's own life. It represents an effort to bring into synthesis his two great experiences—his youthful, serene, idyllic and joyful love for Beatrice, and the sense of chaos and of evil, the failing faith, of his later years.

The *Comedy* begins with Dante "in the middle of the way of our life." He wanders in a dark woods, beset upon by wild animals, symbols of untamed passions. He has lost, as an older man, the guiding principles of his youth.

The theme of the poem thus becomes the poet's quest for his lost peace, for that sense of harmony and order which, as a young man in love, he had once so easily found. Through his journey through Hell, Purgatory and Heaven, Dante comes once more to see that for all the undeniable complexities of the world, for all the

apparent triumphs of vice and confusion, divine love had created
and still rules the universe.

In the *Comedy*, Dante also confronts the great cultural problem
of the central Middle Ages: the reconciliation of human power
and freedom with traditional belief in the supremacy of grace.
Dante places a high dignity upon human reason; he makes it primarily responsible for guiding men to the happy and blessed life
on earth. His symbol for reason is the Roman poet Vergil, and
Vergil guides Dante through Hell and Purgatory to the Earthly
Paradise. In Hell, Vergil introduces Dante to a panorama of human sins and sinners, some mythical figures, others historical personages, and still others Dante's own acquaintances. These are the
persons who took as their supreme value in life something other
than the love of God—greed, perhaps, or lust, gluttony, pride or
some other sin. The moral here is clear: all men in their journey
through life have a comparable choice. It is Vergil's function to
show that reason itself declares that those selfish values cannot provide the substance of a happy life. The *Inferno* thus emerges
as a richly textured allegorical tract, showing the rational foundations of ethics, proudly affirming that reason alone can guide men
past the pitfalls of material existence.

Reason can do more than that. It conducts Dante up the seven-
storied mountain of Purgatory, where the natural virtues are acquired that are the foundation for the Earthly Paradise at its
summit. All this implies that reason can do much in guiding men
to a good life in this world. This high dignity alloted to reason is
the common feature of thirteenth-century intellectual culture. But
common too is Dante's affirmation that reason and its rewards are
still not good enough. Man is destined for something still better.
Here, at the summit of Purgatory, Beatrice, the symbol of revelation and grace, enters the story, to guide Dante upward through
the heavens, into the kingdom of grace. She brings him through
the celestial spheres, where the saints shine like stars in their wisdom and virtue, and leads him to the presence of God "in whom
is our peace."

Like Aquinas' *Summa Theologica*, the *Comedy* may be considered an effort to synthesize and reconcile the great experiences of
medieval society: the low view of man's competence, nurtured in
the desperate years when Rome was in decline, and the new boldness and enterprise bred in the central Middle Ages, when men
again recognized the potentials of nature and the dimensions of

their own powers. Dante, like most thinkers of his age, felt that in spite of their diversity, there was truth in both attitudes concerning man and his destiny. His *Comedy* may well be called the testament of medieval man, and the noblest statement of what that age believed to be wisdom.

RECOMMENDED READINGS

Henry Adams, *Mont-Saint-Michel and Chartres* (Boston and New York: Houghton–Mifflin Co., 1933).

Marc Bloch, *Feudal Society*, trans. L. A. Manyon, with a Foreword by M. M. Postan (Chicago: University of Chicago Press, 1963; Phoenix P 156–57).

G. G. Coulton, *Five Centuries of Religion* (4 vols., Cambridge: Cambridge University Press, 1923–50).

G. G. Coulton, *Medieval Panorama. The English Scene from Conquest to Reformation* (New York: Macmillan Co., 1945).

G. G. Coulton, *The Mediaeval Village, Manor and Monastery* (Cambridge: Cambridge University Press, 1925; New York: Harper Torchbooks, 1960, TB 1022).

Jessie R. Crosland, *The Old French Epic* (Oxford: Blackwell, 1951).

C. H. Haskins, *The Renaissance of the Twelfth Century* (Cambridge: Harvard University Press, 1927; Cleveland: World Publishing Co., Meridian M 49).

C. H. Haskins, *The Rise of the Universities* (New York: Holt and Co., 1923; Ithaca, New York: Great Seal Books, 1957).

Friedrich Heer, *The Medieval World: Europe, 1100–1350* (Cleveland: World Publishing Co., 1962; New York: New American Library, Mentor MQ 524).

C. S. Lewis, *The Allegory of Love. A Study in Medieval Tradition* (London: Oxford University Press, 1959, Galaxy GB 17).

Sydney Painter, *French Chivalry. Chivalric Ideas and Practices in Mediaeval France* (Baltimore: Johns Hopkins Press, 1940, Ithaca, New York: Great Seal Books, 1962).

H. Rashdall, *The Universities of Europe in the Middle Ages*, new ed. by F. M. Powicke and A. B. Emden (London: Oxford University Press, 1958).

R. Southern, *The Making of the Middle Ages* (New Haven: Yale University Press, 1953; Yale Paperbound Y 46).

I. *Countryside and city*

⎍⎍⎍⎍⎍⎍⎍⎍⎍⎍⎍⎍⎍⎍⎍⎍⎍⎍⎍⎍⎍⎍⎍

1. German colonization in the East, according to the chronicler Helmold

The following account by the chronicler Helmold of Bosau describes the efforts of Count Adolf II of Holstein (1128–64) to attract settlers to the lands along the eastern frontier he had just conquered from the Slavic Wagri. It also tells of Adolf's foundation of the city of Lübeck, which was eventually to become one of the largest commercial centers of the region and a leading city in the association of German trading towns known as the Hanseatic League.

The Latin text may be found in Helmold's *Chronica Slavorum*, I, 57, *Monumenta Germaniae Historica, Scriptores*, XXI, pp. 55–56, as reprinted in *Clio. Textes et documents d'histoire*, 2: *Moyen Age*, ed. J. Calmette (2nd ed., Paris: Presses Universitaires, 1953), pp. 93–94. The translation is by D. Herlihy.

ADOLF, the count of Holstein, began to rebuild the castle of Segeberg and he encircled it with a wall. But because the land was deserted, he sent messengers to all regions, that is, Flanders and Holland, Utrecht, Westphalia and Frisia, so that whoever might be in difficult straits because of a shortage of fields should come with their families to accept land which was excellent, spacious, fertile with fruits, abounding in fish and meat, and favorable to pastures.

At this invitation, an uncounted multitude arose from the various nations. Taking their families and possessions, they came to the land of the Wagri to Count Adolf, in order to take possession of the land which he had promised them. First of all, the people from Holstein accepted settlements in protected places in the region west of Segeberg, around the Trave river, and the fields of Schwentinefeld, and the lands which extend from the river Schwale to Tens-

fleder and Lake Plön. The Westphalians settled in the land of
Dargun, the Hollanders in that of Eutin, the Frisians in the country
of Süsel. But the region of Plön has remained deserted to this day.
The count gave Oldenburg and Lütjenburg and other lands near
to the sea to the Slavs to colonize, who thus became his tributaries.
After this, Count Adolf came to the place known as Bucu and
he found there the fortifications of a deserted town, which Cruto,
the tyrant of God, had erected. He also found a wide island surrounded by two rivers. One one side the river Trave flowed past,
and on the other the Wakenitz, and both had a swampy and im-
passable bank. But on the side where the land road passes is a small
hill, next to the fortifications of the castle. Discerning the suitability of the place for the erection of an excellent port, the industri-
ous man began to build a city. He called it Lübeck, for the reason
that it was not far away from the old port and city which Prince
Henry had at one time constructed. He sent messengers to Niclot,
prince of the Obotrites, to make with him a treaty of friendship.
He won over all the nobles with gifts, so that they would rival one
another in loyalty to him and in the cultivation of his land. Thus,
the deserted land of the province of the Wagri began to gain inhabitants, and the number of its settlers multiplied. At a similar
invitation of the count and with his help, the priest Vicelinus also
received the properties which Emperor Lothair had once given to
him near the castle of Segeberg for the construction of a monastery and the support of the servants of God.

2. The statutes of the free village of Lorris

One important means for encouraging the clearance of the land within
Europe was the establishment of "free villages." To encourage reset-
tlement, lords invited peasants to settle on their lands under exception-
ally favorable conditions. In France, one of the earliest of the free
villages was Lorris in the Gâtinais, which received a charter, now lost,
from Louis VI, and confirmations from Louis VII in 1155 and Philip
II in 1187. The privileges of Lorris became a model for many similar
charters. They thus illustrate the liberal conditions widely enjoyed by
colonizers of new lands in the north of France.

The following translation, by D. Herlihy, is based on the confirmation of 1187, given in *Recueil des actes de Philippe Auguste roi de
France*, ed. M. Delaborde, I (Paris: Imprimerie nationale, 1916), no.
202, pp. 243–46. The prologue, conclusion and five clauses dealing
with the technical operation of the courts have been omitted.

1. We concede that whoever owns a house in the parish of Lorris
shall pay for his house and for each arpent of land, if he should
hold it in the same parish, six pennies of quitrent only. And if he
should acquire property [by clearing wastelands] he shall hold it
for the same quitrent as his house.

2. No man of the parish of Lorris shall pay either a tariff or other
tax upon his food. Nor shall he pay any tax for measuring the grain
which he obtains from his own labor or that of his animals. Nor
shall he pay any tax on the wine which he obtains from his own
vineyards.

3. No man need go on an expedition on foot or by horse unless he
can return if he wishes the same day.

4. No man shall pay tolls as far as Etamps nor as far as Orléans,
nor as far as Milly, which is in the Gâtinais.

5. Whoever has his farm in the parish of Lorris, shall lose none of
it by fines, unless he has been fined for offense against us or any
of our new settlers.

6. No one going to or coming from the fairs or the market of
Lorris shall be arrested or disturbed, unless he committed an offense
on that same day. No one, on the day of the market or fair of
Lorris, shall confiscate a bond put up as security, unless the pledge
was made for such a day.

7. Fines of sixty solidi shall be reduced to five solidi, those of five
solidi to twelve pennies, and the fee of the prévôt to four pennies.

8. No man need leave Lorris in order to plead in the court of the
king.

9. No one, neither we ourselves nor any one else, shall demand of
the men of Lorris a taille or requisition or aid.

10. No one shall sell wine at Lorris with a proclamation, except
the king, who may sell his own wine in his cellar with such a
proclamation.

11. We shall have at Lorris credit in food for our own need and
that of the queen for fifteen full days. And if anyone have a pledge

belonging to the lord king, he shall not keep it more than eight days, unless by our will.

.   .   .   .

15. No man of Lorris should labor for us except once a year, to bring our wine to Orléans. Nor are others to do this, but only those who have horses and wagons and have been summoned. They shall not receive lodging from us. The villeins shall bring wood for our kitchen.

16. No one of them should be kept in prison if he is able to furnish bail.

17. If any of them wish to sell their belongings, he may sell them, and with the payments from the sales, may freely and quietly leave the village, if he wishes to leave, unless he has committed a crime in the village.

18. Whoever lives in the parish of Lorris one year and a day with no demand having been made for him, if he was not denied the right by us or by our prévôt, from that time he shall remain free and undisturbed.

.   .   .   .

20. And when the men of Lorris shall go to Orléans with their goods to be sold, they should pay for their wagon only one coin when they leave the city, that is, when they shall go not for reason of the fair. And when for reason of the fair they go in March, in leaving Orléans they should pay four pennies for their wagon, and in entering the city two pennies.

21. In weddings at Lorris, neither the herald nor the watchman shall receive a payment.

22. No peasant of the parish of Lorris who cultivates the land with a plow shall give more than one mina of rye to the sergeants of Lorris at harvest.

23. And if any knight or sergeant shall find horses or other animals of the men of Lorris in our forests, he should bring them only to the prévôt of Lorris.

If any animal of the parish of Lorris, fleeing from bulls or incited by flies, should enter our forest or grove, he whose animal it is shall pay nothing to the prévôts, if he is able to swear that the animal entered against the will of the guard. And if it entered with the knowledge of the guard, he shall give twelve pennies for this.

And if there were several animals, he should pay so much for each.
24. At the furnaces of Lorris there shall be no tax for porters.
25. There shall be no tax for the guard at Lorris.
26. If anyone from Lorris brings salt or wine to Orléans, he shall give one penny for his wagon only.
27. No man of Lorris shall make payment to the prévôt of Etamps, nor to the prévôt of Pithiviers, nor in all the Gâtinais.
28. No one of them shall pay a toll at Ferrières, nor Château-Landon, nor Piuseaux nor Nibelle.
29. The men of Lorris may take dead wood outside the forest for their own use.
30. Whoever in the market of Lorris should buy or sell anything and in forgetfulness retain the toll, let him pay it after eight days, without any prosecution, if he can swear that he did not knowingly retain it.

                       .   .   .   .

32. And if any man of Lorris should be accused of anything, and it cannot be proved by a witness, he shall purge himself by his own oath against the affirmation of the accuser.
33. No one of the same parish from what he may sell or buy over the week, and from what he may buy on Wednesdays in the market for his own use, shall pay a tax.
34. These customs have been conceded to the men of Lorris, and they are the same as those granted to the men who live at Courtpalais, at Chanteloup and in the bailiwick of Harpard.
35. Finally we ordain that every time the prévôt is changed in the village, he shall swear to observe faithfully these customs, and the new sergeants shall do the same every time they are installed.

ᒐᒐᒐᒐᒐᒐᒐᒐᒐᒐᒐᒐᒐᒐᒐᒐᒐᒐᒐ

3. The charter of the town of St. Omer, 1127

In the eleventh and twelfth centuries, towns not only grew in economic importance but many of them were able to win privileges and concessions of self-government from the nobles and bishops who had formerly ruled them. Italy in the south and Flanders in the north were the great centers of medieval urban development. The following charter, issued by William of Normandy, then count of Flanders, in 1127 to the citizens of St. Omer, is one of the oldest such privileges to have survived. The Belgian historian Henri Pirenne called it "the point of departure of the political program of the burghers of Flanders." By it they won recognition of their commune or autonomous urban government, of their guild and court system, and were conceded numerous tax benefits.

The charter, here translated by D. Herlihy, may be found in the *Actes des comtes de Flandre, 1071–1128*, ed. F. Vercauteren (Brussels: Palais des Académies, 1938), no. 128, pp. 299–302, April 14, 1127.

I, WILLIAM, by the grace of God, Count of the Flemings, not wishing to reject the petition of the citizens of St. Omer—especially as they have willingly received my petition about the consulate of Flanders, and because they have always been more honest and faithful than other Flemings to me—grant them the laws and customs written below in perpetuity, and command that these laws remain inviolate.

1. First, that to every man I will show peace, and I will maintain and defend them as my own men without deceit. And I concede that their aldermen [*scabini*] can make right judgment concerning all men, including myself. I grant liberty to those aldermen such as the most favored aldermen of my lands enjoy.

2. If any citizen of St. Omer lend money to anyone, and the borrower freely acknowledges this in the presence of lawful men who hold inheritances in the city, if the debt is unpaid on the agreed date, he or his goods may be detained until all is paid. If he is unwilling to pay, or denies the agreement, he shall be detained until he pays the debt, if he is convicted on the testimony of two aldermen or two sworn men.

3. If anyone is accused under the law of the Church, he need not leave St. Omer to do justice elsewhere, but may do what is right in the city, in the presence of the bishop or his archdeacon or his priest, and by the judgment of the clerics and aldermen. He need answer to no one, except for these three reasons: that is, desecration of a church or temple, an injury of a cleric, or rape and violation of a woman. If a complaint is lodged against him for other reasons, the case should be heard in the presence of the judges and my prévôt. Thus it was decreed in the presence of Count K. [Charles] and Bishop John.

4. I concede to them the liberty which they enjoyed at the time

of my ancestors, that is, that they never must leave their territory on campaign, saving only if a hostile army invade Flanders. Then they must defend me and my land.

5. All those who have their guild and belong to it and reside within the circle of the city, I free from all tolls at the port of Dixmude and Gravelines; and throughout all the land of Flanders I free them of the tax called *sewerp*. I grant them the toll which the men of Arras pay at Bapaume.

6. If any of them go into the land of the emperor for trading, he shall not be required by any of my men to pay the tax known as *hansa*.

7. If it should happen that at any time I should acquire land outside of Flanders, or if a treaty of peace should be made between me and my uncle H[enry], king of England, I shall free them of all tolls in the land acquired or in the entire realm of the English, or I shall make them free of all customs by the terms of such a treaty.

8. In every market of Flanders, if anyone raises a complaint against them, they shall undergo the judgment of the aldermen concerning every complaint without a duel. They shall henceforth be free from the duel.

9. All who live within the walls of St. Omer, or who shall live there in the future, I make free from the *cavagium*, that is, from the head tax, and from payments to the court officials [*advocati*].

10. Their money which after the death of Count K. [Charles] was taken from them, and which because of the fidelity which they hold towards me is still not given them, I shall repay within the year, or I shall have justice done for them according to the judgment of the aldermen.

11. Moreover, they have asked the king of France and Ralph of Péronne that wherever they go in their lands they should be free from all toll, transit duties and passage; this I too wish to grant them.

12. I command that their commune remain undisturbed, just as they created it by oath. I shall let it be dissolved by no one. I concede to them all right and right justice, as it is best available in my land, that is, in Flanders. I wish them to be free henceforth of all customary taxes, as the best and freer townsmen of Flanders. I shall ask of them no scot, no taille, and make no request for their money.

13. I give my mint at St. Omer, from which I have had 30 pounds per year, and whatever I ought to have from it, for the repayment of their losses and the sustenance of their guild. These townsmen should keep the money for all my life stable and good, so that their city may be improved.

14. The guards who every night in the year protect the castle of St. Omer, and who, besides their salary and support as was established in olden times in oats and cheese and in goatskins, are accustomed to demand unjustly and violently one loaf and one or two pennies from each house in the city, at the feasts of St. Omer and St. Bertin and at Christmas, should dare no longer to take anything besides their salary and support.

15. Whoever comes to Nieuport from any place should have permission to come to St. Omer with his goods in whatever ship he pleases.

16. If I make peace with S[tephan] count of Boulogne, I shall in that peace make them free from toll and *sewerp* at Wissant and in all his lands.

17. I grant for their use the pasture adjacent to the city of St. Omer in the forest which is called Lo and in the marshes and meadows, moors and uncultivated lands, except in the land of the lepers, as it was at the time of Count Robert the Bearded.

18. I make free from all tolls the houses which are under the supervision of the advocate of the abbey of St. Bertin, namely those which are inhabited. Each one shall give 12 pennies at the feast of St. Michael, 12 pennies as *brotban* [bread tax], and 12 pennies as *byrban* [beer tax]. Deserted houses shall pay nothing.

19. If any stranger should attack any citizen of St. Omer and bring injury or insult upon him or violently rob him of his property, and with this injury should escape his hands, and is afterwards summoned by the castellan or by his wife or by his steward, if he disdains to come to make satisfaction within three days or should neglect to do so, the commune shall together take the injury of their brother upon themselves. In taking vengeance, if a home should be destroyed or burned, or if anyone should be injured or killed, he who accomplished the vengeance should not incur any danger of person or property nor should he know or fear my displeasure concerning this. If however, whoever made the injury should soon be taken, he shall be judged according to the laws and customs of the city and shall be punished according to the degree

of the crime, that is, he shall render an eye for eyes, a tooth for a tooth, and a head for a head.

20. Concerning the death of Eustache of Steenvoorde, whoever may disturb and molest any citizen of St. Omer should be held guilty of the betrayal and death of Count K. [Charles], since whatever was done was done out of fidelity to me. And as I swore and gave faith, thus I wish them to be reconciled and hold peace towards his relatives.

The following persons under oath promised to uphold this commune and to observe the above-mentioned customs and agreements: Louis, the king of the French; William, the count of Flanders; Ralph of Péronne; Hugh Oatfield; Osto the castellan and William his brother; Robert of Béthune and William his son; Anselm of Hesdin; Stephan, the count of Boulogne; Masasses, the count of Guines; Walter of Lillers; Balduin of Ghent; Ywain his brother; Roger the castellan of Lille, and Robert his son; Rasse of Gavere; Daniel of Termonde; Helias of Saint-Saens; Henry of Bourbourg; Eustache the advocate and Arnulf his son; the castellan of Ghent, Gervais; Peter the steward; Stephan of Steninghem.

This privilege was confirmed by Count William and the above-mentioned barons, by faith and oath approved and accepted. In the year of the Lord's Incarnation 1127, 18 kalends of May, the fifth day of the week, the feast of the saints Tiburtius and Valerian.

4. The guild of fishermen at Worms, ca. 1106

In the early stages of guild development, towns had usually only one large guild, which included all merchants. Specialization came later, and towns, which were commercial before they were industrial centers, were slow to develop and recognize associations of artisans. Artisan or craft guilds become numerous only after the year 1200. The following recognition of a guild of fishermen at Worms, dated about 1106, is therefore exceptional. It is in fact one of the earliest privileges accorded to a craft guild in the whole of Europe.

The charter, here translated by D. Herlihy, may be found in the *Urkundenbuch der Stadt Worms*, ed. H. Boos, I (Berlin: Weidmann, 1886), no. 58, p. 50.

In the name of the Holy and Undivided Trinity. Be it known to
all men of the present and future age that Adalbert, the venerable
bishop of Worms, at the request of Count Wernher and on the persuasion and recommendation of his other chief advisers, has appointed these twenty-three fishermen of Worms, namely these:
Herrich, Sethwin, Satmar, Herrich, Etman, Dietmar, Siegefrit,
Lutwin, Godeschalc, Wolfram, Wilrich, Guntere, Woppelin, Lut-
frit, Gerhart, Luzo, Berchtolt, Luzo, Bernhelm, Truthnit, Ruthart,
Hildebrant and Godeschalch. To them he gave this privilege under
this condition: that if any of them should succumb to death, his
nearest relative may succeed him in this office by hereditary custom;
if however there is no heir, the places should be filled to the above
number by the common counsel of the city [fishermen]. On the
advice of the above-mentioned men, the bishop has also decreed
that if anyone should be found buying fish between Suelntheim
and Altdruphen for the sake of reselling them and should be caught
in this purchase by the said fishermen, the fishes should be taken
from them and divided equally among the city [fishermen]. He
who was caught in this purchase should be brought before the
judges and after conviction should give three pounds, two pounds
to the bishop and the third to the count. Those who catch fish are
not prohibited from selling them, but the said twenty-three fishermen are not allowed to buy any before the hour of prime. Further,
in confirmation of this charter, lest it later be damaged by the advice or disagreement of anyone, the said bishop decreed with his
ban that these twenty-three fishermen in the time of rogations shall
offer three salmon, two to the bishop and the third to the count,
and by this gift they shall confirm their privilege every year. The
witnesses of this charter are the following: [thirty-nine names fol-
low].

5. Florence in 1336–38

The size and social complexity which a medieval city could attain are
excellently illustrated in the following description of Florence in the
years 1336–38. It was written by the contemporary chronicler Gio-

vanni Villani. He has just described the revenues of the city, which he
says were greater than those enjoyed by the kingdoms of southern
Italy, Sicily or Aragon. He then goes on to speak of population.

The translation, by D. Herlihy, is based upon the Italian text in the
Cronica di Giovanni Villani (Florence: Magheri, 1823), VI, pp. 183–88.

Now that we have spoken of the revenues and expenses of the
commune of Florence in these times, I think it appropriate to mention this and the other great things about our city. Thus, our successors, who in times to come shall follow us, may become aware
of the rise and decline of the wealth and power which our city
achieved. Thus they may also, through the wise and courageous
citizens who at various times shall govern her, see to it that she advances in wealth and great power, through the memory and example of this our chronicle.

We have diligently discovered that in these times there were in
Florence about 25,000 men able to bear arms, from 15 years up to
70, all citizens. Among them there were 1500 noble and powerful
citizens who as magnates posted bond with the commune. There
were then in Florence upwards of 75 liveried knights. We have
diligently discovered that before the popular regime, which rules
at present, was established, there were more than 250 knights. Since
the popular government was created, the magnates have not had
the possessions or the power as before, and therefore few become
knights.

It has been estimated that there are in Florence upwards of
90,000 mouths, including men, women and children, from the evidence of the bread which is continuously needed in the city, as one
can well understand. It has been guessed that there were continuously in the city more than 1500 foreigners, transients and soldiers,
not counting in the total religious, friars and cloistered nuns, of
whom we shall make mention soon. It has been estimated that there
were in these times in the countryside and district of Florence upwards of 80,000 men. We have discovered from the priest who baptized the babies that they numbered every year in these times from
5500 to 6000, with the masculine sex larger than the feminine by up
to 500 per year. (The priest sets aside a black bean for every male
baptized in San Giovanni and a white bean for every female, in order to know their number). We have discovered, that the boys and
girls who are learning to read number from 8000 to 10,000. The

boys who are learning the abacus and calculation in six schools number from 1000 to 1200. And those who are learning Latin and logic in four large schools number from 550 to 600.

The churches which were then in Florence and in her suburbs, including the abbeys and the churches of the religious friars, have been found to be 110. Among them are 57 parishes with congregations, five abbeys with two priors and upwards of 80 monks, 24 convents of nuns with upwards of 500 women, 10 houses of friars, 30 hospitals with more than 1000 beds to serve the poor and infirm, and from 250 to 300 ordained chaplains.

The shops of the wool craft were 200 or more, and produced from 70,000 to 80,000 cloths, which were worth upwards of 1,200,000 gold florins. A third of this value remained in the country to pay for labor, without regarding the profit which the wool merchants made from that labor. More than 30,000 persons were supported by it. We have accurately discovered, that thirty years ago there were 300 shops or thereabouts, and that they made every year more than 100,000 cloths. But these cloths were cruder and worth half the present value, since wool from England was not then imported, nor was it known how to work it, as has subsequently been done. The shops of the guild of Calimala, which deals with cloth brought from France and beyond the mountains, number upwards of twenty, and import every year more than 10,000 cloths worth 300,000 gold florins. These they sell entirely in Florence, and we do not include those cloths which are shipped outside of Florence. The tables of money-changers were upwards of eighty. The gold money which was coined was upwards of 350,000 gold florins and sometimes 400,000; and of pennies worth four *piccioli* each, there were coined every year about 20,000 pounds.

The college of judges was upwards of 80. The notaries were more than 600. The pharmacists, physicians and surgeons numbered upwards of 60. The drug stores were more than 100. Merchants and dealers in dry goods were of great number. One cannot estimate the shops of the makers of shoes, slippers and boots. Those who went outside of Florence to trade numbered 300 or more, and many other masters of many crafts, and masters of stone and wood, did likewise. There were then in Florence 146 furnaces. We have discovered by the tax of milling and for the furnaces, that every day the city needed for internal consumption 140 moggia of grain. From this one can estimate what was needed every year. And we do not consider that the greater part of the rich, noble and affluent citizens spent with their families four months every year in the countryside, and some even more. We have discovered that in the year 1280, when the city was in happy and good circumstances, that it needed every week upward of 800 moggia. We have discovered by the tax at the gates that every year Florence imported upwards of 55,000 cogna of wine, and when it was plentiful about 10,000 cogna more. The city required every year about 400 cows and calves; 60,000 muttons and sheep; 20,000 she-goats and he-goats; and 30,000 pigs. In the month of July through the gate of San Frediano there entered 4000 loads of melons, which were all distributed in the city.

In these times there were in Florence the following magistracies held by foreign officials. Each held court and had the authority to torture. They were the podestà, the captain, the defender of the people and the guilds; the executor of the Ordinances of Justice; the captain of the guard, or defender of the people, who had more authority than the others. All these four [*sic*] magistrates had the option of inflicting personal punishment: the judge of auditing and appeals; the judge of taxes; the official supervising women's ornaments; the official over commerce; the official over the wool guild; the ecclesiastical officials; the court of the bishop of Florence; the court of the bishop of Fiesole; the inquisitor concerning heretical depravity. And other high and magnificent offices of our city of Florence ought not to be omitted, but remembered, in order to provide information to those who shall follow us.

The city was well laid out within, and constructed with many beautiful houses. Construction was going on continually in these times. Buildings were improved, to make them comfortable and elegant, and fine examples of all sorts of improvements were sought from outside the city. There were cathedral churches, and churches of brothers of every discipline, and magnificent monasteries. Besides that, there was not a citizen, of popular or magnate status, who had not built or would not build in the countryside great and rich estates, and very rich habitations, with beautiful buildings, much better than in the city. And in this they all sinned, and were considered insane for their extravagant expenditures.

And it was such a magnificent thing to behold, that foreigners coming from afar, not familiar with Florence, believed (or most of them) that the rich buildings and beautiful palaces which were outside the city about three miles were part of the city, as they are at Rome. We do not speak of the rich palaces, towers, courts and walled gardens even farther from the city, which in other regions would be called castles. In conclusion, it has been estimated, that around the city for a distance of six miles there are so many rich and noble habitations that two Florences would not contain as many. We have said enough of the facts of Florence.

II. *Scholasticism*

⎣⌐⎣⌐⎣⌐⎣⌐⎣⌐⎣⌐⎣⌐⎣⌐⎣⌐⎣⌐⎣⌐⎣⌐⎣⌐⎣⌐⎣⌐⎣⌐⌐

6. Peter Abelard's *History of My Misfortunes*

Peter Abelard (1079–1142) was one of the founders of scholasticism, and the teacher who perhaps more than anyone established the reputation of the school of Paris for logical and philosophical studies. He is furthermore one of the first figures of the Middle Ages to leave on the historical record a strong impression of personality. One of his letters, written to an unnamed friend, is a revealing autobiography, called the *History of My Misfortunes*. It gives an unequaled picture of the tumultuous life of students and teachers in the early twelfth century. It also recounts his affair with Heloise, one of the most moving love stories in Western history.

The following selection from the *History* gives in their entirety the first seven and one-half chapters, taking the story to the point where both lovers abandon the world and adopt the monastic life. The Latin text may be found in *Petri Abaelardi opera,* ed. V. Cousin, I (Paris: Durand, 1849), 3–17. The translation is by D. Herlihy.

EXAMPLES often more than words either arouse or calm human passions. Therefore, since the conversation held in your presence was the source of some consolation, I have decided to write to you in your absence a comforting letter, regarding my experience of misfortunes. You may thereby see, that in comparison with my own, your trials are little or nothing; you may therefore the more easily bear them.

1. I was born in a small town, which is built at the approaches to lesser Brittany, and is, I believe, eight miles to the east of the city of Nantes. Its name is Palets. By the nature of my land or the character of my ancestry I was quick of mind, and so, by my native talent I was easily disposed to literary studies. I had a father who had tasted a little of letters before he became a knight. He thus afterwards embraced letters with such love that he was intent on

having whatever sons he had first instructed in letters before they were trained in arms. And so it happened. As he loved me, his first-born, more than the others, so much the more solicitously did he care for my education. I, on the other hand, as I made ever more extensive and easier progress in the study of letters, took to them with the greater enthusiasm. I was captured by so much love for them, that I abandoned to my brothers the pomp of chivalrous glory with the inheritance and prerogatives of the first-born. I preferred altogether to desert the court of Mars, in order to be educated in the lap of Minerva. And since I favored the weapons of dialectic reasoning above all teachings of philosophy, I changed my other arms for these arms, and I preferred the conflict of disputations to the trophies of battle. Then, wandering and disputing through various provinces, wherever I had heard that the study of this art was waxing strong, I became an imitator of the peripatetic philosophers of old.

2. I then came to Paris, where already this discipline was especially flourishing, to William of Champeaux, my teacher, who was then in this instruction famous in fact and repute. I stayed with him a little while and was first accepted by him. Afterwards I became most burdensome to him, since I sought to refute some of his opinions, and rather frequently I stepped forward to reason against him. And sometimes I appeared to be his better in disputing. Therefore, those two scholars who were considered outstanding among our fellows were so much the more indignant, as I was their inferior in age and time of study. From this came the beginnings of my misfortunes, which have lasted to the present. The more widely my reputation spread, the more the envy of others was enkindled against me.

It then happened that I, presuming upon my native talent beyond the strength of my years, aspired while still a young man to the direction of students. I sought a place, where I might accomplish this. At that time the town of Melun was famous, and a royal capital. My aforesaid master anticipated this plan, and tried to move our school as far as possible from his own. He secretly plotted this by all means at his disposal, so that before I left his school, he might obstruct the preparation of our own, and take away from me my chosen place. But since he had some enemies among the powerful of the land, by relying on their help I fulfilled my desire, and his manifest jealousy won me the good will of many.

From the training given at my school, so much did my name in the art of dialectic spread, that the reputation not only of my fellow students, but even of my master himself, declined and was gradually extinguished. Thus it came about that with great self-confidence I quickly transferred my school to the town of Corbeil, which is nearer to the city of Paris. There opportunity might offer more frequent battles of disputation.

But shortly thereafter, stricken by the immoderate burden of my studies and pressed by illness, I returned to my homeland. Exiled, as it were, for some years from France, I was the more ardently sought by those, whom the learning of dialectic was attracting. After a few years had passed, when I had recovered a little from my illness, William, my teacher, an archdeacon of Paris, changed his older habit and joined an order of the regular [monastic] clergy. He did this, as they said, with this intent, that he might be regarded the more religious, and be elevated to a loftier rank in the hierarchy. This soon happened, as he became bishop of Châlons. Nor did this change in habit call him away from the city of Paris or from his usual study of philosophy. But in that same monastery, to which he had taken himself for the sake of religion, he at once held public lectures in his usual manner.

I then returned to him, so that I might learn rhetoric from him. Among other problems of our disputations, I forced him by the clearest marshaling of arguments to change, or rather, to destroy his old opinion concerning universals. For he was of the following opinion concerning the community of universals. He affirmed that the same being was present entirely, essentially and simultaneously in the individuals of its class. Among these individuals, there was no difference in essence, but only variety in the multitude of their accidents. He then, however, corrected his opinion; he henceforth said that the same thing was present not essentially, but identically [*indifferenter*]. This question concerning universals has always been chief among the dialecticians. Porphyry himself, when he wrote of universals in his *Isagoge;* did not presume to define them, but said: "For this is a very advanced business." When William corrected his opinion, or rather abandoned it under pressure, his lectures fell into such neglect, that he was hardly to be conceded a place in the teaching of dialectic. For in this opinion concerning universals stands the sum total of this art.

From this our teaching acquired so much strength and authority, that those who before had violently sided with our master, and especially attacked our doctrine, flocked to our school. He, who in the school of Paris had succeeded to our master's place, offered me his chair, so that with others he might put himself under our instruction, where his own and my master had flourished. Within a few days, after I began reigning there in the study of dialectic, our master began to be consumed with such jealousy, and to heat with such anger, as cannot be easily put into words. He did not bear the heat of the misery he had conceived for very long, and he cunningly sought to get rid of me again. Since he did not have anything which he might openly use against me, he tried to remove the school from him who had given his chair to me, by advancing most base accusations, and to give it in his place to one of my enemies.

Then I went back to Melun, and set up my school there, as before. And the more openly his envy persecuted me, the greater the authority it conferred upon me, as the poet says: "Jealousy seeks the heights, the winds blow through the loftiest places" (Ovid, *Remedium Amoris*, 1.369).

Not long after this, when he learned that almost all the students were very sceptical about his monastic life, and were whispering a good deal about his conversion, in that he had not left the city, he betook himself and his company of brothers, with his school, to a certain village removed from the city. I at once returned from Melun to Paris, hoping that henceforth I should have peace with him. But because, as we have mentioned, he had delivered our chair to our enemy, I placed the battlements of our school outside the city on the mount of Ste. Geneviève. It was as if I was besieging him who had captured our chair.

When he heard this, our master at once shamelessly returned to the city, and brought back his school which he still then had, and the company of brothers, to their former monastery, expecting to rescue his knight, whom he had deserted, from our siege. Truly, in intending to help him, he rather injured him. For before, he had some few students, especially because of his lectures on Priscian, in which he was thought to be very competent. But after his master arrived, he lost almost all his students, and was forced to retire from the direction of his school. Shortly afterwards, as if despairing of worldly glory, he too was converted to the monastic life.

After the return of our master to the city, history has already informed you what conflicts of disputations our students had both

with him and with his disciples, and what results fortune in these
wars gave to our people, or rather to myself. But this saying of
Ajax I may quote with more modesty than he, and boldly pronounce it:

> If you wish to know the result
> Of this fight, I was not beaten by him.

Even if I am silent about it, the facts themselves speak, and the
outcome of the affair reveals it. While these things were going on,
my mother Lucia, who was most dear to me, made me come back
to my home. After my father Berengar had adopted the monastic
life, she was making arrangements to do likewise. With this accomplished, I returned to France, especially that I might be instructed in theology. At that time, our master William, many times
mentioned, was lording it as bishop of Châlons. In this discipline,
his own master, Anselm of Laon, had then held for much time past
the greatest authority.

3. I therefore went to this old man, who had earned his name more
through long habit than through native talent or memory. If anyone came to him in uncertainty to inquire of a problem, he went
away with his uncertainty magnified. He was a wonder in the eyes
of his hearers, but a nothing in the view of those who questioned
him. He had a marvelous facility with words, but they were con-
temptible in meaning and devoid of reason. When he kindled a
fire, he filled his house with smoke, rather than illuminating it with
light. His tree appeared to those viewing it from afar all in foliage,
excellent, but to those up close, and carefully investigating, it was
found to be barren. When I too came to this tree that I might
collect fruit from it, I learned that this was the fig tree which the
Lord cursed, or that old oak, to which Lucan compared Pompey,
saying:

> There stands the shadow of a mighty name
> Like a tall oak in a fruitful field.

When I discovered this, I spent not many days peacefully in
his shadow. But when I gradually began to come ever more rarely
to his lectures, some of his better students began to take offense, as
if I was contemptuous of so great a teacher. Then, secretly
prodding him too against me, they made me by their wicked
innuendos hateful to him.

It happened one day, that we students were playing together after certain exchanges of opinion. One of them, with evil towards me in his heart, asked me what I thought about the reading of sacred Scripture. I, who up until then had studied only physics, answered that it was most advantageous to study the readings where the soul's salvation could be learned, but that I greatly wondered why educated men did not find Scripture itself or the glosses upon them sufficient for the understanding of these holy things, but needed further instruction. Many who were there mocked me, and demanded whether I could or would dare attack the subject. I answered that if they wished to see it tried, I was ready. Then, amid shouts and further mockery, they said, "Certainly, we too are willing. Let's find and impose on you the interpretation of some little used Scripture, and let us test what you promise." And all agreed upon the most obscure prophecy of Ezekiel.

Thus assuming the role of expositor, I at once invited them to my lecture on the morrow. Offering advice to me against my will, they said that one should not hasten into so great a matter, but that I, in my inexperience, should for a long time stand guard, in considering and strengthening my interpretations. I, however, answered indignantly that it was not my habit to make progress by practice but rather by talent. And I added that I would abandon the contest entirely, if they did not, as I wished, come to my lecture without delay.

Few were present at my first lecture, as it seemed laughable to all that I, still almost a neophyte in sacred Scripture, should attack it in such haste. But to all who did attend, my lecture had such appeal, that they praised it with singular commendation, and required me to prepare a gloss according to the sense of our lecture. When they heard this, those who had not attended began to come with eagerness to my second and third lecture. All were equally and extremely solicitous, in the beginning of my lectures to take down the glosses which I had begun the first day.

4. That same old man was thereby moved by violent envy, and from that time was aroused against me, as I have said above, by the arguments of certain students against me. He began to persecute me in sacred Scripture no less than our William had before done in philosophy. There were then in this old man's school two who seemed to excel the others: Alberic of Rheims, and Lotulph a Lombard. The better they thought of themselves, the more

they raged against me. Especially by the suggestions of these two (as was later found out), this old man in his upset shamelessly forbade me to continue the gloss I had begun in his place of teaching. He advanced the pretext that if I, as a person still untrained in this subject, should perchance commit an error, it might be charged to him. When this reached the ears of the students, they were moved by the greatest indignation concerning so manifest a calumny of envy, which had never happened to any man before. But the more manifest it became, so much the more was it a credit to me, and I became the more glorious through persecution.

5. After a few days I returned to Paris. For some years I quietly held the school which a long time before had been intended for me and given me, from which I had first been driven out. I labored to finish there, in the very beginning of my lectures, those glosses on Ezekiel, which I had begun at Laon. They were still so pleasing to readers, that they already believed that I had acquired no less grace in sacred Scripture, than they had seen me acquire in philosophy. From this, by enthusiasm for both courses, our school greatly grew. Surely, rumor has not left you ignorant of how much monetary profit, and how much glory, my school brought.

But prosperity always inflates the imprudent, and worldly peace weakens the vigor of the soul, and easily dissolves it by the attractions of the flesh. Since I already believed that I was the only philosopher left in the world, and since I feared no further disturbance, I began to let lust run free. I had before lived in perfect chastity. The further I advanced in philosophy or sacred Scripture, the more I receded, by the impurity of my life, from philosophers and theologians. For it is certain that philosophers, and theologians too, that is, those intent on exhorting to the sacred Scriptures, have especially shone in the beauty of chastity.

I was therefore in my whole person laboring in pride and lust; divine grace, although against my will, has since given me the remedy for both diseases, first for lust, and then for pride. For lust, by depriving me of those parts by which I practiced it; and for pride, which was conceived in me especially from my knowledge of letters, according to the Apostle's words, *Knowledge puffeth up* (1 Cor. 18.1), by humiliating me with the burning of that book in which I took the greatest pride. I wish you to know the story of this affair truthfully from the fact itself, rather than from rumor, in the order in which the events occurred.

I had always hated the filth of prostitutes, but I was restrained from approaching and visiting noble women by dedication to my scholarly pursuits. I had little experience of conversation even with common women. Wicked fortune, favoring me as the saying goes, offered me a more convenient opportunity, by which she might the more easily cast me down from the peak of this sublimity. Thus might divine grace reclaim this most arrogant person, who had forgotten the grace he had received.

6. For there was in this city of Paris a certain young girl, by the name of Heloise. She was the niece of a certain canon, Fulbert by name, who, because he loved her so much, was so much the more zealous in advancing her in all knowledge of letters, as far as he could. She, while not the meanest in her countenance, was the highest woman by virtue of her wealth of learning. For since this good (I mean a knowledge of letters) is rarely found in women, so much the more did it distinguish the girl, and made her famous in the entire kingdom.

After I discerned in her all the things which are likely to attract lovers, I therefore thought it suitable to join her with me in love, and I believed that I could easily accomplish this. For so great was my reputation then, and so much did I excel in the grace of youth and beauty, that I feared no rejection from whatever woman I might favor with my love. I felt that the girl would yield to me the more readily the more I knew her to possess and to love this knowledge of letters. It would be possible for us, even when separated, to enter each other's presence through written messengers, and often to write more audaciously than we could speak. Thus always we would share sweet conversations.

All afire for the love of this young girl, I sought an opportunity by means of which I might make her familiar with me by domestic and daily conversation, so that I could the more easily bring her to consent. To achieve this, I negotiated with the uncle of the girl, with the support of certain of his friends, that he should receive me into his house, which was next to our school, for whatever he might charge. I used this as an excuse, that the household concern for my servants greatly impeded my studies, and the large expenses weighed too much upon me. For he was very greedy, and also very eager in regard to his niece, that she might continuously make greater progress in the study of letters.

For these two reasons, I easily obtained his assent, and I got what I wanted. For he was entirely panting after money, and thought that his niece would learn something from our instruction.

He energetically exhorted me to this, more than I presumed to hope, and he yielded to my wishes, and so was an aid to love. He gave her over entirely to my instruction, so that as often as, returning from school, I had some leisure, both in day and in night, I might make an effort to teach her, and if I found her negligent, I might harshly punish her. I greatly wondered at the man's simplicity, no less was I amazed within myself, as if he had committed a tender lamb to a ravenous wolf. Since he delivered her to me not only to be taught, but also to be violently punished, what else was he doing, but giving me full license to my wishes, and offering the chance, even if he did not wish it, that I might the more easily sway the girl by threats and blows, if I could not by flattery? For there were two things, which especially kept him from base suspicion, his love for his niece, and my own past reputation for continence.

Why say more? We were first joined in a single house, and then in soul. Under the pretense of study, we gave ourselves entirely to love; the practice of reading offered us the secret hideaways which love desires. With the books open, the words dealt more with love than with letters; more were the kisses than the learned opinions. We moved our hands more often to the breast than to the books. More often love turned our eyes upon itself, than reading directed them to the text. In order that we might have less of suspicion, love (not wrath) gave blows—grace, not anger, which transcends the sweetness of all ointments.

What then? No stage of love escaped our desires. If love could invent some new manner, we tried this too. The less we were experienced in these joys, the more ardently we gave ourselves to them, and the less satiety did they bring.

From the time this pleasure had strongly seized me, I was less able to concentrate on philosophy, and take pains for my school. It was exceedingly wearisome for me to go to school, and to remain there; it was equally exhausting, as I reserved my nightly vigils for love, and my days for study. My lectures then found me negligent and indifferent. I produced nothing from inspiration, but all from routine. I was nothing but a repeater of old discoveries. What poems I allowed myself to compose were of love, and not of the secrets of philosophy. Of these songs, many, as you know, are still popular and sung in many regions, by those especially who seek pleasure in life.

It is not easy to think how much sadness, what groans and what laments our students took from this, when they saw the distraction, or even more the disturbance of my mind. Already this open affair had been successful in deceiving few or no one, saving him, whose shame it principally regarded, I mean the girl's uncle. When some persons occasionally hinted of it to him, he was unable to believe it, both because of his limitless love for his niece, and because of the known continence of my own past life, as I said above. For we do not easily suspect baseness in those whom we love most dearly. Nor in strong love can the disgrace of base suspicion easily take root. St. Jerome says as much in his letter to Sabinianus: "We are usually the last to know the evils of our own household and we ignore the vices of children and spouses, while neighbors sing them." But what is the last to be known, this surely will someday be revealed, and what all have grasped, cannot easily stay hidden from one. Thus, after many months had passed, it happened to us.

Oh, how much sorrow had the uncle in learning this! How much sorrow had the lovers themselves, in their separation! With what shame was I confounded! With what contrition for my mistreatment of the girl was I afflicted! What tides of sorrow had she to bear from my disgrace! We thought not of what had happened to ourselves, but to the other. We wept, not for our own, but for the other's discomfiture. For this division of bodies was the greatest union of our souls, and satisfaction denied so much the more inflamed our love. The past experience of shame made us the more shameless, and as this experience of shame lessened, so the more proper appeared our acts. To us occurred what the poet relates happened to Mars and Venus when they were caught. For not much time later, the girl discovered that she had conceived, and wrote me of this with the highest exultation, asking what I thought should be done concerning this. One night, when her uncle was absent, as we had decided together, I took her secretly from her uncle's house, and without delay I sent her to my homeland. There she lived at the house of my sister, until she gave birth to a male baby, whom she named Astrolabe.

But her uncle after her departure turned nearly mad with anger. The heat with which he burnt, and the shame he felt, no one could know unless he experienced them. What he should do to me, what snares he should lay, he did not know. If he killed me, or in any way injured my body, he especially feared lest his most beloved niece might be punished for it in my homeland. To capture me and force me anywhere against my will he was in no wise able, especially since I had taken precautions against this, because I did not doubt that he would quickly attempt anything he could, or dared to do.

But I took some compassion on his great anxiety, and vehemently accused myself of the deceit which love had caused, as if I had done a supreme betrayal. I went to him, praying and promising the man whatever amends he should set for this. I urged that the affair would appear remarkable to no one who has experienced the power of love, and remembers to what ruin women had cast down even the greatest men, from the very origins of the human race. That I might the better placate him, more than he could have hoped, I offered to satisfy him by joining to me in matrimony the girl I had debased. I asked only that it be kept secret, lest I incur injury to my reputation. He agreed, and by his own faith and that of his people, and by kisses, he entered with me into that concord I asked, in order the more easily to betray me.

7. Then returning to my homeland, I brought back my mistress, that I might make her my wife. She, however, scarcely approved of this. Rather she opposed it for two reasons, both for the danger, and for my own disgrace. She swore that her uncle would never be content with this satisfaction, as was later found to be true. She also asked what glory she could take in me, since she was robbing me of glory, and equally humiliating myself and her. What punishments might the world demand from her, if she deprived it of so great a light? What curses, what injuries to the Church, what tears of philosophers would follow such a wedding? How unfitting, how lamentable it would be, that I, whom nature had intended for all men, should give myself to a single woman, and subject myself to such indignity. She vehemently hated this marriage, since it was shameful for me in every way, and burdensome. She pointed out my infamy and equally the difficulties of marriage, which the Apostle urges us to avoid, saying: *Art thou free from a wife? Do not seek a wife. But if thou takest a wife, thou hast not sinned. And if a virgin marries, she has not sinned. Yet such will have tribulation of the flesh. But I spare you that* (1 Cor. 7.27–28). And again: *I would have you free from care* (*ibid.* v. 32).

If I would accept neither the counsel of the Apostle, nor the exhortations of holy men concerning the great yoke of marriage, I should at least, she said, consult the philosophers, and pay attention to what has been written on this subject by them or concerning them. Often even the saints write thus so to correct us. Such are the words of St. Jerome in the first book *Against Jovinianus.* There he recalls that Theophrastus, after having diligently expounded in great part the unbearable troubles of marriage, and the continuous disturbances, showed with most clear reasons that the wise man should not marry. Then he himself concluded the argument of his philosophic exhortation in these words: "What Christian," he says, "does Theophrastus not confound, reasoning in such a fashion?" Again, in the same book, he says: "Cicero after the divorce of Terentia was asked by Hircius to marry his sister. He altogether refused to do so, saying that he could not give his efforts equally to a wife and philosophy. He does not say 'give his efforts,' but he adds the same idea, not wishing to do anything which could be considered equivalent to the study of philosophy."

But if I now omit this impediment of philosophic study, consider the state itself of honest [family] life. What agreement is there between students and maids, writing desks and cribs, books or tables and distaffs, stiluses or pens and spindles? Who finally, intent on sacred or philosophic meditations, can bear the screams of children, the inane words of nurses who try to sooth them, the tumultuous mob of servants both male and female? Who also shall be able to tolerate the unclean and continuous soilings of babies? That, you will say, the rich can do, whose palaces or ample homes have many rooms, and whose wealth does not feel costs and is not tormented by daily worries. But I say that the status of philosophers is not the same as that of the rich, nor do those who pursue wealth and become engaged in worldly cares devote themselves to theological or philosophical duties. For this reason, the famous philosophers of old despised the world. They did not so much relinquish it as flee it; they renounced all pleasures, that they might rest in the arms of philosophy alone.

Of these philosophers, one and the greatest was Seneca. He so instructed Lucilius: "Not when you have nothing to do should you philosophize. All things are to be abandoned, so that we may pursue this, for which no time is long enough. It doesn't differ much whether you neglect philosophy or interrupt it. For when it is interrupted it does not remain. We must resist distractions; they are not to be extended, but removed." What those among us, who are truly called monks, now endure for the love of God, the noble philosophers among the pagans also bore, for love of philosophy.

For in every people, both pagan and Jewish, or Christian, there have always been some men who excelled in faith or moral distinction over the others, who separated themselves from the people by some special quality of continence or abstinence.

Among the Jews there were of old the Nazarenes, who consecrated themselves to the Lord according to the Law, or the "sons of the prophets," followers of Elias or Eliseus, whom we read were monks in the Old Testament, as blessed Jerome attests. More recently, there were those three sects of philosophy, which Joseph distinguishes in the *Book of Antiquities*, 18, some of whom he calls Pharisees, others Sadducees, and others Essenes. With us, however, the monks either imitated the common life of the apostles, or that older and solitary life of John [the Baptist].

Among the gentiles, however, as has been said, were the philosophers. They applied the name of wisdom or philosophy not so much to the perception of knowledge, as to morality of living, as we learn from the very origin of this name, and also by the witness of holy men. This is what blessed Augustine says, in the eighth book of the *City of God*, as he distinguishes the schools of philosophers: "The Italian school had as its founder Pythagoras the Samian, from whom it is said that the very name philosophy took its origin. Before his time, those who seemed by a certain manner of praiseworthy life to be superior to others were called wise men. When he was asked what was his profession, he answered that he was a philosopher, that is a zealot for and lover of wisdom, since it seemed most arrogant to profess to be wise." Thus, in this place where it is stated, "who seemed by a certain manner of praiseworthy life to be superior to others," it is clearly shown that the wise men of the pagans, that is, the philosophers, were named more in praise of their lives rather than for their knowledge. How soberly and even chastely they lived, it is not our purpose to show by example, lest I seem to be lecturing Minerva herself.

But if laymen and pagans lived in such a fashion, bound by no profession of religion, what should you, as a cleric and canon, do? You should not prefer base pleasures to the divine offices. Let not this Charybdis swallow you headlong. Do not disgracefully and irrevocably sink yourself in these obscenities. If you do not care for the prerogatives of the cleric, defend at least the dignity of the philosopher. If you despise reverence for God, let love for the honest at least temper your rashness.

Remember that Socrates was married, and with how unpleasant

a case did he first wash this stain from philosophy, so that afterwards others by his example should be made more cautious. Nor did Jerome himself omit this point, when he wrote about Socrates in the first book *Against Jovinianus:* "One time, when he had borne up under the unending invective launched against him by Xanthippe from an upper story, he was drenched by dirty water. He said nothing more than this, as he dried his head: 'I knew that after that thunder rain would follow'."

She added finally how perilous it would be for me to marry her, and how much better she would like it, and how much more dignified it would be for me, if she should be called my mistress and not my wife. Then, attractiveness alone would bind me to her, and I would not be constrained by the force of the marriage bond. We would, after we were a while separated, have at our reunions the greater, if rarer joys.

With these and similar arguments, she tried to persuade or dissuade me. When she was not able to bend my stupidity, and did not wish to hurt me, sighing deeply and weeping, she ended her speech with this conclusion: "One thing," she said, "remains at last, that in our mutual ruin, the pain may be no less than the love which preceded it." She did not, as all the world knows, here lack the spirit of prophecy. Commending our baby to the care of my sister, we secretly returned to Paris. Within a few days, after a secret, prayerful vigil held during the night in a certain church, there at the point of morning, in the presence of her uncle and some of my own and his friends, we were joined by the nuptial blessing.

At once we secretly parted, nor did we see each other more, unless rarely and hiddenly, greatly concealing what we had done. But her uncle and his servants, seeking solace for their shame, began to divulge the marriage we had entered, and to violate the faith they had given me in this regard. She, on the other hand, denied it and swore that it was most false. From this the uncle was violently moved, and attacked her with frequent abuse. When I learned this, I sent her to a certain abbey of nuns near Paris, which is called Argenteuil, where she herself once as a young girl had been brought up and instructed. I had prepared for her the habit of a religious, suitable to the convent life, and had her wear it, except the veil. When they heard this, her uncle and his relatives and friends thought that I had now very much deceived them, and had conveniently rid myself of her, by making her a nun. They were greatly disturbed by this, and conspired against me. They bribed one of my servants with money, and one night they took from me a most cruel and shameful vengeance, as I was resting and sleeping in the inner room of my lodging. This punishment the world has learned with the greatest astonishment. For they cut off those parts of my body, by which I had committed the deed which sorrowed them. They turned at once in flight, but two who could be caught lost their eyes and genitals. Of those, one was the servant we have mentioned, who while he remained with me in my service, by greed was led to betray me.

8. At morning, the entire city turned out about me. What shock the populace experienced, what sorrow it suffered, with what shouts they annoyed me, with what complaint they disturbed me, it is difficult, or rather impossible, to express. The clerics above all, and especially our students, tormented me with unbearable laments and groans, so that I suffered more from their compassion than from the pain of the cut. I felt the embarrassment more than the wound, and was more afflicted by shame than by suffering. It occurred to my mind how great my glory once had been, how easily and in a brief incident it had been cast down, or rather entirely extinguished. How I had by the just judgment of God been punished in that part of my body in which I had sinned. How with just betrayal he, whom before I had betrayed, had turned the tables on me. With what praise my enemies would laud such manifest justice. What unending, painful remorse this would bring to my relatives and friends. With what diffusion this singular infamy would spread through the entire world. What way was henceforth open to me, with what face could I go in public, pointed out by the fingers of all, bitten by the tongues of all, destined to be for all a monstrous spectacle.

Nor did it less confound me that according to the killing letter of the Law, so great is God's abomination for eunuchs that men who have been emasculated with the amputation or crushing of their testes are forbidden to enter church, as if they were stinking and unclean. In the sacrifice too, such animals are altogether rejected. The Book of Leviticus says: *You shall not offer to the Lord any beast that hath the testicles bruised, or crushed, or cut and taken away* (Leviticus 22.23). Deuteronomy adds: *A eunuch, whose testicles are broken or cut away, or beard cut off, shall not enter into the church of the Lord* (Deut. 23.1).

The confusion, I admit, of my shame, rather than the devotion of my life compelled me, caught up in so wretched a sorrow, to the recesses of the monastic cloisters. She, who had taken the veil willingly at our command, had first entered a monastery. We thus received at the same time the sacred habit, I in the abbey of Saint-Denis, and she in the monastery of Argenteuil we have mentioned. Many persons, out of sympathy for her, tried in vain to dissuade her youth from the yoke of the monastic rule, as from an intolerable burden. But she, I remember, erupted amid her tears and sighs as best she could, to repeat that complaint of Cornelia, and said:

> Oh greatest husband!
> My bed did not deserve you. Did fortune have
> Power over so great a head? Why did I in impiety marry you,
> If I was to make you wretched? Now accept the penalty
> Which I shall freely pay.   (Lucan, *Pharsalia*, 8.94)

With these words, she moved quickly to the altar, and at once took from it the veil blessed by the bishop. In the eyes of all, she bound herself to the life of a nun.

7. The Preface to Peter Abelard's *Sic et Non*

Sic et Non, Peter Abelard's most famous work, was published in several editions, the first of which appeared probably in 1122. It was an ingenious refutation of the argument that all truth had been stated by the Christian fathers, and that it should be enough for Christians of the present to accept their authority. *Sic et Non* showed the apparent contradictions of patristic and Scriptural texts on 158 questions, and implied that only by intense examination and use of dialectical analysis would their meaning be understood and the truth advanced.

The Preface to *Sic et Non* is taken from *Readings in European History*, ed. James Harvey Robinson (Boston and New York: Ginn and Co., 1904), pp. 450–51.

189. Abelard's Yea and Nay

THERE are many seeming contradictions and even obscurities in the innumerable writings of the Church fathers. Our respect for their authority should not stand in the way of an effort on our part to come at the truth. The obscurity and contradictions in ancient writings may be explained upon many grounds, and may be discussed without impugning the good faith and insight of the fathers. A writer may use different terms to mean the same thing, in order to avoid a monotonous repetition of the same word. Common, vague words may be employed in order that the common people may understand; and sometimes a writer sacrifices perfect accuracy in the interest of a clear general statement. Poetical, figurative language is often obscure and vague.

Not infrequently apocryphal works are attributed to the saints. Then, even the best authors often introduce the erroneous views of others and leave the reader to distinguish between the true and the false. Sometimes, as Augustine confesses in his own case, the fathers ventured to rely upon the opinions of others.

Doubtless the fathers might err; even Peter, the prince of the apostles, fell into error; what wonder that the saints do not always show themselves inspired? The fathers did not themselves believe that they, or their companions, were always right. Augustine found himself mistaken in some cases and did not hesitate to retract his errors. He warns his admirers not to look upon his letters as they would upon the Scriptures, but to accept only those things which, upon examination, they find to be true.

All writings belonging to this class are to be read with full freedom to criticize, and with no obligation to accept unquestioningly; otherwise the way would be blocked to all discussion, and posterity be deprived of the excellent intellectual exercise of debating difficult questions of language and presentation. But an explicit exception must be made in the case of the Old and New Testaments. In the Scriptures, when anything strikes us as absurd, we may not say that the writer erred, but that the scribe made a blunder in copying the manuscripts, or that there is an error in interpretation, or that the passage is not understood. The fathers make a very careful distinction between the Scriptures and later works. They advocate a discriminating, not to say suspicious, use of the writings of their own contemporaries.

In view of these considerations, I have ventured to bring together various dicta of the holy fathers, as they came to mind, and to formulate certain questions which were suggested by the seeming contradictions in the statements. These questions ought to serve to excite tender readers to a zealous inquiry into truth and so sharpen their wits. The master key of knowledge is, indeed, a persistent and frequent questioning. Aristotle, the most clear-sighted of all the philosophers, was desirous above all things else to arouse this questioning spirit, for in his *Categories* he exhorts a student as follows: "It may well be difficult to reach a positive conclusion in these matters unless they be frequently discussed. It is by no means fruitless to be doubtful on particular points." By doubting we come to examine, and by examining we reach the truth.

[Abelard supplies one hundred and fifty-eight problems, carefully balancing the authorities pro and con, and leaves the student to solve each problem as best he may. The following will serve as examples of the questions Abelard raised:]

Should human faith be based upon reason, or no?
Is God one, or no?
Is God a substance, or no?
Does the first Psalm refer to Christ, or no?
Is sin pleasing to God, or no?
Is God the author of evil, or no?
Is God all-powerful, or no?
Can God be resisted, or no?
Has God free will, or no?
Was the first man persuaded to sin by the devil, or no?
Was Adam saved, or no?
Did all the apostles have wives except John, or no?
Are the flesh and blood of Christ in very truth and essence present in the sacrament of the altar, or no?
Do we sometimes sin unwillingly, or no?
Does God punish the same sin both here and in the future, or no?
Is it worse to sin openly than secretly, or no?

ᒫᒪᒫᒪᒫᒪᒫᒪᒫᒪᒫᒪᒫᒪᒫᒪᒫᒪᒫᒪᒫᒪᒫᒪᒫᒪᒫᒪ

8. The Confession of Golias

The world of the medieval student is revealed to us not only through charters and heavy treatises on learned subjects, but also in student songs celebrating the beauties of spring, the joy of youth, and the delights of love and wine. This poetry is called "Goliardic" verse. For unknown reasons, "Golias" came to serve as the mythical hero or patron saint of the wandering students. Goliardic poetry is distinguished by its clever manipulation of rimes, amusing parodies of even sacred phrases, and by its infectious spirit of fun.

Perhaps the most famous of the medieval student songs is the *Confession of Golias*. It was written by a cleric known only under the name of the "archpoet," who wandered through Italy in the company of Reginald von Dassel, archbishop of Cologne and chancellor of the Emperor Frederick I Barbarossa. He died probably about 1165. In tones of joyous irreverence he here defends his characteristic weaknesses for women, gambling and drink.

The translation is taken from John Addington Symonds, *Wine, Women and Song* (New York: G. P. Putnam, 1909), pp. 69–78.

> Boiling in my spirit's veins
> With fierce indignation,
> From my bitterness of soul
> Springs self-revelation:
> Framed am I of flimsy stuff,
> Fit for levitation,
> Like a thin leaf which the wind
> Scatters from its station.
>
> While it is the wise man's part
> With deliberation
> On a rock to base his heart's
> Permanent foundation,
> With a running river I
> Find my just equation,
> Which beneath the self-same sky
> Hath no habitation.
>
> Carried am I like a ship
> Left without a sailor,
> Like a bird that through the air
> Flies where tempests hale her;
> Chains and fetters hold me not,
> Naught avails a jailer;
> Shall I find my fellows out
> Toper, gamester, railer.

To my mind all gravity
   Is a grave subjection;
Sweeter far than honey are
   Jokes and free affection.
All that Venus bids me do,
   Do I with erection,
For she ne'er in heart of man
   Dwelt with dull dejection.

Down the broad road do I run,
   As the way of youth is;
Snare myself in sin, and ne'er
   Think where faith and truth is,
Eager far for pleasure more
   Than soul's health, the sooth is,
For this flesh of mine I care,
   Seek not ruth where ruth is.

Prelate, most discreet of priests,
   Grant me absolution!
Dear's the death whereof I die,
   Sweet my dissolution;
For my heart is wounded by
   Beauty's soft suffusion;
All the girls I come not nigh,
   Mine are in illusion.

'Tis most arduous to make
   Nature's self surrender;
Seeing girls, to blush and be
   Purity's defender!
We young men our longings ne'er
   Shall to stern law render,
Or preserve our fancies from
   Bodies smooth and tender.

Who, when into fire he falls,
   Keeps himself from burning?
Who within Pavia's walls
   Fame of chaste is earning?

Venus with her finger calls
   Youth at every turning,
Snares them with her eyes, and thralls
   With her amorous yearning.

If you brought Hippolitus
   To Pavia Sunday,
He'd not be Hippolitus
   On the following Monday;
Venus there keeps holiday
   Every day as one day;
'Mid these towers in no tower dwells
   Venus Verecunda.

In the second place I own
   To the vice of gaming:
Cold indeed outside I seem,
   Yet my soul is flaming:
But when once the dice-box hath
   Stripped me to my shaming,
Make I songs and verses fit
   For the world's acclaiming.

In the third place, I will speak
   Of the tavern's pleasure;
For I never found nor find
   There the least displeasure;
Nor shall find it till I greet
   Angels without measure,
Singing requiems for the souls
   In eternal leisure.

In the public-house to die
   Is my resolution;
Let wine to my lips be nigh
   At life's dissolution:
That will make the angels cry,
   With glad elocution,
"Grant this toper, God on high,
   Grace and absolution!"

With the cup the soul lights up,
  Inspirations flicker;
Nectar lifts the soul on high
  With its heavenly ichor:
To my lips a sounder taste
  Hath the tavern's liquor
Than the wine a village clerk
  Waters for the vicar.

Nature gives to every man
  Some gift serviceable;
Write I never could nor can
  Hungry at the table;
Fasting, any stripling to
  Vanquish me is able;
Hunger, thirst, I liken to
  Death that ends the fable.

Nature gives to every man
  Gifts as she is willing;
I compose my verses when
  Good wine I am swilling,
Wine the best for jolly guest
  Jolly hosts are filling;
From such wine rare fancies fine
  Flow like dews distilling.

Such my verse is wont to be
  As the wine I swallow;
No ripe thoughts enliven me
  While my stomach's hollow;
Hungry wits on hungry lips
  Like a shadow follow,
But when once I'm in my cups,
  I can beat Apollo.

Never to my spirit yet
  Flew poetic vision
Until first my belly had
  Plentiful provision;

Let but Bacchus in the brain
  Take a strong position,
Then comes Phoebus flowing in
  With a fine precision.

There are poets, worthy men,
  Shrink from public places,
And in lurking-hole or den
  Hide their pallid faces;
There they study, sweat, and woo
  Pallas and the Graces,
But bring nothing forth to view
  Worth the girls' embraces.

Fasting, thirsting, toil the bards,
  Swift years flying o'er them;
Shun the strife of open life,
  Tumults of the forum;
They, to sing some deathless thing,
  Lest the world ignore them,
Die the death, expend their breath,
  Drowned in dull decorum.

Lo! my frailties I've betrayed,
  Shown you every token,
Told you what your servitors
  Have against me spoken;
But of those men each and all
  Leave their sins unspoken,
Though they play, enjoy today,
  Scorn their pledges broken.

Now within the audience-room
  Of this blessèd prelate,
Sent to hunt out vice, and from
  Hearts of men expel it;
Let him rise, nor spare the bard,
  Cast at him a pellet:
He whose heart knows not crime's smart,
  Show my sin and tell it!

I have uttered openly
All I knew that shamed me,
And have spewed the poison forth
That so long defamed me;
Of my old ways I repent,
New life hath reclaimed me;
God beholds the heart—'twas man
Viewed the face and blamed me.

Goodness now hath won my love,
I am wroth with vices:
Made a new man in my mind,
Lo, my soul arises!
Like a babe new milk I drink—
Milk for me suffices,
Lest my heart should longer be
Filled with vain devices.

Thou Elect of fair Cologne,
Listen to my pleading!
Spurn not thou the penitent;
See, his heart is bleeding!
Give me penance! what is due
For my faults exceeding
I will bear with willing cheer,
All thy precepts heeding.

Lo, the lion, king of beasts,
Spares the meek and lowly;
Toward submissive creatures he
Tames his anger wholly.
Do the like, ye powers of earth,
Temporal and holy!
Bitterness is more than's right
When 'tis bitter solely.

Lⁿⁿⁿⁿⁿⁿⁿⁿⁿⁿⁿⁿⁿⁿⁿⁿⁿⁿⁿⁿⁿⁿⁿⁿⁿⁿⁿr

9. Two charters granted to the University of Paris

The following two charters laid the foundations for the immunities
and privileges enjoyed by the masters and students of Paris during the
Middle Ages. The first, granted by King Philip II Augustus of France
in 1200, exempted students from the authority of the city government of Paris. The second, the bull *Parens Scientiarum* of Pope
Gregory IX in 1231, accorded wide autonomy to the masters of Paris
in the government of their affairs. It leaves beyond doubt that the
Parisian masters by that year constituted a true university.

The charters are taken from *Translations and Reprints from the Original Sources of European History*, Vol. II, No. 3 (Philadelphia: University of Pennsylvania, 1902), pp. 4–11.

Royal Privilege of 1200
In the name of the sacred and indivisible Trinity, amen. Philip,
by the grace of God, king of the French. Let all men know, now
and in the future, that for the terrible crime owing to which five
of the clergy and laity at Paris were killed by certain malefactors,
we shall do justice as follows: that Thomas, then provost, concerning whom more than all others the students have complained,
because he denies the deed, we shall consign to perpetual imprisonment, in close confinement, with meager fare, as long as he shall
live; unless, perchance, he shall choose to undergo publicly at
Paris the ordeal by water. If he attempts that and fails, he shall
be condemned. If he succeeds, never henceforth at Paris nor anywhere else in our own land shall he be our provost or bailiff; nor
elsewhere, if we are able to prevent it; nor shall he in the future
enter Paris.

And if through the full and legal examination, which we have
entrusted to two of our faithful servants, Walter, the chamberlain,
and Philip de Levis [to be conducted] without making any exception of persons, by the invocation of the Christian faith and by
the fidelity which they owe to us, their liege lord, and through the
oath which they have sworn to us concerning our honor and ad-

vice, we are able to learn what further we can and ought to do in the matter, we will do it without any hesitation, for God's honor and our own. Moreover, concerning the others who are in prison for the same crime, we will act thus: we will detain them in perpetual imprisonment, in our custody, unless they prefer to undergo the ordeal by water and to prove their innocence by God's witness. If they fail in that, we shall consider them condemned; unless, perchance, some of them having been fully tried shall be found innocent, or being found less guilty, shall be freed from captivity by us, on the intercession of the scholars. Those, moreover, who have fled we consider *ipso facto* condemned, and we shall cause all the counts in our land to swear that they will diligently seek them out and if they are able to seize any one of them, they will seize him and send him to us at Paris.

Also, concerning the safety of the students at Paris in the future, by the advice of our subjects we have ordained as follows: we will cause all the citizens of Paris to swear that if any one sees an injury done to any student by any layman, he will testify truthfully to this, nor will any one withdraw in order not to see [the act]. And if it shall happen that any one strikes a student, except in self-defense, especially if he strikes the student with a weapon, a club or a stone, all laymen who see [the act] shall in good faith seize the malefactor or malefactors and deliver them to our judge; nor shall they withdraw in order not to see the act, or seize the malefactor, or testify to the truth. Also, whether the malefactor is seized in open crime or not, we will make a legal and full examination through clerks or laymen or certain lawful persons; and our count and our judges shall do the same. And if by a full examination we or our judges are able to learn that he who is accused, is guilty of the crime, then we or our judges shall immediately inflict a penalty, according to the quality and nature of the crime; notwithstanding the fact that the criminal may deny the deed and say that he is ready to defend himself in single combat, or to purge himself by the ordeal by water.

Also, neither our provost nor our judges shall lay hands on a student for any offense whatever; nor shall they place him in our prison, unless such a crime has been committed by the student, that he ought to be arrested. And in that case, our judge shall arrest him on the spot, without striking him at all, unless he resists, and shall hand him over to the ecclesiastical judge, who ought to guard him in order to satisfy us and the one suffering the injury. And if a serious crime has been committed, our judge shall go or shall send to see what is done with the student. If, indeed, the student does not resist arrest and yet suffers any injury, we will exact satisfaction for it, according to the aforesaid examination and the aforesaid oath. Also our judges shall not lay hands on the chattels of the students at Paris for any crime whatever. But if it shall seem that these ought to be sequestrated, they shall be sequestrated and guarded after sequestration by the ecclesiastical judge, in order that whatever is judged legal by the Church, may be done with the chattels. But if students are arrested by our count at such an hour that the ecclesiastical judge can not be found and be present at once, our provost shall cause the culprits to be guarded in some student's house without any ill-treatment, as is said above, until they are delivered to the ecclesiastical judge.

Concerning the lay servants of the students, who do not owe to us *burgensiam* or *residentiam*, and do not live by traffic, and through whom the scholars do not do any injury to any one, it shall be as follows: neither we nor our judge shall lay hands on them unless they commit an open crime, for which we or our judge ought to arrest them. In accordance, truly, with the tenor of the privilege which we have granted to the students at Paris, we are not willing that the canons of Paris and their servants should be included in this privilege. But we wish the servants of the canons at Paris and the canons of the same city to have the same liberty which our predecessors ought to have granted to them and which we ought to. Also, on account of the above-mentioned conventions or on account of this charter, we shall not be liable to lawsuit except in our own courts.

In order, moreover, that these [decrees] may be kept more carefully and may be established forever by a fixed law, we have decided that our present provost and the people of Paris shall affirm by an oath, in the presence of the scholars, that they will carry out in good faith all the above-mentioned. And always in the future, whosoever receives from us the office of provost in Paris, among the other initiatory acts of his office, namely, on the first or second Sunday, in one of the churches of Paris,—after he has been summoned for the purpose—shall affirm by an oath, publicly in the presence of the scholars, that he will keep in good faith all the above-mentioned. And that these decrees may be valid forever, we have ordered this document to be confirmed by the authority of our seal and by the characters of the royal name, signed below.

Done near Betisi in the 1200th year of the Incarnation of our Lord, in the 21st year of our reign, those being present in our palace whose names and signs are placed below. The office of Seneschal vacant. Seal of Guy, the Cup-bearer. Seal of Matthew, the Chamberlain. Seal of Drogo, the Constable. Done during a vacancy (monogram) in the Chancellorship.

Parens Scientiarum, 1231

Gregory, the bishop, servant of the servants of God, to his beloved sons, all the masters and students at Paris—greeting and apostolic benediction.

Paris, the mother of sciences, like another Cariath Sepher, a city of letters, stands forth illustrious, great indeed, but concerning herself she causes greater things to be desired, full of favor for the teachers and students. There, as in a special factory of wisdom, she has silver as the beginnings of her veins, and of gold is the spot in which according to law they flow together; from which the prudent mystics of eloquence fabricate golden necklaces inlaid with silver, and making collars ornamented with precious stones of inestimable value, adorn and decorate the spouse of Christ. There the iron is raised from the earth, because, when the earthly fragility is solidified by strength, the breastplate of faith, the sword of the spirit, and the other weapons of the Christian soldier, powerful against the brazen powers, are formed from it. And the stone melted by heat, is turned into brass, because the hearts of stone, enkindled by the fervor of the Holy Ghost, at times glow, burn and become sonorous, and by preaching herald the praises of Christ.

Accordingly, it is undoubtedly very displeasing to God and men that any one in the aforesaid city should strive in any way to disturb so illustrious grace, or should not oppose himself openly and with all his strength to any who do so. Wherefore, since we have diligently investigated the questions referred to us concerning a dissension which, through the instigation of the devil, has arisen there and greatly disturbed the university, we have decided, by the advice of our brethren, that these should be set at rest rather by precautionary measures, than by a judicial sentence.

Therefore, concerning the condition of the students and schools, we have decided that the following should be observed: each chancellor, appointed hereafter at Paris, at the time of his installation, in the presence of the bishop, or at the command of the latter in the chapter at Paris—two masters of the students having been summoned for this purpose and present in behalf of the university—shall swear that, in good faith, according to his conscience, he will not receive as professors of theology and canon law any but suitable men, at a suitable place and time, according to the condition of the city and the honor and glory of those branches of learning; and he will reject all who are unworthy without respect to persons or nations. Before licensing any one, during three months, dating from the time when the license is requested, the chancellor shall make diligent inquiries of all the masters of theology present in the city, and of all other honest and learned men through whom the truth can be ascertained, concerning the life, knowledge, capacity, purpose, prospects and other qualities needful in such persons; and after the inquiries, in good faith and according to his conscience, he shall grant or deny the license to the candidate, as shall seem fitting and expedient. The masters of theology and canon law, when they begin to lecture, shall take a public oath that they will give true testimony on the above points. The chancellor shall also swear, that he will in no way reveal the advice of the masters, to their injury; the liberty and privileges being maintained in their full vigor for the canons at Paris, as they were in the beginning. Moreover, the chancellor shall promise to examine in good faith the masters in medicine and arts and in the other branches, to admit only the worthy and to reject the unworthy.

In other matters, because confusion easily creeps in where there is no order, we grant to you the right of making constitutions and ordinances regulating the manner and time of lectures and disputations, the costume to be worn, the burial of the dead; and also concerning the bachelors, who are to lecture and at what hours, and on what they are to lecture; and concerning the prices of the lodgings or the interdiction of the same; and concerning a fit punishment for those who violate your constitutions or ordinances, by exclusion from your society. And if, perchance, the assessment of the lodgings is taken from you, or anything else is lacking, or an injury or outrageous damage, such as death or the mutilation of a limb, is inflicted on one of you, unless through a suitable admonition satisfaction is rendered within fifteen days, you may suspend your lectures until you have received full satisfaction. And if it happens that any one of you is unlawfully imprisoned, unless the injury ceases on a remonstrance from you, you may, if you judge it expedient, suspend your lectures immediately.

We command, moreover, that the bishop of Paris shall so chastise the excesses of the guilty, that the honor of the student shall be preserved and evil deeds shall not remain unpunished. But in no way shall the innocent be seized on account of the guilty; nay rather, if a probable suspicion arises against any one, he shall be detained honorably and on giving suitable bail he shall be freed, without any exactions from the jailors. But if, perchance, such a crime has been committed that imprisonment is necessary, the bishop shall detain the criminal in his prison. The chancellor is forbidden to keep him in his prison. We also forbid holding a student for a debt contracted by another, since this is interdicted by canonical and legitimate sanctions. Neither the bishop, nor his officials nor the chancellor shall exact a pecuniary penalty for removing an excommunication or any other censure of any kind. Nor shall the chancellor demand from the masters who are licensed an oath, or obedience, or any pledge; nor shall he receive any emolument or promise for granting a license, but be content with the above-mentioned oath.

Also, the vacation in summer is not to exceed one month, and the bachelors, if they wish, can continue their lectures in vacation time. Moreover, we prohibit more expressly the students from carrying weapons in the city, and the university from protecting those who disturb the peace and study. And those who call themselves students, but do not frequent the schools, or acknowledge any master, are in no way to enjoy the liberties of the students.

Moreover, we order that the masters in arts shall alway read one lecture on Priscian, and one book after the other in the regular courses. Those books on natural philosophy which for a certain reason were prohibited in a provincial council, are not to be used at Paris until they have been examined and purged of all suspicion of error. The masters and students in theology shall strive to exercise themselves laudably in the branch which they profess; they shall not show themselves philosophers, but they shall strive to become God's learned. And they shall not speak in the language of the people, confounding the sacred language with the profane. In the schools they shall dispute only on such questions as can be determined by theological books and the writings of the holy fathers.

Also, about the property of the scholars who die intestate or do not commit the arrangement of their affairs to others, we have determined to arrange thus: namely, that the bishop and one of the masters, whom the university shall appoint for this purpose, shall receive all the property of the defunct, and placing it in a suitable and safe spot, shall fix a certain date, before which his death can be announced in his native country, and those who ought to succeed to his property may come to Paris or send a suitable messenger. And if they come or send, the goods shall be restored to them, with the security which shall have been given. If no one appears, then the bishop and masters shall expend the property for the soul of the departed, as seems expedient; unless, perchance, the heirs shall have been prevented from coming by some good reason. In that case, the distribution shall be deferred to a fitting time.

Truly, because the masters and students, who harassed by damages and injuries, have taken a mutual oath to depart from Paris and have broken up the school, have seemed to be waging a contest not so much for their own benefit as for the common good; we, consulting the needs and advantages of the whole Church, wish and command that after the privileges have been granted to the masters and students by our most dearly beloved son in Christ, the illustrious king of the French, and amends have been paid by the malefactors, they shall study at Paris and shall not be marked by any infamy or irregularity on account of their staying away or return.

It is not lawful for any man whatever to infringe this deed of our provision, constitution, concession, prohibition and inhibition or to act contrary to it, from rash presumption. If any one, however, should dare to attempt this, let him know that he incurs the wrath of almighty God and of the blessed Peter and Paul, his apostles.

Given at the Lateran, on the Ides of April, in the fifth year of our pontificate.

10. Thomas Aquinas' proofs for the existence of God

In his *Summa Theologica*, Thomas Aquinas advanced what are perhaps the most famous proofs for the existence of God in the entire history of philosophy. His arguments also give a good example of the characteristic scholastic method of reasoning. The method consisted of four clearly differentiated parts: (1) the question; (2) the objections, giving arguments supporting what will eventually be rejected as the wrong answer; (3) the response to the question, correctly answering it and giving proofs drawn both from authority and reason; and (4) the replies to the objections. It should be understood that "motion," as Thomas uses it, refers not so much to physical movement but to change. He is in fact saying that instability, which we experience at every turn in this life, presumes the existence of an ultimate, stable principle in the universe, which is God.

It is interesting to note that Objection 2, in Question 2, Article 1, is Anselm's famous "ontological" proof for the existence of God, which Aquinas rejects as invalid.

The Latin text may be found in *Sancti Thomae Aquinatis doctoris angelici ordinis praedicatorum opera omnia* (New York: Musurgia, 1948), I, 7–9. The translation is by D. Herlihy.

Question 2
Concerning God, whether there is a God
(divided into three articles)

SINCE therefore the principal aim of sacred learning is to teach the knowledge of God, not only as he is in himself, but also as he is the beginning and the end of things, and especially of the rational creature [man], as is clear from what has been said (Article 7 of the preceding question). In order to explain this teaching, we shall treat (1) concerning God, (2) concerning the movement of the rational creature towards God, and (3) concerning Christ, who, by reason of the fact that he is man, offers us the way of attaining God.

Our consideration of God shall fall into three parts, for we shall consider (1) those things which are characteristic of the divine essence, (2) those things which regard the distinction of the persons, and (3) those things which regard the procession of creatures from God.

Concerning the divine essence, we must consider (1) whether there is a God, (2) how he exists, or rather, how he does not exist, and (3) those things which pertain to his actions, that is, his knowledge, will and power.

Concerning the first point, three things will be investigated: (1) whether it is self-evident that God exists, (2) whether his existence can be proved, and (3) whether there is a God.

The first article:
Whether the existence of God is self-evident.

We thus proceed to the first article.

[Objections:] 1. It seems that the existence of God is self-evident. We say that those things are self-evident a knowledge of which is naturally implanted in us, as is clear in regard to first principles. But, as John Damascene says in the beginning of *De Fide Orthod.* 1.1-3, "An understanding of the existence of God is naturally set within everyone." Therefore the existence of God is self-evident.

2. Moreover, those things are said to be self-evident which are known as soon as the terms are defined, which the Philosopher says is true of the first principles of demonstration, in *Post. Anal.* 1.2. For once it is understood what is the whole, and what a part, it is at once understood that every whole is greater than its part. But once it is understood what the name God means, it is grasped at once that God exists. For this name means that than which a greater cannot be named. But it is a greater thing to exist in fact and in mind, than in the mind alone. Therefore, when the name God is understood and it comes at once to exist in the mind, it follows that it exists also in reality. Therefore the existence of God is self-evident.

3. Moreover, the proposition that truth exists is self-evident, because whoever denies that truth exists, concedes that truth does not exist. If therefore truth does not exist, it is true that truth does not exist. But if anything at all be true, it follows necessarily that truth exists. But God is truth itself; *I am the way, the truth and the life* (John 14.6). Therefore the existence of God is self-evident.

On the contrary, no one can conceive the opposite of that which is self-evident, as is made clear by the Philosopher in *Metaphys.* 4.9 and *Post. Anal.* 1, last passage (towards the middle) and passage 5 (towards the end), in regard to the first principles of demonstration. But it is possible to conceive the opposite of the proposition "God exists," as the Psalmist says: *The fool said in his heart, there is no God* (Ps. 52.1). Therefore the existence of God is not self-evident.

I reply that it must be said that a thing can be self-evident in two ways. In the first way, in itself, but not for us; in the second, in itself, and also for us. A proposition is self-evident when the predicate is included in the meaning of the subject, as: Man is an animal. For animal is part of the meaning of man. If therefore everyone knows the meaning of the predicate and the subject, that proposition shall be self-evident to all, as is clear in regard to the first principles of demonstration, the terms of which are certain common notions known to all, such as being or non-being, whole and part, and the like. If however some persons do not understand what the predicate and subject mean, the proposition, in itself, will be self-evident, but not for those who do not understand the subject and predicate. As Boethius says towards the beginning of his book *De Hebd.* (the title of which is: "Whether everything that is, is good"), there are certain common mental concepts which are self-evident only to the learned, for example, that beings without a body do not exist in space. I therefore say that this proposition, God is, is self-evident in itself, because the predicate is contained in the subject. For God is his own existence, as shall be evident below, Question 3, Article 4. But because we do not know what God is, the existence of God is not self-evident for us. Rather, it must be demonstrated through those things which are better known to us (although less known in their nature), that is, through his effects.

[Replies to objections:] 1. Here it must be said that the knowledge of God's existence in a general and confused way is naturally implanted in us, since God is man's happiness. For man naturally desires happiness. And what is naturally desired by man, is naturally known by him. But this is not absolutely to recognize the existence of God, just as to recognize that someone is coming is not to recognize Peter, although it is Peter who is coming. For some men think that man's greatest good, which is happiness, consists in riches; others in pleasures, and others in something else.

2. Here it must be said that perhaps he who hears the name God does not understand that it means something than which a greater cannot be conceived. For some may believe that God is a body. But let it be conceded that a person understands that the name God means that which has been said, namely, that than which a greater cannot be conceived. It does not, however, follow from this, that he recognizes that that which is meant by the name exists in the world of nature, but only in the understanding of the intellect. For it cannot be argued that it exists in nature, unless it is conceded that there is something in nature than which a greater cannot be conceived. But this is not conceded by those who affirm that God does not exist.

3. Here it must be said that the existence of truth in general is self-evident, but the existence of a First Truth is not self-evident for us.

The second article:
Whether the existence of God can be proved.

We thus proceed to the second article.

[Objections:] 1. It seems that the existence of God cannot be proved. For the existence of God is an article of faith. But those things which are of faith cannot be proved, because proof brings certain knowledge. Faith however concerns those things which are not seen, as is evident in Paul, *Heb.* 11. Therefore the existence of God cannot be proved.

2. Moreover, the means of proof is that which is. But we cannot know concerning God what he is, but only what he is not, as John Damascene says, *De Fide Orthod.* 1.4. Therefore we cannot prove that God exists.

3. Moreover, if it could be proved that God exists, this could only be from his effects. But his effects are not proportionate to him, since he is infinite, and his effects finite. There is, however, no proportion between the finite and the infinite. Since, therefore, a cause cannot be demonstrated through effects not proportionate to it, it seems that the existence of God cannot be proved.

On the contrary, the Apostle says: *The invisible things of him are clearly seen, being understood by the things that are made* (*Rom.* 1.20). But this would not be, unless through the things which are made it was possible to prove the existence of God. For the first thing which must be known of anything is whether it exists.

I reply that it must be said that there are two types of proof. One is through the cause, and it is called *propter quid*, and this is to argue through what comes before absolutely. The other is through effect, and is called the demonstration *quia*, and this is to argue through those things which come earlier in our own regard. For when an effect is more evident to us than its cause, we proceed through the effect to an understanding of the cause. From any effect it is possible to prove the existence of a proper cause for it, if its effects are better known in our regard. For since effects depend on a cause, if the effect is posited, the cause must have existed before it. Whether there is a God, in as much as it is not self-evident to us, can be proved through his effects which are known to us.

[Replies to objections:] 1. Here it must be said that the existence of God, and other, similar propositions, which can be known through natural reason concerning God (as is said in Rom. 1) are not articles of faith, but preambles to the articles. For faith presupposes natural knowledge, just as grace presupposes nature, and perfection the perfectible. But nothing prevents anyone, who cannot understand a proof, from accepting on faith that which in itself is provable and knowable.

2. Here it must be said that when a cause is proved by an effect, it is necessary to use the effect in place of a definition of the cause in proving its existence. And this especially applies in regard to God, because to prove that something exists is to accept as the middle term the meaning of its name, not however what it is (because the question what it is follows the question whether it is). But the names of God are given him from his effects, as shall later be shown (Question 13, Article 1). Therefore, in proving that God exists from his effect, we may take as the middle term the meaning of the name God.

3. Here it must be said that through effects not proportionate to their cause, a perfect knowledge of the cause cannot be had. However, from the effect it can be manifestly proved to us that there is a cause, as has been said (in the body of the article). Thus, from the effects of God it can be proved that there is a God, although through them we cannot perfectly know him in his essence.

The third article:
Whether there is a God.
We thus proceed to the third article.

[Objections:] 1. It seems that there is no God. For if one of two contraries were infinite, the other would be totally destroyed. But this is understood in the name God, that is, that he is a certain infinite good. If therefore there were a God, there would be no evil to be found. But evil is found in the world. Therefore there is no God.

2. Moreover, whatever can be explained through fewer principles, should not be explained through more. But it seems that everything which appears in the world can be explained through other principles, on the assumption that God does not exist. For those things which are natural are explained by the principle which is nature. Those things which are volitional are explained by the principle which is human reason, or will. There is therefore no necessity to posit the existence of God.

On the contrary, it is said in *Exod.* 3.14 concerning the person of God: *I am who am.*

I reply that the existence of God can be shown in five ways.

The first and more evident way is that which is taken from motion. It is certain, and established by the senses, that some things are being moved in this world. But everything which is moved is moved by another. For nothing is moved, unless it is in potency to that to which it is moved. A being does the moving, to the extent that it is in act. For motion is nothing else but the bringing of something from potency to act. A being can be brought from potency to act only through a being which is in act. Thus, something actually hot, like fire, makes something potentially hot, like wood, to be actually hot. Thus it moves and changes it. It is not, however, possible that the same being be at the same time in potency and in act in regard to the same quality, but only in regard to different qualities. That which is actually hot, cannot at the same time be potentially hot, but is rather at that time potentially cold. It is therefore impossible that anything, in regard to the same quality, and in the same fashion, be both mover and moved, that is, that it move itself. Therefore, everything which is moved must be moved by another. If then that by which it is moved should also be moved, it too must be moved by another, and that by another. This however cannot go on forever, for if there were not any first mover, there then would be no other mover moving anything else. For the secondary movers move only by virtue of the fact that they are moved by the first mover. Thus the staff moves only by reason of the fact that it is moved by the hand. Therefore it is necessary to arrive at a certain first mover, which is moved by nothing. And this being everyone knows to be God.

The second way is by reason of efficient cause. For we find in sensible things that there is an order of efficient causes. But it is not found, nor is it possible, that something be the efficient cause of itself, for it would have to be prior to itself, which is impossible. Nor is it possible in regard to efficient causes to proceed into infinity. For in all ordered efficient causes, the first is cause of the middle, and the middle of the last, whether there be many middle causes, or only one. But if the cause be removed, so also is the effect. Therefore, if there were not a first among the efficient causes, there would not be a last, nor a middle. But if one proceeds into eternity in regard to efficient causes, there would not be a first efficient cause, and thus there would not be a final effect, nor intermediary efficient causes. But this is evidently false. Therefore it is necessary to posit some first efficient cause, which all men name as God.

The third way is taken from the possible and the necessary, which is the following. We find in nature some beings which are able to be and not to be, since such things are found to be generated and to decay. Consequently, they can be and not be. But it is impossible that all things which are so constituted always were, because that which is able not to exist, at some time did not exist. If therefore all things were able not to be, at one time nothing was. But if this were true, even now nothing would exist, because that which has no existence cannot begin to exist unless through something which does exist. If therefore there was [at some time] nothing in existence, it was impossible that anything began to be, and thus nothing would now be. But this is clearly false. Therefore not all beings can be possible beings, but there must be a necessary being in nature. Every necessary being either has the cause of its necessity elsewhere, or it does not. It is however not possible to proceed into eternity in regard to necessary beings which have a cause of their necessity, any more than with regard to efficient causes, as has been proved (in this article). Therefore it is necessary to posit that something exists which is necessary in itself, not having the cause of its necessity elsewhere, but which is the cause of the necessity of other beings. This all men call God.

The fourth way is taken from the gradations which are found in nature. For there are found in nature things which are more or less good, and true, and noble, and thus for other similar qualities. But more and less are said of variants, according to the extent that they approach in different measure something which is the highest. Thus, the hotter is that which more closely approaches the highest heat. There is therefore a being which is most true, and excellent and noble; which is consequently a being in the truest sense. For those things which are supreme in truth, are supreme in being, as is said *Metaphs*. 2.4. What is said to be the supreme in any genus, is the cause of all things which are of that genus. Thus fire, which is supremely hot, is the cause of all hot things, as is said in the same book. Therefore, there is something which is to all beings the cause of their being, and their goodness, and any other perfection. And this being we call God.

The fifth way is taken from the governance of things. For we see that some things which lack intelligence, such as natural bodies, operate for an end. This is evident for the reason that always, or usually, they operate in the same fashion, so that they obtain that which is best. From this it is clear that they arrive at their purpose not by accident, but by intention. Those things however which do not have understanding, do not move towards an end unless directed by a being which does understand and think, as the arrow is directed by the marksman. There is therefore some intelligent being, by which all natural things are ordered to their end. And this being we call God.

[Replies to objections:] 1. Here it must be said with Augustine in *Enchir.* 11 (at the beginning), "Since God is supremely good, he would by no means allow anything evil among his works, unless he was so powerful and good, that he can bring good even out of evil."

2. Here it must be said that since nature for a determined end acts from the direction of some superior agent, it is necessary that those things which are done by nature be explained by God as their first cause. So likewise, whatever is done voluntarily, must be explained by some higher cause, which could not be human reason or will. For these are changeable and fallible. For all things changeable and fallible must be brought back to some first, immovable principle, necessary in itself, as has been shown (in the body of the article).

III. The literature of feudal society

ЛЛЛЛЛЛЛЛЛЛЛЛЛЛЛЛЛЛЛЛ

11. Troubadour lyric poetry

The troubadour lyric poetry of southern France was written in a great variety of forms. The most important were the *canso* or "song," usually dealing with love; the *tenso*, or debate, again usually on a point of love; the *sirventes*, or poem dealing with political, religious or moral topics; and the *alba*, or "dawn song," which describes the parting of lovers at sunrise. The poets also produced a wide variety of verse and rime schemes, as it was felt that a metrical pattern once used should not be repeated.

The most important source of inspiration of troubadour poetry was love. Conceiving of love as a redemptive passion, the theoreticians of the art of love also divided the experience into distinct steps or stages. One common division singled out four stages of love. The first was "hesitating," during which the lover could not find the courage or the words to make his feelings known. In the second stage, "pleading," he finally does proclaim his love. In the third stage, "hearing," it is the lady's turn to hesitate, as she considers the lover's request and by her ambiguous responses kindles in him alternate feelings of joy and despair. The last stage is *druerie*, or "service," when the lady accepts the lover's suit and he becomes her devoted servant. He lives in perfect joy, goes about the countryside singing the lady's praises (although it was considered bad form to mention her name). He does great deeds in her honor, and receives in recompense one kiss per year.

These stages of love each had their characteristic mood, and these moods were endlessly explored in the love poetry of the troubadours. It is not too much to say that these poets firmly established the great clichés which have since remained a familiar and expected part of love declarations in the West. Perhaps the reader can judge in the first three following selections where the lover finds himself in relation to his lady. The fourth selection, on the joys of war, is a *sirventes* which expresses the delight of the nobles in the color and excitement of battle.

Bernart of Ventadorn's "So Filled with Happiness" is taken from Justin H. Smith, *The Troubadours at Home* (New York: Knicker-

bocker Press, 1899), II, 185–87, and Peirol's "Like the Swan" from
ibid., II, 98–99. Peire Vidal's "Great Joy" is taken from Ida Farnell,
The Lives of the Troubadours (London: David Nott, 1896), pp. 88–89.
Bertran's "The Joys of War" comes from J. F. Rowbotham, *The
Troubadours and Courts of Love* (New York: Macmillan, 1895), pp.
84–85.

So Filled with Happiness

So filled with happiness am I
    Earth wears another face;
Rich flowers of many a brilliant dye
    For me the frost displace;
When rains descend and tempests fly,
    My joy but gains in grace,—
They only help my song rise high,
    My glory mount apace;
      For in my loving heart
      So sweetly joy doth start,
      Meseems the flowers make ice depart,
    To verdure snow give place.

My garments I could all unlace
    And winter's harshness dare,
For burning love my strength would brace
    Against the bitter air;
Yet they but earn the fool's disgrace,
    Who self-control forbear,
And this is very near my case,
    And hence my grievous care;
      The Peerless tries my heart
      Who might instead impart,
      Richer than gold in Frisian mart,
    A wealth beyond compare.

Her heart she yields me not,—my Fair,
    Yet token grants she me,
That something hath been conquered there
    As like love as could be;
And such delightful hopes prepare
    My eyes her face to see,

That I am sure complete despair
　　Is not my destiny;
　　　　Toward her—so fond my heart—
　　　　My thoughts fly like a dart,
　　　　Yet love and I must dwell apart,
　　Since far from France is she.

So rich the hoped felicity,
　　Compared with what I gain,
I only rise to sink alee
　　Like ships upon the main;
From present woe to get me free
　　I seek escape in vain;
All night in anxious misery
　　I writhe and toss in pain;
　　　　The pangs that wring my heart
　　　　Are more than Tristan's smart,
　　　　When, forced from blonde Yseult to part,
　　His soul was rent in twain.

O God, were I a bird! I'd fain
　　Across the earth take flight,
And ere the stars of night should wane
　　By her would I alight;
Your lover for your love is slain,
　　Fair lady, gay and bright;
No heart can long such woe contain,—
　　Soon mine will break outright;
　　　　Before your love my heart
　　　　Adores, and stands apart!
　　　　Alas, fair form, fresh cheeks, your art
　　Hath brought me grievous blight!

For nothing else can give delight,
　　Of nothing else I dream;
'Tis bliss if one but speak or write
　　A word on this dear theme,—
At once my face is all alight,
　　Though small the word might seem,
And that I can be glad and light,
　　You'd see by that quick gleam;

Such love fills up my heart
That often tears do start,
And to my sighs these tears impart
A savor more supreme.

Haste, messenger, depart;
Go tell her peerless heart,
My woeful pain and smart
A martyr would beseem.

[Bernart of Ventadorn]

Like the Swan

Like the swan when death is nigh,
    Dying I will sing;
'T will be comeliest so to die,
    Least will be the sting;
For Love hath caught me in his net,
And many woes my heart beset;
    But this I gain: that o'er and o'er
    I've learned I never loved before.

Ceaselessly to plead and sigh
    Ends by wearying,—
From my looks, when she is by,
    Silent prayers shall spring;
Whate'er she wills I then shall get,
And joy and love are sweeter yet
    When heart, come nigh to heart, doth pour,
    Unasked, what each would fain implore.

Song, to greet my fair one fly,
    Asking not a thing,
Yet with prudent sighs tell why
    I am languishing;
Beseech her never to forget
My loyal heart on her is set;
    Her vassal, I will e'er adore,—
    Or die, if that would please her more.

[Peirol]

Great Joy

GREAT joy have I to greet the season bright,
And joy to greet the blessed summer days,
And joy when birds do carol songs of praise,
And joy to mark the woods with flowerets dight,
And joy at all whereat to joy were meet,
And joy unending at the pleasaunce sweet
That yonder in my joy I think to gain,
There where in joy my soul and sense remain.

'Tis Love that keeps me in such dear delight,
'Tis Love's clear fire that keeps my breast ablaze,
'Tis Love that can my sinking courage raise,
Even for Love am I in grievous plight;
With tender thoughts Love makes my heart to beat,
And o'er my every wish has rule complete—
Virtue I cherish since began his reign,
And to do deeds of Love am ever fain.

                                    [Peire Vidal]

The Joys of War

Well do I love the lusty spring,
When leaves and flow'rets peep to light!
I love to hear the songbirds sing
Among the leafage in delight
    Which forms their airy dwelling.
And when on tented fields I spy
Tall tents and proud pavilions high,
    My breast with joy is swelling;
Or when I see in legions lie
Squadrons of armored chivalry.

What joy when scouts are skirmishing,
And scatter craven knaves in flight!
What joy to hear the fighters fling
High words and cries about the fight!
    What bliss is in me welling,
When castle walls that flout the sky
Stagger to their foundations nigh!
    What joys are me impelling,

When gallant troops a city try,
With trenches fenced impregnably!

And equal pleasure does it bring
When some gay gallant is in sight,
On lordly charger galloping,
Who cheers his men from base affright,
    Of rich rewards them telling.
And when the camp he cometh nigh,
Then must his men their prowess ply,
    Their very lifeblood selling.
For not a man is rated high
Until to blows he can reply.

Swords, spears, and helmets glittering,
Shields shivered, and in sorry plight—
Such sights and sounds does battle bring;
With crowds of vassals left and right
    Their master's foemen felling,
And horses mad, with rolling eye,
Who frenzied through the battle fly.
    The man of race excelling
Thinks but of blood and butchery,
And yearns for death or victory.

                              [Bertran de Born]

⌐˩˩˩˩˩˩˩˩˩˩˩˩˩˩˩˩˩˩˩˩⌐

12. Courtesy, according to the Romance of the Rose

Courtly society imposed upon its members a new code of behavior
known as "courtesy." This was literally the art of proper deportment
at court, and it included as its highest skill the art of wooing ladies.
    One of the most extended tracts on courtly love and courtly manners
was the thirteenth-century French poem, the *Romance of the Rose*.
It was a huge work, ultimately reaching over 20,000 lines of poetry.
Its purpose was defined as follows:

This is the Romance of the Rose
Where the art of love is all enclosed (vv. 37–38).

The first part of the poem, consisting of a little more than 4000 lines, was written by Guillaume de Lorris about 1237. He describes, with considerable color and pageantry, the dream of a lover. He sets out to win his lady, who is allegorically represented as a rose within a walled garden. The lover is aided in his quest by mirth, courtesy, gladness, wealth, largesse and other qualities, and is obstructed by danger, jealousy and shame. All are presented as allegorical figures. Guillaume did not finish the poem, and an anonymous poet contributed 78 additional lines, which brought it to a rapid conclusion.

This abbreviated dénouement apparently did not satisfy the literate public. About 1277, another author, Jean de Meun, wrote a vast new conclusion which finally gave the lover his rose after more than 16,000 additional lines of verse. Jean, who was educated at the University of Paris and was steeped in scholastic learning, made of the work an encyclopedia of contemporary science, lore and opinion. Its large dimensions and lavish embellishments have led critics to compare it with contemporary Gothic cathedrals, or at least to the scholastic Summas.

Jean, however, differed sharply from Guillaume in his views of love. He was cynical rather than idealistic, and manifested the same low opinion concerning women as is characteristic of the contemporary French *fabliaux*. He was no more favorably disposed towards the clergy, and he was bitterly critical of the mendicant orders. The summation of his advice is the need for sexual activity, as much of it as possible, if the world is to be replenished.

In the first of the following two selections from the *Romance*, the god of Love instructs the lover on the manners he must cultivate if he is to make himself acceptable to his lady. This part, written by Guillaume de Lorris, illustrates the importance of the courtly tradition in the emergence of a "polite" and sophisticated society in the Middle Ages. In the second selection by Jean de Meun, the "Old Nurse" (simply called *La Vieille* in the poem) gives with some cynicism instructions on how women can capture men. The influence of Ovid's *Art of Love* is here apparent.

Of many Old-French editions of the *Romance*, the most elaborate is *Le Roman de la Rose par Guillaume de Lorris et Jean de Meun*, ed. E. Langlois (Paris: Société des Anciens Testes Français, 1914–24). The translation here is by David and Patricia Herlihy.

I

[lines 2055–2212]
The god of Love then charged me
Such as you shall hear,
Word for word, his commandments.
This romance explains them well.
Who wishes to love, now let him heed,
For the romance henceforth improves.
From now on it makes good listening,
For here is one who can tell a tale!
The dream's conclusion is very nice,
And its subject is new.
The one who shall hear the end of the dream,
I tell you well, he'll be able
To be master of the games of love,
Provided that he listens well
To what I explain in my romance,
And of the dream the significance.
The truth which is hidden here
Then shall be revealed to you,
When you have heard me expound the dream,
For there is no word of untruth here.
    "Villainy, first of all,"
Says Love, "I wish and command
That you avoid without relapse,
If you do not wish to offend me.
Be cursed and excommunicated
All those who love villainy.
Villainy makes villains.
I have no reason to love that vice.
Villains are traitors and void of pity,
Who can neither serve nor love.
    "Then, guard yourself well from repeating
Things about people better left in silence.
It isn't gentlemanly to slander.
Consider Kay the seneschal
Who once for his mockery
Gained bad repute and hatred.
But from Gawain you well could learn,
Who by courtesy had as much of praise,

As Kay acquired of blame,
Since he was vile and cruel,
A mocking, evil-tongued man,
Above all other knights.
"Be courteous and accommodating,
With soft and reasonable words,
To people great and humble.
When you are passing through the streets,
Be sure you act politely.
Be first to greet the people.
If another be first in greeting,
Don't let your mouth be silent.
Be ready with a salutation
Without delay or hesitation.
"Then, take care that you never say
Those vulgar words or smutty jokes.
To name a vulgar thing,
Never let your mouth be opened.
I don't call that man courteous,
Who mentions what's nasty and bad.
All women serve and honor,
Spare no pain and effort in their service;
And if you hear one speaking ill,
Who mouths contempt for women,
Rebuke him, and bid him be quiet.
Do, if you can, something which pleases
Women and girls,
So that of you good news
They will hear told and repeated.
By this you'll be the better prized.
"Besides all this, beware of pride.
For the man who heeds and understands,
Pride is foolishness and a sin.
Whoever is pride's victim
Cannot apply his heart
To service or to pleading.
Proud men do the contrary
To that which the good lover must do.
But he who wishes to succeed in love,
Must conduct himself with grace.
The man who seeks love's ultimate service

Can do nothing without refinement.
Polish is never pride.
Whoever is elegant is worth the more,
For the reason that he has not pride,
And isn't a conceited fool.
Dress yourself handsomely, as you can afford
Both in coat and trousers.
Fine cloths and embellishments
Greatly improve the man.
You should entrust your clothing to
Someone who knows how to tailor,
Who cuts his edges well
And turns out sleeves fit and fine.
Laced shoes and boots
Wear often fresh and new.
See to it that they fit so well
That the common folk will argue
By what means you got them on,
And where you entered them.
With gloves and purse of silk
And belt, bedeck yourself.
And if your riches be not great,
Do the best with what you have.
But try for the maximum elegance
That you can reach this side of bankruptcy.
A garland of flowers, which little costs,
Or of roses at Pentecost,
Anyone can well afford
Since much expense is not involved.
   "Suffer no filth upon your person,
Wash your hands, scrub your teeth.
If your nail rims are black
Don't let them so remain.
Lace your sleeves, comb your hair,
But do not paint nor rouge yourself.
It's not even fitting for women,
Or even women of ill fame,
Who have found by evil paths
Love against the law.
   "After this you must recall
To keep a cheerful mien.

Surround yourself with joy and gladness.
Love doesn't like a dour man;
Love is a gentle illness,
Which prompts to joy and laughs and fun.
Thus it is with lovers:
Joy and pain change with the hours.
Lovers know the ills of loving.
One hour sweet, one touched with gall.
The ills of loving are quite extreme:
Now the lover is at play,
Now he is distraught, now he raves.
He cries one hour, the other he sings.
If you know how to cause delight,
By which you can please people,
I command that so you do.
All must do in every place,
That which he knows will there be best,
From this comes honor, praise and grace.
    "If you feel yourself quick and agile,
Don't fear the risk in jumping.
If you are good on horseback,
You should spur your horse and ride.
If you know how to break a lance,
You can win from it goodly praise;
And if at arms you excel,
For this you'll be ten times loved.
If you have a voice clear and true,
You should never seek excuse
From singing, should they ask you.
For good singing raises delight.
It's profitable to a bachelor
That he know how to play the strings,
To pipe the flute, and how to dance.
By this he can make much advance.
    "Don't make yourself seem miserly,
For that can wound you much.
It's very fitting that lovers
Give from their own more liberally
Than any villain or oaf.
That man is ignorant of love
Whom it pleases not to give.

Whoever seeks advance in love,
Must of avarice beware.
For he who for a single glance,
Or for a smile sweet and serene
Has given up his heart entire,
Must surely follow so rich a gift
With treasure in abundance.
  "Now I wish briefly to review
That which I've said for remembrance.
For advice better impresses
The memory, when it is brief.
Whoever wants Love to be his lord,
Courteous and without pride must be,
Elegant and affable,
And endowed with generosity.
  "Then you ought in penitence
Night and day without surcease
Let love be your single thought.
Retain those thoughts for all the days,
Keep in your heart that happy hour,
When joy so strongly dwelt with you;
And that you may excel in love,
I wish and I command that you
Have set all your heart in just one place,
So that it never be released,
Thus all entire with no deceit.
For I do not love divided service.
Who leaves his heart in many spots
Gives to all a tiny part.
But never doubt the lover who
In one place wholly sets his heart.
For this wish that in one place you put it,
But watch well that you do not lend it.
For if you would lend it out,
I would hold this scandalous.
But give it with no strings attached,
If you would have the larger merit.
For the profit from a loaned thing
Is soon paid and acquitted.
But for something given as a gift,
Great should be the rewards therefrom.

So give it all without conditions,
If you wish to do it graciously,
For a thing ought to be especially dear,
Which is given in good cheer.
For I don't care beans for any gift
That weighs hard on the donor."

II

[The old Nurse gives instructions on how a lady
can succeed in love, lines 13,879–14,444.]
"If she is not fair, let her groom herself.
The homelier she is, let her be the better dressed;
And if she should see shedding
(Which is always great sorrow ever to behold),
The beautiful curls of her blonde head,
Or if it's needed that she cut them
For some grave malady,
(By which her beauty is soon injured),
Or if by chance through anger
Some villain tears out her tresses,
So that not enough remains
To give covering of thick braids,
She must at once have brought to her
The hair of some dead women,
Or chignons of blonde silk
To place beneath her headdress.
Over her ears she should wear such horns,
That neither buck nor bull nor unicorn,
If they should chance to meet her,
Could with their own surpass in height.
And if her hair have need of dye,
Let her take the sap of many herbs.
For fruit, wood, leaf, bark and root
Have much power and corrective force.
    "If she should see her color fade,
Which gives the heart much sorrow,
She should have moist ointments ready
In jars within her boudoir
Daily to paint herself in secret.
But take great care lest a lover
Might learn or see.

There might be trouble there!
If her neck be lovely and white her throat,
See to it that her seamstress so cuts her dress,
And so reveals a décolletage,
That her skin appears white and clear,
Six inches in back and front,
If she would be the more seductive.
If her shoulders are too broad
To please at dances and at balls,
Let her dress be made of thin cloth.
If her hands lack loveliness,
And if they are not fair and smooth,
Or with calluses or warts,
She does not let them there remain.
Have her remove them with a needle,
Else hide her hands in gloves,
So that wart or blemish does not appear.
And if she be too bosomy,
Let her take a band or cloth
To stretch across her chest,
And binding tight all around her ribs,
Then to attach, to sew or knot,
That she may go her merry way.
    "And like every good maiden,
She should keep her Venus' chamber clean,
If she is refined and well brought up.
Let her leave no spiderwebs about
Which she won't burn, remove, sweep out,
So that no scum can be gathered there.
If her feet be ugly, she always keeps on her shoes,
Fat legs need dainty shoes.
In brief, should she know of any flaw,
She should disguise it, if she isn't simple.
And if she knows that her breath be bad,
There needn't be here grief nor pain.
'Tis to be watched that while she fasts,
That she refrains from words as well,
And watch, if she can, that her mouth doesn't get
Too close to the noses of others.
If there comes occasion to smile,
Let her do so wisely and well,

That she reveals two dimples
On both sides of her face.
Not by laughing does she puff her cheeks,
Nor does she hold her lips too pressed.
Nor does laughter too widely part her mouth
As to disclose her teeth.
A woman should laugh with her mouth closed,
For it is never a lovely sight
When she laughs with jaws agape,
They seem too widely split.
If her teeth are too irregular,
Ugly and crooked from birth,
If she shows them by her smile
She's apt to be less prized.
In crying let her know the manner;
But every woman is expert enough
On how to cry for all occasions.
It doesn't require
Grief, shame, unpleasantness.
They always have tears ready.
All weep, and are wont to weep
In the way that they prefer.
But a man ought not be much impressed,
If he sees these tears pour forth
As thickly as ever rain has fallen.
Only then to women come the tears,
Those sorrows and those griefs,
When there are deceptions there.
Woman's tears are nothing but an ambush;
They only dissemble sorrow.
But see that not by word nor deed,
You ever reveal this thought!
   "It matters much that when at table,
She wear an agreeable face.
But before she takes her place,
She makes herself seen by the guests.
To each she gives to understand
That she has done her duty well.
She goes and comes here and there,
And seats herself the very last,
And she takes a little pause

Before she's ready to assume her place.
And when she's sitting at table,
She does, if she can, service to all.
Before the others she ought to break
Some bread, and pass it around.
And should, in order to merit grace,
Place before her guest
Something to eat upon his plate.
Before him she puts a leg or wing,
Or beef or pork, she cuts it then
According to what he'll have for food,
Be it of fish or be it of flesh.
She has no taste for stingy service;
If he allows, she gives him more.
And well she watches that she doesn't wet
Her fingers in the sauce up to the joints.
Never let her mouth be smeared
With soup, with garlic or fatty meat.
Let her bites be dainty-sized,
She never stuffs her mouth.
With fingertips only she touches the food
Which is to be dipped in the sauce,
(Whether green, or brown, or yellow).
And so well carries her morsel
That no drop falls upon her breast
Of soup or sauce or pepper.
And so gracefully she ought to drink
That no drop trickles on her.
For some may well consider her
Ill-mannered and a glutton,
Who see such things occur.
And watch lest the goblet touch her lips
While she has food within her mouth.
She ought so well her mouth to wipe
That no drop of grease adheres
To the upper lip at least.
For when the grease remains on that lip,
Upon the wine drops of grease appear
Which are neither nice nor neat.
She drinks a little at a time,
No matter how great her thirst.

She doesn't gulp with a single breath
An entire goblet or cup;
Rather she drinks little and often
That she does not move the others
To say that she swallows too much,
Or that she drinks with a glutton's throat.
But she lets it delicately trickle in.
From the rim of the goblet she doesn't gulp too much
As do so many nurses
Who are such gluttons and sots
That they pour wine into their filled throats,
Just as if it were a barrel.
With such great gulps they load themselves
That they grow stunned and confused.
She watches well that she doesn't get drunk.
For a drunken man or woman
Can never a secret keep;
For when a woman has drunk too much,
She's utterly without defense,
And babbles out all she thinks.
She is at the mercy of all
When she's given herself to this trouble.
She is careful not to sleep at table;
For that would be too disagreeable.
Many ugly things occur
To those who take these naps.
For there is no point in sleeping
In places intended for wakeful people.
Many have been injured,
And many times have they fallen
Forwards, backwards, or to the side.
They break arm or head or rib.
She watches that such naps do not lay hold of her.
Remember Palinurus
Who piloted Aeneas' ship.
While awake he steered it well.
But when sleep invaded him,
He fell from the tiller into the sea
And drowned in view of the crew
Who mourned much after him.
   "A woman ought to be concerned

Not too late to play at love.
For she could wait so very long,
That no one will want her tender hand.
She ought to seek the pleasure of love
While youth still delights her.
For when old age assails a woman,
She loses the joy and battle of love.
The fruit of love, if a woman is wise,
She picks in the flower of her years.
For what she loses of time (unhappy one!)
That much passes without the joy of love.
And if she does not heed my counsel
Which I make for our common profit,
Let her know that she'll be sorry
When old age flails her.

. . . .

    "She watches that she is not too secluded;
For when she stays much at home,
She is less seen by many people.
Her beauty gains less renown,
And she is less desired and sought.
Often she goes to the principal church,
And makes visits
To weddings, processions,
To games, parties, carolings,
For the god of love (the goddess too)
In such place holds his school,
And sings Mass for his disciples.
But first she consults her reflection
To learn if she's well attired.
And when she feels that everything's right,
Then through the streets she shall go.
Let her be of such lovely carriage,
Not too lax and not too stiff,
Not fast, and not too slow,
But very pleasing in every crowd.
She moves her shoulders and her hips,
So nobly, that one cannot find
A more lovely movement;
And she walks prettily
In her tiny, handsome slippers

Which she shall have made so fine
That they will fit her feet so closely,
That there shall be no wrinkle at all.
And if she trails her dress,
Or leans over near the pavement,
She lifts it on side or front
As if to take a bit of breeze,
Or have a freer gait.
Then she sees that she frees the foot
That all who pass may see
The beautiful form of visible foot.
    "And if she's one who carries a coat
She should wear it in such a fashion
Which doesn't too much encumber the view
Of the beautiful body to which it gives shade.
And in order that the body better appear,
And the clothes with which it is embellished,
The coat should neither too wide nor skimpy be,
Embroidered with silver and tiny pearls
And the purse in the open
So that it is right for all to see.
She should take her cloak with both her hands,
Extend her arms and spread them,
Whether on a good road or in the mud,
And let her think of the arc
Which the peacock makes with his tail.
She makes thus of her coat her own
Whether the lining be of ermine white or grey,
Or whatever she shall choose,
To show all her body in the open
To all that she sees gazing at her.
    "If she is not fair of face,
She must the more in wisdom turn
To show her lovely locks, blonde, dear,
And all the tresses at her nape
To show how lovely and well plaited they are.
It's a very pleasing thing,
That beauty of the hair.
The woman should all days give care
That she can imitate the wolf
Who wishes to snare the lamb.

Lest she fail utterly,
For a single prize she wishes to attack a thousand.
She doesn't know which one she'll get
Before she seizes the young one.
Thus ought the woman spread everywhere
Her nets to take all men.
For since she cannot ever know
To whom she'll pleasing be,
At least to seize one for herself,
She ought to sink her hooks in all.
Then it will not come to pass
That she won't have someone taken
Of the fools, among the thousands
Who will rub her sides,
Maybe many with some luck,
For art helps nature quite a bit.
    "And if she gets several on her hook
Who wish to place her on the skewer,
Do what the situation requires.
Don't give to both the same appointment,
For they may consider themselves deceived
When several gather together;
They may well then leave her.
That could be quite demeaning.
For from her hand there might escape
That which each has brought her,
And she ought to leave them nothing
From which they might grow fatter,
But place them in such poverty,
That they die miserable and poor.
And she will be left a rich proprietress,
For she loses what she doesn't get.
To love a poor man isn't fit;
For poor men are worth nothing.
Were he Ovid or Homer,
He wouldn't be worth a pear.
Let her never love a stranger.
For, as he places and feeds
His body in many inns,
Just as vagabond is his heart.
I never urge to love a stranger,

But all the time in his passing,
If he offers her money or jewels,
She should take them all and put them in her coffer,
And let him take his pleasure
All in haste or at leisure.
And let her watch that she takes
No man of too great an elegance,
Nor one who vaunts his beauty.
For it's pride which tempts such a one.
Such are placed in the wrath of God;
The man who loves himself I greatly fear.
For thus says Ptolemy,
Who greatly loved learning,
They are not able to love well,
So wicked and so bitter are their hearts,
That which he'll tell to one woman,
He'll say as much to another.
And many he seeks to flatter,
The better to despoil and rob them.
Much complaint have I heard
Of a girl thus deceived.
    "And if arrives a man who promises,
Whether he be true or false,
Who beseeches for her love,
And by promises binds himself to her,
So too can she promise in return.
But she well watches that she doesn't give herself
For nothing into his power,
Unless she holds first the cash.
And if he sends a note,
She sees if it is written with deception,
Or if he has a good intention,
And an honest heart without deceit.
Then write him in a few hours,
But do not do so right away.
Delay arouses lovers.
But let it not take too long.
And when she hears the lover's request,
She arranges that she doesn't hasten
To grant everything of love,
Nor should she deny him all.

Thus she holds him in suspense,
That he has both hope and fear.
"And when he again makes his plea,
And she does not offer him
Her love which binds him tightly,
The lady defends herself that she does enough
By her design and by strength,
That daily he increases hope,
And little by little goes away
The fear until it completely fails.
And let them make peace and concord.
She who then concedes to him,
And who knows enough of deceptive wiles,
Ought swear to God and saints, male and female,
That never has she wished to grant herself
To any man, however much he begged.
And says: 'Sire, this is the ultimate,
Faith which I owe to Saint Peter of Rome,
For pure love I give myself to you;
It is not for your gifts.
There is no man born for whom I would do this,
Nor for any gift, however great I view it.
Many a valiant man have I refused,
For much have many men courted me.
I believe you have enchanted me.
You have cast a wicked spell on me.'
Then she should hug him tightly,
And kiss him, the better to daze him.
But if she wishes to have my counsel,
She considers nothing but property.
She's a fool not to pluck her lover
Right to the last feather.
For she who knows best how to pluck,
It's she who'll have the best of it.
And she'll be the dearer held
Who sells herself more dearly.
For what one gets for nothing,
The more they will despise it.
One doesn't prize a piece of rind,
If it is lost, there is no fuss.
At least if large, one notes the loss

Of what's been purchased dearly.
    "But plucking takes a certain art;
Her servants and her chambermaid,
Her sister and her nurse,
And her mother, if she isn't stupid,
In order to cooperate
Make sure that they receive
Dresses, coats, mittens, gloves,
And seize just as the vultures
Whatever they can grasp,
So that he can't escape
From their clutches by any means
Until he has paid his last penny.
And as if he were playing with tokens,
He should give them that much coins and jewels.
Much booty is soon acquired,
When it is taken by many hands.
Other times they say to him, 'Sire,
Since it is proper to tell you this,
See how my lady is lacking clothes.
How can you permit this want?
If she wishes to do it, by St. Giles,
There is a man in this town,
He would dress her like a queen
And have her ride with a great retinue.
Lady, why do you delay so long?
Why don't you ask him?
You're too modest in his regard,
When he lets you so to suffer.'
And she, however much it pleases her,
Should bid them hold their peace.
For so much has been taken from him,
That he has been too badly injured,
And if she notes that he perceives
That he gives more than he ought,
And he thinks himself greatly injured
By the great gifts which he knows she has consumed,
And she senses that to give more
Persuasion will not move him,
Then she should ask that he grant a loan.
She swears to him that she is all prepared

To pay him back on the day he names,
As much as he shall give her.
But I do solemnly forbid
That anything ever be returned.
  "But if another lover comes
(Of whom she has several, if it pleases God),
But to none of them has given her heart,
She calls them all her lovers.
Then she'll complain, if she is wise,
That her best dress is in hock.
More usury is sought each day
From which she is in so bad a state,
Such sadness has her heart,
That she will do nothing which pleases him
If he does not redeem her pledges.
And the young man, if he's not very wise,
For this money he'll be the source.
He'll place at once his hand to his purse
Or take some suitable action
By which the pledges will be delivered
Which have no need to be redeemed,
But are, I hope, concealed within,
From the bachelor locked away
In some well sealed trunk.
Let her not mind, I hope, that he look
Within her cupboard or closet,
In order to be the better convinced,
As long as she gets the money.
For the third she saves another trick.
Let her ask of him a belt of silver,
Or a dress or wimple,
And then money which she'll spend.
And if he has nothing with him,
He should swear to comfort her,
And promises by foot and hand,
That he'll bring it on the morrow,
Let her turn deaf ears,
Not believing anything, for these are fibs.
Too many men are found to be liars.
More have flatterers failed me
In faith and oaths in times past,

Than there are saints in Paradise.
Then at least, if he has nothing to pay,
Let him hock his property
For two pennies or three or four,
Or let him go elsewhere to have his fun.
"The woman ought, if she isn't stupid,
To seem to be a coward,
To tremble, to fear,
To be distraught and anxious
When she is to receive her lover.
She should make him clearly see
In what great peril she receives him,
Since her husband she deceives for him,
Or her guardians or relatives;
And if the affair becomes known,
Which she wishes to be done in secret,
She shall die without fail.
And she swears that he cannot remain,
If he wishes her still to live.
Then he will stay willingly
When she has so beguiled him.
"It's important for her to remember well
When her lover is supposed to come.
If she sees that no one perceives him,
By the window let her receive him,
Although the door would have served as well.
Let her swear that she is destroyed and dead,
And that nothing would be left of him,
If any knew he was within.
No arms in motion can guard them,
Helmets, hauberks, pike or ax,
Nor hutch nor closet nor chamber
From being torn apart limb by limb.
Then must the lady sigh,
And seem to be angry
And assail and trample him,
And say that so long an absence,
He has not done without reason,
And that he's keeping in his house
Another woman, whoever she may be,
Who gives him greater solace,

And that now she's well betrayed,
Since he hates her for reason of another.
She ought to be called unhappy,
Since she loves without being loved.
When he shall hear this word,
He, who has a weak head,
Shall believe quite in error
That she loves him too loyally,
And that she is more jealous of him
Than ever was the spouse of Venus:
Vulcan, when he chanced to find
Her caught and proved with Mars
In his chains of forged brass
Which held them very tightly,
Joined and bound in the game of love,
So well had the fool watched them."

13. The *Song of Roland*

The greatest of the medieval heroic epics, and the oldest masterpiece of French literature, is the *Song of Roland*. It is based on a historical event. In 778, as recorded by Charlemagne's biographer Einhard (and only by Einhard), Basques ambushed the rear guard of the Frankish army at Roncesvalles in the Pyrenees. In the epic, however, this story is much transformed by time and the poetic imagination. For the *Song* was put down in its present form probably in the last quarter of the eleventh century, three hundred years after the event it purports to describe. The unknown author wrote in the language of northern France, but little specific can be said about him. He shows familiarity with the pilgrim routes leading from northern France to the great shrine of St. James of Compostela in Spain. He probably made use of popular legends, and perhaps even written saints' lives, which had grown up in glorification of the many shrines along the way. The poem was probably first heard by knights and pilgrims, on their way to Compostela or to do battle against the Saracens in Spain. They would have had occasion to see first hand the historic locales mentioned in the poem.

The setting of the *Song of Roland* is Spain, where Charlemagne has been waging a victorious war for seven years. Only Saragossa holds out against him, and its King Marsila, without hope of defeating Charles, attempts to trick him into leaving Spain. Through ambassadors, he sends rich presents, and asks that Charles return home. He falsely promises to follow him, accept Christianity, and become his vassal. Charles, with the urging of his nephew Roland, sends Ganelon (Roland's stepfather) to Marsila's court to negotiate the settlement. Ganelon is incensed that this dangerous mission falls upon him. To gain revenge upon Roland, Ganelon advises Marsila to ambush with his 400,000 knights the rear guard of Charlemagne's army as it passes over the Pyrenees. Roland will be in command of it, and Roland's death will "smite off the right hand of Charles." Peace will then be assured. The poet then recounts the ambush at Roncesvalles, the death of the Frankish heroes Oliver, the archbishop Turpin, and Roland himself, and Charlemagne's revenge.

The *Song of Roland* tells a fast-paced and exciting tale, but its greatness rests rather on the analysis it offers of its two chief characters, Roland and Charlemagne.

In depicting Roland, the poem dwells upon the conflict between the freedom of the hero and the restrictions coming to be imposed upon him by the new feudal order. Roland's dominant personality trait is his irrepressible boldness, which verges on arrogance. He provokes Ganelon by his insults into plotting his treasonous revenge. At the crucial battle at Roncesvalles, he at first haughtily refuses to signal Charlemagne with his horn, when there was yet time for the king to return, rescue the rearguard, and win a decisive victory over the faithless Marsila. Though even the brave Oliver urges him to sound his horn, he rejects the act as cowardly, pronouncing that "thereby would I lose all fame in sweet France."

This decision ultimately spells tragedy for Roland and his men, but without this haughty courage the hero would hardly have been the man that he was. The poet, on the other hand, is well aware that this traditional, reckless bravery, however admirable, is now inconsistent with the demands of the emerging feudal society and state. Roland was no longer, like Beowulf, a lonely hero who could depend only upon himself. He was a vassal and a comrade, with responsibilities to the feudal order of which he was a member. Roland's pride and individualism cost Charlemagne the services of many good men, and damaged the cause of Frank and Christian. The tragedy of Roncesvalles was thus rooted in the clash of two high social ideals, traditional heroism, and the new social discipline required in the construction of an effectively governed state.

Charlemagne is also a principal hero of the poem, and the work might be described as an incident in his life. He is more than two hundred years old, and his life has been dominated by exertions and sorrows. After the bitter experience of Roncesvalles, he returns to sweet France. Exhausted, he sleeps in his vaulted chamber. But the angel Gabriel comes to him in his dreams, and orders him at once to assemble his army. He and his men must be off on the morrow to the land of Bire (did he even know where it was?). There heaven once more had need of the presence of his arms. The great king, with little will to go, weeps and tears his beard. On this pathetic note, the poem ends.

Charlemagne represents the man who has been selected, half without willing it, as an instrument of a higher destiny. He knows the dignity of his role, but he cannot repress a human protest about the weight he must carry. He resembles Vergil's Aeneas, who similarly is the tired, bruised, unhappy, driven instrument of destiny. Many knights and crusaders of the late eleventh century found themselves battling in distant lands, driven by what they took to be the will of God. They had reason to sympathize with the fatigue, loneliness and sadness of the great and aged king.

The *Song of Roland* is written in ten-syllable, assonanced verses. These in turn are grouped in irregular stanzas or "laisses." The paragraphs of the following prose translation correspond pretty much to the laisses of the original French.

The following selection presents the most dramatic part of the poem: Roland's death at Roncesvalles. It is adapted from *The Song of Roland*, trans. Isabel Butler (Cambridge, Mass.: Riverside Press, 1904), pp. 63–87.

WHEN Count Roland is aware of the great slaughter of his men, he turns to Oliver, saying: "Sir comrade, as God may save thee, see how many a good man of arms lies on the ground; we may well have pity on sweet France, the fair, that must now be desolate of such barons. Ah, king and friend, would thou wert here! Oliver, my brother, what shall we do? How shall we send him tidings?" "Nay, I know not how to seek him," saith Oliver; "but I would rather die than bring dishonor upon me."

Then saith Roland: "I will sound my horn of ivory, and Charles, as he passes the mountains, will hear it; and I pledge thee my faith the Franks will return again." Then saith Oliver: "Therein would be great shame for thee, and dishonor for all thy kindred, a reproach that would last all the days of their life. Thou wouldst not sound it when I bid thee, and now thou shalt not by my counsel. And if thou dost sound it, it will not be hardily, for now both thy arms are stained with blood." "Yea," the count answers him, "I have dealt some goodly blows."

Then saith Roland: "Sore is our battle, I will blow a blast, and Charles the king will hear it." "That would not be knightly," saith Oliver; "when I bid thee, comrade, thou didst disdain it. Had the king been here, we had not suffered this damage; but they who are afar off are free from all reproach. By this my beard, if I see again my sister, Aude the Fair, never shalt thou lie in her arms."

Then saith Roland: "Wherefore art thou wroth with me?" And Oliver answers him, saying: "Comrade, thou thyself art to blame. Wise courage is not madness, and measure is better than rashness. Through thy folly these Franks have come to their death; nevermore shall Charles the king have service at our hands. Hadst thou taken my counsel, my liege lord would be here, and this battle had been ended, and King Marsila had been or taken or slain. Woe worth thy prowess, Roland! Henceforth Charles shall get no help of thee; never till God's Judgment Day shall there be such another man; but thou must die, and France shall be shamed thereby. And this day our loyal fellowship shall have an end; before this evening grievously shall we be parted."

The archbishop, hearing them dispute together, spurs his horse with his spurs of pure gold, and comes unto them, and rebukes them, saying: "Sir Roland, and thou, Sir Oliver, in God's name I pray ye, let be this strife. Little help shall we now have of thy horn; and yet it were better to sound it; if the king come, he will revenge us, and the paynims shall not go hence rejoicing. Our Franks will light off their horses, and find us dead and maimed, and they will lay us on biers, on the backs of donkeys, and will weep for us with sorrow and pity; and they will bury us in the courts of churches, that our bones may not be eaten by wolves and swine and dogs." "Sir, thou speakest well and truly," quoth Roland.

And therewith he sets his ivory horn to his lips, grasps it well and blows it with all the might he hath. High are the hills, and the sound echoes far, and for thirty full leagues they hear it resound. Charles and all his host hear it, and the king saith: "Our men are at battle." But Count Ganelon denies it, saying: "Had any other said so, we had deemed it great falsehood."

With dolor and pain, and in sore torment, Count Roland blows his horn of ivory, that the bright blood springs out of his mouth, and the temples of his brain are broken. Mighty is the blast of the horn, and Charles, passing the mountains, hears it, and Naymes hears it, and all the Franks listen and hear. Then saith the king: "I hear the horn of Roland; never would he sound it, if he were not at battle." But Ganelon answers him, saying: "Battle is there none; thou art old and white and hoary, and thy words are those of a child. Well thou knowest the great pride of Roland;—a marvel it is that God hath suffered it thus long. Aforetime he took Noples against thy commandment, and when the Saracens came out of the city and set upon Roland the good knight, (he slew them with Durendal his sword); thereafter with water he washed away the blood which stained the meadow, that none might know of what he had done. And for a single hare he will blow his horn all day long; and now he but boasts among his fellows, for there is no folk on earth would dare do him battle. I prithee ride on. Why tarry we? The Great Land still lies far before us."

Count Roland's mouth has burst out a-bleeding, and the temples of his brain are broken. In dolor and pain he sounds his horn of ivory; but Charles hears it and the Franks hear it. Saith the king: "Long drawn is the blast of that horn." "Yea," Naymes answers, "for in sore need is the baron who blows it. Surely, our men are at battle; and he who now dissembles hath betrayed Roland. Take your arms and cry your war cry, and succor the men of your house. Dost thou not hear Roland's call?"

The Emperor has commanded that his trumpets be sounded, and now the Franks light down from their horses and arm themselves with hauberks and helms and swords adorned with gold; fair are their shields, and goodly and great their lances, and their banners are scarlet and white and blue. Then all the barons of the host get them to horse, and spur through the passes; and each saith to the other: "If we may but see Roland a living man, we will strike good blows at his side." But what avails it? for they have delayed too long.

Clear is the evening as was the day, and all their armor glistens in the sun, and there is great shining of hauberks, and helms, and shields painted with flowers, and lances, and gilded banners. The emperor rides on in wrath, and the Franks are full of care and foreboding; and not a man but weeps full sore and hath great fear for Roland. Then the king had Count Ganelon seized and gave him over to the cooks of his household; and he called Besgon their

chief, saying: "Guard him well, as beseems a felon who hath
betrayed my house." Besgon took him, and set a watch about
him of a hundred of his fellows of the kitchen, both best and worst.
They plucked out the hairs of Ganelon's beard and mustache, and
each one dealt him four blows with his fist, and hardily they beat
him with rods and staves; then they put about his neck a chain,
and bound him even as they would a bear, and in derision they
set him upon a donkey. So they guard him till they return him
unto Charles.

High are the hills and great and dark, deep the valleys, and
swift the waters. To answer Roland's horn all the trumpets are
sounded, both rear and van. The Emperor rides on in wrath, and
the Franks are full of care and foreboding; there is not a man but
weepeth and maketh sore lament, praying to God that he spare
Roland until they come unto the field, that at his side they may
deal good blows. But what avails it? They have tarried too long,
and may not come in time.

Charles the king rides on in great wrath, and over his hauberk
is spread his white beard. And all the barons of France spur mightily, not one but is full of wrath and grief that he is not with
Roland the captain who is at battle with the Saracens of Spain.
If he be wounded, what hope that one soul be left alive? God, what
a sixty he still hath in his fellowship; no king or captain ever had
better.

Roland looks abroad over hill and heath and sees the great multitude of the Frankish dead, and he weeps for them as beseems a
gentle knight, saying: "Lords and barons now may God have
mercy upon you, and grant Paradise to all your souls, that ye may
rest among the blessed flowers. Man never saw better men of arms
than ye were. Long and well, year in and year out, have ye
served me, and many wide lands have ye won for the glory of
Charles. Was it to such an end that he nourished you? O France,
fair land, today art thou made desolate by rude slaughter. Ye
Frankish barons, I see ye die through me, yet can I do naught to
save or defend you. May God, who knows no lie, aid you! Oliver,
brother, I must not fail thee; yet I shall die of grief, and I be not
slain by the sword. Sir comrade, let us get us into battle."

So Count Roland falls a-smiting again. He holds Durendal in
his hand, and lays on right valiantly, that he cleaves in twain
Faldron de Pui, and slays four and twenty of the most worship-
ful of the paynims. Never shall ye see man more desirous to re-

venge himself. And even as the hart flies before the hounds, so flee the heathen from before Roland. "Thou dost rightly," then said the archbishop; "such valor well beseems a knight who bears arms and mounts a good horse; in battle such a one should be fierce and mighty, or he is not worth four deniers, and it behooves him to turn monk and get him into a monastery to pray the livelong day for our sins." And Roland answered him, saying: "Smite and spare not." And at these words the Franks go into battle again; but great is the slaughter of the Christians.

That man who knows he shall get no mercy defends him savagely in battle. Wherefore the Franks are fierce as lions. Marsila like a true baron mounts his horse Gaignon; he spurs him well and rides on Bevon—lord he was of Beaune and Dijon—and breaks his shield, and rends his hauberk, that without other hurt he smites him dead to ground. And thereafter he slew Ivon and Ivory, and with them Gerard the Old of Roussillon. Now nigh at hand is Count Roland, and he saith to the paynim: "May the Lord God bring thee to mishap! And because thou hast wrongfully slain my comrades thou shalt thyself get a buffet before we twain separate, and this day thou shalt learn the name of my sword." And therewith he rides upon him like a true baron, and smites off his right hand, and thereafter he takes off the head of Jurfaleu the Fair, the son of King Marsila. Thereat the paynims cry: "Now help us, Mahound! O ye, our gods, revenge us upon Charles! He has sent out against us into our marches men so fierce that though they die they will not yield." And one saith to another: "Let us fly." At these words a hundred thousand turn and flee, and let whosoever will, call them, they will not return again.

But alack, what avails it? for though Marsila be fled his uncle the caliph yet abides, he who ruled Aferne, Carthage, Garmalie, and Ethiopia, a cursed land; under his lordship he has the black folk, great are their noses and large their ears, and they are with him to the number of fifty thousand. And now they come up in pride and wrath, and cry aloud the war cry of the paynims. Then saith Roland: "Now must we needs be slain, and well I know we have but a little space to live; but cursed be he who doth not sell himself right dear. Lay on, lords, with your burnished swords, and debate both life and death; let not sweet France be brought to shame through us. When Charles, my liege lord, shall come into this field, he will see such slaughter of the Saracens, that he shall find fifteen of them dead over against each man of ours, and he will not fail to bless us."

When Roland sees the cursed folk whose skin is blacker than any ink, and who have naught of white about them save their teeth, he saith: "Now I know in very sooth that we shall die this day. Lay on, lords, and yet again I bid thee, smite." "Now foul fall him who lags behind," quoth Oliver. And at this word the Franks haste into the fray.

Now when the paynims see how few are the Franks, they have great pride and joy thereof; and one saith to another: "Surely, the emperor is in the wrong." The caliph bestrides a sorrel horse, he pricks him on with his spurs of gold, and smites Oliver from behind, amid the back, that he drives the mails of his white hauberk into his body, and his lance passes out through his breast: "Now hast thou got a good buffet," quoth the caliph. "On an ill day Charles the Great left thee in the passes; much wrong hath he done us, yet he shall not boast thereof, for on thee alone have I well revenged us."

Oliver feels that he is wounded unto death; in his hand he holds Halteclere, bright was its blade, and with it he smites the caliph on his golden pointed helmet, that its flowers and gems fall to earth, and he cleaves the head even unto the teeth, and with the force of the blow smote him dead to earth, and said: "Foul fall thee, paynim! Say not that I am come to my death through Charles: and neither to thy wife, nor any other dame, shalt thou ever boast in the land from which thou art come, that thou hast taken from me so much as one farthing's worth, or hast done any hurt to me or to others." And thereafter he called to Roland for succor.

Oliver feels that he is wounded unto death; never will he have his fill of vengeance. In the thick of the press he smites valiantly, cleaving lances and embossed shields, and feet and hands and flanks and shoulders. Whosoever saw him thus dismember the Saracens, and hurl one dead upon another, must call to mind true valiance; nor did he forget the war cry of Charles, but loud and clear he cries out Montjoy! And he calls to Roland, his friend and peer: "Sir comrade, come stand thou beside me. In great sorrow shall we twain soon be parted."

Roland looks Oliver in the face, pale it is and livid and all discolored; the bright blood flows down from amid his body and falls in streams to the ground. "God," saith the count, "now I know

not what to do. Sir comrade, woe worth thy valor! Never shall
the world see again a man of thy might. Alas, fair France, today
art thou stripped of goodly vassals, and fallen and undone. The
emperor will suffer great loss thereby." And so speaking he swoons
upon his horse.

Lo, Roland has swooned as he sits his horse, and Oliver is
wounded unto death, so much has he bled that his sight is dark-
ened, and he can no longer distinguish any living man whether far
off or near at hand; and now, as he meets his comrade, he smites
him upon the helm set with gold and gems, and cleaves it down to
the nasal, but does not come unto the head. At the blow Roland
looks up at him, and asks him full softly and gently: "Comrade,
dost thou this wittingly? I am Roland who so loves thee. Never
yet hast thou mistrusted me." Then saith Oliver: "Now I hear
thee speak, but I cannot see thee; may the Lord God guard thee.
I have struck thee, but I pray thy pardon." "Thou hast done me
no hurt," Roland answers him; "I pardon thee before God, as here
and now." So speaking each leans forward towards the other, and
lo, in such friendship they are separated.

Oliver feels the anguish of death come upon him; his two eyes
turn in his head; and his hearing goes from him, and all sight. He
lights down from his horse and lies upon the ground, and again
and again he confesses his sins; he holds out his clasped hands
toward heaven and prays God that he grant him Paradise, and he
blesses Charles and sweet France, and Roland, his comrade, above
all men. Then his heart fails him, and his head sinks upon his
breast, and he lies stretched at all his length upon the ground.
Dead is the count and gone from hence. Roland weeps for him
and is sore troubled; never on the earth shall ye see a man so
sorrowful.

When Count Roland sees his friend lie prone and dead, facing
the east, gently he begins to lament him: "Sir comrade, woe worth
thy hardiness! We twain have held together for years and days,
never didst thou me wrong or I thee. Since thou art dead, alack
that I yet live." So speaking, the count swoons as he sits upon
Veillantif his horse, but his golden spurs hold him firm, and let him
go where he will, he cannot fall.

So soon as Roland comes to his senses, and is restored from his
swoon, he is aware of the great slaughter about him. Slain are the
Franks, he has lost them all save only Gualter del Hum and the
archbishop. Gualter has come down from the mountains where

he fought hardily with those of Spain; the paynims conquered, and his men are slain, and howsoever unwillingly, he must perforce flee down into the valley and call upon Roland for succor. "O gentle count, brave captain, where art thou? for where thou art I have no fear. It is I, Gualter, who conquered Maëlgut, I the nephew of Droön the old, the hoary, I whom thou wert wont to love for my hardihood. Now my shield is pierced, and the shaft of my lance is broken, and my hauberk rent and unmailed; I have the wounds of eight lances in my body, and I must die, but dear have I sold myself." So he saith, and Roland hears him, and spurs his horse and rides towards him.

Full sorrowful is Roland and of great wrath; he falls a-smiting in the thick of the press, and of those of Spain he cast twenty to the ground dead, and Gualter slew six, and the archbishop five. Then say the paynims: "Fierce and brave are these men. Take ye heed, lords, that they go not hence alive. He who doth not set upon them is traitor, and recreant he who lets them go hence." Then the hue and cry begins again, and from all sides they close about the three Franks.

Count Roland is a full noble warrior, and a right good knight is Gualter del Hum, the archbishop is of good valor and well tried; not one would leave aught to his fellows, and together, in the thick of the press, they smite the paynims. A thousand Saracens get them to foot, and there are still forty thousand on horseback, yet in sooth they dare not come nigh unto the three, but they hurl upon them lances and spears, arrows and darts and sharp javelins. In the first storm they slew Gualter, and sundered the shield of Turpin of Rheims, broke his helmet and wounded him in his head, and rent and tore his hauberk that he was pierced in the body by four spears; and his horse was slain under him. The archbishop falls; great is the pity thereof.

But so soon as Turpin of Rheims finds himself beaten down to earth with the wounds of four lances in his body, he right speedily gets him afoot again; he looks toward Roland, and hastes to him, and saith: "I am nowise vanquished; no good vassal yields him so long as he is a living man." And he draws Almace, his sword of brown steel, and in the thick of the press he deals well more than a thousand buffets. Afterwards Charles bore witness that Turpin spared himself no whit, for around him they found four hundred dead, some wounded, some cut in twain amid the body, and some whose heads had been smitten off; so saith the Geste and he who was on the field, the valiant Saint Gilles, for whom God wrought miracles; he it was who wrote the annals of the monastery of Laon. And he who knows not this, knows nought of the matter.

Count Roland fights right nobly, but all his body is a-sweat and burning hot, and in his head he hath great pain and torment, for when he sounded his horn he rent his temples. But he would fain know that Charles were coming, and he takes his horn of ivory, and feebly he sounds it. The emperor stops to listen: "Lords," he saith, "now has great woe come upon us, this day shall we lose Roland my nephew, I wot from the blast of his horn that he is nigh to death. Let him who would reach the field ride fast. Now sound you all the trumpets of the host." Then they blew sixty thousand, so loud that the mountains resound and the valleys give answer. The paynims hear them and have no will to laugh, but one saith to another: "We shall have ado with Charles anon."

Say the paynims: "The emperor is returning, we hear the trumpets of France; if Charles come hither, we shall suffer sore loss. Yet if Roland live, our war will begin again, and we shall lose Spain our land." Then four hundred armed in their helmets, and of the best of those on the field, gather together, and on Roland they make onset fierce and sore. Now is the count hard pressed.

When Count Roland sees them draw near he waxes hardy and fierce and terrible; never will he yield as long as he is a living man. He rides his horse Veillantif, and spurs him well with his spurs of fine gold, and charges into the fray. At his side is Archbishop Turpin. And the Saracens saith one to another: "Now save yourselves, friends. We have heard the trumpets of France; Charles the mighty king is returning."

Count Roland never loved the cowardly, or the proud, or the wicked, or any knight who was not a good vassal, and now he calls to Archbishop Turpin, saying: "Lord, you are on foot and I am on horseback; for love of you, I will take my stand, and together we will take the good and the ill; I will not abandon you for any living man; the blows of Almace and of Durendal shall give back this assault to the paynims." Then saith the Archbishop: "A traitor is he who does not smite; Charles is returning, and well will he revenge us."

"In an evil hour," saith the paynims, "were we born; woeful is the day that has dawned for us! We have lost our lords and our peers. Charles the valiant comes hither again with his great host,

we hear the clear trumpets of those of France, and great is the
noise of their cry of Montjoy. Count Roland is of such might he
cannot be vanquished by any mortal man. Let us hurl our missiles
upon him, and then leave him." Even so they did; and cast upon
him many a dart and javelin, and spears and lances and feathered
arrows. They broke and rent the shield of Roland, tore open and
unmailed his hauberk, but did not pierce his body: but Veillantif
was wounded in thirty places, and fell from under the count, dead.
Then the paynims flee, and leave him; Count Roland is left alone
and on foot.

The paynims flee in anger and wrath, and in all haste they turn
toward Spain. Count Roland did not pursue after them, for he
has lost his horse Veillantif, and whether he will or no, is left on
foot. He went to the help of Archbishop Turpin, and unlaced
his golden helm from his head, and took off his white hauberk of
fine mail, and he tore his tunic into strips and with the pieces
bound his great wounds. Then he gathers him in his arms, and
lays him down full softly upon the green grass, and gently he
beseeches him: "O gracious baron, I pray thy leave. Our comrades whom we so loved are slain, and it is not meet to leave them
thus. I would go seek and find them, and range them before thee."
"Go and return again," quoth the archbishop. "Thank God, this
field is thine and mine."

Roland turns away and goes on alone through the field; he
searches the valleys and the hills; (and there he found Ivon and
Ivory,) and Gerin, and Gerier his comrade (and he found Engelier
the Gascon,) and Berengier, and Oton, and he found Anseïs and
Samson, and Gerard the Old of Rousillon. One by one he hath
taken up the barons, and hath come with them unto the archbishop, and places them in rank before him. The archbishop cannot
help but weep; he raises his hand and gives them benediction, and
thereafter saith: "Alas for ye, lords! May God the Glorious receive
your souls, and bring them into Paradise among the blessed flowers.
And now my own death torments me sore; never again shall I see
the great emperor."

Again Roland turned away to search the field; and when he
found Oliver his comrade, he gathered him close against his breast,
and as best he might returned again unto the archbishop, and
laid his comrade upon a shield beside the others; and the archbishop
absolved and blessed him. Then their sorrow and pity broke forth
again, and Roland saith: "Oliver, fair comrade, thou wert son of

the great Duke Reinier, who held the Marches of Rivier and Genoa; for the breaking of lances or the piercing of shields; for vanquishing and affrighting the proud, for upholding and counseling the good, never in any land was there a better knight."

When Roland sees the peers, and Oliver whom he so loved, lying dead, pity takes him and he begins to weep; and his face is all discolored; so great is his grief he cannot stand upright, but helplessly falls to the ground in a swoon. Saith the archbishop: "Alack for thee, good baron."

When the archbishop sees Roland swoon, he has such sorrow as he has never known before. He stretches out his hand and takes the horn of ivory, for in Roncevals there is a swift streamlet, and he would go to it to bring of its water to Roland. Slowly and falteringly he sets forth, but so weak he is he cannot walk, his strength has gone from him, too much blood has he lost, and before a man might cross an acre his heart faileth, and he falls forward upon his face, and the anguish of death comes upon him.

When Count Roland recovers from his swoon he gets upon his feet with great torment; he looks up and he looks down, and beyond his comrades, on the green grass, he sees that goodly baron, the archbishop, appointed of God in his stead. Turpin saith his *mea culpa*, and looks up, and stretches out his two hands towards heaven, and prays God that he grant him Paradise. And so he dies, the warrior of Charles. Long had he waged strong war against the paynims, both by his mighty battling and his goodly sermons. May God grant him his holy blessing.

Count Roland sees the archbishop upon the ground; his bowels have fallen out of his body, and his brains are oozing out of his forehead; Roland takes his fair, white hands and crosses them upon his breast between his two collar bones; and lifting up his voice, he mourns for him, after the manner of his people: "Ah gentle man, knight of high parentage, now I commend thee to the heavenly Glory; never will there be a man who shall serve him more willingly; never since the days of the apostles hath there been such a prophet to uphold the law, and win the hearts of men; may thy soul suffer no pain or torment, but may the doors of Paradise be opened to thee."

Now Roland feels that death is near him, and his brains flow out at his ears; he prays to the Lord God for his peers that he will receive them, and he prays to the angel Gabriel for himself. That he may be free from all reproach, he takes his horn of ivory in the one hand, and Durendal, his sword, in the other, and farther than a crossbow can cast an arrow, through a cornfield he goeth on towards Spain. At the crest of a hill, beneath two fair trees, are four stairs of marble; there he falls down on the green grass in a swoon, for death is close upon him.

High are the hills and very tall are the trees; the four stones are of shining marble; and there Count Roland swoons upon the green grass. Meantime a Saracen is watching him; he has stained his face and body with blood, and feigning death, he lies still among his fellows; but now he springs to his feet and hastens forward. Fair he was, and strong, and of good courage; and in his pride he breaks out into mighty wrath, and seizes upon Roland, both him and his arms, and he cries: "Now is the nephew of Charles overthrown. This his sword will I carry into Arabia." But at his touch the count recovered his senses.

Roland feels that his sword hath been taken from him, he opens his eyes, and saith: "Surely, thou art not one of our men." He holds his horn of ivory which he never lets out of his grasp, and he smites the Saracen upon the helm which was studded with gold and gems, and he breaks steel and head and bones that his two eyes start out, and he falls down dead at his feet. Then saith Roland: "Coward, what made thee so bold to lay hands upon me, whether right or wrong? No man shall hear it but shall hold thee a fool. Now is my horn of ivory broken in the bell, and its gold and its crystals have fallen."

Now Roland feels that his sight is gone from him. With much striving he gets upon his feet; the color has gone from his face; before him lies a brown stone, and in his sorrow and wrath he smites ten blows upon it. The sword grates upon the rock, but neither breaks nor splinters; and the count saith: "Holy Mary, help me now! Ah Durendal, alas for your goodness! Now am I near to death, and have no more need of you. Many a fight in the field have I won with you, many a wide land have I conquered with you, lands now ruled by Charles with the white beard. May the man who would flee before another, never possess you. For many a day have you been held by a right good lord, never will there be such another in France the free."

Roland smote upon the block of hard stone, and the steel grates, but neither breaks nor splinters. And when he sees that he can in nowise break it, he laments, saying: "O Durendal, how fair and bright thou art, in the sunlight how thou flashest and shinest!

Charles was once in the valley of Moriane, when God commanded him by one of his angels that he should give thee to a chieftain count; then the great and noble king girded thee upon me; and with thee I won for him Anjou and Bretagne, and I conquered Poitou and Maine for him, and for him I conquered Normandy the free, and Provence, and Acquitaine; and Lombardy, and all of Romagna; and I conquered for him Bavaria, and Flanders, and Bulgaria, and all of Poland; Constantinople which now pays him fealty, and Saxony, where he may work his will. And I conquered for him Wales, and Scotland, and Ireland, and England which he holds as his demesne. Many lands and countries have I won with thee, lands which Charles of the white beard rules. And now am I heavy of heart because of this my sword; rather would I die than that it should fall into the hands of the paynims. Lord God our Father, let not this shame fall upon France."

And again Roland smote upon the brown stone and beyond all telling shattered it; the sword grates, but springs back again into the air and is neither dented nor broken. And when the count sees he may in no wise break it, he laments, saying: "O Durendal, how fair and holy a thing thou art! In thy golden hilt is many a relic,—a tooth of Saint Peter, and some of the blood of Saint Basil, and hairs from the head of my lord, Saint Denis, and a bit of the raiment of the Virgin Mary. It is not meet that thou fall into the hands of the paynims, only Christians should wield thee. May no coward ever possess thee! Many wide lands have I conquered with thee, lands which Charles of the white beard rules; and thereby is the emperor great and mighty."

Now Roland feels that death has come upon him, and that it creeps down from his head to his heart. In all haste he moves under a pine tree, and hath cast himself down upon his face on the green grass. Under him he laid his sword and his horn of ivory; and he turned his face towards the paynim folk, for he would that Charles and all his men should say that the gentle count had died a conqueror. Speedily and full often he confesses his sins, and in atonement he offers his glove to God.

Roland lies on a high peak looking towards Spain; he feels that his time is spent, and with one hand he beats upon his breast: "O God, I have sinned; forgive me through thy might the wrongs, both great and small, which I have done from the day I was born even to this day on which I was smitten." With his right hand he holds out his glove to God; and lo, the angels of heaven come down to him.

Count Roland lay under the pine tree; he has turned his face towards Spain, and he begins to call many things to remembrance, —all the lands he had won by his valor, and sweet France, and the men of his lineage, and Charles, his liege lord, who had brought him up in his household; and he cannot help but weep. But he would not wholly forget himself, and again he confesses his sins and begs forgiveness of God: "Our Father, who art truth, who raised up Lazarus from the dead, and who defended Daniel from the lions, save thou my soul from the perils to which it is brought through the sins I wrought in my life days." With his right hand he offers his glove to God, and Saint Gabriel has taken it from his hand. Then his head sinks on his arm, and with clasped hands he hath gone to his end. And God sent him his cherubim, and Saint Michael of the Seas, and with them went Saint Gabriel, and they carried the soul of the count into Paradise.

14. The *Romance of Tristan and Iseult*

Medieval romances differed from the heroic epic in the great importance they conceded to love, and perhaps the most moving of all the medieval love stories was the *Romance of Tristan and Iseult*. Many poets treated of this "high tale of love and of death," and they told many adventures concerning these tragic lovers. In 1900, the great French scholar Joseph Bédier put together from various sources the history of Tristan and Iseult, and his reconstruction is followed here.

Tristan is the nephew of King Mark of Cornwall, and his loyal vassal. He is sent to Ireland to bring to Mark his chosen bride, Iseult. On the voyage home, through a tragic blunder, Tristan shares with Iseult a love potion intended for her future husband Mark. They fall in love, desperately and forever. With Iseult's marriage to Mark, their love involves them in the betrayal of an uncle and husband, the treason of a vassal, and adultery against Christian marriage. The lovers experience numerous close escapes, but are eventually captured. They succeed in escaping once more, but now must flee to the wilderness. The moral here seems to be that the anarchy of illicit love cannot abide within an ordered society, but only in the wild forest. Still, the lovers are not presented as callous sinners, but as the unhappy victims of a power stronger than themselves.

They return and try to separate. Tristan wanders widely through Europe, reaches Brittany, and there marries another girl, named Iseult of the White Hands. But his passion gives him no peace, and he grows ill in body and mind. A friend sails away to bring back his loved one, and tells him that if he succeeds, his returning ship will bear a white sail. Iseult does return with him, and the ship approaches Brittany with a white sail. But Tristan is too weak to view the sea himself, and Iseult of the White Hands lies to him about its color. He dies in grief, and Iseult, when she finds him, follows him in death.

The following selection tells of the discovery of the lovers by King Mark, their condemnation and flight to the wilderness. The scene is Mark's castle in Cornwall. Brangien is Iseult's faithful maid, who knew about the love affair and tried to protect the lovers from themselves. The Morholt was a terrible monster which Tristan had slain in an earlier episode. The selection is taken from *The Romance of Tristan and Iseult*, retold by J. Bédier and trans. by H. Belloc (London: George Allen and Co., 1913), pp. 53–87.

The Tall Pine Tree

As King Mark came down to greet Iseult upon the shore, Tristan took her hand and led her to the king and the king took seizin of her, taking her hand. He led her in great pomp to his castle of Tintagel, and as she came in hall amid the vassals her beauty shone so that the walls were lit as they are lit at dawn. Then King Mark blessed those swallows which, by happy courtesy, had brought the Hair of Gold, and Tristan also he blessed, and the hundred knights who, on that adventurous bark, had gone to find him joy of heart and of eyes; yet to him also that ship was to bring sting, torment and mourning.

And on the eighteenth day, having called his barony together he took Iseult to wife. But on the wedding night, to save her friend, Brangien took her place in the darkness for her remorse demanded even this from her; nor was the trick discovered.

Then Iseult lived as a queen, but lived in sadness. She had King Mark's tenderness and the barons' honor; the people also loved her; she passed her days amid the frescoes on the walls and floors all strewn with flowers; good jewels had she and purple cloth and tapestry of Hungary and Thessaly too, and songs of harpers, and curtains upon which were worked leopards and eagles and popinjays and all the beasts of sea and field. And her love too she had, love high and splendid, for as is the custom among great lords, Tristan could ever be near her. At his leisure and his dalliance, night and day: for he slept in the King's chamber as great lords do, among the lieges and the councilors. Yet still she feared; for though her love were secret and Tristan unsuspected (for who suspects a son?) Brangien knew. And Brangien seemed in the queen's mind like a witness spying; for Brangien alone knew what manner of life she led, and held her at mercy so. And the queen thought: Ah, if some day she should weary of serving as a slave the bed where once she passed for queen . . . If Tristan should die from her betrayal! So fear maddened the queen, but not in truth the fear of Brangien who was loyal; her own heart bred the fear.

Not Brangien who was faithful, not Brangien, but themselves had these lovers to fear, for hearts so stricken will lose their vigilance. Love pressed them hard, as thirst presses the dying stag to the stream; love dropped upon them from high heaven, as a hawk slipped after long hunger falls right upon the bird. And love will not be hidden. Brangien indeed by her prudence saved them well, nor ever were the queen and her lover unguarded. But in every hour and place every man could see Love terrible, that rode them, and could see in these lovers their every sense overflowing like new wine working in the vat.

The four felons at court who had hated Tristan of old for his prowess, watched the queen; they had guessed that great love, and they burnt with envy and hatred and now a kind of evil joy. They planned to give news of their watching to the king, to see his tenderness turned to fury, Tristan thrust out or slain, and the queen in torment; for though they feared Tristan their hatred mastered their fear; and, on a day, the four barons called King Mark to parley, and Andret said: "Fair king, your heart will be troubled and we four also mourn; yet are we bound to tell you what we know. You have placed your trust in Tristan and Tristan would shame you. In vain we warned you. For the love of one man you have mocked ties of blood and all your barony. Learn then that Tristan loves the queen; it is truth proved and many a word is passing on it now."

The royal king shrank and answered: "Coward! What thought

was that? Indeed I have placed my trust in Tristan. And rightly, for on the day when the Morholt offered combat to you all, you hung your heads and were dumb, and you trembled before him; but Tristan dared him for the honor of this land, and took mortal wounds. Therefore do you hate him, and therefore do I cherish him beyond thee, Andret, and beyond any other; but what then have you seen or heard or known?"

"Naught, lord, save what your eyes could see or your ears hear. Look you and listen, sire, if there is yet time."

And they left him to taste the poison.

Then King Mark watched the queen and Tristan; but Brangien noting it warned them both and the king watched in vain, so that, soon wearying of an ignoble task, but knowing (alas!) that he could not kill his uneasy thought, he sent for Tristan and said: "Tristan, leave this castle; and having left it, remain apart and do not think to return to it, and do not repass its moat or boundaries. Felons have charged you with an awful treason, but ask me nothing; I could not speak their words without shame to us both, and for your part seek you no word to appease. I have not believed them . . . had I done so . . . But their evil words have troubled all my soul and only by your absence can my disquiet be soothed. Go, doubtless I will soon recall you. Go, my son, you are still dear to me."

When the felons heard the news they said among themselves, "He is gone, the wizard; he is driven out. Surely he will cross the sea on far adventures to carry his traitor service to some distant king."

But Tristan had not strength to depart altogether; and when he had crossed the moats and boundaries of the castle he knew he could go no further. He stayed in Tintagel town and lodged with Gorvenal in a burgess' house, and languished oh! more wounded than when in that past day the shaft of the Morholt had tainted his body.

In the close towers Iseult the Fair drooped also, but more wretched still. For it was hers all day long to feign laughter and all night long to conquer fever and despair. And all night as she lay by King Mark's side, fever still kept her waking, and she stared at darkness. She longed to fly to Tristan and she dreamt dreams of running to the gates and of finding there sharp scythes, traps of the felons, that cut her tender knees; and she dreamt of weakness and falling, and that her wounds had left her blood upon the ground. Now these lovers would have died, but Brangien succored them. At peril of her life she found the house where Tristan lay. There Gorvenal opened to her very gladly, knowing what salvation she could bring.

So she found Tristan, and to save the lovers she taught him a device, nor was ever known a more subtle ruse of love.

Behind the castle of Tintagel was an orchard fenced around and wide and all closed in with stout and pointed stakes and numberless trees were there and fruit on them, birds and clusters of sweet grapes. And furthest from the castle, by the stakes of the palisade, was a tall pine tree, straight and with heavy branches spreading from its trunk. At its root a living spring welled calm into a marble round, then ran between two borders winding, throughout the orchard and so, on, till it flowed at last within the castle and through the women's rooms.

And every evening, by Brangien's counsel, Tristan cut him twigs and bark, leapt the sharp stakes and, having come beneath the pine, threw them into the clear spring; they floated light as foam down the stream to the women's rooms; and Iseult watched for their coming, and on those evenings she would wander out into the orchard and find her friend. Lithe and in fear would she come, watching at every step for what might lurk in the trees observing, foes or the felons whom she knew, till she spied Tristan; and the night and the branches of the pine protected them.

And so she said one night: "Oh, Tristan, I have heard that the castle is faëry and that twice a year it vanishes away. So is it vanished now and this is that enchanted orchard of which the harpers sing." And as she said it, the sentinels bugled dawn.

Iseult had refound her joy. Mark's thought of ill-ease grew faint; but the felons felt or knew which way lay truth, and they guessed that Tristan had met the queen. Till at last Duke Andret (whom God shame) said to his peers: "My lords, let us take counsel of Frocin the Dwarf; for he knows the seven arts, and magic and every kind of charm. He will teach us if he will the wiles of Iseult the Fair."

The little evil man drew signs for them and characters of sorcery; he cast the fortunes of the hour and then at last he said: "Sirs, high good lords, this night shall you seize them both."

Then they led the little wizard to the king, and he said: "Sire, bid your huntsmen leash the hounds and saddle the horses, proclaim a seven days' hunt in the forest and seven nights abroad

therein, and hang me high if you do not hear this night what con-
verse Tristan holds."

So did the king unwillingly; and at fall of night he left the hunt
taking the dwarf in pillion, and entered the orchard, and the dwarf
took him to the tall pine tree, saying: "Fair king, climb into these
branches and take with you your arrows and your bow, for you
may need them; and bide you still."

That night the moon shone clear. Hid in the branches the king
saw his nephew leap the palisades and throw his bark and twigs
into the stream. But Tristan had bent over the round well to throw
them and so doing had seen the image of the king. He could not
stop the branches as they floated away, and there, yonder, in the
women's rooms, Iseult was watching and would come.

She came, and Tristan watched her motionless. Above him in
the tree he heard the click of the arrow when it fits the string.

She came, but with more prudence than her wont, thinking,
"What has passed, that Tristan does not come to meet me? He has
seen some foe."

Suddenly, by the clear moonshine, she also saw the king's
shadow in the fount. She showed the wit of women well, she did
not lift her eyes. "Lord God," she said, low down, "grant I may
be the first to speak."

"Tristan," she said, "what have you dared to do, calling me
hither at such an hour? Often have you called me—to beseech, you
said. And queen though I am, I know you won me that title—and
I have come. What would you?"

"Queen, I would have you pray the king for me."

She was in tears and trembling, but Tristan praised God the
Lord who had shown his friend her peril.

"Queen," he went on, "often and in vain have I summoned you;
never would you come. Take pity; the king hates me and I know
not why. Perhaps you know the cause and can charm his anger.
For whom can he trust if not you, chaste queen and courteous,
Iseult?"

"Truly, Lord Tristan, you do not know he doubts us both. And
I, to add to my shame, must acquaint you of it. Ah! but God
knows if I lie, never went out my love to any man but he that first
received me. And would you have me, at such a time, implore your
pardon of the king? Why, did he know of my passage here tonight
he would cast my ashes to the wind. My body trembles and I am
afraid. I go, for I have waited too long."

In the branches the king smiled and had pity.

And as Iseult fled: "Queen," said Tristan, "in the Lord's name help me, for charity."

"Friend," she replied, "God aid you! The king wrongs you but the Lord God will be by you in whatever land you go."

So she went back to the women's rooms and told it to Brangien, who cried: "Iseult, God has worked a miracle for you, he is compassionate and will not hurt the innocent in heart."

And when he had left the orchard, the king said smiling: "Fair nephew, that ride you planned is over now."

But in an open glade apart, Frocin, the Dwarf, read in the clear stars that the king now meant his death; he blackened with shame and fear and fled into Wales.

The Discovery

King Mark made peace with Tristan. Tristan returned to the castle as of old. Tristan slept in the king's chamber with his peers. He could come or go, the king thought no more of it.

Mark had pardoned the felons, and as the seneschal, Dinas of Lidan, found the dwarf wandering in a forest abandoned, he brought him home, and the king had pity and pardoned even him.

But his goodness did but feed the ire of the barons, who swore this oath: If the king kept Tristan in the land they would withdraw to their strongholds as for war, and they called the king to parley.

"Lord," said they, "drive you Tristan forth. He loves the queen as all who choose can see, but as for us we will bear it no longer."

And the king sighed, looking down in silence.

"King," they went on, "we will not bear it, for we know now that this is known to you and that yet you will not move. Parley you, and take counsel. As for us if you will not exile this man, your nephew, and drive him forth out of your land forever, we will withdraw within our bailiwicks and take our neighbors also from your court: for we cannot endure his presence longer in this place. Such is your balance: choose."

"My lords," said he, "once I hearkened to the evil words you spoke of Tristan, yet was I wrong in the end. But you are my lieges and I would not lose the service of my men. Counsel me therefore, I charge you, you that owe me counsel. You know me for a man neither proud nor overstepping."

"Lord," said they, "call then Frocin hither. You mistrust him

for that orchard night. Still, was it not he that read in the stars of
the queen's coming there and to the very pine tree too? He is very
wise, take counsel of him."

And he came, did that hunchback of hell: the felons greeted
him and he planned this evil.

"Sire," said he, "let your nephew ride hard tomorrow at dawn
with a brief drawn up on parchment and well sealed with a seal:
bid him ride to King Arthur at Carduel. Sire, he sleeps with the
peers in your chamber; go you out when the first sleep falls on
men, and if he love Iseult so madly, why, then I swear by God
and by the laws of Rome, he will try to speak with her before he
rides. But if he do so unknown to you or to me, then slay me. As
for the trap, let me lay it, but do you say nothing of his ride to
him until the time for sleep."

And when King Mark had agreed, this dwarf did a vile thing.
He bought of a baker four farthings' worth of flour, and hid it in
the turn of his coat. That night, when the king had supped and
the men-at-arms lay down to sleep in hall, Tristan came to the
king as custom was, and the king said: "Fair nephew, do my will:
ride tomorrow night to King Arthur at Carduel, and give him this
brief, with my greeting, that he may open it: and stay you with
him but one day."

And when Tristan said: "I will take it on the morrow;"

The king added: "Aye, and before day dawn."

But, as the peers slept all round the king their lord, that night,
a mad thought took Tristan that, before he rode, he knew not for
how long, before dawn he would say a last word to the queen.
And there was a spear length in the darkness between them. Now
the dwarf slept with the rest in the king's chamber, and when he
thought that all slept he rose and scattered the flour silently in
the spear length that lay between Tristan and the queen; but
Tristan watched and saw him, and said to himself:

"It is to mark my footsteps, but there shall be no marks to
show."

At midnight, when all was dark in the room, no candle nor any
lamp glimmering, the king went out silently by the door and with
him the dwarf. Then Tristan rose in the darkness and judged the
spear length and leapt the space between, for his farewell. But
that day in the hunt a boar had wounded him in the leg, and in this
effort the wound bled. He did not feel it or see it in the darkness,
but the blood dripped upon the couches and the flour strewn be-

tween; and outside in the moonlight the dwarf read the heavens
and knew what had been done and he cried: "Enter, my king, and
if you do not hold them, hang me high."

Then the king and the dwarf and the four felons ran in with
lights and noise, and though Tristan had regained his place there
was the blood for witness, and though Iseult feigned sleep, and
Perinis too, who lay at Tristan's feet, yet there was the blood
for witness. And the king looked in silence at the blood where
it lay upon the bed and the boards and trampled into the flour.

And the four barons held Tristan down upon his bed and
mocked the queen also, promising her full justice; and they bared
and showed the wound whence the blood flowed.

Then the king said: "Tristan, now nothing longer holds. Tomorrow you shall die."

And Tristan answered: "Have mercy, lord, in the name of God
that suffered the cross!" But the felons called on the king to take
vengeance, saying: "Do justice, king: take vengeance."

And Tristan went on, "Have mercy, not on me—for why should
I stand at dying?—Truly, but for you, I would have sold my
honor high to cowards who, under your peace, have put hands on
my body—but in homage to you I have yielded and you may do
with me what you will. But, lord, remember the queen!"

And as he knelt at the king's feet he still complained: "Remember the queen; for if any man of your household make so bold as
to maintain the lie that I loved her unlawfully, I will stand up
armed to him in a ring. Sire, in the name of God the Lord, have
mercy on her."

Then the barons bound him with ropes, and the queen also. But
had Tristan known that trial by combat was to be denied him,
certainly he would not have suffered it.

For he trusted in God and knew no man dared draw sword
against him in the lists. And truly he did well to trust in God,
for though the felons mocked him when he said he had loved
loyally, yet I call you to witness, my lords who read this, and
who know of the philter drunk upon the high seas, and who understand whether his love were disloyalty indeed. For men see this
and that outward thing, but God alone the heart, and in the heart
alone is crime and the sole final judge is God. Therefore did he
lay down the law that a man accused might uphold his cause by
battle, and God himself fights for the innocent in such a combat.

Therefore did Tristan claim justice and the right of battle and

therefore was he careful to fail in nothing of the homage he owed
King Mark, his lord.

But had he known what was coming, he would have killed the
felons.

The Chantry Leap

Dark was the night, and the news ran that Tristan and the queen
were held and that the king would kill them; and wealthy burgess,
or common man, they wept and ran to the palace.

And the murmurs and the cries ran through the city, but such
was the king's anger in his castle above that not the strongest nor
the proudest baron dared move him.

Night ended and the day drew near. Mark, before dawn, rode
out to the place where he held pleas and judgment. He ordered
a ditch to be dug in the earth and knotty vine-shoots and thorns
to be laid therein.

At the hour of Prime he had a ban cried through his land to
gather the men of Cornwall; they came with a great noise and the
king spoke them thus: "My lords, I have made here a faggot of
thorns for Tristan and the queen; for they have fallen." But they
cried all, with tears: "A sentence, lord, a sentence; an indictment
and pleas; for killing without trial is shame and crime." But Mark
answered in his anger: "Neither respite, nor delay, nor pleas, nor
sentence. By God that made the world, if any dare petition me, he
shall burn first!"

He ordered the fire to be lit, and Tristan to be called.

The flames rose, and all were silent before the flames, and the
king waited.

The servants ran to the room where watch was kept on the two
lovers; and they dragged Tristan out by his hands though he wept
for his honor; but as they dragged him off in such a shame, the
queen still called to him:

"Friend, if I die that you may live, that will be great joy."

Now, hear how full of pity is God and how he heard the lament
and the prayers of the common folk, that day.

For as Tristan and his guards went down from the town to
where the faggot burned, near the road upon a rock was a chantry,
it stood at a cliff's edge steep and sheer, and it turned to the sea-
breeze; in the apse of it were windows glazed. Then Tristan said to
those with him: "My lords, let me enter this chantry, to pray for
a moment the mercy of God whom I have offended; my death is

near. There is but one door to the place, my lords, and each of you
has his sword drawn. So, you may well see that, when my prayer
to God is done, I must come past you again: when I have prayed
God, my lords, for the last time."

And one of the guards said: "Why, let him go in."

So they let him enter to pray. But he, once in, dashed through
and leapt the altar rail and the altar too and forced a window of
the apse, and leapt again over the cliff's edge. So might he die, but
not of that shameful death before the people.

Now learn, my lords, how generous was God to him that day.
The wind took Tristan's cloak and he fell upon a smooth rock at
the cliff's foot, which to this day the men of Cornwall call "Tristan's leap."

His guards still waited for him at the chantry door, but vainly,
for God was now his guard. And he ran, and the fine sand
crunched under his feet, and far off he saw the faggot burning, and
the smoke and the crackling flames; and fled.

Sword girt and bridle loose, Gorvenal had fled the city, lest
the king burn him in his master's place: and he found Tristan on
the shore.

"Master," said Tristan, "God has saved me, but oh! master, to
what end? For without Iseult I may not and I will not live, and
I rather had died of my fall. They will burn her for me, then I
too will die for her."

"Lord," said Gorvenal, "take no counsel of anger. See here this
thicket with a ditch dug round about it. Let us hide therein where
the track passes near, and comers by it will tell us news; and, boy,
if they burn Iseult, I swear by God, the Son of Mary, never to
sleep under a roof again until she be avenged."

There was a poor man of the common folk that had seen Tristan's fall, and had seen him stumble and rise after, and he crept to
Tintagel and to Iseult where she was bound, and said: "Queen,
weep no more. Your friend has fled safely."

"Then I thank God," said she, "and whether they bind or loose
me, and whether they kill or spare me, I care but little now."

And though blood came at the cord-knots, so tightly had the
traitors bound her, yet still she said, smiling: "Did I weep for that
when God has loosed my friend I should be little worth."

When the news came to the king that Tristan had leapt that leap
and was lost he paled with anger, and bade his men bring forth
Iseult.

They dragged her from the room, and she came before the crowd, held by her delicate hands, from which blood dropped, and the crowd called: "Have pity on her—the loyal queen and honored! Surely they that gave her up brought mourning on us all—our curses on them!"

But the king's men dragged her to the thorn faggot as it blazed. She stood up before the flame, and the crowd cried its anger, and cursed the traitors and the king. None could see her without pity, unless he had a felon's heart: she was so tightly bound. The tears ran down her face and fell upon her gray gown where ran a little thread of gold, and a thread of gold was twined into her hair.

Just then there had come up a hundred lepers of the king's, deformed and broken, white horribly, and limping on their crutches. And they drew near the flame, and being evil, loved the sight. And their chief Ivan, the ugliest of them all, cried to the king in a quavering voice: "O king, you would burn this woman in that flame, and it is sound justice, but too swift, for very soon the fire will fall, and her ashes will very soon be scattered by the high wind and her agony be done. Throw her rather to your lepers where she may drag out a life for ever asking death."

And the king answered: "Yes; let her live that life, for it is better justice and more terrible. I can love those that gave me such a thought."

And the lepers answered: "Throw her among us, and make her one of us. Never shall lady have known a worse end. And look," they said, "at our rags and our abominations. She has had pleasure in rich stuffs and furs, jewels and walls of marble, honor, good wines and joy, but when she sees your lepers always, king, and only them for ever, their couches and their huts, then indeed she will know the wrong she has done, and bitterly desire even that great flame of thorns."

And as the king heard them, he stood a long time without moving; then he ran to the queen and seized her by the hand, and she cried: "Burn me! rather burn me!"

But the king gave her up, and Ivan took her, and the hundred lepers pressed around, and to hear her cries all the crowd rose in pity. But Ivan had an evil gladness, and as he went he dragged her out of the borough bounds, with his hideous company.

Now they took that road where Tristan lay in hiding, and Gorvenal said to him: "Son, here is your friend. Will you do naught?"

Then Tristan mounted the horse and spurred it out of the bush, and cried: "Ivan, you have been at the queen's side a moment, and too long. Now leave her if you would live."

But Ivan threw his cloak away and shouted: "Your clubs, comrades, and your staves! Crutches in the air—for a fight is on!"

Then it was fine to see the lepers throwing their capes aside, and stirring their sick legs, and brandishing their crutches, some threatening: groaning all; but to strike them Tristan was too noble. There are singers who sing that Tristan killed Ivan, but it is a lie. Too much a knight was he to kill such things. Gorvenal indeed, snatching up an oak sapling, crashed it on Ivan's head till his blood ran down to his misshapen feet. Then Tristan took the queen.

Henceforth near him she felt no further evil. He cut the cords that bound her arms so straightly, and he left the plain so that they plunged into the wood of Morois; and there in the thick wood Tristan was as sure as in a castle keep.

And as the sun fell they halted all three at the foot of a little hill: fear had wearied the queen, and she leant her head upon his body and slept.

But in the morning, Gorvenal stole from a woodman his bow and two good arrows plumed and barbed, and gave them to Tristan, the great archer, and he shot him a fawn and killed it. Then Gorvenal gathered dry twigs, struck flint, and lit a great fire to cook the venison. And Tristan cut him branches and made a hut and garnished it with leaves. And Iseult slept upon the thick leaves there.

So, in the depths of the wild wood began for the lovers that savage life which yet they loved very soon.

IV. *The literature of towns*

15. A French *fabliau*

The French *fabliaux*, poetic short stories written in eight-syllable verses, present lively (and often salacious) narratives with little character development but with much wit and comedy. The following tale, "The Peasant Doctor," gives a good example of the genre's robust good humor. The selection is taken from *Fabliaux: Ribald Tales from the Old French for the First Time Done into English*, by Robert Hellman and Richard O'Gorman. Copyright © 1965 by Robert Hellman and Richard O'Gorman. Thomas Y. Crowell Company, New York, publishers. Pp. 71–80. The editor is grateful for permission to reprint it here.

THERE was once a rich peasant who was very avaricious and stingy. He was never without a plow, which he worked himself with the air of a mare and an old nag; he had plenty of meat and bread and wine and whatever else he needed. But his friends and everyone else found fault with him because he had no wife. He said that he would take a good one willingly, if he could find one; and they said that they would search until they found the best one they could.

In that country there lived a knight, an old man and a widower. He had a daughter who was a very beautiful and well-mannered young lady. But, because he lacked money, the knight could not find anyone who would ask for his daughter's hand, although he would very willingly have married her off, she being of an age and disposition to wed. The peasant's friends went to this knight and asked for his daughter's hand on behalf of the peasant, who had so much gold and silver, such an abundance of grain, and such great plenty of linens. He gave her to them straightway and agreed to this marriage. The daughter, who was motherless and

very dutiful, did not dare oppose her father, and so she agreed to
do as he wished. So the peasant, as soon as he could, made his
wedding and took to wife this girl, who was much grieved at the
marriage and who, if she dared, would have done anything not to
go through with it.

After the wedding had taken place and all that went with it,
the peasant was not long in thinking that he had made a bad
bargain. For it did not suit his trade at all to have a knight's daughter
at home when he went out to plow. A young lord, for whom every
day is a holiday, can go strolling down the street; perhaps when
he was away from the house, the priest would come to visit, today,
tomorrow, and the day after, until he had seduced his wife. Nor
would she ever love him or hold him dearer than two loaves of
bread.

"Alas, poor wretch that I am!" he said. "Now I don't know
where to look for advice; for it's no use being sorry now." Then
he began to think how he could keep what he feared from happening. "My God!" he cried, "if I should beat her in the morning
when I get up, she would weep all day and I could go and work
my land. I'm sure that as long as she wept no one would come
courting her. In the evening when I come back, I shall ask her
forgiveness, for the love of God. I shall make her happy in the
evening, but in the morning she shall sulk. I'll take leave of her
then, when I have had a bite to eat."

Then the peasant asked for something to eat, and his wife
hastened to bring it to him. They did not have salmon or partridge,
but bread and wine they had, and fried eggs and cheese in great
abundance, which the peasant had stored up. And when the table
was cleared, with the palm of his hand, which was large and wide,
the peasant struck his wife across the face so hard that he left the
marks of his fingers there. Then this churl, who was very strong,
seized her by the hair and beat her just as if she had deserved it.
Then he went straight to his fields, and his wife remained there
weeping.

"Alas!" she said. "What shall I do? And how shall I be comforted? I do not know any more what to say. My father indeed
betrayed me when he gave me to that baseborn fellow. Was I afraid
that I would die of hunger? Surely I must have had madness in my
heart when I agreed to such a marriage. God, why did my mother
die!" So pitifully did she lament that everyone who came to see
her turned away again.

Thus did she grieve until the sun had set and the peasant returned home. Then he fell at her feet and begged her forgiveness for God's sake. "Know," he said, "that the Adversary did this to me; it was he who made me do violence. See here, I give you my word that I will never raise a hand to you again. I am grieved and distressed that I beat you." This stinking peasant pleaded so much that his wife pardoned him and gave him the supper which she had prepared; and when he had had enough to eat, they went to bed in peace. But in the morning this stinkard once again beat his wife so hard that he almost crippled her. Then he went again to plow his fields. The lady began to weep. "Alas!" said she. "What shall I do and how shall I be comforted? I can see that evil has befallen me. Has my husband ever been beaten? Not he, he does not know what blows are. If he did, not for all the world would he give me so many of them."

While she was sorrowing thus, behold, two of the king's messengers, each on a white palfrey, came riding toward her. They greeted her in the king's name and asked her to give them something to eat, for they were in great need of food. Willingly she gave them something, and then she asked them: "Where are you going and where do you come from? And tell me, what are you looking for?" One of them answered: "Madam, in faith, we are messengers of the king, who has sent us to look for a physician. We must go over to England." "What for?" said the wife. "Because Mistress Aude, the king's daughter, is sick. It is eight days since she was able to eat or drink, for a fishbone is stuck in her throat. Now, the king is very grieved; if he loses her he will never be happy again."

Then the lady said: "You will not go as far as you think; for my husband, I assure you, is a fine physician. Really, he knows more about medicines and how to judge truly from urine than ever Hippocrates did." "Lady, are you joking?" "I have no wish to joke," she said, "but my husband is of such a humor that he won't do anything for anybody unless he is first beaten soundly." And they answered: "Well, it's not likely he'll remain behind for lack of a beating. Lady, where can we find him?" "You'll find him in the fields. When you come out of this courtyard, follow right along the course of the brook on the other side of that abandoned road, and the first plow you come to is ours. Go," she said. "To Saint Peter the apostle I commend you."

And they went riding off until they found the peasant. They

greeted him in the king's name, and then, without further ado, they said to him: "Come immediately to speak to the king." "What for?" said the peasant. "Because of the wisdom that's in you. There is not such a fine doctor in this country. We have come a great distance to find you." When the peasant heard himself called a doctor, his blood began to boil, and he said that where such things were concerned he didn't know beans from onions. "Now then," said the first messenger, "what are we waiting for?" And the second one said: "You know that before he says or does anything worthwhile he expects to be beaten." The first one struck him on the ear, and the second struck him square in the back with a big thick staff he had; they beat him shamefully. Then they mounted him on a horse, his face to the tail, and led him to the king.

The king came to meet them and said to them: "Have you found anything?" "Yes, sire," they said together; and the peasant trembled with fear. One of the messengers spoke up and told the king about the peasant's peculiar foibles: that he was full of trickery and would do nothing for anyone if he were not beaten soundly first. "What a wretched physician we have here," said the king. "Never before have I heard tell of such a one." And one of the servants said: "Let him be beaten then, if that's the way it is. I am ready. You have only to say the word and I shall give him what he deserves." The king addressed the peasant. "Master doctor," he said, "listen. I shall send for my daughter, for she is in great need of a cure." The peasant cried for mercy. "For God's sake, sire," he said, "before God, who does not lie, I tell you that I know nothing of medicine, nor am I of the physician's trade." And the king said: "What wonders do I hear! Beat him for me!" His servants, who went willingly about their work, seized the peasant; and when he felt the blows, he thought he was going mad. "Mercy!" he began to cry. "I will cure her at once."

The girl was brought into the hall, all pale and flushed, and the peasant wondered how he could cure her, for he well knew that he must either do so or die. Then he thought that if he wanted to cure her and save her, what he had to do was say or do something to make her laugh; and that would make the bone jump out of her throat, for she had not swallowed it down into her body. So he said to the king: "Have a fire made in that room which lies apart. You will see what I shall do and how, if it please God, I shall cure her."

The king had a roaring fire made; the squires and servants

hopped to it and quickly lit the fire where the king had ordered it. And the maiden came and sat by the fire on a stool which they had brought for her. The peasant took off his breeches and stripped himself all naked. Then he stretched out across the fire and scratched and curried himself. He had long nails and a tough skin, and know, you couldn't find a better scratcher from here to Saumur. The maiden, when she saw this, in spite of all the pain she felt, wanted to laugh; and she strained so hard that the bone flew out of her throat and onto the coals. At once the peasant put on his clothes, took up the bone, and ran out of the room in great joy. When he saw the king, he cried out loud: "Sire, your daughter is cured! Here is the bone, thanks to God!"

The king was overjoyed and said: "Now know that I love you above all things. Now you shall have robes and linens." "Thank you, sire," said the peasant, "but I don't want them and I can't stay. I must go back home." "That you shall not do," said the king. "You will be my physician and my friend." "Thanks, sire, but by Saint German, there was no bread at my house when I left yesterday morning. I was to have gone and got some at the mill." The king called two boys. "Beat him for me," he said, "and he'll stay." The boys leapt on him at once and began to beat him. When the peasant felt the blows on his arms and on his legs and on his back, he began to cry for mercy: "I'll stay, let me be!"

So the peasant remained at court. His hair and whiskers were trimmed, and he wore a robe of scarlet. But how embarrassed he was when the sick of that country, more than eighty of them, I believe, came before the king on a certain holiday, and each of them told his misfortune. The king called the peasant. "Doctor," he said, "take care of these people; do it quickly and cure them for me." "Sire," the peasant said, "may God help me, there are too many of them. I can't accomplish so much or cure them all." The king called two boys, and each of them picked up a rod for they well knew why the king called them. When the peasant saw them coming, his blood began to freeze. "Mercy!" he cried. "I will cure them immediately."

The peasant asked for some wood, of which there was more than enough, and a fire was built in the hall, which he kindled himself. He assembled all the sick people, and then he said to the king: "Sire, you must leave the room and all those who are not sick." The king left the hall very willingly, he and all his household. Then the peasant said to the sick people: "My lords,

by the God who made me, there is a great deal to cure you of. I do
not think I can do it all. I shall select the sickest one and put him
on that fire; I shall burn him up there, and the others will benefit
from this, for all who swallow the powder of the man who has been
burned will be cured immediately." They looked at one another,
and the most hunchbacked or dropsical one among them would
not admit, for all of Normandy, that he was the sickest one there.
The peasant said to the first: "I see that you have grown very
weak. You are the worst afflicted of the lot." "No, thank you,
my lord, I am quite healthy. I am relieved of the great pain which
I suffered for a long time. I wouldn't lie to you about it in any
way." "Go out then," said the peasant. "What were you looking
for here?" The sick man made for the door, and when he came
out the king asked him: "Are you cured?" "Yes, sire, I am sounder
than an apple. You have a very worthy man in that doctor."

But why should I make a long story of it? Not one of them,
large or small, would agree, for all the world, to be thrown into
the fire; they chose rather to go away just as if they had been
cured. And when the king saw them, he was beside himself with
joy. He said to the peasant: "I wonder at how you cured them
so quickly!" "Thank you, sire," said the peasant. "I cast a spell
on them. I know a spell that is worth more than ginger or setwall."
And the king said: "Now you may go home whenever you like,
and you will take with you money and horses, both palfreys and
war steeds. And when I send for you again, you will do what I
want. You will be my dear good friend, and I shall love you more
than anyone in the land. But don't be foolish any more and cause
yourself to be beaten, for it is a shame to strike you." "Thank you,
sire," said the peasant. "I am your man evening and morning,
and so I shall be as long as I live. Nor will I ever go back on my
word."

He took his leave of the king and joyfully returned home.
Never had there been a richer landholder. He no longer went
to the plow, nor did he ever again beat his wife; rather, he loved
and cherished her. So it happened as I have told you: because
of his wife and his own cunning, he was a good physician without
learning.

16. Isegrim's fishing, from the *Romance of Reynard the Fox*

The following selection from the *Romance of Reynard* illustrates one of its favorite themes: the superiority of the fox's wit and cunning over the unthinking strength of Isegrim the wolf.

The French original, written in rimed couplets of eight syllables, may be found in *Le Roman de Renart. Analyse et meilleures pages*, ed. Rémy Beaurieux (Paris: Jean Gillequin, 1911), pp. 67–70. The translation is by D. Herlihy.

It was shortly before Christmas
When the sides of pork are salted.
The heavens were clear and starry
And the fish ponds were so frozen
Where Isegrim used to fish,
That one could have danced upon them.
Some distance out there was a hole
Which some peasants cut and kept
Where they led their cattle
Each night to exercise and drink.
They had left a bucket there.
Reynard comes in great haste,
And he looks at his comrade.
"Sir," he said, "go over there.
There is plenty of fish
And the instrument by which you can catch
Eels and carp
And other good and lovely fish."
Isegrim said: "Brother Reynard,
Now take the bucket behind me,
Tie it tightly to my tail."
Reynard took it and bound it
Around his tail as best he could.
"Brother," he said, "now it's up to you

To handle yourself very prudently
In order to have the fish come."
There is nearby a hidden bush.
Reynard put his snout between his paws,
So that he saw what was in front of him.
And Isegrim is on the ice.
The bucket is in the water
Filled by good fortune with broken ice.
The water begins to freeze
And to surround the bucket
Which was tied to the tail.
The tail, which was submerged in the ice
Is frozen in the water,
And is sealed to the ice.
He thought he would lift himself
And pull the bucket to him.
He tries this in many ways.
He doesn't know what to do.
He begins to worry.
He begins to call to Reynard
That he should no longer hide,
For already the dawn is breaking.
Reynard with his head raised up
Looks at him with widened eyes.
"Brother," he says, "let's leave the work.
Let us depart, good sweet friend,
We have caught enough fish."
And Isegrim cries to him.
"Reynard," he says, "there are too many fish.
I have caught so many I do not know what to say."
And Reynard began to laugh
As if he had said openly,
"He who desires all, loses all."
The night passes, the dawn breaks;
The sun rises in the morning.
The paths are white with snow,
And Monsieur Constance des Granches,
A very rich knight,
Who lived near the pond,
Arose together with his household
Which was very joyous and gay.

He has taken a horn, calls his dogs
And commands that his horses be saddled
And he shouts and calls for his servants.
And Reynard hears him and turns and flees,
So hard that he gives no thought to being quiet.
Isegrim remains in trouble.
He tries very hard; he tugs and pulls.
He almost rips his skin off.
If he wishes to leave that place,
He'll have to leave his tail behind.
As Isegrim was continuing to struggle,
Here comes a boy running.
He holds two greyhounds on a leash.
He sees Isegrim (he was hurrying toward him)
All frozen on the ice,
With his mangy neck.
He looks at him and then he cries,
"Ha, ha, the wolf, help, help!"
The hunters, when they hear him,
From the house they go out
With all the dogs by one gate.
Now Isegrim is in a pickle.
Before him Constance now comes
On a horse with great haste.
He cries aloud while riding,
"Let them go, let the dogs go."
The attendants loose the dogs,
And the hounds attack the wolf.
Isegrim bristles much.
The hunters urge on the dogs,
And threaten them harshly.
Isegrim defends himself well;
In the teeth of death, what else could he do?
He much preferred peace.
Then Constance with his sword drawn
Approaches him to strike him hard.
On foot he descends towards the place
And comes to the wolf across the ice.
He has attacked him in the rear.
He wishes to strike him, but he missed his blow.
The blow threw Constance to one side,

And then he fell backwards
So that the back of his neck was bloodied.
He lifted himself with great pain.
With great earnestness he rejoined the battle.
Now could you hear fierce warfare.
He thought to get him in the head,
But on his other side the blow came to rest.
The sword descended towards the tail.
Quite cleanly it cut it off.
And Isegrim, who has felt it,
Leaps to the side, then turns
Biting the dogs, one by one,
Who kept coming at his heels.
But the tail remains behind, in pawn.
And many he catches and many he wounds.
His heart almost breaks from pain.
He can take no more, he turns in flight
Until he rests his back upon a knoll.

. . . .

The dogs are tired, overcome with fatigue,
And Isegrim loses no time
Fleeing, he goes (he so looks after himself)
Right towards the woods with great haste.
He rails, exclaims and swears
That he will avenge himself on Reynard,
Nevermore will he love him.

V . *Religious literature*

17. Our Lady's Tumbler

Our Lady's Tumbler is perhaps the most charming of many tales which grew up in the twelfth and thirteenth centuries around the figure of the Virgin Mary. It reflects the deep devotion to the Virgin, which was then becoming one of the most characteristic features of medieval piety. It should be noted that tumbling and other forms of public entertainment were looked upon with grave suspicion by the medieval Church. In suggesting that a good heart could make even these disreputable acts pleasing to God, the story implies that the interior spiritual disposition of the believer, more even than his external behavior, defined the character of true holiness.

This legend has been retold in a popular modern version by the French author Anatole France (1844–1924), under the title *Le Jongleur de Notre-Dame.*

The translation of the thirteenth-century original is taken from Eugene Mason, *Aucassin and Nicolette and Other Mediaeval Romances and Legends* (New York: E. P. Dutton and Co., 1910), pp. 53–66.

Amongst the lives of the ancient fathers, wherein may be found much profitable matter, this story is told for a true ensample. I do not say that you may not often have heard a fairer story, but at least this is not to be despised, and is well worth the telling. Now therefore will I say and narrate what chanced to this minstrel.

He erred up and down, to and fro, so often and in so many places, that he took the whole world in despite, and sought rest in a certain holy order. Horses and raiment and money, yea, all that he had, he straightway put from him, and seeking shelter from the world, was firmly set never to put foot within it more. For this cause he took refuge in this holy order, amongst the monks of Clairvaux. Now, though this dancer was comely of face and shapely of person, yet when he had once entered the monastery he found that he was master of no craft practiced therein. In the world he had gained his bread by tumbling and dancing and feats of address. To leap, to spring, such matters he knew well, but of greater things he knew nothing, for he had never spelled from book—nor Paternoster, nor canticle, nor creed, nor Hail Mary, nor aught concerning his soul's salvation.

When the minstrel had joined himself to the order he marked how the tonsured monks spoke amongst themselves by signs, no words coming from their lips, so he thought within himself that they were dumb. But when he learned that truly it was by way of penance that speech was forbidden to their mouths, and that for holy obedience were they silent, then considered he that silence became him also; and he refrained his tongue from words, so discreetly and for so long a space, that day in, day out, he spake never, save by commandment; so that the cloister often rang with the brothers' mirth. The tumbler moved amongst his fellows like a man ashamed, for he had neither part nor lot in all the business of the monastery, and for this he was right sad and sorrowful. He saw the monks and the penitents about him, each serving God, in this place and that, according to his office and degree. He marked the priests at their ritual before the altars; the deacons at the gospels; the subdeacons at the epistles; and the ministers about the vigils. This one repeats the introit; this other the lesson; cantors chant from the Psalter; penitents spell out the Miserere—for thus are all things sweetly ordered—yea, and the most ignorant amongst them yet can pray his Paternoster. Wherever he went, here or there, in office or cloister, in every quiet corner and nook, there he found five, or three, or two, or at least one. He gazes earnestly, if so he is able, upon each. Such an one laments; this other is in tears; yet another grieves and sighs. He marvels at their sorrow. Then he said, "Holy Mary, what bitter grief have all these men that they smite the breast so grievously! Too sad of heart, meseems, are they who make such bitter dole together. Ah, St. Mary, alas, what words are these I say! These men are calling on the mercy of God, but I—what do I here! Here there is none so mean or vile but who serves God in his office and degree, save only me, for I work not, neither can I preach. Caitiff and shamed was I when I thrust myself herein, seeing that I can do nothing well, either in labor or in prayer. I see my brothers upon their errands, one behind the other; but I do naught but fill my belly with the meat that they provide. If they perceive this thing, certainly shall I be in an evil case, for they will cast me out amongst the dogs, and none will take pity on the glutton and the idle man. Truly am I a caitiff, set in a high place for a sign." Then he wept for very woe, and would that he was quiet in the grave. "Mary, Mother," quoth he, "pray now your heavenly Father that he keep me in his pleasure, and give me such good counsel that I may truly serve both him and you; yea, and may deserve that meat which now is bitter in my mouth."

Driven mad with thoughts such as these, he wandered about the abbey until he found himself within the crypt, and took sanctuary by the altar, crouching close as he was able. Above the altar was carved the statue of Madame St. Mary. Truly his steps had not erred when he sought that refuge; nay, but rather, God who knows his own had led him thither by the hand. When he heard the bells ring for mass he sprang to his feet all dismayed. "Ha!" said he; "now am I betrayed. Each adds his mite to the great offering, save only me. Like a tethered ox, naught I do but chew the cud, and waste good victuals on a useless man. Shall I speak my thought? Shall I work my will? By the Mother of God, thus am I set to do. None is here to blame. I will do that which I can, and honor with my craft the Mother of God in her monastery. Since others honor her with chant, then I will serve with tumbling."

He takes off his cowl, and removes his garments, placing them near the altar, but so that his body be not naked he dons a tunic, very thin and fine, of scarce more substance than a shirt. So, light and comely of body, with gown girt closely about his loins, he comes before the Image right humbly. Then raising his eyes, "Lady," said he, "to your fair charge I give my body and my soul. Sweet Queen, sweet Lady, scorn not the thing I know, for with the help of God I will essay to serve you in good faith, even as I may. I cannot read your Hours nor chant your praise, but at the least I can set before you what art I have. Now will I be as the lamb that plays and skips before his mother. Oh, Lady, who art nowise bitter to those who serve you with a good intent, that which thy servant is, that he is for you."

Then commenced he his merry play, leaping low and small, tall and high, over and under. Then once more he knelt upon his knees before the statue, and meekly bowed his head. "Ha!" said he, "most gracious Queen, of your pity and your charity scorn not this my service." Again he leaped and played, and for holiday

and festival, made the somersault of Metz. Again he bowed before
the Image, did reverence, and paid it all the honor that he might.
Afterwards he did the French vault, then the vault of Champagne,
then the Spanish vault, then the vaults they love in Brittany, then
the vault of Lorraine, and all these feats he did as best he was able.
Afterwards he did the Roman vault, and then, with hands before
his brow, danced daintily before the altar, gazing with a humble
heart at the statue of God's Mother. "Lady," said he, "I set before
you a fair play. This travail I do for you alone; so help me God,
for you, Lady, and your Son. Think not I tumble for my own
delight; but I serve you, and look for no other guerdon on my
carpet. My brothers serve you, yea, and so do I. Lady, scorn not
your villein, for he toils for your good pleasure; and, Lady, you
are my delight and the sweetness of the world." Then he walked on
his two hands, with his feet in the air, and his head near the ground.
He twirled with his feet, and wept with his eyes. "Lady," said he,
"I worship you with heart, with body, feet and hands, for this I
can neither add to nor take away. Now am I your very minstrel.
Others may chant your praises in the church, but here in the crypt
will I tumble for your delight. Lady, lead me truly in your way,
and for the love of God hold me not in utter despite." Then he
smote upon his breast, he sighed and wept most tenderly, since he
knew no better prayer than tears. Then he turned him about,
and leaped once again. "Lady," said he, "as God is my Savior,
never have I turned this somersault before. Never has tumbler
done such a feat, and, certes, it is not bad. Lady, what delight is
his who may harbor with you in your glorious manor. For God's
love, Lady, grant me such fair hostelry, since I am yours, and am
nothing of my own." Once again he did the vault of Metz; again
he danced and tumbled. Then when the chants rose louder from
the choir, he, too, forced the note, and put forward all his skill.
So long as the priest was about that mass, so long his flesh endured
to dance, and leap and spring, till at the last, nigh fainting, he could
stand no longer upon his feet, but fell for weariness on the ground.
From head to heel sweat stood upon him, drop by drop, as blood
falls from meat turning upon the hearth. "Lady," said he, "I can
no more, but truly will I seek you again." Fire consumed him
utterly. He took his habit once more, and when he was wrapped
close therein, he rose to his feet, and bending low before the
statue, went his way. "Farewell," said he, "gentlest Friend. For
God's love take it not to heart, for so I may I will soon return.

Not one Hour shall pass but that I will serve you with right good-will, so I may come, and so my service is pleasing in your sight." Thus he went from the crypt, yet gazing on his Lady. "Lady," said he, "my heart is sore that I cannot read your Hours. How would I love them for love of you, most gentle Lady! Into your care I commend my soul and my body."

In this fashion passed many days, for at every Hour he sought the crypt to do service, and pay homage before the Image. His service was so much to his mind that never once was he too weary to set out his most cunning feats to distract the Mother of God, nor did he ever wish for other play than this. Now, doubtless, the monks knew well enough that day by day he sought the crypt, but not a man on earth—save God alone—was aware of aught that passed there; neither would he, for all the wealth of the world, have let his goings in be seen, save by the Lord his God alone. For truly he believed that were his secret once espied he would be hunted from the cloister, and flung once more into the foul, sinful world, and for his part he was more fain to fall on death than to suffer any taint of sin. But God considering his simplicity, his sorrow for all he had wrought amiss, and the love which moved him to this deed, would that this toil should be known; and the Lord willed that the work of his friend should be made plain to men, for the glory of the Mother whom he worshipped, and so that all men should know and hear, and receive that God refuses none who seeks his face in love, however low his degree, save only he love God and strive to do his will.

Now think you that the Lord would have accepted this service, had it not been done for love of him? Verily and truly, no, how-ever much this juggler tumbled; but God called him friend, because he loved him much. Toil and labor, keep fast and vigil, sigh and weep, watch and pray, ply the sharp scourge, be diligent at Matins and at mass, owe no man anything, give alms of all you have—and yet, if you love not God with all your heart, all these good deeds are so much loss—mark well my words—and profit you naught for the saving of your soul. Without charity and love, works avail a man nothing. God asks not gold, neither for silver, but only for love unfeigned in his people's hearts, and since the tumbler loved him beyond measure, for this reason God was willing to accept his service.

Thus things went well with this good man for a great space. For more years than I know the count of, he lived greatly at his

ease, but the time came when the good man was sorely vexed, for
a certain monk thought upon him, and blamed him in his heart
that he was never set in choir for Matins. The monk marveled
much at his absence, and said within himself that he would never
rest till it was clear what manner of man this was, and how he
spent the Hours, and for what service the convent gave him bread.
So he spied and pried and followed, till he marked him plainly,
sweating at his craft in just such fashion as you have heard. "By
my faith," said he, "this is a merry jest, and a fairer festival than
we observe altogether. Whilst others are at prayers, and about the
business of the House, this tumbler dances daintily, as though one
had given him a hundred silver marks. He prides himself on being
so nimble of foot, and thus he repays us what he owes. Truly it is
this for that; we chant for him, and he tumbles for us. We throw
him largesse: he doles us alms. We weep his sins, and he dries our
eyes. Would that the monastery could see him, as I do, with their
very eyes; willingly therefore would I fast till Vespers. Not one
could refrain from mirth at the sight of this simple fool doing
himself to death with his tumbling, for on himself he has no pity.
Since his folly is free from malice, may God grant it to him as
penance. Certainly I will not impute it to him as sin, for in all
simplicity and good faith, I firmly believe, he does this thing, so
that he may deserve his bread." So the monk saw with his very
eyes how the tumbler did service at all the Hours, without pause or
rest, and he laughed with pure mirth and delight, for in his heart
was joy and pity.

The monk went straight to the abbot and told him the thing from
beginning to end, just as you have heard. The abbot got him on his
feet, and said to the monk, "By holy obedience I bid you hold
your peace, and tell not this tale abroad against your brother. I
lay on you my strict command to speak of this matter to none, save
me. Come now, we will go forthwith to see what this can be, and
let us pray the heavenly King, and his very sweet, dear Mother, so
precious and so bright, that in her gentleness she will plead with
her Son, her Father, and her Lord, that I may look on this work—
if thus it pleases him—so that the good man be not wrongly blamed,
and that God may be the more beloved, yet so that thus is his good
pleasure." Then they secretly sought the crypt, and found a privy
place near the altar, where they could see, and yet not be seen.
From there the abbot and his monk marked the business of the
penitent. They saw the vaults he varied so cunningly, his nimble

leaping and his dancing, his salutations of Our Lady, and his springing and his bounding, till he was nigh to faint. So weak was he that he sank on the ground, all outworn, and the sweat fell from his body upon the pavement of the crypt. But presently, in this his need, came she, his refuge, to his aid. Well she knew that guileless heart.

Whilst the abbot looked, forthwith there came down from the vault a Dame so glorious, that certainly no man had seen one so precious, nor so richly crowned. She was more beautiful than the daughters of men, and her vesture was heavy with gold and gleaming stones. In her train came the hosts of heaven, angel and archangel also; and these pressed close about the minstrel, and solaced and refreshed him. When their shining ranks drew near, peace fell upon his heart; for they contended to do him service, and were the servants of the servitor of that Dame who is the rarest Jewel of God. Then the sweet and courteous Queen herself took a white napkin in her hand, and with it gently fanned her minstrel before the altar. Courteous and debonair, the Lady refreshed his neck, his body and his brow. Meekly she served him as a handmaid in his need. But these things were hidden from the good man, for he neither saw nor knew that about him stood so fair a company.

The holy angels honor him greatly, but they can no longer stay, for their Lady turns to go. She blesses her minstrel with the sign of God, and the holy angels throng about her, still gazing back with delight upon their companion, for they await the hour when God shall release him from the burden of the world and they possess his soul.

This marvel the abbot and his monk saw at least four times, and thus at each Hour came the Mother of God with aid and succor for her man. Never doth she fail her servants in their need. Great joy had the abbot that this thing was made plain to him. But the monk was filled with shame, since God had shown his pleasure in the service of his poor fool. His confusion burnt him like fire. "Dominus," said he to the abbot, "grant me grace. Certainly this is a holy man, and since I have judged him amiss, it is very right that my body should smart. Give me now fast or vigil or the scourge, for without question he is a saint. We are witnesses to the whole matter, nor is it possible that we can be deceived." But the abbot replied, "You speak truly, for God has made us to know that he has bound him with the cords of love. So I lay my commandment upon you, in virtue of obedience, and under pain of your person,

that you tell no word to any man of that you have seen, save to
God alone and me." "Lord," said he, "thus I will do." On these
words they turned them, and hastened from the crypt; and the
good man, having brought his tumbling to an end, presently
clothed himself in his habit, and joyously went his way to the
monastery.

Thus time went and returned, till it chanced that in a little while
the abbot sent for him who was so filled with virtue. When he
heard that he was bidden of the abbot, his heart was sore with grief,
for he could think of nothing profitable to say. "Alas!" said he, "I
am undone; not a day of my days but I shall know misery and
sorrow and shame, for well I trow that my service is not pleasing
to God. Alas! plainly doth he show that it displeases him, since
he causes the truth to be made clear. Could I believe that such
work and play as mine could give delight to the mighty God! He
had no pleasure therein, and all my toil was thrown away. Ah me,
what shall I do? What shall I say? Fair, gentle God, what portion
will be mine? Either shall I die in shame, or else shall I be banished
from this place, and set up as a mark to the world and all the evil
thereof. Sweet Lady, St. Mary, since I am all bewildered, and since
there is none to give me counsel, Lady, come thou to my aid. Fair,
gentle God, help me in my need. Stay not, neither tarry, but come
quickly with your Mother. For God's love, come not without
her, but hasten both to me in my peril, for truly I know not what
to plead. Before one word can pass my lips, surely will they bid
me 'Begone.' Wretched that I am, what reply is he to make who
has no advocate? Yet, why this dole, since go I must?" He came
before the abbot, with the tears yet wet upon his cheeks, and he
was still weeping when he knelt upon the ground. "Lord," prayed
he, "for the love of God deal not harshly with me. Would you
send me from your door? Tell me what you would have me do,
and thus it shall be done." Then replied the abbot, "Answer me
truly. Winter and summer have you lived here for a great space;
now, tell me, what service have you given, and how have you deserved your bread?" "Alas!" said the tumbler, "well I knew that
quickly I should be put upon the street when once this business was
heard of you, and that you would keep me no more. Lord," said
he, "I take my leave. Miserable I am, and miserable shall I ever be.
Never yet have I made a penny for all my juggling." But the abbot
answered, "Not so said I; but I ask and require of you—nay, more,
by virtue of holy obedience I command you—to seek within your

conscience and tell me truly by what craft you have furthered the business of our monastery." "Lord," cried he, "now have you slain me, for this commandment is a sword." Then he laid bare before the abbot the story of his days, from the first thing to the last, whatsoever pain it cost him; not a word did he leave out, but he told it all without a pause, just as I have told you the tale. He told it with clasped hands, and with tears, and at the close he kissed the abbot's feet, and sighed.

The holy abbot leaned above him, and, all in tears, raised him up, kissing both his eyes. "Brother," said he, "hold now your peace, for I make with you this true covenant, that you shall ever be of our monastery. God grant, rather, that we may be of yours, for all the worship you have brought to ours. I and you will call each other friend. Fair, sweet brother, pray you for me, and I for my part will pray for you. And now I pray you, my sweet friend, and lay this bidding upon you, without pretense, that you continue to do your service, even as you were wont heretofore—yea, and with greater craft yet, if so you may." "Lord," said he, "truly is this so?" "Yea," said the abbot, "and verily." So he charged him, under peril of discipline, to put all doubts from his mind; for which reason the good man rejoiced so greatly that, as telleth the rime, he was all bemused, so that the blood left his cheeks, and his knees failed beneath him. When his courage came back, his very heart thrilled with joy; but so perilous was that quickening that therefrom he shortly died. But theretofore with a good heart he went about his service without rest, and Matins and Vespers, night and day, he missed no Hour till he became too sick to perform his office. So sore was his sickness upon him that he might not rise from his bed. Marvelous was the shame he proved when no more was he able to pay his rent. This was the grief that lay the heaviest upon him, for of his sickness he spake never a word, but he feared greatly lest he should fall from grace since he travailed no longer at his craft. He reckoned himself an idle man, and prayed God to take him to himself before the sluggard might come to blame. For it was bitter to him to consider that all about him knew his case, so bitter that the burden was heavier than his heart could bear, yet there without remedy he must lie. The holy abbot does him all honor; he and his monks chant the Hours about his bed, and in these praises of God he felt such delight that not for them would he have taken the province of Poitou, so great was his happiness therein. Fair and contrite was his confession, but still he was not at peace; yet why say more of this, for the hour had struck, and he must rise and go.

The abbot was in that cell with all his monks; there, too, was company of many a priest and many a canon. These all humbly watched the dying man, and saw with open eyes this wonder happen. Clear to their very sight, about that lowly bed, stood the Mother of God, with angel and archangel, to wait the passing of his soul. Over against them were set, like wild beasts, devils and the Adversary, so they might snatch his spirit. I speak not to you in parable. But little profit had they for all their coming, their waiting, and their straining on the leash. Never might they have part in such a soul as his. When the soul took leave of his body, it fell not in their hands at all, for the Mother of God gathered it to her bosom, and the holy angels thronging round, quired for joy, as the bright train swept to heaven with its burthen, according to the will of God. To these things the whole of the monastery was witness, besides such others as were there. So knew they and perceived that God sought no more to hide the love he bore to his poor servant, but rather would that his virtues should be plain to each man in that place; and very wonderful and joyful seemed this deed to them. Then with meet reverence they bore the body on its bier within the abbey church, and with high pomp commended their brother to the care of God; nor was there monk who did not chant or read his portion that day within the choir of the mighty church.

Thus with great honor they laid him to his rest, and kept his holy body amongst them as a relic. At that time spake the abbot plainly to their ears, telling them the story of this tumbler and of all his life, just as you have heard, and of all that he himself beheld within the crypt. No brother but kept awake during that sermon. "Certes," said they, "easy is it to give credence to such a tale; nor should any doubt your words, seeing that the truth bears testimony to itself, and witness comes with need; yea, without any doubt have we full assurance that his discipline is done." Great joy amongst themselves have all within that place.

Thus endeth the story of the minstrel. Fair was his tumbling, fair was his service, for thereby gained he such high honor as is above all earthly gain. So the holy fathers narrate that in such fashion these things chanced to this minstrel. Now, therefore, let us pray to God—he who is above all other—that he may grant us so to do such faithful service that we may win the guerdon of his love.

Here endeth the Tumbler of Our Lady.

▁⌐▁⌐▁⌐▁⌐▁⌐▁⌐▁⌐▁⌐▁⌐▁⌐▁⌐▁⌐▁⌐▁⌐▁⌐▁⌐

18. Perfect happiness, according to the *Little Flowers of St. Francis*

Although late in composition (it was not written down in its present form until about 1330), the collection of stories known as the *Little Flowers of St. Francis* still preserves probably our best insight into the character of Franciscan piety. One of the best of the many stories they contain is Francis' definition of perfect happiness, given one winter's day as he traveled from Perugia to Portiuncula near Assisi.

The Italian text is taken from *I Fioretti di S. Francesco, con una introduzione storico-critica,* ed. P. Giacinto Pagnani, O.F.M. (Rome: Bibliotheca Fides, 1962), pp. 65–67, the eighth chapter of the *Fioretti.* The translation is by D. Herlihy.

O NE day, in winter time, as St. Francis was coming with Brother Leo from Perugia to St. Mary of the Angels, and the bitter cold cut them keenly, he called to Brother Leo, who was going a little ahead, and he said this: "O Brother Leo, even if we Brothers in every country should give great example of holiness and edification, nonetheless, write it down and note it carefully, that not in this is perfect happiness."

And going on a little farther, St. Francis called to him a second time: "O Brother Leo, even if we Brothers should give sight to the blind, cure the crippled, cast out demons, make the deaf to hear, the lame to walk and the dumb to speak and (which is a greater thing) should raise up the dead after four days, write that not in this is perfect happiness." And going a little farther on, St. Francis cried aloud: "O Brother Leo, if we Brothers should know all the languages and all sciences and all writings, so that we knew how to prophesy and to reveal not only future things, but also the secrets of consciences and of souls, write that not in this is perfect

happiness." Going a little farther along, St. Francis again called
loudly: "O Brother Leo, you little lamb of God, even if we
Brothers should speak with the tongues of angels and know the
movements of the stars and the powers of herbs, and even if all
the treasures of the earth were revealed to us and we knew the
natures of birds and fishes, and of all animals, and of men, and of
trees, and of stones and roots and waters, write that not in this is
perfect happiness." And again going on a little while, Francis cried
loudly: "O Brother Leo, even if we Brothers should know how to
preach so excellently that we might convert all infidels to the faith
of Christ, write that not in this is perfect happiness."

After he had spoken in such a fashion for fully two miles,
Brother Leo with great amazement asked him, and said: "Father,
for God's sake I pray that you tell me where is perfect happiness."

And St. Francis answered him: "When we reach St. Mary of
the Angels, thus drenched with the rain and chilled by the cold
and splattered by mud and afflicted with hunger, and we knock
at the door of the convent, and the porter comes in anger and
says: 'Who are you?' And we reply: 'We are two of your
brothers.' And he says: 'You do not speak the truth; rather you
are two rascals who go about deceiving the world and robbing the
poor of their alms. Go away.' And he does not open to us but
makes us stand outside in the snow and water, in cold and in
hunger, until night. Then, if we patiently bear such injuries,
cruelties and insults without being upset and without murmuring
against him, and if we think in humility and charity that the porter
truly knows us for what we are, and that God makes him speak
against us, O Brother Leo, write that there is perfect happiness.

"And if we persist in our knocking and he comes out in great
anger and drives us away like shameless scoundrels with insults
and blows, with these words: 'Get away from here, you worthless thieves. Go stay with the sick. You'll get no food or lodging
here.' If we bear this patiently and with joy and good love, O
Brother Leo, write that there is perfect happiness. And if we,
driven by hunger, and by the cold and night, again knock and cry
and pray with great pleading, for the love of God will he please
open for us, and let us stand a little within the door. And he in
even greater anger says: 'These are nervy bums. I shall give them
what they well deserve.' And he rushes out with a knotty stick and
seizing us by our cowls throws us on the ground and rolls us in
the snow and beats us nearly to death with that stick. If we bear

all these things patiently and with joy, thinking on the wounds of the blessed Christ, which we ought to bear for his love, O Brother Leo, write that in this is perfect happiness.

"And now hear the end, Brother Leo. Above all the graces and gifts of the Holy Spirit, which Christ gives to his friends, is the conquest of self, and the willing forbearance, for love of Christ, of wounds, injuries, insults and hardships. For in all the other gifts of God, we cannot take glory for ourselves, because they do not belong to us, but to God. Hence the Apostle says: 'What have you that you have not received? But after you have received it, why do you take credit for it, as if you had it of yourselves?' But in the cross of suffering and of affliction, we can take credit for this is our own. And so the Apostle says: 'I will not glory save in the cross of our Lord Jesus Christ.' To whom be honor and glory for all ages to come. Amen."

19. The *Canticle of Brother Sun,* of St. Francis of Assisi

The Franciscan joy in nature is sublimely expressed in this famous poem. The translation is taken from *St. Francis of Assisi: the Legends and Lauds,* trans. N. Wydenbruck and ed. Otto Karrer (copyright 1948, Sheed & Ward, New York), and is reprinted with the permission of the publisher.

Most high, omnipotent, merciful Lord,
Thine is all praise, the honor and the glory and every benediction
To thee alone are they confined,
And no man is worthy to speak thy name.

Praised be thou, my Lord, with all thy creatures,
Especially for Sir Brother Sun.
Through him thou givest us the light of day,
And he is fair and radiant with great splendor,
Of thee, Most High, giving signification.

Praised be thou, my Lord, for Sister Moon and the stars
Formed in the sky, clear, beautiful, and fair.
Praised be thou, my Lord, for Brother Wind,
For air, for weather cloudy and serene and every weather
By which thou to thy creatures givest sustenance.

Praised be thou, my Lord, for Sister Water,
Who is very useful and humble, precious and chaste.

Praised be thou, my Lord, for Brother Fire,
By whom thou dost illuminate the night;
Beauteous is he and jocund, robustious, and strong.
Praised be thou, my Lord, for our Mother Earth,

Who sustains and rules us
And brings forth divers fruits and colored flowers and herbs.
Praised be thou, my Lord, for those who grant forgiveness through
    thy love
And suffer infirmities and tribulation.
Blessed are they who bear them with resignation,
Because by thee, Most High, they will be crowned.

Praised be thou, my Lord, for our sister bodily Death,
From whom no living man can ever 'scape.
Woe unto those who die in mortal sin.
Blessed those who are found in thy most holy will;
To them the second death will bring no ill.
Praise and bless my Lord, render thanks to him
And serve him with great humility.

20. The *Dies Irae*

The *Dies Irae* is widely considered to be the greatest of the medieval
Latin hymns. It is of uncertain authorship, but dates from the thirteenth
century and is traditionally attributed to Thomas of Celano, one of
Francis' disciples and the author of two lives of his master. The poem

certainly reflects Franciscan influence. Dealing with the Last Judgment, the poem in the first seven stanzas depicts Christ as the awesome, terrible judge. Then the tone shifts to a sentimental, even pathetic appeal to the human redeemer.

The *Dies Irae* has been translated many times into English, but even more than other medieval hymns it has defied an entirely satisfactory rendition. The following translation, by Franklin Johnson, preserves the meter of the original, and is one of the better efforts at capturing its spirit in English verse.

The translation is taken from *Great Hymns of the Middle Ages*, compiled by Eveline Warner Brainerd (New York: Century Co., 1909), pp. 104–07.

Day of wrath, that day of burning!
Earth shall end, to ashes turning:
Thus sing saint and seer, discerning.

Ah, the dread beyond expression
When the Judge in awful session
Searcheth out the world's transgression.

Then is heard a sound of wonder:
Mighty blasts of trumpet-thunder
Rend the sepulchers asunder.

What can e'er that woe resemble,
Where even death and nature tremble
As the rising throngs assemble!

Vain, my soul, is all concealing;
For the book is brought, revealing
Every deed and thought and feeling.

On his throne the Judge is seated,
And our sins are loud repeated,
And to each is vengeance meted.

Wretched me! How gain a hearing,
When the righteous falter, fearing,
At the pomp of his appearing?

King of majesty and splendor,
Fount of pity, true and tender,
Be, thyself, my strong defender.

From thy woes my hope I borrow:
I did cause thy way of sorrow:
Do not lose me on that morrow.

Seeking me, thou weary sankest,
Nor from scourge and cross thou shrankest;
Make not vain the cup thou drankest.

Thou wert righteous even in slaying:
Yet forgive my guilty straying,
Now, before that day dismaying.

Though my sins with shame suffuse me,
Though my very moans accuse me,
Canst thou, Loving One, refuse me!

Blessed hope! I have aggrieved thee:
Yet, by grace the thief believed thee,
And the Magdalen received thee.

Though unworthy my petition,
Grant me full and free remission,
And redeem me from perdition.

Be my lot in love decreed me;
From the goats in safety lead me;
With thy sheep forever feed me.

When thy foes are all confounded,
And with bitter flames surrounded,
Call me to thy bliss unbounded.

From the dust I pray thee, hear me:
When my end shall come, be near me;
Let thy grace sustain and cheer me.

Ah, that day, that day of weeping,
When, no more in ashes sleeping,
Man shall rise and stand before thee!
Spare him, spare him, I implore thee!
(Trans. Franklin Johnson)

⎍⎍⎍⎍⎍⎍⎍⎍⎍⎍⎍⎍⎍⎍⎍⎍⎍⎍⎍⎍⎍⎍⎍⎍

21. The life of St. Nicholas the bishop, according to the *Golden Legend*

The *Golden Legend*, composed between 1258 and 1270 by Iacobus de
Voraggine (or Voragine), bishop of Genoa, presented a collection of
saints' lives intended for the edification, and entertainment, of a lay
audience. The following Life of St. Nicholas (the original Santa Claus)
is typical of the genre. The historical St. Nicholas lived during the
reigns of Diocletian and Constantine, but almost nothing is known for
certain about him.

The following selection is based upon the translation published in
1483 by the English printer William Caxton. It is taken from Iacobus
de Voragine, *The Golden Legend. Lives of the Saints,* trans. William
Caxton and selected and edited by George V. O'Neill, S.J. (Cambridge:
Cambridge University Press, 1914), pp. 62–71.

Nicholas, citizen of the city of Patras, was born of rich and holy
kin, and his father was Epiphanes and his mother Johane. In his
young age he eschewed the plays and japes of other young children.
He used and haunted gladly holy Church; and all that he might
understand of holy Scripture he executed it in deed and work after
his power. And when his father and mother were departed out of
this life, he began to think how he might distribute his riches, and
not to the praising of the world but to the honor and glory of
God. And it was so that one, his neighbor, had then three daughters, virgins, and he was a nobleman: but for the poverty of them
together, they were constrained and in very purpose to abandon
them to sin. And when the holy man Nicholas knew hereof he
had great horror of this, and threw by night secretly into the house
of the man a mass of gold wrapped in a cloth. And when the man

arose in the morning, he found this mass of gold, and rendered to God therefor great thankings, and therewith he married his oldest daughter. And a little while after this holy servant of God threw in another mass of gold; which the man found, and thanked God, and purposed to wake for to know him that so had aided him in his poverty. And after a few days Nicholas doubled the mass of gold, and cast it into the house of this man. He awoke by the sound of the gold, and followed Nicholas, which fled from him, and he said to him: "Sir, flee not away so but that I may see and know thee." Then he ran after him more hastily, and knew that it was Nicholas; and anon he kneeled down, and would have kissed his feet, but the holy man would not, but required him not to tell nor discover this thing as long as he lived.

After this the bishop of Mirea died and other bishops assembled for to purvey to this church a bishop. And there was, among the others, a bishop of great authority, and all the election was in him. And when he had warned all for to be in fastings and in prayers, this bishop heard that night a voice which said to him that, at the hour of matins, he should take heed to the doors of the church, and him that should come first to the church and have the name of Nicholas they should sacre him bishop. And he showed this to the other bishops and admonished them for to be all in prayers; and he kept the doors. And this was a marvelous thing, for at the hour of matins, like as he had been sent from God, Nicholas arose tofore all other. And the bishop took him when he was come and demanded of him his name. And he, which was simple as a dove, inclined his head, and said: "I have to name Nicholas." Then the bishop said to him: "Nicholas, servant and friend of God, for your holiness ye shall be bishop of this place." And sith they brought him to the church, howbeit that he refused it strongly, yet they set him in the chair. And he followed, as he did tofore in all things, in humility and honesty of manners. He woke in prayer and made his body lean, he eschewed company of women, he was humble in receiving all things, profitable in speaking, joyous in admonishing, and cruel in correcting.

It is read in a chronicle that the blessed Nicholas was at the Council of Nice; and on a day, as a ship with mariners were in perishing on the sea, they prayed and required devoutly Nicholas, servant of God, saying: "If those things that we have heard of thee said be true, prove them now." And anon a man appeared in his likeness, and said: "Lo! see ye me not? ye called me"; and then he began to help them in their exploit of the sea, and anon the tempest ceased. And when they were come to his church, they knew him without any man to show him to them, and yet they had never seen him. And then they thanked God and him of their deliverance. And he bade them to attribute it to the mercy of God and to their belief, and nothing to his merits.

It was so on a time that all the province of S. Nicholas suffered great famine, in such wise that vitaille failed. And then this holy man heard say that certain ships laden with wheat were arrived in the haven. And anon he went thither and prayed the mariners that they would succor the perished at least with an hundred muyes of wheat of every ship. And they said: "Father we dare not, for it is meted and measured, and we must give reckoning thereof in the garners of the emperor in Alexandria." And the holy man said to them: "Do this that I have said to you, and I promise, in the truth of God, that it shall not be lessed or minished when ye shall come to the garners." And when they had delivered so much out of every ship, they came into Alexandria and delivered the measure that they had received. And then they recounted the miracle to the ministers of the emperor, and worshipped and praised strongly God and his servant Nicholas. Then this holy man distributed the wheat to every man after that he had need, in such wise that it sufficed for two years, not only for to sell but also to sow.

And in this country the people served idols and worshipped the false image of the cursed Diana. And to the time of this holy man many of them had some customs of the paynims, for to sacrifice to Diana under a sacred tree; but this good man made them of all the country to cease then these customs, and commanded to cut off the tree. Then the devil was angry and wroth against him, and made an oil that burned, against nature, in water and burned stones also. And then he transformed him in the guise of a religious woman and put him in a little boat, and encountered pilgrims that sailed in the sea towards this holy saint, and areasoned them thus and said: "I would fain go to this holy man, but I may not; wherefore I pray you to bear this oil into his church, and for the remembrance of me that ye anoint the walls of the hall"; and anon he vanished away. Then they saw anon after another ship with honest persons, among whom there was one like to S. Nicholas, which spake to them softly: "What hath this woman said to you, and what hath she brought?" And they told to him all by order. And he said to them: "This is the evil and foul Diana; and, to the end that ye know that I say truth, cast that oil into the sea." And when they had cast it, a great fire caught it in the sea, and they saw it long burn against nature. Then they came to this holy man and said to him: "Verily thou art he that appeared to us in the sea and deliveredst us from the sea and awaits of the devil."

And in this time certain men rebelled against the emperor; and the emperor sent against them three princes, Nepotian, Ursyn and Apollyn. And they came into the port Andrien for the wind, which was contrary to them; and the blessed Nicholas commanded them to dine with him, for he would keep his people from the ravin that they made. And whilst they were at dinner, the consul, corrupt by money, had commanded three innocent knights to be beheaded. And when the blessed Nicholas knew this, he prayed these three princes that they would much hastily go with him. And when they were come where they should be beheaded, he found them on their knees, and blindfold, and the righter brandished his sword over their heads. Then S. Nicholas, embraced with the love of God, set him hardily against the righter, and took the sword out of his hand, and threw it from him, and unbound the innocents, and led them with him all safe. And anon he went to the judgment to the consul, and found the gates closed, which anon he opened by force. And the consul came anon and saluted him: and this holy man having this salutation in despite, said to him: "Thou enemy of God, corrupter of the law, wherefore hast thou consented to so great evil and felony? How darest thou look on us?" And when he had sore chidden and reproved him, he repented, and at the prayer of the three princes he received him to penance. After, when the messengers of the emperor had received his benediction, they made their gear ready and departed, and subdued their enemies to the empire without shedding of blood, and sith returned to the emperor and were worshipfully received. And after this it happed that some other in the emperor's house had envy on the weal of these three princes, and accused them to the emperor of high treason, and did so much by prayer and by gifts that they caused the emperor to be so full of ire that he commanded them to prison, and without other demand, he commanded that they should be slain that same night. And when they knew it by their keeper, they rent their clothes and wept bitterly; and then Nepotian remembered him how S. Nicholas had delivered the three innocents, and admonested the others that they should require his aid and help. And thus as they prayed S. Nicholas appeared to them, and after appeared to Constantine the emperor, and said to him: "Wherefore hast thou taken these three princes with so great wrong, and hast judged them to death without trespass? Arise up hastily, and command that they be not executed, or I shall pray to God that he move battle against thee, in which thou shalt be overthrown and shalt be made meat to beasts." And the emperor demanded: "What art thou that art entered by night into my palace and durst say to me such words?" And he said to him: "I am Nicholas bishop of Mirea." And in like wise he appeared to the provost, and feared him, saying with a fearful voice: "Thou that hast lost mind and wit, wherefore hast thou consented to the death of innocents? Go forth anon and do thy part to deliver them, or else thy body shall rot and be eaten with worms, and thy meiny shall be destroyed." And he asked him: "Who art thou that so menacest me?" And he answered: "Know thou that I am Nicholas, the bishop of the city of Mirea." Then that one awoke that other, and each told to other their dreams, and anon sent for them that were in prison, to whom the emperor said: "What art, magic or sorcery can ye, that ye have this night by illusion caused us to have such dreams?" And they said that they were none enchanters ne knew no witchcraft, and also that they had not deserved the sentence of death. Then the emperor said to them: "Know ye well a man named Nicholas?" And when they heard speak of the name of the holy saint, they held up their hands towards heaven, and prayed Our Lord that by the merits of S. Nicholas they might be delivered of this present peril. And when the emperor had heard of them the life and miracles of S. Nicholas, he said to them: "Go ye forth, and yield ye thankings to God, which hath delivered you by the prayer of this holy man, and worship ye him; and bear ye to him of your jewels, and pray ye him that he threaten me no more, but that he pray for me and for my royame unto Our Lord." And a while after, the said princes went unto the holy man, and fell down on their knees humbly at his feet, saying: "Verily thou art the sergeant of God, and the very worshipper and lover of Jesu Christ." And when they had all told this said thing by order, he lift up his hands to heaven and gave thankings and praisings to God, and sent again the princes, well informed, into their countries.

And when it pleased Our Lord to have him depart out this world, he prayed Our Lord that he would send him his angels; and inclining his head he saw the angels come to him, whereby he knew well that he should depart, and began this holy Psalm: "In te domine speravi," unto "in manus tuas," and so saying: "Lord, into thine hands I commend my spirit," he rendered up his soul and died, the year of Our Lord three hundred and forty-three, with great melody sung of the celestial company. And when he was buried in a tomb of marble, a fountain of oil sprang out from the head unto his feet; and unto this day holy oil issueth out of his body, which is much available to the health of sicknesses of many men. And after him in his see succeeded a man of good and holy life, which by envy was put out of his bishopric. And when he was out of his see the oil ceased to run, and when he was restored again thereto the oil ran again.

Long after this the Turks destroyed the city of Mirea, and then came thither forty-seven knights of Bari, and four monks showed to them the sepulchre of S. Nicholas. And they opened it and found the bones swimming in the oil, and they bare them away honorably into the city of Bari, in the year of our Lord ten hundred and eighty-seven.

There was a Jew that saw the virtuous miracles of S. Nicholas, and did do make an image of the saint, and set it in his house, and commanded him that he should keep well his house when he went out, and that he should keep well all his goods, saying to him: "Nicholas, lo! here be all my goods, I charge thee to keep them, and if thou keep them not well, I shall avenge me on thee in beating and tormenting thee." And on a time, when the Jew was out, thieves came and robbed all his goods, and left unborne away only the image. And when the Jew came home he found him robbed of all his goods. He areasoned the image, saying these words: "Sir Nicholas, I had set you in my house for to keep my goods from thieves, wherefore have ye not kept them? Ye shall receive sorrow and torments, and shall have pain for the thieves. I shall avenge my loss and refrain my woodness in beating thee." And then took the Jew the image, and beat it, and tormented it cruelly. Then happed a great marvel, for when the thieves departed the goods, the holy saint, like as he had been in his array, appeared to the thieves, and said to them: "Wherefore have I been beaten so cruelly for you and have so many torments? See how my body is hewed and broken; see how that the red blood runneth down by my body; go ye fast and restore it again, or else the ire of God Almighty shall make you as to be one out of his wit, and that all men shall know your felony, and that each of you shall be hanged."

And they said: "Who art thou that sayest to us such things?" And he said to them: "I am Nicholas the servant of Jesu Christ, whom the Jew hath so cruelly beaten for his goods that ye bare away." Then they were afeard, and came to the Jew, and heard what he had done to the image, and they told him the miracle, and delivered to him again all his goods. And thus came the thieves to the way of truth, and the Jew to the way of Jesu Christ.

A man, for the love of his son, that went to school for to learn, hallowed, every year, the feast of S. Nicholas much solemnly. On a time it happed that the father had do make ready the dinner, and called many clerks to this dinner. And the devil came to the gate in the habit of a pilgrim for to demand alms; and the father anon commanded his son that he should give alms to the pilgrim. He followed him as he went for to give to him alms, and when he came to the quarfox the devil caught the child and strangled him. And when the father heard this he sorrowed much strongly and wept, and bare the body into his chamber, and began to cry for sorrow, and say: "Bright sweet son, how is it with thee? S. Nicholas, is this the guerdon that ye have done to me because I have so long served you?" And as he said these words, and other semblable, the child opened his eyes, and awoke like as he had been asleep, and arose up tofore all, and was raised from death to life.

22. Cantos from the *Divine Comedy*

The *Divine Comedy* of Dante Alighieri (1265–1321) is the supreme religious poem and probably the greatest literary masterpiece of the Middle Ages. It describes the poet's journey, under the guidance first of Vergil and then of Beatrice, through Hell, Purgatory and Heaven, into the presence of God. The place of this theme in medieval cultural history has already been discussed (see above, p. 172).

In Dante's conception of the universe, Hell took the form of a deep pit plunging to the center of the earth, divided into nine circles or levels. The worse the sin, the lower the place alloted to those guilty of it. In the very depth of hell stands Satan, the supreme betrayer, who is frozen in ice, but still devours sinners with his three mouths.

Purgatory is a seven-storied mountain, rising up from the earth on the side opposite the pit of hell. As the soul passes through each of these seven levels, a particular vice is expunged from it. At the summit stands the earthly paradise, which Adam lost by his sin.

Heaven consists of eight spheres, which hold up the moon, sun, five visible planets, and the fixed stars; beyond them is the empyrean, the abode of God.

The *Comedy* is written in the verse form known as *terza rima*. It consists of iambic verses of eleven syllables each, with three verses forming a stanza. Stanzas are linked according to the rime scheme ABA, BCB, CDC, and so forth. The entire poem is divided into a hundred cantos or chapters, thirty-four depicting Hell, and thirty-three each for Purgatory and Heaven.

The *Comedy* is a difficult poem, overflowing with erudite allusions, and its compensating music is difficult to convey in translation. The nobility of its theme and the grace of its presentation, however, make it one of literature's most rewarding works. The following prose translation, together with the notes, is taken from Charles Eliot Norton, *The Divine Comedy of Dante Alighieri* (Boston: Houghton Mifflin Co., 1941), pp. 1–34 of Hell, and pp. 231–57 of Paradise, the opening and closing cantos of the Comedy. It is reprinted here with permission of the publishers.

Hell

Canto I
Dante, astray in a wood, reaches the foot of a hill which he begins to ascend; he is hindered by three beasts; he turns back and is met by Vergil, who proposes to guide him into the eternal world.

Midway upon the journey of our life I found myself in a dark wood, where the right way was lost.[1] Ah! how hard a thing it is to tell what this wild and rough and difficult wood was, which in thought renews my fear! So bitter is it that death is little more. But in order to treat of the good that I found in it, I will tell of the other things that I saw there.

I cannot well report how I entered it, so full was I of slumber at that moment when I abandoned the true way. But after I had

---

[1] v. 3. The action of the poem begins on the night before Good Friday of the year 1300, as we learn from Canto XXI. 112–114. Dante was thirty-five years old, midway on the road of life, or, as he says in the *Convito*, IV. 24, 30, at "the summit of the arch of life." The dark wood is the forest of the world of sense, "the erroneous wood of this life" (Id. I. 124), that is, the wood in which man loses his way.

reached the foot of a hill,[2] where that valley ended which had pierced my heart with fear, I looked upward, and saw its shoulders clothed already with the rays of the planet [3] which leads man aright along every path. Then was the fear a little quieted which had lasted in the lake of my heart through the night that I had passed so piteously. And even as one who with spent breath, issued forth from the sea upon the shore, turns to the perilous water and gazes, so did my mind, which still was flying, turn back to look again upon the pass which never left person alive.[4]

After I had rested a little my weary body, I again took my way along the desert slope,[5] so that the firm foot was always the lower. And lo! almost at the beginning of the steep a she-leopard,[6] light and very nimble, which was covered with a spotted coat. And she did not withdraw from before my face, nay, hindered so my road that I often turned to go back.

The time was the beginning of the morning, and the Sun was mounting up with those stars that were with him when the Love Divine first set in motion those beautiful things;[7] so that the hour of the time and the sweet season were occasion to me of good hope concerning that wild beast with the dappled skin; but not so that the sight which appeared to me of a lion[8] did not give me

[2] v. 13. The hill is the type of the true course of life, opposed to the false course in the wood of the valley. The man conscious of having lost his moral way, alarmed for his soul, seeks to escape from the sin and cares in which he is involved, by ascending the hill of virtue whose summit is "lighted by dayspring from on high."

[3] v. 17. According to the Ptolemaic system the sun was a planet.

[4] v. 27. The pass is the dangerous road through the dark wood, "the end whereof are the ways of death," for he who walks therein is "dead in trespasses and sins."

[5] v. 29. Desert, because "narrow is the way that leadeth unto life, and few there be that find it." *Matthew* vii. 14.

[6] v. 32. The leopard is the type of the temptations of the flesh, the pleasures of sense with their fair, varied outside seeming.

[7] v. 40. It was a common belief, which existed from early Christian times, that the Spring was the season of the Creation. By the Julian Calendar, March 25th was the date of the Vernal Equinox, and it was assumed that on this day the Sun was created and placed in the sign of the Zodiac, Aries, to begin his course. The same date was assigned to the Annunciation and to the Crucifixion. March 25th was thus what may be called the ideal Good Friday. But in the year 1300 the actual Good Friday fell on April 8th. This is the date which Dante, following the calendar of the Church, adopted for that of his journey. The sun was rising on the morning of Good Friday, when Dante began his attempt to ascend the hill.

[8] v. 47. The lion is the type of pride, the disposition which is the root of the sins of violence.

fear. He appeared to be coming against me, with his head high and with ravening hunger, so that it appeared that the air was affrighted at him; and a she-wolf,[9] which in her leanness seemed laden with all cravings, and ere now had made many folk to live forlorn,—she brought on me so much heaviness, with the fear that came from sight of her, that I lost hope of the height. And such as is he who gains willingly, and the time arrives which makes him lose, so that in all his thoughts he laments and is sad, such did the beast without peace make me, which, coming on against me, was pushing me back, little by little, thither where the Sun is silent.

While I was falling back to the low place, one who appeared faint-voiced through long silence presented himself before my eyes. When I saw him in the great desert, "Have pity on me!" I cried to him, "whatso thou be, whether shade or real man." He answered me: "Not man; man once I was, and my parents were Lombards, and both Mantuans by country. I was born *sub Julio*, though late,[10] and I lived at Rome under the good Augustus, at the time of the false and lying gods. I was a poet, and sang of that just son of Anchises[11] who came from Troy, after proud Ilion had been burned. But thou, why dost thou return to such great annoy? Why dost thou not ascend the delectable mountain which is the source and cause of all joy?" "Art thou then that Vergil and that fount which pours forth so broad a stream of speech?" replied I with bashful front to him: "O honor and light of the other poets! may the long study avail me and the great love, which have made me search thy volume! Thou art my master and my author;[12] thou

---

[9] v. 49. The wolf is the type of avarice, that covetousness of earthly goods which turns the heart from seeking the goods of heaven, and is the main source of sins of fraud.

The imagery of these three beasts seems to have been suggested by *Jeremiah* v. 6. "A lion out of the forest shall slay them, and a wolf of the evenings shall spoil them, a leopard shall watch over their cities."

These three beasts, which hinder the progress of him who would ascend the hill of virtue, correspond with the triple division of sins into those of incontinence, of violence, and of fraud which Vergil makes in the eleventh Canto, according to which the sinners in Hell are divided into three main classes.

[10] v. 70. Vergil was twenty-five years old at the time of Caesar's death, B. C. 44.

[11] v. 73. "Aeneas, than whom none was more just." *Aeneid*, I. 544.

[12] v. 85. In the *Convito* Dante says that the word *autore*, here translated "author," has a double origin and meaning. According to the one, it signifies only the poets who practice the art of the Muses; according to the other, it means "every one worthy of being believed and obeyed," and from this is derived the word *Authority*. *Conv.* IV. 6. 14–49.

alone art he from whom I took the fair style that has done me
honor. Behold the beast because of which I turned; help me against
her, famous sage, for she makes my veins and pulses tremble." "It
behoves thee to hold another course," he replied, when he saw
me weeping, "if thou wouldst escape from this savage place; for
this beast, because of which thou criest out, lets not any one pass
along her way, but so hinders him that she kills him; and she has
a nature so malign and evil that she never sates her greedy will, and
after food has more hunger than before. Many are the animals with
which she wives, and there shall be more yet, until the hound [13]
shall come that will make her die of grief. He shall not feed on
land or pelf,[14] but wisdom and love and valor, and his birthplace
shall be between Feltro and Feltro.[15] Of that low Italy shall he
be the salvation, for which the virgin Camilla died, and Euryalus,
Turnus and Nisus of their wounds.[16] He shall hunt her through
every town till he shall have put her back again in Hell, there
whence envy[17] first sent her forth. Wherefore I think and deem
it for thy best that thou follow me, and I will be thy guide, and
will lead thee hence through the eternal place where thou shalt
hear the despairing shrieks, shalt see the ancient spirits woeful who
each proclaim the second death.[18] And then thou shalt see those
who are contented in the fire,[19] because they hope to come, when-

[13] v. 101. After centuries of controversy, it is still doubtful of whom
the hound is the symbol.

[14] v. 103. Literally, "he shall not feed on land or pewter." The word
peltro, pewter, is a rhyme-word, used in a forced meaning, perhaps analo-
gous to our colloquial, vulgar use of "tin."

[15] v. 105. No satisfactory explanation has been given of the meaning of
"between Feltro and Feltro."

[16] v. 108. Camilla and Turnus died for Italy fighting against the Trojans,
Euryalus and Nisus died on the Trojan side. Vergil commemorates them all
in the *Aeneid*.

[17] v. 111. "The devil seeing that man through obedience might ascend
whence he through pride had fallen, envied him; and he who first through
pride had been the devil, that is the fallen one, became through envy Satan,
that is the adversary." Petri Lombardi, *Sententiae*, II. 21.

[18] v. 117. That is, who each by their misery proclaim the torments of
the second death. The appellation of "the second death," given to the
sufferings endured by the sinners in Hell, is derived from *Revelation* xx.
10, 14; xxi. 8. "The souls of the good separated from the body by death
are at rest; but those of the wicked suffer punishment; and the bodies of the
good live again in eternal life, while those of the wicked revive for eternal
death, which is called the second death." S. Augustine, *De Civitate Dei*,
XIII. 8.

[19] v. 118. "Contented in the fire," that is, contented in the purifying pains
of Purgatory, by which they are made fit for Paradise.

ever it may be, to the blessed folk; to whom if thou wouldst then
ascend, there shall be a soul [20] more worthy than I for that. With
her I will leave thee at my departure; for that Emperor who reigns
thereabove wills not, because I was rebellious[21] to His law, that
through me any one should come into His city. In all parts He
governs and there He reigns: there is His city and His lofty seat.
O happy the man whom thereto He elects!" And I to him: "Poet,
I beseech thee by that God whom thou didst not know, in order
that I may escape this ill and worse, that thou lead me thither
where thou now hast said, so that I may see the gate of St. Peter,[22]
and those whom thou reportest so afflicted."

Then he moved on, and I held behind him.

Canto II

*Dante, doubtful of his own powers, is discouraged at the outset.
—Vergil cheers him by telling him that he has been sent to his aid
by a blessed Spirit from Heaven, who revealed herself as Beatrice.
—Dante casts off fear, and the poets proceed.*

The day was going, and the dusky air was taking the living things
that are on earth from their fatigues, and I alone was preparing to
sustain the war alike of the journey and of the woe, which my
memory that errs not shall retrace.

O Muses, O lofty genius, now assist me! O memory that didst
inscribe that which I saw, here shall thy nobility appear!

I began:—

"Poet, who guidest me, consider my power, if it be sufficient,
before thou trust me to the deep pass. Thou sayest [1] that the parent
of Silvius while still corruptible went to the immortal world and
was there in the body; and truly if the Adversary of every ill was
courteous to him, it seems not unmeet to the man of understanding,
thinking on the high effect that should proceed from him, and on

---

[20] v. 121. Beatrice.

[21] v. 125. Not actively rebellious, but "one who did not duly worship
God." See Canto iv. 36.

[22] v. 134. The gate of St. Peter is the gate of Purgatory, which is un-
locked by the keys of the Kingdom of Heaven that Christ gave to Peter.
See *Purgatory*, Canto ix. 127. Whoever passes through this gate is admitted
to that Kingdom.

[1] v. 13. In the sixth book of the *Aeneid*.

the who and the what;[2] for in the empyrean heaven he was chosen for father of revered Rome and of her empire; both which (would one say truth) were ordained for the holy place[3] where the successor of the greater Peter has his seat. Through this going, whereof thou givest him vaunt, he learned things which were the cause of his victory and of the papal mantle. Afterward the Chosen Vessel[4] went thither to bring thence comfort to that faith which is the beginning of the way of salvation. But I, why go I thither? or who concedes it? I am not Aeneas, I am not Paul; neither I nor others believe me worthy of this; wherefore if I yield myself to go, I fear lest the going may be mad. Thou art wise, thou understandest better than I speak."

And as is he who unwills what he willed, and by reason of new thoughts changes his purpose, so that he withdraws wholly from what he had begun, such I became on that dark hillside: because in my thought I abandoned the enterprise which had been so hasty in its beginning.

"If I have rightly understood thy speech," replied that shade of the magnanimous one, "thy soul is hurt by cowardice, which oftentimes encumbers a man so that it turns him back from honorable enterprise, as false seeing does a beast when it shies. In order that thou loose thee from this fear I will tell thee why I came, and what I heard at the first moment that I grieved for thee. I was among those who are suspended,[5] and a Lady blessed and beautiful called me, such that I besought her to command. Her eyes were more shining than the star, and she began to say to me sweet and clear, with angelic voice, in her speech: 'O courteous Mantuan soul! of whom the fame yet lasts in the world, and shall last so long as motion continues,[6] my friend, and not of fortune, is so hindered on his road upon the desert hillside that he has turned for fear, and I am afraid, through that which I have heard of him in heaven, lest he be already so astray that I may have risen late to his succor.

---

[2] v. 18. It is not strange that God was thus gracious to him, since he was the Father of the Roman people (the Who), and founder of the Roman empire (the What).

[3] v. 23. Rome as well as Jerusalem was a holy city, the Empire as well as the Church a divine institution. All profane no less than all sacred history was the divinely ordered course of events leading up to the Incarnation and Redemption. See *Il Convito*, iv. 5, and *De Monarchia*, ii. 4 and 5.

[4] v. 28. St. Paul. See *Acts* ix. 15, and 2 *Corinthians* xii. 1–4.

[5] v. 52. In Limbo, neither in the proper Hell nor in Heaven.

[6] v. 60. That is: so long as time shall last. "Time is the reckoning of the motion of the heavens." *Il Convito*, iv. 2, 49.

Now do thou move, and with thy ornate speech and with whatever is needful for his deliverance, assist him so that I may be consoled thereby. I am Beatrice who make thee go. I come from a place whither I desire to return. Love moved me, that makes me speak. When I shall be before my Lord, I will often praise thee to Him.' Then she was silent, and thereon I began: 'O Lady of Virtue! through whom alone the human race excels all contained within that heaven which has the smallest circles,[7] thy command so pleases me that to obey it, were it already done, were slow to me. There is no need for thee further to open to me thy will; but tell me the reason why thou dost not beware of descending down here into this centre, from the ample place[8] whither thou burnest to return.' 'Since thou wishest to know so inwardly, I will tell thee briefly,' she replied to me, 'wherefore I fear not to come here within. One need be afraid only of those things that have power to do one harm, of others not, for they are not fearful. I am made by God, thanks be to Him, such that your misery touches me not,[9] nor does the flame of this burning assail me. A gentle Lady[10] is in heaven who feels compassion for this hindrance whereto I send thee, so that she breaks stern judgment there above. She summoned Lucia[11] in her request, and said, "Thy faithful one now has need of thee, and I commend him to thee." Lucia, the foe of every cruel one, moved and came to the place where I was, seated with the ancient Rachel.[12] She said, "Beatrice, true praise of God, why dost thou not succor him who so loved thee that for thee he came forth from the vulgar throng? Dost thou not hear the pity of his plaint? Dost

[7] v. 78. The heaven of the moon, the innermost of the nine revolving heavens, the nearest to the earth. Through Beatrice, as symbol of the knowledge of the things of God revealed to man, and by reason of man's capacity to receive the revelation, the human race is exalted above all other created things save the angels alone.

[8] v. 84. The Empyrean.

[9] v. 92. "The blessed in glory will have no compassion for the damned, . . . for it would impugn the justice of God." S. T. Suppl. xciv. 2.

[10] v. 94. The Virgin Mary, the fount of mercy, never spoken of by name in Hell.

[11] v. 100. Whether any real person is intended by Lucia is doubtful, but as an allegorical figure she is the symbol, as her name indicates, of illuminating Grace.

[12] v. 102. Rachel was adopted by the Church, from a very early period, as the type of the contemplative life, that life in which the soul withdrawing itself from earthly concerns, and devoting itself to the consideration of the things of God, attains to heights above the reach of reason, and has a foretaste of the felicity of heaven. The place of Beatrice, the type of instruction in the divine mysteries, is therefore rightly at the side of Rachel.

thou not see the death that combats him on the stream where the
sea has no vaunt?" [13] Never were persons in the world swift to do
their good, or to fly their harm, as I, after these words were uttered,
came down here from my blessed seat, putting my trust in thy
upright speech, which honors thee and them who have heard it.'
After she had said this to me, weeping she turned her lucent eyes,
whereby she made me more quick to come. And I came to thee
thus as she willed. I withdrew thee from before that wild beast
which took from thee the short way on the beautiful mountain.
What is it then? Why, why dost thou hold back? why dost thou
harbor such cowardice in thy heart? why hast thou not daring
and assurance, since three such blessed Ladies care for thee in the
court of Heaven, and my speech pledges thee such good?"

As the flowerets, bent and closed by the chill of night, when the
sun brightens them erect themselves all open on their stem, so I
became with my drooping courage, and such good daring ran to
my heart that I began like a person enfreed: "O compassionate
she who succored me, and courteous thou who didst speedily obey
the true words that she addressed to thee! Thou by thy words hast
so disposed my heart with desire of going, that I have returned to
my first intent. Now go, for one sole will is in us both: thou leader,
thou lord, and thou master." Thus I said to him; and when he
moved on, I entered along the deep and savage road.

Canto III

*The gate of Hell.—Vergil leads Dante in.—The punishment of
those who had lived without infamy and without praise.—Acheron, and the sinners on its bank.—Charon.—Earthquake.—Dante
swoons.*

"Through me is the way into the woeful city; through me is the
way into the eternal woe; through me is the way among the lost
people. Justice moved my lofty maker: the divine Power, the
supreme Wisdom and the primal Love made me. Before me were
no things created, save eternal, and I eternal last. Leave every
hope, ye who enter!" [1]

---

[13] v. 108. Dost thou not see him in danger of death from the sins that
assail him in the flood of human life, a flood more stormy with passion and
darker with evil than the ocean with its tempests?

[1] v. 8. "Creation," says St. Thomas Aquinas, "is the joint act of the whole
Trinity." *S. T.* i. 45. 6. This is indicated in these verses by the enumeration

These words of obscure color I saw written at the top of a gate; whereat I: "Master, their meaning is dire to me."

And he to me, like a person well advised: "Here it behoves to leave every fear; it behoves that all cowardice should here be dead. We have come to the place where I have told thee that thou shalt see the woeful people, who have lost the good of the understanding." [2]

And when he had put his hand on mine with a cheerful look, wherefrom I took courage, he brought me within to the secret things. Here sighs, laments, and deep wailings were resounding through the starless air; wherefore at first I wept thereat. Strange tongues, horrible utterances, words of woe, accents of anger, voices high and faint, and sounds of hands with them, were making a tumult which whirls always in that air forever dark, like the sand when the whirlwind breathes.

And I, who had my head girt with horror, said: "Master, what is that which I hear? and what folk is it that seems so overcome with its woe?"

And he to me: "The wretched souls of those who lived without infamy and without praise maintain this miserable mode. They are mingled with that caitiff choir of the angels, who were not rebels, nor were faithful to God, but were for themselves.[3] The heavens chased them out in order to be not less beautiful, nor does the deep Hell receive them, for the damned would have some boast of them."

And I: "Master, what is so grievous to them, that makes them lament so bitterly?"

He answered: "I will tell thee very briefly. These have not hope of death; and their blind life is so debased, that they are envious of every other lot. Fame of them the world permits not to be; mercy and justice disdain them. Let us not speak of them, but do thou look and pass on."

And I, who was gazing, saw a banner, which, whirling, ran so swiftly that it seemed to me disdainful of any pause, and behind it came so long a train of folk, that I should never have believed death had undone so many. After I had recognized some among

---

of the attributes ascribed respectively to the three persons of the Trinity, according to the common teaching of the doctors of the Church. *Id.* i. 39. 8.

[2] v. 18. The ultimate end and felicity of human life is to see God and the truth in him (*S. T. Suppl.* xcii. 1); this is the supreme good of the understanding.

[3] v. 39. This class of angels seems to have been an invention of the poet's.

them, I saw and knew the shade of him who made, through cowardice, the great refusal.[4] At once I understood and was certain,
that this was the sect of the caitiffs displeasing to God and to his
enemies. These wretches, who never were alive, were naked, and
much stung by gad-flies and by wasps that were there; these
streaked their faces with blood, which, mingled with tears, was
gathered at their feet by loathsome worms.

And when I gave myself to looking onward, I saw people on
the bank of a great river; wherefore I said: "Master, now grant
to me that I may know who these are, and what rule makes them
appear so ready to pass over, as I discern through the faint light."
And he to me: "The things will be clear to thee, when we shall
stay our steps on the sad shore of Acheron." Then with eyes
ashamed and downcast, fearing lest my speech might be trouble-
some to him, far as to the river I refrained from speaking.

And behold! coming toward us in a boat, an old man, white
with ancient hair, crying: "Woe to you, wicked souls! hope not
ever to see the Heavens! I come to carry you to the other bank,
into the eternal darkness, into heat and into frost. And thou who
art there, living soul, depart from these that are dead." But when
he saw that I did not depart, he said: "By another way, by other
ports thou shalt come to the shore, not here, for passage; a lighter
bark must carry thee." [5]

And my Leader to him: "Charon, vex not thyself; it is thus
willed there where is power for that which is willed; and ask no
more." Thereon were quiet the fleecy jaws of the ferryman of the
livid marsh, who round about his eyes had wheels of flame.

But those souls, who were weary and naked, changed color and
gnashed their teeth, soon as they heard his cruel words. They
blasphemed God and their parents, the human race, the place, the
time and the seed of their sowing and of their birth. Then, all of
them bitterly weeping, drew together to the evil bank, which

[4] v. 60. By him "who made the great refusal" is probably intended Pope
Celestine V., who, after having held the papacy for five months in 1294,
abdicated. His successor, Boniface VIII., Dante's great enemy, put Celestine
in prison, where he died in 1296.
[5] v. 93. The boat that bears the souls of the redeemed to Purgatory.
Charon recognizes that Dante is not among the damned. The gods and other
personages of heathen mythology were held by the Church to have been
demons who had a real existence; they were adopted into the Christian
mythology, and hence appear with entire propriety as characters in Hell.
Charon and other beings of this order were familiar to the readers of the
sixth book of the *Aeneid*.

awaits every man who fears not God. Charon the demon, with eyes of glowing coal, beckoning to them, collects them all; he beats with his oar whoever lingers.

As in autumn the leaves depart one after the other, until the bough sees all its spoils upon the earth, in like wise the evil seed of Adam throw themselves from that shore one by one, at signals, as the bird at his recall. Thus they go over the dusky wave, and before they have landed on the farther side, already on this a new throng is assembled.

"My son," said the courteous Master, "those who die in the wrath of God, all come together here from every land; and they are eager to pass over the stream, for the divine justice spurs them so that fear is turned to desire. A good soul never passes this way; and therefore if Charon fret at thee, well mayest thou now know what his speech signifies."

This ended, the gloomy plain trembled so mightily, that the memory of the terror even now bathes me with sweat. The tearful land gave forth a wind that flashed a crimson light which vanquished all sensation in me, and I fell as a man whom slumber seizes.

Canto IV

The further side of Acheron.—Vergil leads Dante into Limbo, the First Circle of Hell, containing the spirits of those who lived virtuously but without faith in Christ.—Greeting of Vergil by his fellow poets.—They enter a castle, where are the shades of ancient worthies.—After seeing them Vergil and Dante depart.

A heavy thunder broke the deep sleep in my head, so that I started up like a person who is waked by force, and, risen erect, I moved my rested eye round about, and looked fixedly to distinguish the place where I was. True it is, that I found myself on the brink of the woeful valley of the abyss which collects a thunder of infinite wailings. It was so dark, deep, and cloudy, that, though I fixed my sight on the depth, I did not discern anything there.

"Now let us descend here below into the blind world," began the Poet all deadly pale, "I will be first, and thou shalt be second."

And I, who had observed his color, said: "How shall I come, if thou fearest, who art wont to be the comfort to my doubting?"

And he to me: "The anguish of the folk who are here below paints on my face that pity which thou takest for fear. Let us go on, for the long way urges us."

Thus he placed himself,[1] and thus he made me enter into the first circle[2] that girds the abyss. Here, as one listened, there was no lamentation but that of sighs which made the eternal air to tremble; this came of the woe without torments felt by the crowds, which were many and great, of infants and of women and of men.

The good Master to me: "Thou dost not ask what spirits are these that thou seest. Now I would have thee know, before thou goest farther, that these did not sin; and though they have merits it suffices not, because they did not have baptism,[3] which is part of the faith that thou believest; and if they were before Christianity, they did not duly worship God: and of such as these am I myself. For such defects, and not for other guilt, are we lost, and only so far harmed that without hope we live in desire."

Great woe seized me at my heart when I heard him, because I knew that people of much worth were suspended in that limbo. "Tell me, my Master, tell me, Lord," I began, with wish to be assured of that faith which vanquishes every error,[4] "did ever any one who afterwards was blessed go forth from here, either by his own or by another's merit?" And he, who understood my covert speech, answered: "I was new in this state[5] when I saw a Mighty One come hither crowned with sign of victory. He drew out hence the shade of the first parent, of Abel his son, and that of Noah, of Moses the law-giver and obedient, Abraham the patriarch, and David the King, Israel with his father and with his offspring, and with Rachel, for whom he did so much, and many others; and He made them blessed: and I would have thee know that before these, human spirits were not saved."[6]

We ceased not going on because he spoke, but all the while were passing through the wood, the wood, I mean, of crowded

[1] v. 23. In the lead, in front of Dante.
[2] v. 24. The Limbo (Lat. *limbus*, edge, hem, border).
[3] v. 35. Such merit as they might have could not secure salvation for them, for only he who receives baptism becomes a member of Christ, and through His merits is freed alike from the fault and from the penalty of original sin.
[4] v. 48. Wishing especially to be assured in regard to the descent of Christ into Hell.
[5] v. 52. Vergil died B. C. 19.
[6] v. 62. The sin of Adam infected all his descendants with the offence of original sin, and subjected them to its eternal punishment, from which none could be saved except by faith in Christ. Adam and the fathers of the chosen people had held implicitly the faith in Christ to come, but they were excluded from the life of glory, until the redemption of the human race by the passion of Christ. After his passion he descended into Hell, to deliver them. (*S. T.* iii. 52. 5.)

spirits; nor yet had our way been long from the place of my slumber, when I saw a fire, which overcame a hemisphere of darkness.[7] We were still a little distant from it, yet not so far but that I could in part discern that honorable folk possessed that place. "O thou who honorest both science and art, who are these, who have such honor that it separates them from the manner of the others?" And he to me: "The honorable renown of them which sounds above in thy life wins grace in heaven which thus advances them." At this a voice was heard by me: "Honor the loftiest Poet! his shade returns which had departed." When the voice had stopped and was quiet, I saw four great shades coming to us; they had a semblance neither sad nor glad. The good Master began to say: "Look at him with that sword in hand who comes before the three, even as lord; he is Homer, the sovereign poet; the next who comes is Horace, the satirist; Ovid is the third, and the last is Lucan. Since each shares with me the name which the single voice sounded, they do me honor, and in that do well."

Thus I saw assembled the fair school of that Lord of the loftiest song who soars above the others like an eagle. After they had discoursed somewhat together, they turned to me with sign of salutation; and my Master smiled thereat. And far more of honor yet they did me, for they made me of their band, so that I was the sixth amid so much wisdom. Thus we went on as far as the light, speaking things concerning which silence is becoming, even as was speech there where I was.

We came to the foot of a noble castle, seven times circled by high walls,[8] defended round about by a fair streamlet. This we passed as if hard ground; through seven gates[9] I entered with these

---

[7] v. 69. The fire may be the symbol of the partial light afforded by philosophy to the virtuous heathen, whose abode the poets are approaching.

[8] v. 107. The castle is the symbol of the abode of Philosophy, or human wisdom unenlightened by revelation; its seven high walls may perhaps signify the four moral and three intellectual virtues,—prudence, temperance, fortitude and justice, understanding, knowledge and wisdom, all which could be attained by the virtuous heathen. (*S. T.* ii. 65. 2.)

[9] v. 110. The seven gates may typify the seven liberal arts of the *Trivium* and the *Quadrivium,* by which names the courses of instruction in them were known in the schools of the Middle Ages. The *Trivium* included Grammar, Logic and Rhetoric; the *Quadrivium,* Music, Arithmetic, Geometry and Astronomy. The following rude mnemonic verses set forth their order and meaning:

> Gram. loquitur, Dia. verba docet, Rhe. verba ministrat;
> Mus. canit, Ar. numert, Ge. ponderat, As. colit astra.

sages; we came to a meadow of fresh verdure. People were there with slow and grave eyes, of great authority in their looks; they spoke seldom, and with soft voices. Thereon we withdrew ourselves upon one side, into an open, luminous, and high place, so that they all could be seen. There before me upon the green enamel were shown to me the great spirits, whom for having seen I inwardly exalt myself.

I saw Electra with many companions, among whom I recognized Hector and Aeneas, Caesar in armor, with his gerfalcon eyes; I saw Camilla and Penthesilea, on the other side I saw the King Latinus, who was sitting with Lavinia his daughter. I saw that Brutus who drove out Tarquin; Lucretia, Julia, Marcia, and Cornelia; and alone, apart, I saw the Saladin. When I raised my brows a little more, I saw the Master of those who know,[10] seated amid the philosophic family; all regard him, all do him honor. Here I saw Socrates and Plato, who in front of the others stand nearest to him; Democritus, who ascribes the world to chance; Diogenes, Anaxagoras, and Thales, Empedocles, Heraclitus, and Zeno; and I saw the good collector of the qualities, Dioscorides, I mean;[11] and I saw Orpheus, Tully, and Linus, and moral Seneca, Euclid the geometer, and Ptolemy, Hippocrates, Avicenna, and Galen, and Averrhoës, who made the great comment.[12] I cannot report of all in full, because the long theme so drives me that many times the speech comes short of the fact.

The company of six is reduced to two. By another way the wise guide leads me out from the quiet into the air that trembles, and I come into a region where is nothing that can give light.

Canto V

The Second Circle, that of Carnal Sinners.—Minos—Shades renowned of old.—Francesca da Rimini.

Thus I descended from the first circle down into the second, which girdles less space, and so much more woe that it goads to wailing. There stands Minos horribly, and snarls; he examines the transgressions at the entrance; he judges, and he sends according as he entwines himself. I mean, that when the ill born soul comes there

---

[10] v. 131. Aristotle.

[11] v. 140. Dioscorides, a physician in Cilicia, of the first century A. D., who in his treatise *de materia medica* wrote of the qualities of plants.

[12] v. 144. The great comment on Aristotle.

before him, it confesses itself wholly, and that discerner of the sins sees what place of Hell is for it; he girds himself with his tail so many times as the grades he wills that it be sent down. Always many of them stand before him; they go, in turn, each to the judgment; they speak and hear, and then are whirled below.

"O thou that comest to the woeful inn," said Minos to me, when he saw me, leaving the act of so great an office, "beware how thou enterest, and to whom thou trustest thyself; let not the amplitude of the entrance deceive thee." And my Leader to him: "Wherefore dost thou too cry out? [1] Hinder not his fated going; thus is it willed there where is power for that which is willed; and ask no more."

Now the notes of woe begin to make themselves heard by me; now I am come where much wailing smites me. I had come into a place mute of all light, that bellows as the sea does in a tempest, if it be combated by contrary winds. The infernal hurricane which never rests carries along the spirits with its rapine; whirling and smiting it molests them.[2] When they arrive before its rush, here are the shrieks, the complaint, and the lamentation; here they blaspheme the divine power. I understood that to such torment are condemned the carnal sinners who subject the reason to the appetite. And as their wings bear along the starlings in the cold season in a large and full troop, so did that blast the evil spirits; hither, thither, down, up it carries them; no hope ever comforts them, neither of repose, nor of less pain.

And as the cranes go singing their lays, making in air a long line of themselves, so I saw come, uttering wails, shades borne along by the aforesaid strife. Wherefore I said: "Master, who are these folk whom the black air so castigates?" "The first of those of whom thou wishest to have knowledge," said he to me then, "was empress of many tongues. She was so abandoned to the vice of luxury[3] that lust she made licit in her law, to take away the blame into which she had been brought. She is Semiramis, of whom it is read that she succeeded Ninus and had been his wife; she held the land which the Sultan rules. That other is she[4] who, for love, slew herself, and broke faith to the ashes of Sichaeus; next is Cleopatra,

[1] v. 21. As Charon had done.

[2] v. 33. The storm and darkness are symbols of the tempest of the passions. "Wherewithal a man sinneth, by the same also shall he be punished." *Wisdom of Solomon*, xi. 16.

[3] v. 55. Luxury in the obsolete, Shakespearean sense of lasciviousness.

[4] v. 61. Dido.

the luxurious. See Helen, for whom so long a time of ill revolved; and see the great Achilles, who fought to the end with love.[5] See Paris, Tristan,—" and more than a thousand shades whom love had parted from our life he showed me, and, pointing to them, named to me.

After I had heard my Teacher name the dames of eld and the cavaliers, pity overcame me, and I was well nigh bewildered. I began: "Poet, willingly would I speak with those two that go together, and seem to be so light upon the wind." [6] And he to me: "Thou shalt see when they are nearer to us, and do thou then pray them by that love which leads them, and they will come." Soon as the wind sways them toward us, I lifted my voice: "O wearied souls, come to speak with us, if Another[7] deny it not."

As doves, called by desire, with wings open and steady, come through the air borne by their will to their sweet nest, these issued from the troop where Dido is, coming to us through the malign air, so strong was the compassionate cry.

"O living creature, gracious and benign, that goest through the black air visiting us who stained the world blood-red, if the King of the universe were a friend we would pray Him for thy peace, since thou hast pity on our perverse ill. Of what it pleases thee to hear, and what to speak, we will hear and we will speak to you, while the wind, as now, is hushed for us. The city where I was born sits upon the seashore, where the Po, with his followers, descends to have peace. Love, which quickly lays hold on gentle heart, seized this one for the fair person that was taken from me, and the mode still hurts me. Love, which absolves no loved one from loving, seized me for the pleasing of him so strongly that, as thou seest, it does not even now abandon me. Love brought us to one death. Cain awaits him who quenched our life." These words were borne to us from them.

Soon as I had heard those injured souls I bowed my face, and

---

[5] v. 66. According to the post-Homeric account of the death of Achilles, which was current in the Middle Ages, he was slain by Paris in the temple of Apollo in Troy, "whither he had been lured by the promise of a meeting with Polyxena, the daughter of Priam, with whom he was enamored."

[6] v. 75. These two are Francesca da Rimini, daughter of Guido Vecchio da Polenta, lord of Ravenna; and her lover, Paolo, the brother of her husband, the son of Malatesta da Verrucchio, lord of Rimini. Their death, at the hands of her husband, took place about 1285.

[7] v. 81. The name of God is never spoken by the spirits in Hell, save once, in blasphemous defiance, by Vanni Fucci (xxv. 3); nor by Dante in addressing them.

held it down so long until the Poet said to me: "What art thou thinking?" When I replied, I began: "Alas! how many sweet thoughts, how great desire, led these unto the woeful pass." Then I turned me again to them, and spoke, and began: "Francesca, thy torments make me sad and piteous to weeping. But tell me, at the time of the sweet sighs, by what and how did love concede to thee to know thy dubious desires?" And she to me: "There is no greater woe than the remembering in misery the happy time, and that thy Teacher knows.[8] But if thou hast so great desire to know the first root of our love, I will do like one who weeps and tells.

"We were reading one day, for delight, of Lancelot, how love constrained him. We were alone and without any suspicion. Many times that reading urged our eyes, and took the color from our faces, but only one point was it that overcame us. When we read of the longed-for smile being kissed by such a lover, this one, who never shall be divided from me, kissed my mouth all trembling. Gallehaut was the book, and he who wrote it.[9] That day we read no farther in it."

While the one spirit said this, the other was so weeping that through pity I swooned as if I had been dying, and fell as a dead body falls.

Paradise

Canto XXXI

The Rose of Paradise.—St. Bernard.—Prayer to Beatrice.—The glory of the Blessed Virgin.

In form then of a pure white rose the holy host was shown to me, which, in His own blood, Christ made His bride. But the other,[1] which, flying, sees and sings the glory of Him who enamours it, and the goodness which made it so great, like a swarm of bees which one while inflower themselves and one while return to where their work acquires savor, were descending into the great flower which is adorned with so many leaves, and thence rising up again to where their love always abides. They had their faces all of living

---

[8] v. 123. Thy Teacher who lives sorrowfully in Limbo without hope, but with memory of the life lighted by the Sun.

[9] v. 137. In the Romance, it was Gallehaut that prevailed on Guenever to give a kiss to Lancelot.

[1] v. 4. The angelic host.

flame, and their wings of gold, and the rest so white that no snow reaches that limit. When they descended into the flower, from bench to bench, they imparted of the peace and of the ardor which they acquired as they fanned their sides. Nor did the interposing of so great a flying plenitude, between what was above and the flower, impede the sight or the splendor; for the divine light penetrates through the universe, according as it is worthy, so that naught can be an obstacle to it. This secure and joyous realm, thronged with ancient and with modern folk, had its look and love all on one mark.

O Trinal Light, which in a single star, scintillating on their sight, dost so satisfy them, look down here upon our tempest!

If the Barbarians, coming from a region such that every day it is covered by Helicé,[2] revolving with her son of whom she is fond, when they beheld Rome and her lofty work,—what time Lateran rose above mortal things,[3]—were wonder-struck, I, who to the divine from the human, to the eternal from the temporal, had come, and from Florence to a people just and sane, with what amazement must I have been full! Truly what with it and with the joy I was well pleased not to hear, and to stand mute. And as a pilgrim who is refreshed within the temple of his vow as he looks around, and hopes some day to report how it was, so, journeying through the living light, I carried my eyes over the ranks, now up, now down, and now circling about. I saw faces persuasive to love, beautified by the light of Another and by their own smile, and actions graced with every dignity.

My look had now comprehended the general form of Paradise as a whole, and on no part had my sight as yet been fixed; and I turned me with rekindled wish to ask my Lady about things as to which my mind was in suspense. One thing I purposed, and another answered me; I was thinking to see Beatrice, and I saw an old man, robed like the people in glory. His eyes and his cheeks were overspread with benignant joy, his mien kindly such as befits a tender father. And: "Where is she?" on a sudden said I. Whereon he: "To terminate thy desire, Beatrice urged me from my place, and if

2 v. 32. The nymph Callisto, or Helicé, bore to Zeus a son, Arcas; she was metamorphosed by Hera into a bear, and then transferred to Heaven by Jupiter as the constellation of the Great Bear, while her son was changed into the constellation of Arctophylax or the lesser Bear. In the far north these constellations are always high in the heavens.

3 v. 36. When Rome was mistress of the world, and the Lateran the seat of imperial or papal power.

thou lookest up to the third circle from the highest rank, thou wilt again see her upon the throne which her merits have allotted to her." Without answering I lifted up my eyes, and saw her as she made for herself a crown reflecting from herself the eternal rays. From that region which thunders highest up no mortal eye is so far distant, in whatsoever sea it lets itself sink deepest,[4] as there from Beatrice was my sight. But this was naught to me, for her image did not descend to me blurred by aught between.

"O Lady, in whom my hope is strong, and who, for my salvation, didst endure to leave thy footprints in Hell, of all those things which I have seen through thy power and through thy goodness, I recognize the grace and the virtue. Thou hast drawn me from servitude to liberty by all those ways, by all the modes whereby thou hadst the power to do it. Guard thou in me thine own magnificence so that my soul, which thou hast made whole, may, pleasing to thee, be unloosed from the body." Thus I prayed; and she, so distant, as it seemed, smiled and looked at me; then turned to the eternal fountain.

And the holy old man said: "In order that thou mayst complete perfectly thy journey, for which end prayer and holy love sent me, fly with thine eyes through this garden; for seeing it will prepare thy look to mount further through the divine radiance. And the Queen of Heaven, for whom I burn wholly with love, will grant us every grace, because I am her faithful Bernard." [5]

As is he who comes perchance from Croatia to see our Veronica,[6] who by reason of its ancient fame is never sated, but says in thought, so long as it is shown: "My Lord Jesus Christ, true God, was then your semblance like to this?" [7] such was I, gazing on the living charity of him who, in this world, in contemplation, tasted of that peace.

"Son of Grace, this glad existence," began he, "will not be

---

[4] v. 75. From the highest region of the air to the lowest depth of the sea.

[5] v. 102. St. Bernard of Clairvaux, to whom, because of his fervent devotion to her, the Blessed Virgin had deigned to show herself during his life.

[6] v. 104. The likeness of the Saviour miraculously impressed upon the kerchief presented to him by a holy woman, on his way to Calvary, wherewith to wipe the sweat and dust from his face, and now religiously preserved at Rome, and shown at St. Peter's, on certain of the chief holydays.

[7] v. 108. The pilgrim, who has long heard of the Veronica and desired to see it, cannot sate his desire in gazing at it, and in his thought says: "This, then, Lord Jesus, is your likeness."

known to thee holding thine eyes only down here at the base, but look on the circles even to the most remote, until thou seest upon her seat the Queen to whom this realm is subject and devoted." I lifted up my eyes; and as at morning the eastern parts of the horizon surpass that where the sun declines, thus, as if going with my eyes from valley to mountain, I saw a part on the extreme verge vanquishing in light all the rest of the front.[8] And even as there where the pole which Phaëton guided ill is awaited,[9] the glow is brightest, and on this side and that the light diminishes, so that pacific oriflamme[10] was vivid at the middle, and on each side in equal measure the flame slackened. And at that mid part I saw more than a thousand jubilant Angels with wings outspread, each distinct both in effulgence and in act. I saw there, smiling at their sports and at their songs, a Beauty[11] which was joy in the eyes of all the other saints. And if I had such wealth in speech as in imagining, I should not dare to attempt the least of its delightfulness.

Bernard, when he saw my eyes fixed and intent upon the object of his own burning glow, turned his own with such affection to it, that he made mine more ardent to gaze anew.

Canto XXXII

St. Bernard describes the order of the Rose, and points out many of the Saints.—The children in Paradise.—The angelic festival.— The patricians of the Court of Heaven.

With affection set on his Delight, that contemplator freely assumed the office of a teacher, and began these holy words: "The wound which Mary closed up and anointed, that one who is so beautiful at her feet is she who opened it and who pierced it. Beneath her, in the order which the third seats make, sits Rachel with Beatrice, as thou seest. Sara, Rebecca, Judith, and she[1] who was great-grand-

---

[8] v. 123. All the rest of the circumference.

[9] v. 125. Where the chariot of the sun is about to rise.

[10] v. 127. This oriflamme of peace is the part of the rose of Paradise where the Virgin is seated, and its mid point is the Virgin herself. It is called 'the pacific' in contrast with the warlike oriflamme, the banner given by the archangel Gabriel to the ancient kings of France, which bore a flame on a field of gold, whence its name, *aurea flamma*.

[11] v. 134. The Blessed Virgin.

[1] v. 10. Ruth.

mother of the singer who, through sorrow for his sin, said *Miserere mei,*[2] thou mayst see thus from rank to rank in gradation downward, as with the name of each I go downward through the rose from leaf to leaf. And from the seventh row downwards, even as down to it, Hebrew women follow in succession, dividing all the tresses of the flower; because these are the wall by which the sacred stairs are separated according to the look which faith turned on Christ. On this side, where the flower is mature with all its leaves, are seated those who believed in Christ about to come. On the other side, where the semicircles are broken by empty spaces, are those who turned their faces on Christ already come.[3] And as on this side the glorious seat of the Lady of Heaven, and the other seats below it, make so great a division, thus, opposite, does the seat of the great John, who, ever holy, endured the desert and martyrdom, and then Hell for two years,[4] and beneath him Francis and Benedict and Augustine and others are allotted thus to divide, far down as here from circle to circle. Now behold the high divine foresight; for one and the other aspect of the faith will fill this garden equally. And know that downwards from the row which midway cleaves[5] the two divisions, they are seated for no merit of their own, but for that of others, under certain conditions; for all these are spirits absolved ere they had true power of choice. Well canst thou perceive it by their faces, and also by their childish voices, if thou lookest well upon them and if thou listenest to them. Now thou art perplexed, and in perplexity art silent; but I will loose for thee the strong bond in which thy subtle thoughts fetter

[2] v. 12. "Have mercy upon me." *Psalm* li. 1.
[3] v. 27. The circle of the Rose is divided vertically in two equal parts. In the upper tiers of the one half, far as midway down the flower, the saints of the Old Dispensation, who believed in Christ about to come, are seated. These benches are full. On the corresponding benches of the other half, on which are some empty spaces, sit the redeemed of the New Dispensation who have believed in Christ already come. On one side the line of division between the semicircles is made by the Hebrew women from the Virgin Mary downwards; on the opposite side the line is made by St. John Baptist and other saints who had rendered special service to Christ and his Church. The lower tiers of seats are occupied by innocent children elect to bliss.
[4] v. 33. The two years from the death of John to the death of Christ and his descent to Hell, to draw from the *limbus patrum* the souls predestined to salvation.
[5] v. 40. Those who are seated below the row which cleaves horizontally the two halves are children too young to have merit of their own.

thee.[6] Within the amplitude of this realm a casual point can have no place,[7] any more than sadness, or thirst, or hunger; for whatever thou seest is established by eternal law, so that here the ring answers exactly to the finger. And therefore this folk, hastened to true life, is not *sine causa* more and less excellent here among themselves.[8] The King, through whom this realm reposes in such great love and in such great delight that no will dares for more, creating all the minds in His own glad aspect, endows with grace diversely according to His pleasure; and here let the fact suffice.[9] And this is expressly and clearly noted for you in the Holy Scripture in the case of those twins who, within their mother, had their anger stirred.[10] Therefore, according to the color of the hair of such grace,[11] the highest light must needs befittingly crown them. Without, then, merit from their own ways, they are placed in different grades, differing only in their primary keenness of vision.[12] In the early centuries, indeed, the faith of parents alone sufficed, together with innocence, to secure salvation; after the first ages were complete, it was needful for males, through circumcision, to acquire power for their innocent wings. But after the time of grace had come, without perfect baptism in Christ, such innocence was held back there below.[13]

"Look now upon the face which most resembles Christ, for only its brightness can prepare thee to see Christ."

I saw raining down on her such great joy, borne in the holy minds created to fly across through that height, that whatsoever I

[6] v. 51. The perplexity was, How can there be difference of merit in the innocent, assigning them to different seats in Paradise?

[7] v. 53. No least thing can here be matter of chance.

[8] v. 60. It is not "without cause" that these children enjoy different measures of bliss.

[9] v. 66. Without attempt to account for it or to seek the "wherefore" of the will of God.

[10] v. 69. Jacob and Esau. See *Genesis* xxv. 22. "For the children being not yet born, neither having done any good or evil, that the purpose of God, according to election, might stand, not of works, but of him that calleth; it was said unto her, The elder shall serve the younger." *Romans* ix. 11–12.

[11] v. 71. This strange metaphor has been apparently suggested by the reference to Jacob and Esau, who differed in color and skin. See *Genesis* xxv. 25. The argument is, that God imparts grace to one or another according to his pleasure; and as the hair of children differs in color without apparent reason, so the endowment of grace differs in measure for each, and in proportion to this diversity, does the light of Heaven crown them.

[12] v. 75. In their innate capacity to see God, which is in proportion to the grace vouchsafed to them before birth.

[13] v. 84. In the limbo of children.

had seen before held me not suspended in such great wonder, nor showed to me such likeness unto God. And that Love which had before descended to her,[14] in front of her spread wide his wings, singing "*Ave, Maria, gratia plena*." The blessed Court responded to the divine song from all sides, so that every countenance became thereby the more serene.

"O holy Father, who for me endurest to be here below, leaving the sweet place in which thou sittest by eternal allotment, who is that Angel who with such joy looks into the eyes of our Queen, so enamoured that he seems of fire?" Thus did I again recur to the teaching of him who was deriving beauty from Mary, as the morning star from the sun. And he to me, "Confidence and grace as much as there can be in Angel and in soul, are all in him, and we would have it so, for he it is[15] who bore the palm down to Mary, when the Son of God willed to load Himself with our burden.

"But come now with thine eyes, as I shall proceed speaking, and note the great patricians of this most just and pious empire. Those two who sit there above, most happy through being nearest to the Empress, are, as it were, two roots of this rose. He who on the left is next her is the Father because of whose audacious tasting the human race tastes so much bitterness. On the right see that ancient Father of Holy Church, to whom Christ entrusted the keys of this lovely flower. And he[16] who saw before his death all the grievous times of the fair bride, who was won with the spear and with the nails, sits at his side; and by the other rests that leader, under whom the ingrate, fickle and stubborn people lived on manna. Opposite Peter see Anna sitting, so content to gaze upon her daughter, that she moves not her eyes as she sings Hosannah; and opposite the eldest father of a family sits Lucia,[17] who moved thy Lady, when thou didst bend thy brow to rush downward.[18]

"But because the time flies which holds thee slumbering,[19] here

[14] v. 94. In the heaven of the Fixed Stars; Canto xxiii. 94.

[15] v. 112. The angel Gabriel; Luke i. 26.

[16] v. 127. St. John, the Evangelist, who in his long life witnessed and suffered from the persecutions which the early Church had to endure.

[17] v. 137. The introduction of Lucia here is not less enigmatic than the choice of her for the functions which she performs in the other parts of the poems, *Hell*, ii. 97–108; *Purgatory*, ix. 55–63.

[18] v. 138. When in despair of reaching the height thou wert speeding down into the low place. See *Hell*, i. 61.

[19] v. 139. Dante has told us at the beginning of his ascent through the Heavens that he knows not whether he was there in body or only in spirit (Cantos i. 73–75; ii. 37–39). The hint of slumber let fall thus *obiter* in this

will we make a stop, like a good tailor who makes the gown according as he has cloth, and we will direct our eyes to the First Love, so that, looking towards Him, thou mayst penetrate so far as is possible through His effulgence. But, lest perchance, moving thy wings, thou go backward, believing to advance, it is needful that grace be obtained by prayer; grace from her who has the power to aid thee; and do thou follow me with thy affection so that thy heart depart not from my speech."

And he began this holy prayer.

Canto XXXIII
Prayer to the Virgin.—The beatific Vision.—The Ultimate Salvation.

"Virgin Mother, daughter of thine own Son, humble and exalted more than any creature, fixed term of the eternal counsel, thou art she who didst so ennoble human nature that its own Maker disdained not to become its creature. Within thy womb was rekindled the Love through whose warmth this flower has thus blossomed in the eternal peace. Here thou art to us the noonday torch of charity, and below, among mortals, thou art the living fount of hope. Lady, thou art so great, and so availest, that whoso would have grace, and has not recourse to thee, would have his desire fly without wings. Thy benignity not only succors him who asks, but oftentimes freely foreruns the asking. In thee mercy, in thee pity, in thee magnificence, in thee whatever of goodness is in any creature, are united. Now doth this man, who, from the lowest abyss of the universe, far even as here, has seen one after one the spiritual lives, supplicate thee of grace, for power such that he may be able with his eyes to uplift himself higher toward the Ultimate Salvation. And I, who never for my own vision burned more than I do for his, proffer to thee all my prayers, and pray that they be not scant, that with thy prayers thou wouldst dispel for him every cloud of his mortality, so that the Supreme Pleasure may be displayed to him. Further I pray thee, Queen, who canst whatso thou wilt, that, after so great a vision, thou wouldst preserve his affections sound. May thy guardianship vanquish human impulses.

---

verse affords, perhaps, the clue to his real conception. The body was lying in apparent physical sleep, while the soul, far from the body, was actually visiting the spiritual world. The journey through Paradise is the type of the deliverance of the soul from captivity to the law of sin, and from the body of this death.

Behold Beatrice with all the Blessed for my prayers clasp their hands to thee." [1]

The eyes beloved and venerated by God, fixed on the speaker, showed to us how pleasing unto her are devout prayers. Then to the Eternal Light were they directed, to which it may not be believed that eye so clear of any creature enters in.

And I, who to the end of all desires was approaching, even as I ought, ended within myself the ardor of my longing.[2] Bernard made a sign to me, and smiled, that I should look upward; but I was already, of myself, such as he wished; for my sight, becoming pure, was entering more and more through the radiance of the lofty Light which in Itself is true.

Thenceforward my vision was greater than our speech, which yields to such a sight, and the memory yields to such excess.[3]

As is he who dreaming sees, and after the dream the passion remains imprinted, and the rest returns not to the mind, such am I; for my vision almost wholly departs, while the sweetness that was born of it yet distils within my heart. Thus the snow is by the sun unsealed; thus by the wind, on the light leaves, was lost the saying of the Sibyl.

O Supreme Light, that so high upliftest Thyself from mortal conceptions, re-lend to my mind a little of what Thou didst appear, and make my tongue so powerful that it may be able to leave one single spark of Thy glory for the folk to come; for, by returning somewhat to my memory and by sounding a little in these verses, more of Thy victory shall be conceived.

I think that by the keenness of the living ray which I endured, I should have been dazed if my eyes had been averted from it; and I remember that on this account I was the more hardy to sustain it till I conjoined my gaze with the Infinite Goodness.

O abundant Grace, whereby I presumed to fix my look through the Eternal Light till that there I consummated the seeing!

[1] v. 39. In the *Second Nun's Tale* Chaucer has rendered, with great beauty, the larger part of this prayer.

[2] v. 48. The ardor of longing ceased in the consummation and enjoyment of desire.

[3] v. 57.

"Vague words! but ah, how hard to frame
In matter-moulded forms of speech,
Or ev'n for intellect to reach
Thro' memory that which I became."

In Memoriam, XCV.

I saw that in its depth is enclosed, bound up with love in one volume, that which is dispersed in leaves through the universe; substance and accidents and their modes, fused together, as it were, in such wise, that that of which I speak is one simple Light. The universal form of this knot [4] I believe that I saw, because, in saying this, I feel that I rejoice more spaciously. One single moment only is greater oblivion for me than five and twenty centuries to the emprise which made Neptune wonder at the shadow of Argo.[5]

Thus my mind, wholly rapt, was gazing fixed, motionless, and intent, and ever with gazing grew enkindled. In that Light one becomes such that it is impossible he should ever consent to turn himself from it for other sight; because the Good which is the object of the will is all collected in it, and outside of it that is defective which is perfect there.

Now will my speech fall more short, even in respect to that which I remember, than that of an infant who still bathes his tongue at the breast. Not because more than one simple semblance was in the Living Light wherein I was gazing, which is always such as it was before; but through my sight, which was growing strong in me as I looked, one sole appearance, as I myself changed, was altering itself to me.

Within the profound and clear subsistence of the lofty Light appeared to me three circles of three colors and of one dimension; and one seemed reflected by the other, as Iris by Iris,[6] and the third seemed fire which from the one and from the other is equally breathed forth.

O how inadequate is speech, and how feeble toward my conception! and this toward what I saw is such that it suffices not to call it little.

O Light Eternal, that sole abidest in Thyself, sole understandest Thyself, and, by Thyself understood and understanding, lovest and smilest on Thyself! That circle, which appeared in Thee generated

[4] v. 91. This union of substance and accident and their modes; the unity of creation in the Creator.

[5] v. 96. The larger joy felt in the mention of what he saw, is proof that it was seen, but the vision so surpassed human faculties, though their power was exalted by grace, that they could not retain it in its completeness, but lost more of it in a single moment, than any loss which long lapse of time may work for past events.

Neptune wondered at the shadow of Argo because it was the first vessel that sailed the sea.

[6] v. 118. As one arch of the rainbow by the other.

as a reflected light, being awhile surveyed by my eyes, seemed to me depicted with our effigy within itself, of its own very color; wherefore my sight was wholly set upon it. As is the geometer who wholly applies himself to measure the circle, and finds not by thinking that principle of which he is in need, such was I at that new sight. I wished to see how the image was conformed to the circle, and how it has its place therein; but my own wings were not for this, had it not been that my mind was smitten by a flash in which its wish came.

To the high fantasy here power failed; but now my desire and my will were revolved, like a wheel which is moved evenly, by the Love which moves the sun and the other stars.[7]

[7] v. 145. By the grace of God Dante's desire was fulfilled in this vision, and his beatitude perfected in the conformity of his will with the Divine.

Part Three

The Late Middle Ages,

ca. 1350–1500

Introduction

⊓⊔⊓⊔⊓⊔⊓⊔⊓⊔⊓⊔⊓⊔⊓⊔⊓⊔⊓⊔⊓⊔⊓⊔⊓⊔⊓⊔

In the late Middle Ages (ca. 1350–1500), European society entered upon a time of troubles which severely affected the character of its civilization. The population fell drastically, and the economy entered upon a period of protracted slump. Numerous and destructive wars erupted all over Europe. The institutions, the ways of doing things, which had apparently worked so well in the thirteenth and earlier centuries, seemed no longer able to cope with the mounting problems of the age.

The character of late medieval culture, as it unfolds against this dismal background, is difficult to evaluate. To many historians, the fourteenth and fifteenth centuries were a period of decadence, of excessive ripeness, an "autumn" following the high summer of the thirteenth century. But it would be wrong to interpret the closing Middle Ages exclusively in terms of an effete and dying culture. Its spirit, at once critical and searching, undermined the confident and unified cultural attitudes of the thirteenth century and prepared the way for the cultural pluralism of the modern world. In rejecting, at least partially, many of the ideas and values of the earlier period, it cleared the way for new cultural experiments and departures, and initiated currents which were to gain in strength in the coming centuries. It therefore played a role of no little importance in lending character and content to the civilization of the modern West.

A. Spectacular catastrophes

The prosperity of the central Middle Ages had ridden a high wave of population growth which had persisted from at least the year 1000 to probably the late thirteenth century. The troubles of the closing Middle Ages, in their turn, were poised upon an acute and protracted population collapse.

The size of the late medieval population fall cannot be measured exactly, and it differed among the various regions of Europe. Losses seem usually to have been more than a third, and ranged in some unhappy areas to two-thirds or more. The decline was also protracted. The population may have stabilized as early as 1300, but it did not experience serious losses until the middle fourteenth century. Then it plummeted and continued to slide until well past the year 1400. It stabilized at much lower levels in the early or middle fifteenth century, and not until the century's end was it able again to register significant gains.

Historians are not sure of all the forces which influenced this substantial decline, nor of their relative importance. Some factors are evident enough: the Black Death of 1348, and the other numerous onslaughts of plague which followed it; the frequent famines; and widespread wars. But some scholars feel that these troubles were only manifestations of a deeper crisis. Perhaps they show an underlying excess of population within the medieval community, which by 1300 was on the verge of provoking, and eventually did provoke, a true Malthusian crisis. Still other historians feel that a major root of the population decline and stagnation was a low and sluggish birth rate, which crippled the population's efforts to make good its losses. The low birth rate may have been in turn a product of the poor social conditions under which the masses of the people had come to live by the thirteenth century. Perhaps it also reflected a widespread psychological discouragement and malaise, which compromised the desire of a large segment of the population to bring children into the world. All these possible influences upon the late medieval population collapse are currently the subjects of much scholarly research and discussion.

The results of these huge population losses were understandably profound. With dwindling numbers of people, wages tended to increase and rents decline, as landlords and employers had to compete with favorable terms to attract needed laborers. High costs and low returns ruined the prosperity which rentiers and businessmen had enjoyed in the thirteenth century. Ultimately, to be sure, the population decline brought better conditions for the diminished number of poor who survived. But its more immediate impact was an acute dislocation of economic production and of social relationships. The rich, unwilling to meet the high labor costs demanded, tried to hold down wages through legislation and even sought to limit the movement of peasants, creating a kind of neo-serfdom. These efforts in turn provoked social unrest and even revolt among the laboring classes. Perhaps the best known of these social uprisings are the Peasants' War in England (1381), and the *Ciompi* rebellion (1378), which involved the wool workers of Florence. Similar manifestations of social dissatisfactions are widely found in this unsettled age.

Economic and social dislocations were paralleled by political crises, to which they undoubtedly contributed. The greatest such crisis was the Hundred Years' War between France and England, which was fought intermittently between 1339 and 1453. Its origins were complex, but it may be considered fundamentally a struggle between the king of France and his chief vassal, who happened also to be the king of England. It thus represents a breakdown in the feudal constitution of France, which, in the thirteenth century, had apparently worked so well. Italy in the same period faced the crisis involving the decline of the free city, the rise of the despot and the coalescence of larger territorial principalities. For Italy too, the age was one of incessant strife.

The Church similarly experienced acute constitutional difficulties. The long residence of the popes at Avignon rather than at Rome (1309–78) compromised papal prestige, and helped inspire protests from all over Europe concerning the papacy's growing fiscal exactions. The still greater scandal of the Great Schism (1378–1417), when two and eventually three popes battled for supremacy, further aggravated the plight of the see of Peter. Demands for reform were constant, but little was actually accomplished.

Against the background of these repeated disasters, late medieval culture also shows some basic transformations. We can distinguish two major trends in the cultural history of the age: an exaggerated, even unbalanced pursuit of traditional ideals; and a critical reevaluation of them, leading to a search for new values to take their place.

B. Chivalry, thought and religion

The argument that the culture of the late Middle Ages grew over-ripe and decadent is probably best supported by a consideration of the ideals of the noble class, which are conveniently summarized under the term, chivalry.

The experience of the noble in this tumultuous age was paradoxical. The heavily armed, mounted fighter was losing his former military pre-eminence, and was in fact becoming technologically obsolete. The great English victories in the Hundred Years' War at Crécy (1346), Poitiers (1356) and Agincourt (1415) showed the superiority of the foot soldier, armed with his longbow, over the mounted armies of France. The emergence of the Swiss pikemen as the most effective fighters of Europe, and the continuing improvement of firearms, confirmed that in the fifteenth century infantry was becoming the queen of battles.

But as their military importance declined, the pretensions and self-adulation of Europe's nobles acquired a new extravagance. The courts of Europe vied with one another in the pomp of their ceremonies and lavishness of display; the court of the dukes of Burgundy probably ranked as the most sumptuous of the age. This is the period of the foundation of the great knightly orders, such as the English Knights of the Garter (founded in 1346), or still more typical, the Burgundian Knights of the Golden Fleece (founded in 1430). It was confidently assumed that such orders and the virtues they cultivated would save the world. This is also the age of the dashing hero, such as the model knight, the Fleming Jacques de Lalaing, and of the dramatic *beau geste*, the brilliant deed, done by a single brave man, which turns the tide of battle, while thousands stand in awe.

The literature of feudal society in the closing Middle Ages tends to view both life and history through blinders formed by its chivalrous ideals. The important events of history were summarized in the doings of the "Nine Worthies" (three pagan heroes, three Jewish and three Christian). Chroniclers such as Jean Froissart record battles largely in terms of the combat of knights, and ignore such factors as resources, wealth, men and weapons on which victory or defeat really depended.

Balance too was lost in the cult of love. Attitudes towards love varied between the cynical eroticism already manifest in Jean de Meun's section of the *Romance of the Rose*, and an artificial and unbalanced devotion to all women, no matter how undeserving, characteristic of the model knights.

The attitudes and behavior of the nobles in the late Middle Ages betray a weakening sense of proportion, a defective understanding of the world, a failure (or perhaps unwillingness) to come to grips with the realities around them. The culture of this noble class has all the aspects of a colorful, entertaining, but fundamentally impossible dream.

The history of late medieval scholasticism also shows a slipping sense of proportion, but combines this with a powerful current of criticism, directed against its own traditional assumptions.

St. Thomas continued to attract supporters and defenders in the schools of the late Middle Ages, but their work was distinguished by few new insights. Rather their interest in puerile questions (how many angels could dance on the head of a pin?), their highly elaborate and complex reasoning, their exaggerated subtleties helped give scholasticism a reputation for futility it was not soon to lose.

Opposed to the traditionalists were the promoters of a new, critical approach to philosophy, which came to be called the *via moderna*. One of the first and probably the greatest figure in the movement was the English Franciscan William of Ockham, who after an active and harried life died in Germany, perhaps in 1349. He is best known for his critical logic, and a principle advanced by him has come to be called "Ockham's razor." It can be stated in several ways, but says in essence that in reasoning the simpler explanation is always to be preferred. This principle of parsimony was used to hack away at the multiplied forms and essences with which traditional scholasticism had crowded the universe.

The new critical logic was also nominalist in inspiration, that is, it located the only knowable reality in the individual object as it was perceived by the senses. It denied the possibility of getting beyond the individual into a world of common essences or supersensory forms.

The new logic thus favored an empirical and even experimental approach to reality, and created a favorable milieu for the growth of a new, non-Aristotelian natural science. At Paris in the fourteenth century, scholastics such as Nicholas of Oresme and Jean Buridan were experimenting with the nature of acceleration, and advancing non-Aristotelian explanations for it. The center of such interests shifted to Padua in Italy in the fifteenth century, and linked directly with the scientific tradition that eventually produced Galileo. (This father of modern science was for part of his life professor at Padua.)

Religion too, in the late Middle Ages, shows these characteristic features of loss of proportion in pious practices, and a tendency critically to re-evaluate former assumptions.

Late medieval piety was touched by an intense preoccupation with death and its ravages. Literature and art became crowded with depictions of the *danse macabre*, the dance of death, and with lurid portraits of the putrefaction of the grave. It has well been observed that this perverted concern with the decay of matter does not reflect a religious delight in the spiritual world but a true materialism, an excessive attachment to the fleeting character of sensual beauty. This kind of troubled, tortured religion could well be interpreted not as a triumphant, but as a failing faith.

So also, such traditional religious practices as penance and self-mortification, the veneration of relics, or the quest for indulgences, exceeded all prior bounds, and invited the critical attacks even of those fundamentally orthodox.

On a more positive note, the age also witnessed efforts to develop new forms and styles of piety. The piety of the late Middle Ages was marked by a profound mystical bent, which perhaps surpassed in its depth and fervor all prior mystical movements. It stressed the importance of the inner life, the need of cultivating within the soul a sensitivity to the presence of God. It tended to discount the importance of precisely defined dogmatic systems and punctilious rules of conduct. Unless the believer first felt the love of God and returned it, it mattered little what he thought or did.

Mystics appeared all over Europe, but perhaps the most influential were Germans and Dutch of the Rhineland, who had a particular appeal to laymen. The first prominent name in this group is Meister Eckhart (ca. 1260–1327). A devoted student of St. Thomas, he rose to high office in the Dominican order, and won fame for his inspiring sermons. The goal of his mysticism was the preparation for God's "eternal birth" within the soul. To receive God within him, the Christian should first exclude from his mind all thoughts of the world, and should not even think about God in the traditional categories of dogma. He should cultivate a state of complete passivity. God will then be born within him, and kindle a divine spark in his soul. This spark, when nurtured, would bring the believer to eventual union with God.

Eckhart's theories of eternal birth and reunion with God seemed to verge on pantheism. After his death, Pope John XXII in 1329 condemned seventeen articles drawn from his works as heretical, and declared eleven others suspect.

But Eckhart's emphasis on the cultivation of an interior spiritual disposition found continued expression, although in more moderate form, in the works of his fellow Dominican preachers John Tauler (ca. 1300–61) and Henry Suso (ca. 1295–1366). The believer could find within himself, if not a divine spark, at least a kind of mystical wisdom.

One of the most influential of these Rhenish mystics was the Dutchman Gerard Groote (1340–81), who was born at Deventer and educated at Paris and Cologne. Shortly after his death, a group of men inspired by him formed a new religious congregation, known as the Brethren of the Common Life. They established schools in Germany and the Low Countries, and played a role in fifteenth-century education comparable to that of the Jesuits in the sixteenth and seventeenth centuries. The great humanist Erasmus was one of their students.

The Brethren tried to instill a kind of piety known as the *devotio moderna*, or "modern devotion." It finds its richest expression in one of the great religious classics of the Middle Ages, the *Imitation of Christ*, by Thomas à Kempis. Thomas wrote his meditations (which may have been based directly upon the teachings of Groote) about 1425, and a copy in Thomas' own hand dates from 1441.

The *Imitation* is critical of a formal approach to religion, even formal theology: "Let all teachers hold their peace . . ." it says, "do Thou alone speak to me." It is particularly disdainful of the precise logic of scholastic theology: "I would rather feel compunction than know how to define it." The *Imitation* rather emphasizes the calling to the inner life, and the inward consolation that comes from it. Even after the Reformation, this work retained its appeal to Christians of every confessional persuasion.

The difficulties of the ecclesiastical government, the demands for reform, the excesses evident in many traditional practices and the search for an interior religion contributed not only to new forms of orthodox piety, but to open heretical revolts against the medieval Church. Heresy had been a familiar problem, particularly since the twelfth century, but never before had the Church faced so powerful a challenge to its system.

Foremost among the heretics of the late Middle Ages was the Englishman John Wycliffe (ca. 1320–80). Educated at Oxford and eventually a professor there, he reveals a distinctively conservative, Augustinian cast to his thought. He dwells upon the weakness of human nature and the all-important role of grace in the government of the world.

Wycliffe attacked with ferocity the authority claimed by the established hierarchy. He argued that grace alone conferred dominion, that is, that only the good had a right to rule. The pope and cardinals, manifestly not in the state of grace, had no right either to dominate kings, exercise jurisdiction, or even own property. He looked to the secular prince or magistrate as God's chief instrument in ruling and reforming his visible Church, and thus anticipated the policy of "magisterial reformation" which many Protestant reformers later also supported. He further denied the dogma of transubstantiation, which affirmed that at Mass the species of bread and wine lost their natural substances and took on the substance, the body, blood, soul and divinity, of Christ. Transubstantiation conceded to priests the power to work a miracle, and its denial thus undermined their distinct and privileged status within Christian society. Finally, he defended the supremacy of Scripture, and denied that the pope and cardinals could authoritatively define its meaning. He began the translation of the Bible into English, and the work was continued by his followers.

Wycliffe's supporters in England, known as Lollards, were eventually suppressed by the king and Church. His ideas appealed to another university professor, John Hus (ca. 1370–1415) in Bohemia. Hus was burned at the stake for his views at the Council of Constance in 1415, but his death helped inspire the formation in Bohemia of a Czech national Church. In spite of crusades declared against it and compromises offered to it (and in spite of its own internal divisions), this national Church was never entirely suppressed. The religious defiance of the Bohemians represents the first permanent division within the fabric of medieval Christianity. It was thus a landmark along the way from the unity of medieval Christian civilization to the pluralism of the modern age.

In discussing the culture of the late Middle Ages, recognition should also be given to the humanist movement, which gained strength in Italy from the fourteenth century and spread to encompass all Europe in the late fifteenth and sixteenth centuries. Humanism is, however, amply represented in a separate volume of this series. We need only note here that humanism was one other product of late medieval civilization which was to influence profoundly the culture of the modern world.

The Middle Ages thus ended amid disasters and disunion, but with some important creations. When all is considered, medieval men left behind them an impressive heritage. The modern world in no small measure was built upon their efforts. And in their literature, thought and art, they examined with insight, imagination and passion problems which to thinking men should still be alive today.

RECOMMENDED READINGS

H. S. Bennett, *Chaucer and the Fifteenth Century* (Oxford: Clarendon Press, 1961).

Otto Cartellieri, *The Court of Burgundy* (New York: Knopf, 1929).

E. K. Chambers, *English Literature at the Close of the Middle Ages* (Oxford: Clarendon Press, 1961).

J. M. Clark, *The Great German Mystics: Eckhart, Tauler, Suso* (Oxford: Blackwell, 1949).

A. C. Flick, *The Decline of the Medieval Church* (2 vols., London: Paul, Trench and Trubner, 1930).

Johan Huizinga, *The Waning of the Middle Ages* (London: Arnold, 1924; New York: Doubleday, Anchor A 42).

Kenneth B. McFarlane, *John Wycliffe and the Beginnings of English Nonconformity* (New York: Macmillan, 1953).

W. A. Pantin, *The English Church in the Fourteenth Century* (Cambridge: Cambridge University Press, 1955).

L. Thorndike, *Science and Thought in the Fifteenth Century* (New York: Hafner, 1963).

I. *Late medieval society*

⎍⎏⎍⎏⎍⎏⎍⎏⎍⎏⎍⎏⎍⎏⎍⎏⎍⎏⎍⎏⎍⎏⎍⎏⎍⎏⎍⎏⎍⎏⎍⎏

1. Giovanni Boccaccio's description of the Black Death at Florence

In his Preface to his *Decameron*, which was written between 1348 and 1353, the Florentine author Giovanni Boccaccio has left us one of the most detailed descriptions of the onslaught of the Black Death in 1348. His precise estimate of a hundred thousand dead at Florence may be somewhat exaggerated, but there is no denying that the carnage reached terrible dimensions.

The *Decameron* itself, the most famous of Boccaccio's works, is a collection of a hundred short stories, narrated by seven women and three men who have fled to a country estate to escape the plague. The stories are close in spirit to the French *fabliaux*, and like them are primarily intended to entertain.

The *Decameron* has a reputation for realism, because of its frank and frequent treatment of sex. But as the author says, his effort is not to treat life realistically, but to present "sweetness and delight." The *Decameron* rather represents an effort to escape the grim realities of a plague-swept world by conjuring up amusing tales of fantasy, from which the more unpleasant aspects of contemporary life were largely excluded. This imaginative flight from reality into an ideal world of make-believe is one of the prominent features in late medieval culture.

The Italian text of the following passage may be found in Giovanni Boccaccio, *Il Decameron*, ed. Luigi Russo (Florence: Sansoni, 1939), pp. 5–15. The translation is by David and Patricia Herlihy.

Preface to the Ladies

How many times, most gracious ladies, have I considered in my innermost thoughts how full of pity you all are by nature. As often as I have thought this, I recognized that this present work will have in your judgment a depressing and unpleasant beginning. For it bears in its initial pages a disheartening remembrance of the past mortal pestilence, which was irksome and painful to all who saw it or otherwise knew it. But I do not wish that this should frighten you from going further, as if your reading will continuously carry you through sighs and tears. Let this horrid beginning be to you not otherwise than a rugged and steep mountain to travelers, next to which lies a lovely and delightful plain. The plain is all the more pleasing to them, in proportion to the great difficulties of climbing and descending. For just as sorrow drives out extreme happiness, so miseries are ended by supervening joy. To this brief unpleasantness (I say brief since it is contained in few words) there shall at once follow sweetness and delight. I have promised it to you in advance; for it might not have been expected from such a beginning, if it hadn't been told you. In truth, if I could have in honesty led you where I want by a way other than a path as rough as this, I would willingly have done so. But without this recollection I could not have shown you the reason why the things took place, of which you soon will be reading. Thus constrained, as if by necessity, I brought myself to write of them.

I say, then, that it was the year of the bountiful Incarnation of the Son of God, 1348. The mortal pestilence then arrived in the excellent city of Florence, which surpasses every other Italian city in nobility. Whether through the operations of the heavenly bodies, or sent upon us mortals through our wicked deeds by the just wrath of God for our correction, the plague had begun some years before in Eastern countries. It carried off uncounted numbers of inhabitants, and kept moving without cease from place to place. It spread in piteous fashion towards the West. No wisdom or human foresight worked against it. The city had been cleaned of much filth by officials delegated to the task. Sick persons were forbidden entrance, and many laws were passed for the safeguarding of health. Devout persons made to God not just modest supplications and not just once, but many, both in ordered processions and in other ways. Almost at the beginning of the spring of that year, the plague horribly began to reveal, in astounding fashion, its painful effects.

It did not work as it had in the East, where anyone who bled from the nose had a manifest sign of inevitable death. But in its early stages both men, and women too, acquired certain swellings, either in the groin or under the armpits. Some of these swellings reached the size of a common apple, and others were as big as an egg, some more and some less. The common people called them plague-boils. From these two parts of the body, the deadly swellings began in a short time to appear and to reach indifferently every part of the body. Then, the appearance of the disease began to change into black or livid blotches, which showed up in many on the arms or thighs and in every other part of the body. On some they were large and few, on others small and numerous. And just as the swellings had been at first and still were an infallible indication of approaching death, so also were these blotches to whomever they touched. In the cure of these illnesses, neither the advice of a doctor nor the power of any medicine appeared to help and to do any good. Perhaps the nature of the malady did not allow it; perhaps the ignorance of the physicians (of whom, besides those trained, the number had grown very large both of women and of men who were completely without medical instruction) did not know whence it arose, and consequently did not take required action against it. Not only did very few recover, but almost everyone died within the third day from the appearance of these symptoms, some sooner and some later, and most without any fever or other complication. This plague was of greater virulence, because by contact with those sick from it, it infected the healthy, not otherwise than fire does, when it is brought very close to dry or oily material.

The evil was still greater than this. Not only conversation and contact with the sick carried the illness to the healthy and was cause of their common death. But even to handle the clothing or other things touched or used by the sick seem to carry with it that same disease for those who came into contact with them. You will be amazed to hear what I now must tell you. If the eyes of many, including my own, had not seen it, I would hardly dare to believe it, much less to write it, even if I had heard it from a person worthy of faith. I say that the character of the pestilence we describe was of such virulence in spreading from one person to another, that not only did it go from man to man, but many times it also apparently did the following, which is even more remarkable. If an animal outside the human species contacted the belongings of a man sick or dead of this illness, it not only caught the disease, but within a brief time was killed by it. My own eyes, as I said a little while ago, saw one day (and other times besides) this occurrence. The rags of a poor man dead from this disease had been thrown in a public street. Two pigs came to them and they, in their accustomed manner, first rooted among them with their snouts, and then seized them with their teeth and tossed them about with their jaws. A short hour later, after some staggering, as if the poison was taking effect, both of them fell dead to earth upon the rags which they had unhappily dragged.

Such events and many others similar to them or even worse conjured up in those who remained healthy diverse fears and imaginings. Almost all were inclined to a very cruel purpose, that is, to shun and to flee the sick and their belongings. By so behaving, each believed that he would gain safety for himself. Some persons advised that a moderate manner of living, and the avoidance of all excesses, greatly strengthened resistance to this danger. Seeking out companions, such persons lived apart from other men. They closed and locked themselves in those houses where no sick person was found. To live better, they consumed in modest quantities the most delicate foods and the best wines, and avoided all sexual activity. They did not let themselves speak to anyone, nor did they wish to hear any news from the outside, concerning death or the sick. They lived amid music and those pleasures which they were able to obtain.

Others were of a contrary opinion. They affirmed that heavy drinking and enjoyment, making the rounds with singing and good cheer, the satisfaction of the appetite with everything one could, and the laughing and joking which derived from this, were the most effective medicine for this great evil. As they recommended, so they put into practice, according to their ability. Night and day, they went now to that tavern and now to another, drinking without moderation or measure. They did even more in the houses of others; they had only to discern there things which were to their liking or pleasure. This they could easily do, since everyone, as if he was destined to live no more, had abandoned all care of his possessions and of himself. Thus, most houses had become open to all, and strangers used them as they happened upon them, as their proper owner might have done. With this inhuman intent, they continuously avoided the sick with all their power.

In this great affliction and misery of our city, the revered authority of both divine and human laws was left to fall and decay by those who administered and executed them. They too, just as other men, were all either dead or sick or so destitute of their families, that they were unable to fulfill any office. As a result everyone could do just as he pleased.

Many others held a middle course between the two mentioned

above. Not restraining themselves in their diet as much as the first group, nor letting themselves go in drinking and other excesses as the second, they satisfied their appetites sufficiently. They did not go into seclusion but went about carrying flowers, fragrant herbs and various spices which they often held to their noses, believing it good to comfort the brain with such odors since the air was heavy with the stench of dead bodies, illness and pungent medicines. Others had harsher but perhaps safer ideas. They said that against plagues no medicine was better than or even equal to simple flight. Moved by this reasoning and giving heed to nothing but themselves, many men and women abandoned their own city, their houses and homes, their relatives and belongings in search of their own country places or those of others. Just as if the wrath of God, in order to punish the iniquity of men with the plague, could not pursue them, but would only oppress those within city walls! They were apparently convinced that no one should remain in the city, and that its last hour had struck.

Although these people of various opinions did not all die, neither did they all live. In fact many in each group and in every place became ill, but having given example to those who were still well, they in turn were abandoned and left to perish.

We have said enough of these facts: that one townsman shuns another; that almost no one cares for his neighbor; that relatives rarely or never exchange visits, and never do they get too close. The calamity had instilled such terror in the hearts of men and women that brother abandoned brother, uncle nephew, brother sister, and often wives left their husbands. Even more extraordinary, unbelievable even, fathers and mothers shunned their children, neither visiting them nor helping them, as though they were not their very own.

Consequently, for the enormous number of men and women who became ill, there was no aid except the charity of friends, who were few indeed, or the avarice of servants attracted by huge and exorbitant stipends. Even so, there weren't many servants, and those few men and women were of unrefined capabilities, doing little more than to hand the sick the articles they requested and to mark their death. Serving in such a capacity, many perished along with their earnings. From this abandonment of the sick by neighbors, relatives and friends and from the scarcity of servants arose an almost unheard-of custom. Once she became ill, no woman, however attractive, lovely or well-born, minded having as her servant a man, young or old. To him without any shame she exhibited any part of her body as sickness required, as if to another woman. This explains why those who were cured were less modest than formerly. A further consequence is that many died for want of help who might still be living. The fact that the ill could not avail themselves of services as well as the virulence of the plague account for the multitude who died in the city by day and by night. It was dreadful to hear tell of it, and likewise to see it. Out of necessity, therefore, there were born among the survivors customs contrary to the old ways of the townspeople.

It used to be the custom, as it is today, for the female relatives and neighbors of the dead man to gather together with those closest to him in order to mourn. Outside the house of the dead man his friends, neighbors and many others would assemble. Then, according to the status of the deceased, a priest would come with the funeral pomp of candles and chants, while the dead man was borne on the shoulders of his peers to the church chosen before death. As the ferocity of the plague increased, such customs ceased either totally or in part, and new ones took their place. Instead of dying amidst a crowd of women, many left this life without a single witness. Indeed, few were conceded the mournful wails and bitter tears of loved ones. Instead, quips and merrymaking were common, and even normally compassionate women had learned well such habits for the sake of their health. Few bodies had more than ten or twelve neighbors to accompany them to church, and even those were not upright citizens, but a species of vulture sprung from the lowly who called themselves "grave-diggers," and sold their services. They shouldered the bier and with hurried steps went not to the church designated by the deceased, but more often than not to the nearest church. Ahead were four or six clerics with little light or sometimes none, who with the help of the grave-diggers placed the dead in the nearest open grave without straining themselves with too long or solemn a service.

Much more wretched was the condition of the poor people and even perhaps of the middle class in large part. Because of hope or poverty, these people were confined to their houses. Thus keeping to their quarters, thousands fell ill daily and died without aid or help of any kind, almost without exception. Many perished on the public streets by day or by night, and many more ended their days at home, where the stench of their rotting bodies first notified their neighbors of their death. With these and others dying all about, the city was full of corpses. Now a general procedure was followed more out of fear of contagion than because of charity felt for the dead. Alone or with the help of whatever porters they could find, they dragged the corpses from their houses and piled them in front so, particularly in the morning, anyone abroad could see countless bodies. Biers were sent for and when they were lacking, ordinary planks carried the bodies. It was not an isolated bier which carried two or three together. This happened not just once, but many biers could be counted which held in fact a wife and husband, two or three brothers, or father and son. Countless times, it happened that two priests going forth with a cross to bury someone were joined by three or four biers carried behind by bearers, so that whereas the priests thought they had one corpse to bury, they found themselves with six, eight or even more. Nor were these dead honored with tears, candles or mourners. It had come to such a pass that men who died were shown no more concern than dead goats today.

All of this clearly demonstrated that although the natural course of events with its small and occasional stings had failed to impress the wise to bear such trials with patience, the very magnitude of evils now had forced even the simple people to become indifferent to them. Every hour of every day there was such a rush to carry the huge number of corpses that there was not enough blessed burial ground, especially with the usual custom of giving each body its own place. So when the ground was filled, they made huge trenches in every churchyard, in which they stacked hundreds of bodies in layers like goods stowed in the hold of a ship, covering them with a bit of earth until the bodies reached the very top.

And so I won't go on searching out every detail of our city's miseries, but while such hard times prevailed, the surrounding countryside was spared nothing. There, in the scattered villages (not to speak of the castles which were like miniature cities) and across the fields, the wretched and impoverished peasants and their families died without any medical aid or help from servants, not like men but like beasts, on the roads, on their farms, and about the houses by day and by night. For this reason, just like the townspeople, they became lax in their ways and neglected their chores as if they expected death that very day. They became positively ingenious, not in producing future yields of crops and beasts, but in ways of consuming what they already possessed. Thus, the oxen, the asses, sheep, goats, pigs and fowl and even the dogs so faithful to man, were driven from the houses, and roamed about the fields where the abandoned wheat grew uncut and unharvested. Almost as if they were rational, many animals having eaten well by day returned filled at night to their houses without any shepherding.

To leave the countryside and to return to the city, what more can be said? Such was heaven's cruelty (and perhaps also man's) that between March and the following July, the raging plague and the absence of help given the sick by the fearful healthy ones tore from this life more than one hundred thousand human beings within the walls of Florence. Who would have thought before this deadly calamity that the city had held so many inhabitants? Oh, how many great palaces, how many lovely houses, how many noble mansions once filled with families of lords and ladies remained empty even to the lowliest servant! Alas! How many memorable families, how many ample heritages, how many famous fortunes remained without a lawful heir! What number of brave men, beautiful ladies, lively youths, whom not only others, but Galen, Hippocrates, and Aesculapius themselves would have pronounced in the best of health, breakfasted in the morning with their relatives, companions and friends, only to dine that very night with their ancestors in the other world!

2. The Ordinance of Laborers of Edward III, 1349

The plague and accompanying population fall dislocated production and exerted an upward pressure on wages and most prices. All over Europe, governments, guilds and other makers of economic policies tried to resist these trends by imposing wage and price ceilings or other rigid economic controls. These efforts seem to have been for the most part futile, but they did strain the relationships between the propertied and working classes. They were one principal reason for the widespread social unrest and frequent uprisings which mark the fourteenth century.

In summer, 1349, Edward III of England issued the following proclamation concerning the laborers of his realm. It was reissued as a parliamentary "Statute of Laborers" in 1351, and was thereafter several times reenacted by subsequent Parliaments. It well illustrates the dislocations brought on by the scarcity of workers and the efforts of medieval governments to counter them. The text is taken from *Translations and Reprints from the Original Sources of European History*, Vol. II, No. 5 (Philadelphia: University of Pennsylvania, 1902), pp. 3–5.

THE king to the sheriff of Kent, greeting. Because a great part of the people, and especially of workmen and servants, have lately died in the pestilence, many seeing the necessities of masters and great scarcity of servants, will not serve unless they may receive excessive wages, and others preferring to beg in idleness rather than by labor to get their living; we, considering the grievous incommodities which of the lack especially of plowmen and such laborers may hereafter come, have upon deliberation and treaty with the prelates and the nobles and learned men assisting us, with their unanimous counsel ordained:

That every man and woman of our realm of England, of what condition he be, free or bond, able in body, and within the age of sixty years, not living in merchandize, nor exercising any craft, nor having of his own whereof he may live, nor land of his own about whose tillage he may occupy himself, and not serving any other; if he be required to serve in suitable service, his estate considered, he shall be bound to serve him which shall so require him; and take only the wages, livery, meed, or salary which were accustomed to be given in the places where he oweth to serve, the twentieth year of our reign of England, or five or six other common years next before. Provided always, that the lords be preferred before others in their bondmen or their land tenants, so in their service to be retained; so that, nevertheless, the said lords shall retain no more than be necessary for them. And if any such man or woman being so required to serve will not do the same, and that be proved by two true men before the sheriff, bailiff, lord, or constable of the town where the same shall happen to be done, he shall immediately be taken by them or any of them, and committed to the next gaol, there to remain under strait keeping, till he find surety to serve in the form aforesaid.

If any reaper, mower, other workman or servant, of what estate or condition he be, retained in any man's service, do depart from the said service without reasonable cause or license, before the term agreed, he shall have pain of imprisonment; and no one, under the same penalty, shall presume to receive or retain such a one in his service.

No one, moreover, shall pay or promise to pay to anyone more wages, liveries, meed, or salary than was accustomed, as is before said; nor shall anyone in any other manner demand or receive them, upon pain of doubling of that which shall have been so paid, promised, required or received, to him who thereof shall feel himself aggrieved; and if none such will sue, then the same shall be applied to any of the people that will sue; and such suit shall be in the court of the lord of the place where such case shall happen.

And if lords of towns or manors presume in any point to come against this present ordinance, either by them or by their servants, then suit shall be made against them in the form aforesaid, in the counties, wapentakes, and trithings, or such other courts of ours, for the penalty of treble that so paid or promised by them or their servants. And if any before this present ordinance hath covenanted with any so to serve for more wages, he shall not be bound, by reason of the said covenant, to pay more than at another time was wont to be paid to such a person; nor, under the same penalty, shall presume to pay more.

Item. Saddlers, skinners, white tawyers, cordwainers, tailors, smiths, carpenters, masons, tilers, shipwrights, carters, and all other artificers and workmen, shall not take for their labor and workmanship above the same that was wont to be paid to such persons the said twentieth year, and other common years next preceding, as before is said, in the place where they shall happen to work; and if any man take more he shall be committed to the next gaol, in manner as before is said.

Item. That butchers, fishmongers, hostelers, brewers, bakers, poulterers, and all other sellers of all manner of victuals, shall be bound to sell the same victuals for a reasonable price, having respect to the price that such victuals be sold at in the places adjoining, so that the same sellers have moderate gains, and not excessive, reasonably to be required according to the distance of the place from which the said victuals be carried; and if any sell such victuals in any other manner, and thereof be convicted, in the manner and form aforesaid, he shall pay the double of the same that he so received to the party injured, or in default of him, to any other that will sue in this behalf. And the mayors and bailiffs of cities, boroughs, merchant towns, and others, and of the ports and maritime places, shall have power to inquire of all and singular, which shall in any thing offend against this, and to levy the said penalty to the use of them at whose suit such offenders shall be convicted. And in case the same mayors and bailiffs be negligent in doing execution of the premises, and thereof be convicted before our justices, by us to be assigned, then the same mayors and bailiffs shall be compelled by the same justices to pay the treble of the thing so sold to the party injured, or in default of him, to any other that will sue; and nevertheless they shall be grievously punished on our part.

And because many strong beggars, as long as they may live by begging, do refuse to labor, giving themselves to idleness and vice, and sometimes to theft and other abominations; none upon the said pain of imprisonment, shall, under the color of pity or alms, give anything to such, who are able to labor, or presume to favor them in their idleness, so that thereby they may be compelled to labor for their necessary living.

3. Chaucer's picture of medieval society

Geoffrey Chaucer (ca. 1340–1400) is the greatest English poet of the late Middle Ages, and one of the most gifted then writing in any European language. He was the son of a London vintner, and spent most of his adult life in government service, first traveling widely on the continent as a soldier and diplomat, then holding several high administrative offices at home.

Chaucer shows the continuing strong influence of French courtly literature; he translated a portion of the *Romance of the Rose* as well as several French tales of chivalry. But he was also the first major English writer to reflect Italian influences, especially the popularity of the short narrative or *novella*, best represented by Boccaccio's *Decameron*.

The *Canterbury Tales*, Chaucer's greatest work, tells of the journey of twenty-nine pilgrims from the Tabard Inn in Southwark to the tomb of St. Thomas at Canterbury. For entertainment on the road, all the pilgrims are to relate two tales each and two more on returning. The work was, however, unfinished, as we have only twenty complete stories, and fragments of four others.

In the Prologue to the tales, Chaucer describes the participants in the pilgrimage, and has left us an unexcelled picture of the English society of his age. It is not, to be sure, comprehensive. Great barons and prelates are not present, and the very poor are also slighted. The pilgrims predominantly represent the middle ranges of English medieval society.

Chaucer describes his figures with frequent irony and humor, but he is no true social critic or reformer. All the pilgrims, including the monk and friar, are judged in the light of their own professed ideals. Chaucer shows no influence of the new humanism gaining strength in Italy, or even of the movements of religious criticism current in the England of his day. He is a medieval poet, surveying the medieval social world and judging it according to its own standards. This lack of any tendentious purpose adds to the accuracy of his portraits, and also to their lasting human appeal.

Among the figures on the pilgrimage, the "franklin" was a large landholder. The "manciple" was a steward employed at the London law schools (the inns of court). The "reeve" was a manager of a lord's estate. The "summoner" was an official of an ecclesiastical court who summoned delinquents, and the "pardoner" sold papal dispensations and indulgences.

The selection is taken from Geoffrey Chaucer, *The Canterbury Tales*, trans. Frank E. Hill, School Edition, pp. 117–24, 219 (New York, 1960). Used by permission of David McKay Company, Inc.

The Prologue

When April with his showers hath pierced the drought
Of March with sweetness to the very root,
And flooded every vein with liquid power
That of its strength engendereth the flower;
When Zephyr also with his fragrant breath
Hath urged to life in every holt and heath
New tender shoots of green, and the young sun
His full half course within the Ram hath run,
And little birds are making melody
That sleep the whole night through with open eye,
For in their hearts doth Nature stir them so,
Then people long on pilgrimage to go,
And palmers to be seeking foreign strands,
To distant shrines renowned in sundry lands.

And then from every English countryside
Especially to Canterbury they ride,
There to the holy sainted martyr kneeling
That in their sickness sent them help and healing.

Now in that season it befell one day
In Southwark at the Tabard as I lay,
Ready upon my pilgrimage to start
Toward Canterbury, reverent of heart,
There came at night into that hostelry
Full nine and twenty in a company,
People of all kinds that had chanced to fall
In fellowship, and they were pilgrims all
Riding to Canterbury. The stables there
Were ample, and the chambers large and fair,
And well was all supplied us of the best,
And by the time the sun had gone to rest
I knew them and had talked with every one,
And so in fellowship had joined them soon,
Agreeing to be up and take our way
Where I have told you, early with the day.
    But none the less, while I have space and time,
Before I venture farther with my rime,
It seems to me no more than reasonable
That I should speak of each of them and tell
Their characters, as these appeared to me,
And who they were, and what was their degree,
And something likewise of their costumes write;
And I will start by telling of a knight.

THE KNIGHT

A KNIGHT there was, and that a noble man,
Who from the earliest time when he began
To ride forth, loved the way of chivalry,
Honor and faith and generosity.
Nobly he bare himself in his lord's war,
And he had ridden abroad (no man so far),
In many a Christian and a heathen land,
Well honored for his worth on every hand.
    He was at Alexandria when that town
Was won, and many times had sat him down

Foremost among the knights at feast in Prussia.
In Lithuania had he fought, and Russia,
No Christian more. Well was his worth attested
In Spain when Algeciras was invested,
And at the winning of Lyeys was he,
And Sataly, and rode in Belmarie;
And in the Great Sea he had been at hand
When many a noble host had come to land.
Of mortal battles he had known fifteen,
And jousted for our faith at Tramessene
Thrice in the lists, and always slain his foe.
And he had been in Turkey, years ago,
Lending the prince of Palaty his sword
In war against another heathen lord;
And everywhere he went his fame was high.
And though renowned, he bore him prudently;
Meek was he in his manner as a maid.
In all his life to no man had he said
A word but what was courteous and right:
He was a very perfect noble knight.
But now to tell you what array he had—
His steeds were good, but he himself was clad
Plainly; in fustian doublet he was dressed,
Discolored where his coat of mail had pressed,
For he was lately come from his voyage,
And went at once to do his pilgrimage.

THE SQUIRE

WITH him there went a SQUIRE, that was his son,—
A lover and soldier, full of life and fun,
With locks tight-curled, as if just out of press;
His age in years was twenty, I should guess.
In stature he appeared of middle height,
And great of strength, and wondrous quick and light.
And he had gone campaigning recently
In Flanders, in Artois, and Picardy,
And in this short space bore a gallant part,
Hoping for favor in his lady's heart.
His raiment shone as if he were a mead
Broidered with flowers fresh and white and red.
Singing or fluting was he all the day;

He was as lusty as the month of May.
Short was his gown, with sleeves both long and wide,
Well could he sit a horse and fairly ride;
He could make songs, and prettily indite,
And joust and dance as well, and draw and write.
So fierce by night did love his heart assail
He slept no more than doth a nightingale.
Courteous he was, humble, willing and able,
And carved before his father at the table.

THE YEOMAN

HE had a YEOMAN there, and none beside
In service, for it pleased him so to ride;
And he was clad in coat and hood of green.
He bore a sheaf of arrows, bright and keen,
And wings of peacock feathers edged the wood.
He kept his gear the way a yeoman should—
No shafts of his with feathers dragging low!—
And in his hand he bare a mighty bow.
Close-cropped his head was, and his face was brown,
He knew well all the woodcraft that was known.
Gay on his arm an archer's guard he wore;
A buckler at one side and sword he bore;
Upon the other side a dagger swung,
Sharp as a spear's point, richly wrought and hung.
Saint Christopher on his breast made silver sheen.
He bore a horn; his baldric was of green;
In truth, he was a forester, I should guess.

THE PRIORESS

ALSO there was a nun, a PRIORESS,
And she went smiling, innocent and coy;
The greatest oath she swore was by Saint Loy;
And she was known as Madame Eglentine.
Full well she sang the services divine,
Intoning through her nose right prettily,
And fair she spoke her French and fluently
After the school of Stratford-at-the-Bow;
(The French that Paris spoke she didn't know).

Well-taught she was at table; she would let
No food fall from her lips; she never wet
Her fingers deeply in the sauce; with care
She raised each morsel; well would she beware
Lest any drop upon her breast should fall;
In manners she delighted above all.
Always she wiped her upper lip so clean
That never a fleck of grease was to be seen
Within her cup when she had drunk. When she
Reached for her food, she did it daintily.
Pleasant she was, and loved a jest as well,
And in demeanor she was amiable.
Ever to use the ways of court she tried,
And sought to keep her manner dignified,
That all folk should be reverent of her.
But, speaking of her heart and character,
Such pity had she, and such charity
That if she saw a trapp'd mouse she would cry—
If it had died, or even if it bled;
And she had little dogs to which she fed
Fine roasted meat, or milk, or dainty bread;
How would she weep if one of them were dead,
Or any one should strike it viciously:
She was all heart and sensibility!
Her face was fair in pleated wimple draped,
Her eyes were gray as glass, her nose well-shaped,
Her mouth full small and thereto soft and red,
But of a truth she had a fair forehead,
A span in breadth or I should be surprised,
For certainly she was not undersized.
Handsome her cloak, as I was well aware;
And wrought of coral round her arm she bare
A bracelet all of beads and green gauds strung,
And down from this a golden pendant hung—
A brooch on which was written a crown'd *A*
Followed by *Amor Vincit Omnia.*

THE NUN   THE THREE PRIESTS

ANOTHER NUN rode in her retinue,
That as her chapelaine served, and THREE PRIESTS too.

THE MONK

A Monk there was, as fair as ever was born,
An out-rider, that loved the hounds and horn,
A manly man, to be an abbot able.
Full many a dainty horse he had in stable,
And when he rode ye might his bridle hear
Jingle upon the whistling wind as clear
And all as loud as sounds the chapel bell
Where this same lord was keeper of the cell.
The rules of Maurice and of Benedict,
These being ancient now, and rather strict,
This monk ignored, and let them go their ways,
And laid a course by rules of newer days.
He held that text worth less than a plucked hen
Which said that hunters were not holy men,
Or that a monk who follows not the rule
Is like a fish when it is out of pool—
That is to say, a monk out of his cloister.
Indeed, he held that text not worth an oyster;
And his opinion here was good, I say.
For why go mad with studying all day,
Poring over a book in some dark cell,
And with one's hands go laboring as well,
As Austin bids? How shall the world be served?
Let Austin's work for Austin be reserved!
Therefore he hunted hard and with delight;
Greyhounds he had as swift as birds in flight;
To gallop with the hounds and hunt the hare
He made his joy, and no expense would spare.
I saw his sleeves trimmed just above the hand
With soft gray fur, the finest in the land;
And fastening his hood beneath his chin,
Wrought out of gold, he wore a curious pin—
A love-knot at the larger end there was!
His head was wholly bald and shone like glass,
As did his face, as though with ointment greased
He was full fat and sleek, this lordly priest.
His fierce bright eyes that in his head were turning
Like flames beneath a copper cauldron burning,
His supple boots, the trappings of his steed,

Showed him a prelate fine and fair indeed!
He was not pale like some tormented ghost.
He loved a fat swan best of any roast.
His palfrey was as brown as is a berry.

THE FRIAR

THERE was a FRIAR, a wanton and a merry,
Licensed to beg—a gay, important fellow.
In all four orders no man was so mellow
With talk and dalliance. He had brought to pass
The marrying of many a buxom lass,
Paying himself the priest and the recorder:
He was a noble pillar to his order!
He was familiar too and well-beloved
By all the franklins everywhere he moved
And by good women of the town withal,
For he had special powers confessional
As he himself would let folk understand:
He had been licensed by the Pope's own hand!
Full sweetly would he listen to confession,
And very pleasantly absolved transgression;
He could give easy penance if he knew
There would be recompense in revenue;
For he that to some humble order hath given—
Is he not by that token all but shriven?
For if he gave, then of a certain, said he,
He knew the man was penitent already!
For many a man may be so hard of heart
He may not weep, though sore may be his smart,
Therefore his case no tears and prayers requires:
Let him give silver to the needy friars!
Always he kept his tippet stuffed with knives
And pins, that he could give to comely wives.
And of a truth he had a merry note,
For he could sing and play upon the rote—
There he would take the prize for certainty.
His neck was white as is the *fleur-de-lys*.
He was as strong as any champion.
As for the inns, he knew them every one,
Their hosts and barmaids too—much better than
He'd know a leper or a beggar-man;

For it was not for such a one as he
To seek acquaintance in the company
Of loathsome lepers—no, not for a minute!
There was no decency or profit in it.
One should avoid such trash and cultivate
Vendors of food and folk of rich estate.
And if a profit was to be expected
No courtesy or service he neglected.
There was no man so able anywhere—
As beggar he was quite beyond compare.
He paid a fee to get his hunting ground;
None of his brethren dared to come around;
For though a widow might not own a shoe,
So pleasant was his *In principio*,
That he would have a farthing ere he went;
His profits more than paid him back his rent!
And like a puppy could he romp; yet he
Could work on love days with authority,
For he was not a monk threadbare of collar,
Out of some cloister, like a half-starved scholar,
But rather like a master or a pope.
Of double worsted was his semi-cope,
And rounded like a bell hot from the press.
Somewhat he lisped his words, in playfulness,
To make his English sweet upon his tongue.
And in his harping, after he had sung,
Deep in his head his eyes would twinkle bright,
As do the stars upon a frosty night.
Hubert this begging friar was called by name.

THE MERCHANT

NEXT, all in motley garbed, a MERCHANT came,
With a forked beard. High on his horse he sat,
Upon his head a Flanders beaver hat;
His boots were buckled fair and modishly.
He spoke his words with great solemnity,
Having in mind his gain in pounds and pence.
He wished the sea, regardless of expense,
Kept safe from Middleburg to Orëwell.
Cunningly could he buy French crowns, or sell,
And great sagacity in all ways showed;

No man could tell of any debt he owed,
So stately was his way in everything,
His loans, his bargains, and his trafficking.
In truth, a worthy man withal was he,
And yet I know not what his name might be.

THE STUDENT

THERE was a STUDENT out of Oxford town,
Indentured long to logic and the gown.
Lean as a rake the horse on which he sat,
And he himself was anything but fat,
But rather wore a hollow look and sad.
Threadbare the little outer-coat he had,
For he was still to get a benefice
And thoughts of worldly office were not his.
For he would rather have beside his bed
Twenty books arrayed in black or red
Of Aristotle and his philosophy
Than robes or fiddle or jocund psaltery.
Yet though he was philosopher, his coffer
Indeed but scanty store of gold could offer,
And any he could borrow from a friend
On books and learning straightway would he spend,
And make with prayer a constant offering
For those that helped him with his studying.
He gave to study all his care and heed,
Nor ever spoke a word beyond his need,
And that was said in form, respectfully,
And brief and quick and charged with meaning high.
Harmonious with virtue was his speech,
And gladly would he learn and gladly teach.

THE LAWYER

A SERJEANT OF THE LAW, wise and discreet,
There was as well, who often held his seat
In the church porch; an excellent man was he,
Prudent indeed, and great of dignity—
Or so he seemed, his speeches were so wise.
Oftimes he had been justice at assize
By patent and by full commission too.
For his renown and for the law he knew

He won good fees, and fine robes many a one.
Conveyancer to match him was there none:
All turned fee simple underneath his hand;
No work of his but what was made to stand.
No busier person could ye find than he,
Yet busier than he was he seemed to be;
He knew the judgments and the cases down
From the first day King William wore his crown;
And he could write, and pen a deed in law
So in his writing none could pick a flaw,
And every statute could he say by rote.
He wore a simple, vari-colored coat,
Girt with a fine-striped sash of silken stuff:
This, as to his array, will be enough.

THE FRANKLIN

A FRANKLIN in his company appeared;
As white as any daisy shone his beard;
Sanguine was his complexion; he loved dearly
To have his sop in wine each morning early.
Always to pleasure would his custom run,
For he was Epicurus's own son,
Who held opinion that in pleasure solely
Can man find perfect bliss and have it wholly.
Householder he, a mighty and a good;
He was Saint Julian in his neighborhood;
His bread, his ale, were always prime, and none
Had better store of vintage than his own.
Within his house was never lack of pasty
Or fish or flesh—so plenteous and tasty
It seemed the place was snowing meat and drink,
All dainty food whereof a man could think.
And with the changing seasons of the year
Ever he changed his suppers and his fare.
Many fat partridges were in his mew,
And bream in pond, and pike in plenty, too.
Woe to his cook if all his gear were not
In order, or his sauce not sharp and hot!
And in his hall the plenteous platters lay
Ready upon the table all the day.
At sessions he would play the lord and sire;

He went to parliament as knight-of-shire.
A dagger and a purse of woven silk
Hung at his girdle, white as morning milk.
As sheriff he had served, and auditor;
Nowhere was any vassal worthier.

THE HABERDASHER   THE CARPENTER
THE WEAVER   THE DYER   THE UPHOLSTERER

A Haberdasher and a Carpenter,
A Weaver, Dyer and Upholsterer
Were with us too, clad all in livery
Of one illustrious great fraternity.
All fresh and shining their equipment was;
None of their dagger-sheathes was tipped with brass,
But all with silver, fashioned well and new;
So with their girdles and their pouches, too.
Each of them seemed a burgess proud, and fit
In guildhall on a dais high to sit;
And in discretion each was qualified
To be an alderman, and had beside
Income and goods sufficient for the station,
Which would have filled their wives with jubilation,
Or else for certain they had been to blame.
Full fair it is when one is called "Ma Dame,"
And at the vigils leads the company,
And has one's mantle carried royally.

THE COOK

They brought a Cook for this occasion, who
With marrow-bones would boil their chicken stew,
With powder-marchant tart and galingale.
Well could he judge a draught of London ale.
And he could roast and seethe and broil and fry,
And brew good soup, and well could bake a pie.
But it was pity, as it seemed to me,
That he should have a sore below his knee.
His fowl-in-cream—he made that with the best!

THE SHIPMAN

There was a Shipman hailing from the west,
From Dartmouth possibly, for aught I know.

He rode his nag as well as he knew how;
His gown of falding hung about his knee.
A dagger hanging on a slip had he,
Slung from his neck under his arm and down.
The summer heat had burned his visage brown.
He was a right good fellow; many a draught
Of wine the merry rogue had drawn and quaffed
This side of Bordeaux, the while the merchant slept.
Nice conscience was a thing he never kept.
And if he fought and had the upper hand,
By water he sent 'em home to every land.
But as to skill in reckoning the tides,
The ocean streams, the risks on divers sides;
Harbors and moons and pilotage and such—
No one from Hull to Carthage knew so much.
Bold and yet wise in what he undertook,
With many a bitter storm his beard had shook;
He knew well all the harbors as they were
From Gothland to the Cape of Finisterre,
And every creek in Brittany and Spain.
The ship he sailed was called the *Madelaine*.

THE DOCTOR

A DOCTOR OF PHYSIC there was with us, too.
In all the world was not another who
Matched him in physic and in surgery,
For he was grounded in astrology.
Much could he help his patients with his powers,
Selecting well the most auspicious hours,
When the ascendant ruled, and he was sure
To prosper in the making of his cure.
He knew the cause of every malady,
Were it from Hot or Cold or Moist or Dry,
And where begun, and what its humor too;
He was a perfect doctor and a true.
The cause once known, the root of his disease,
At once he gave the patient remedies.
For he would have at call apothecaries
Ready to send him drugs and lectuaries,
For each of them from the other profit won;
Their friendship was not something just begun.

The ancient Æsculapius he knew,
Haly and Rufus and Serapion, too,
Avicenna, and great Hippocrates,
Rhasis and Galen, Dioscorides,
Averroes, Damascene, and Constantine,
Bernard and Gatisden and Gilbertine.
As for his diet, moderate was he,
And never ate to superfluity,
But for digestion and for nourishment.
Upon the scriptures little time he spent.
Sky-blue and sanguine was his whole array,
Well-lined with sarcenet and taffeta;
Yet he spent little, and with providence
Had saved his fees during the pestilence.
For gold in physic is a cordial; he
Loved gold on that account especially.

THE WIFE OF BATH

A GOOD WIFE was there from beside the city
Of Bath—a little deaf, which was a pity.
Such a great skill on making cloth she spent
That she surpassed the folk of Ypres and Ghent.
No parish wife would dream of such a thing
As going before her with an offering,
And if one did, so angry would she be
It put her wholly out of charity.
Her coverchiefs were woven close of ground,
And weighed, I lay an oath, at least ten pound
When of a Sunday they were on her head.
Her stockings were a splendid scarlet red
And tightly laced, with shoes supple and new.
Bold was her face, and fair and red of hue.
She was a worthy woman all her life;
Five times at church door had she been a wife,
Not counting other company in youth—
But this we need not mention here, in truth.
Thrice at Jerusalem this dame had been,
And many a foreign river she had seen,
And she had gone to Rome and to Boulogne,
To Saint James' in Galicia, and Cologne.
Much lore she had from wandering by the way;

Still, she was gap-toothed, I regret to say.
Upon a gentle, ambling nag she sat,
Well-wimpled, and upon her head a hat
As broad as is a buckler or a targe.
A mantle hung about her buttocks large
And on her feet a pair of pointed spurs.
No tongue was readier with a jest than hers.
Perhaps she knew love remedies, for she
Had danced the old game long and cunningly.

THE PARSON

THERE was a PARSON, too, that had his cure
In a small town, a good man and a poor;
But rich he was in holy thought and work.
Also he was a learned man, a clerk,
Seeking Christ's gospel faithfully to preach;
Most piously his people would he teach.
Benign and wondrous diligent was he,
And very patient in adversity—
Often had he been tried to desperation!
He would not make an excommunication
For tithes unpaid, but rather would he give—
Helping his poor parishioners to live—
From the offerings, or his own small property;
In little he would find sufficiency.
Broad was his parish, with houses far apart,
Yet come it rain or thunder he would start
Upon his rounds, in woe or sickness too,
And reach the farthest, poor or well-to-do,
Going on foot, his staff within his hand—
Example that his sheep could understand—
Namely, that first he wrought and after taught.
These words from holy gospel he had brought,
And used to add this metaphor thereto—
That if gold rust, what then shall iron do?
For if the priest be bad, in whom we trust,
What wonder is it if a layman rust?
And shame to him—happy the priest who heeds it—
Whose flock is clean when he is soiled who leads it!
Surely a priest should good example give,
Showing by cleanness how his sheep should live.

He would not put his benefice to hire,
Leaving his sheep entangled in the mire,
While he ran off to London, to Saint Paul's,
To take an easy berth, chanting for souls,
Or with some guild a sinecure to hold,
But stayed at home and safely kept his fold
From wolves that else had sent it wandering;
He was a shepherd and no hireling.
And virtue though he loved, and holiness,
To sinful men he was not pitiless,
Nor was he stern or haughty in his speech,
But wisely and benignly would he teach.
To tempt folk unto heaven by high endeavor
And good example was his purpose ever.
But any person who was obstinate,
Whoever he was, of high or low estate,
Him on occasion would he sharply chide;
No better priest doth anywhere reside.
He had no thirst for pomp or reverence,
Nor bore too sensitive a consciënce,
But taught Christ's and his twelve apostles' creed,
And first in living of it took the lead.

THE PLOWMAN

WITH him his brother, a simple PLOWMAN, rode,
That in his time had carted many a load
Of dung; true toiler and a good was he,
Living in peace and perfect charity.
First he loved God, with all his heart and will,
Always, and whether life went well or ill;
And next—and as himself—he loved his neighbor.
And always for the poor he loved to labor,
And he would thresh and ditch and dyke, and take
Nothing for pay, but do it for Christ's sake.
Fairly he paid his tithes when they were due,
Upon his goods and on his produce, too.
In plowman's gown he sat astride a mare.

THE MILLER   THE REEVE

A MILLER and a REEVE were also there,

THE SUMMONER   THE MANCIPLE   THE PARDONER
A SUMMONER, MANCIPLE, and PARDONER,
And these, beside myself, made all there were.
THE MILLER, big alike of bone and muscle,
Was a stout fellow, fit for any tussle,
And proved so, winning, everywhere he went,
The prize ram in the wrestling tournament.
He was thick-shouldered, knotty, broad and tough;
There was no door but he could tear it off
Its hasps, or with his head could butt it through.
His beard was red as any fox or sow,
And broad in shape as if it were a spade,
And at his nose's very tip displayed
There sat a wart, on which a tuft of hairs
Rose like the bristles on a red sow's ears;
The nostrils underneath were black and wide.
He bore a sword and buckler at his side.
Broad gaped his mouth as some great furnace door.
He would go babbling boastfully, or roar
Jests full of sin and vile scurrility.
He stole, and multiplied his toll by three,
Yet had a golden thumb, as God is true!
He wore a white coat and a hood of blue.
Upon the bagpipes he could blow a ditty,
And piped us out that morning from the city.

THE MANCIPLE

THERE was a MANCIPLE from an inn of court,
And many a buyer might to him resort
To mark a steward's life the way he led it.
For whether he would pay or take on credit
Always he schemed so well and carefully,
That first in stock and well prepared was he.
Now is not that a gift of God indeed,
That one unlettered man should so exceed
The wisdom of a group of learnèd men?
For he had masters more than three times ten,
Expert in law and diligent as well,
Whereof a dozen in the house did dwell
Fit stewards for the land and revenues

Of any lord in England ye might choose,
To make him live upon the rents he had,
Debt-free with honor, if he were not mad,
Or live as plainly as he might desire;
And able to administer a shire
In all emergencies that might befall,
And yet this maniple would fool them all.

THE REEVE

SLENDER and choleric the REEVE appeared;
As close as ever he could he shaved his beard;
Around his ears the hair was closely shorn,
And docked on top, the way a priest's is worn;
His legs were long and lean, with no more calf
Then ye would find upon a walking staff.
Well could he keep a garner and a bin;
There was no auditor could do him in.
And he could estimate by drought and rain
What he would get from seed, and how much grain.
The horses, swine, and cows his lord possessed,
Stock, dairy, poultry, sheep, and all the rest—
Of all such things this reeve had full control,
And made report by contract on the whole,
Because his lord had yet but twenty years.
No man there was could find him in arrears.
No bailiff, herd or hind but he could tell
Their shifts and trickeries—he knew them well;
These fellows feared him as they feared the death.
His dwelling stood full fair upon a heath;
Green trees made shadow there on all the sward.
He picked up money better than his lord,
Rich were the hidden stores he called his own.
And he could please his master with a loan
That came from what were justly his own goods,
Get thanks, and also get some coats and hoods!
In youth he had applied himself with care
To learn a trade; he was a carpenter.
This reeve upon a stallion had installed him;
He was a dapple gray and Scot he called him.
A sky-blue surcoat good of length he wore,
And by his side a rusty blade he bore;

From Norfolk came this reeve of whom I tell,
Close to a town that men call Baldeswell.
Like to a friar's his dress was tucked about,
And ever he rode the hindmost of our rout.

THE SUMMONER

THERE was a SUMMONER with us in that place,
That had a fiery red cherubic face,
With pimples, and his eyes were small and narrow;
As hot he was and lecherous as a sparrow;
Black scabby brows he had, and scraggly beard;
His was a face that all the children feared.
No brimstone, borax, mercury, ceruse,
White lead, or cream of tartar was of use,
Or any ointment that would cleanse or bite,
To rid him of his little pimples white,
Or of the knobs that sat upon his cheeks.
Garlic he loved, and onions, too, and leeks,
And wine as red as blood and wondrous strong.
Then like a madman would he shout ere long,
And when the wine within him held its sway,
Then not a word but Latin would he say.
He had some phrases, only two or three,
Such things as he had learned from some decree—
No wonder, for he heard it all the day;
Besides, ye know full well how any jay
Can cry his "Wat!" as well as the pope can.
But in some other matter probe the man,
Then he had spent all his philosophy:
And "*Questio quid juris*" would he cry!
He was a decent rascal and a kind;
A better fellow nowhere could ye find.
Let any man give him a quart of wine,
He might a twelve month have a concubine
Unscathed. But let him catch some fool in sin
And he would slyly fleece him to the skin.
And if he made a comrade anywhere,
Then would he teach him not to have a care
In such a case for the archdeacon's curse—
Unless, indeed, his soul were in his purse,
For in his purse his punishment should be.

"Your purse—that's the archdeacon's hell!" said he.
But here I hold it was a lie he said;
Let guilty men of curses be afraid—
They slay the soul as absolutions save it;
Also he should beware a *significavit*.
All the young people in the diocese
The man could frighten or could leave at peace,
Their secrets knew, and was their counsellor.
A monstrous garland on his head he wore,
That might have hung upon an alehouse stake.
He had made himself a buckler of a cake.

THE PARDONER

THE summoner brought a noble PARDONER
Of Rouncyvalle, his fellow traveller
And crony, lately from the court at Rome,
Loudly he sang, "Come hither, love, O come!"
The summoner bore him bass—a mighty voice:
Never made trumpet half so loud a noise.
This pardoner had hair yellow as wax,
But smooth it hung, as hangs a hank of flax,
And down in strings about his neck it fell
And all about his shoulders spread as well;
Yet thin in wisps it lay there, one by one.
But hood, for jollity, the man would none,
Safe in his wallet it was packed away;
He thought he kept the fashion of the day;
Hair loose, save for his cap, his head was bared.
His bulging eyeballs like a rabbit's glared.
He had a vernicle sewed on his cap.
His wallet lay before him in his lap,
Brim full of pardons piping hot from Rome.
As small as any goat's his voice would come,
Yet no beard had he nor would ever have,
But all his face shone smooth as from a shave;
I think he was a gelding or a mare.
But at his trade, from Berwick unto Ware
There was no pardoner could go his pace.
For in his bag he kept a pillow-case
That was, he said, our Blessed Lady's veil;
He claimed to own the fragment of the sail

That Peter had the time he walked the sea
And Jesu saved him in his clemency.
He had a cross of latten set with stones,
And in a glass a handful of pig's bones.
But with these relics when he had in hand
Some humble parson dwelling in the land,
In one day he could get more revenue
Than would the parson in a month or two.
And thus with tricks and artful flattery
He fooled both flock and parson thoroughly.
But let us say, to make the truth less drastic,
In church he was a fine ecclesiastic;
Well could he read a lesson or a story,
But best of all he sang an offertory;
For well he knew that when the song was sung
Then he must preach, and smoothly file his tongue
For silver, as he could full cunningly—
Therefore he sang so loud and merrily.

Now in few words I have rehearsed for you
Number, array, and rank, and told you too
Wherefore they came to make a company
In Southwark, at this noble hostelry,
The Tabard, standing close beside the Bell.
But now the time is come when I should tell
Of how we bore ourselves that night when we
Had all alighted at that hostelry;
Then shall I say what on the road befell,
And all else of our pilgrimage as well.
But first I pray that in your courtesy
Ye will not deem it my vulgarity
If I am wholly frank in my narration
Both of their manners and their conversation,
And give their words exactly as they fell;
For this I know—and ye must know as well—
That whoso tells a tale after a man
He must repeat as closely as he can
What has been said, and every word include,
Though much of what he writes be broad and rude;
Else must he make the tale he tells untrue,
Invent, or shape the words of it anew.

None may he spare, not though it be his brother,
Nor slight one word more than he does another.
For Christ himself speaks plain in holy writ;
Ye know well there is nothing base in it.
And Plato says, to any that can read,
The words must be the cousin of the deed.
Also I pray that ye will pardon me
That I have nowise set in their degree
The people in this tale, as they should stand;
My wit is scant, ye well can understand.

  Great cheer our good host made us every one,
And straightway to the supper set us down,
And choicest of his food before us placed;
Strong was the wine and goodly to our taste.
Our host, a seemly man, was fit withal
To be a marshall in a banquet hall,
For he was large, with eyes that brightly shone:
In Cheapside fairer burgess was there none.
Bold of his speech he was, wise and well-taught;
In short, in ways of manhood lacked for naught.
Also he was a gladsome, merry man,
And when the meal was ended he began
To jest and speak of mirth with other things
(When we had settled all our reckonings),
And thus he said: "Lordings, for certainty
Ye have been welcome here and heartily;
For on my word, if I shall tell no lie,
I never saw so merry a company
This year together in my house as now.
Fain would I please you did I know but how.
And now I have bethought me of a way
To give you mirth, and ye shall nothing pay.
Ye go to Canterbury—now God speed you!
With good reward the blessèd martyr heed you!
And well I know that, as ye go along
Ye shall tell tales, and turn to play and song,
For truly joy or comfort is there none
To ride along the road dumb as a stone;
And therefore I will fashion you some sport
To fill your way with pleasure of a sort.
And now if, one and all, it likes you well

To take my judgment as acceptable,
And each to do his part as I shall say,
Tomorrow, as we ride along the way,
Then by the soul of my father that is dead,
Ye shall be merry, or I will give my head!
Up with your hands now, and no more of speech!"
Agreement took us little time to reach.
We saw no reason for an argument,
But gave at once and fully our consent,
And bade him shape his verdict as he chose.
"Lordings," quoth he, "hear now what I propose,
But take it not, I pray you, in disdain;
This is the point, to speak both brief and plain:
Each one, to make your travelling go well,
Two tales upon this pilgrimage shall tell—
Going to Canterbury. And each of you
Journeying home shall tell another two,
Of happenings that long ago befell.
And he of us that best his tales shall tell—
That is, that telleth tales which are the best
In profit and in pleasant interest,
Shall have a supper (we to pay the cost),
Here in this place, sitting beside this post,
When we are come again from Canterbury.
And with design to make you the more merry
Myself along with you will gladly ride,
All at my own expense, and be your guide.
And whoso dares my judgment to withsay
Shall pay what we may spend along the way.
And if ye grant the matter shall be so,
Tell me without more words, that I may go
And quickly shape my plans to suit your need."
And we assented, and by oath agreed
Gladly, and also prayed our host that he
Would pledge to give his service faithfully—
That he would be our governor, and hold
In mind and judge for us the tales we told,
And set a supper at a certain price,
We to be ruled in all by his device,
In things both great and small. So to a man
We gave our full agreement to his plan.

And then the wine was fetched, and every guest
Drank of it straightway, and we went to rest,
And there was nothing further of delay.
   And on the morn, with brightening of day,
Up rose our host, and busily played the cock,
And gathered us together in a flock,
And forth we rode, just barely cantering,
Until we reached St. Thomas' Watering.
And there it was our host at length drew rein,
And said, "Now Lordings, hearken me again;
Here will I call your pact to memory.
If even-song and morning-song agree,
Let us see now who first begins his tale!
As I may ever drink of wine or ale
Whoso rebels at anything I say
Shall stand for all we spend along the way.
Now draw your lots before we take us hence,
And he that draws the shortest shall commence.
Sire knight," he said, "my master and my lord,
Draw now your lot, for here ye have my word.
Come near," quoth he, "my lady prioress,
And ye, sir clerk, have done with bashfulness!
Don't study here! Fall to now, every man!"
Then each at once to draw his lot began,
And briefly, as to how the matter went,
Whether it were by chance or accident,
The truth is this—the lot fell to the knight;
And all were blithe and there was much delight.
And now in reason he could hardly fail
According to the pact, to tell his tale,
As ye have heard—what more is there to say?
And when this good man saw how matters lay,
As one resolved in sense and courtesy,
His compact made, to keep it cheerfully,
He said: "Since it is I begin the game,
Come, let the cut be welcome, in God's name!
Now let us ride, and hearken what I say."
And with that word we went upon our way,
And all in merry mood this knight began
To tell his tale, and thus the story ran.

II. *Chivalry, thought and religion*

⊔⎍⊓

4. The Battle of Crécy, according to Jean Froissart

Jean Froissart (1338–ca. 1410) has left us our most detailed account of the first half of the Hundred Years' War. His work also offers rich insight into the character of late medieval chivalry. This historian of knightly virtues was, paradoxically, a bourgeois by birth. He was born at Valenciennes in Flanders, where his father was a painter. In 1361 he joined the court of Queen Philippa at Westminster in England. He traveled widely while in her service, visiting Scotland, Italy and France. At the queen's urging, he began to collect his histories. He continued his historical work even after his patroness' death (1369), eventually carrying his account up to 1400.

Froissart felt that the principal duty of historians was to preserve the memory of knightly heroes and their valorous deeds. There is an atmosphere of extravagance and even unreality about his work, as he wrote at a time when the military and social importance of the knights were already declining. He was careful, however, in gathering his material, relying chiefly upon interviews and, when possible, upon his own direct experience. His colorful and often exciting narrative has helped impart to the Middle Ages their lasting reputation as the period when knighthood flowered and little else.

The following selection describes the battle of Crécy, the first great English victory of the Hundred Years' War. The English king Edward III has just landed his army in France, and Philip VI Valois marches against him.

The translation is taken from Sir John Froissart, *Chronicles of England, France, Spain and the Adjoining Countries,* trans. Thomas Johnes (New York: Colonial Press, 1901) I, 36–45.

THE first important battle after landing took place at Caen, which town made an obstinate resistance, and upward of 500 English were killed in the narrow streets by the stones and benches which were thrown upon them from the tops of the houses. The king was so much enraged at his loss, that he gave orders that all the inhabitants should be put to the sword and the town burned; but Sir Godfrey de Harcourt prevailed with him to reverse this order, and with the inhabitants to submit to a quiet surrender. Much wealth and many prisoners were taken and sent over to England under charge of the earl of Huntingdon, with 200 men-at-arms and 400 archers.

After the taking of Caen, the English committed serious ravages in Normandy; Sir John Chandos and Sir Reginald Cobham became greatly distinguished for their bravery, and also for their humane treatment of the sufferers. For a time the king of England avoided as much as he could any open engagement with the army of France, and contented himself with plundering the country through which he passed. The two armies, however, now arrived near to Cressy, and it was told Edward that the king of France desired to give him battle. "Let us post ourselves here," said King Edward to his people, "I have good reason to wait for the enemy on this spot; I am now on the lawful inheritance of my lady-mother, which was given her as her marriage portion, and I am resolved to defend it against Philip of Valois." As Edward had not more than an eighth part of the forces which the king of France had, he was, of course, anxious to fix on the most advantageous position; and after he had carefully disposed his forces, he lost no time in sending scouts toward Abbeville to learn if the king of France meant to take the field that day; these, however, soon returned, saying, that they saw no appearance of it; upon which the king dismissed his men to their quarters with orders to be in readiness betimes in the morning, and to assemble at the same place. The king of France remained all Friday at Abbeville, waiting for more troops; during the day he sent his marshals, the Lord of St. Venant and Lord Charles of Montmorency, out of the town to examine the country and get some certain intelligence respecting the English. They returned about vespers with information that the English were encamped on the plain.

That night the king of France entertained at supper, in Abbeville, all the princes and chief lords of his army. There was much conversation relative to the war; and after supper the king entreated them always to remain in friendship with each other; "to be friends without jealousy, and courteous without pride." All the French forces had not yet arrived, for the king was still expecting the earl of Savoy, who ought to have been there with a thousand lances, as he had well paid for them at Troyes in Champaign, three months in advance. That same evening the king of England also gave a supper to his earls and barons, and when it was over he withdrew into his oratory, where, falling on his knees before the altar, he prayed to God that if he should combat his enemies on the morrow, he might come off with honor. About midnight he retired to rest, and rising early the next day, he and the prince of Wales heard mass and communicated. The greater part of his army did the same. After mass the king ordered his men to arm themselves and assemble on the ground which he had before fixed upon.

There was a large park near a wood, on the rear of the army, which King Edward enclosed, and in it placed all his baggage, wagons, and horses; for his men-at-arms and archers were to fight on foot. He afterward ordered, through his constable and his two marshals, that the army should be divided into three battalions. In the first, he placed the young prince of Wales, and with him the earls of Warwick and Oxford, Sir Godfrey de Harcourt, the Lord Reginald Cobham, Lord Thomas Holland, Lord Stafford, Lord Mauley, the Lord Delaware, Sir John Chandos, Lord Bartholomew Burgherst, Lord Robert Neville, Lord Thomas Clifford, the Lord Bouchier, the Lord Latimer, and many other knights and squires whom I cannot name. There might be, in this first division, about 800 men-at-arms, 2000 archers, and 1000 Welshmen; all of whom advanced in regular order to their ground, each lord under his banner and penron, and in the center of his men. In the second battalion were the earl of Northampton, the earl of Arundel, the Lords Ross, Willoughby, Basset, Saint Albans, Sir Lewis Tufton, Lord Multon, the Lord Lascels, and many others, amounting in the whole to about 800 men-at-arms, and 1200 archers. The third battalion was commanded by the king in person and was composed of about 700 men-at-arms and 2000 archers. The king was mounted on a small palfrey, having a white wand in his hand, and attended by his two marshals. In this manner he rode at a foot's pace, through all the ranks, encouraging the army and entreating that they would guard his honor and defend his right; so sweetly and with such a cheerful countenance did he speak, that all who had been before dispirited were directly comforted by hearing him. By the time he had thus visited all the battalions it was nearly ten o'clock; he then retired to his own division, having ordered the men to regale themselves, after which all returned to their own battalions, according to the marshals' orders, and seated themselves on the ground, placing their helmets and bows before them, in order that they might be the fresher when their enemies should arrive.

That same Saturday the king of France also rose betimes, heard mass in the monastery of St. Peter's in Abbeville, where he lodged; and having ordered his army to do the same, left that town after sunrise. When he had marched about two leagues from Abbeville and was approaching the enemy, he was advised to form his army in order of battle, and to let those on foot march forward that they might not be trampled on by the horses. This being done, he sent off four knights, the Lord Moyne, of Bastleberg, the Lord of Noyers, the Lord of Beaujeu, and the Lord of Aubigny, who rode so near to the English that they could clearly distinguish their position. The English plainly perceived that these knights came to reconnoiter; however, they took no notice of it, but suffered them to return unmolested.

When the king of France saw them coming back, he halted his army, and the knights pushing through the crowds came near to the king, who said to them, "My lords, what news?" Neither chose to speak first; at last the king addressed himself personally to the Lord Moyne, who said, "Sir, I will speak, since it pleases you to order me, but under correction of my companions. We have advanced far enough to reconnoiter your enemies. Know, then, that they are drawn up in three battalions, and are waiting for you. I would advise, for my part (submitting, however, to your better counsel), that you halt your army here and quarter them for the night; for before the rear shall come up, and the army be properly drawn up, it will be very late, and your men will be tired and in disorder, while they will find your enemies fresh and properly arrayed. On the morrow you may draw up your army more at your ease, and may at leisure reconnoiter on what part it will be most advantageous to begin the attack, for be assured they will wait for you." The king commanded that it should so be done; and the two marshals rode, one to the front and the other to the rear, crying out, "Halt banners, in the name of God and St. Denis." Those that were in front halted; but those that were behind said they would not halt until they were as forward as the front. When the front perceived the rear pressing on, they pushed forward; and as neither the king nor the marshals could stop them, they marched on without any order until they came in sight of their enemies. As soon as the foremost rank saw the English they fell back at once in great disorder, which alarmed those in the rear, who thought they had been fighting. All the roads between Abbeville and Cressy were covered with common people, who, when they were come within three leagues of their enemies, drew their swords, bawling out, "Kill, kill!" and with them were many lords eager to make a show of their courage.

There is no man, unless he had been present, that can imagine or describe truly the confusion of that day, especially the bad management and disorder of the French, whose troops were out of number. What I know, and shall relate in this book, I have learned chiefly from the English, and from those attached to Sir John of Hainault, who was always near the person of the king of France. The English, who, as I have said, were drawn up in three divisions, and seated on the ground, on seeing their enemies advance, rose up undauntedly and fell into their ranks. The prince's battalion, whose archers were formed in the manner of a portcullis, and the men-at-arms in the rear, was the first to do so. The earls of Northampton and Arundel, who commanded the second division, posted themselves in good order on the prince's wing to assist him if necessary.

You must know that the French troops did not advance in any regular order, and that as soon as their king came in sight of the English his blood began to boil, and he cried out to his marshals, "Order the Genoese forward and begin the battle in the name of God and St. Denis." There were about 15,000 Genoese crossbow men; but they were quite fatigued, having marched on foot that day six leagues, completely armed and carrying their crossbows, and accordingly they told the constable they were not in a condition to do any great thing in battle. The earl of Alençon hearing this, said, "This is what one gets by employing such scoundrels, who fall off when there is any need for them." During this time a heavy rain fell, accompanied by thunder and a very terrible eclipse of the sun; and, before this rain, a great flight of crows hovered in the air over all the battalions, making a loud noise; shortly afterward it cleared up, and the sun shone very bright; but the French had it in their faces, and the English on their backs. When the Genoese were somewhat in order they approached the English and set up a loud shout, in order to frighten them; but the English remained quite quiet and did not seem to attend to it. They then set up a second shout, and advanced a little forward; the English never moved. Still they hooted a third time, advancing with their crossbows presented, and began to shoot. The English archers then advanced one step forward, and shot their arrows with such force and quickness that it seemed as if it snowed. When the Genoese felt these arrows, which pierced through their armor, some of them cut the strings of their crossbows, others flung them to the ground, and all turned about and retreated quite discomfited.

The French had a large body of men-at-arms on horseback to support the Genoese, and the king, seeing them thus fall back, cried out, "Kill me those scoundrels, for they stop up our road without any reason." The English continued shooting, and some of their arrows falling among the horsemen, drove them upon the Genoese, so that they were in such confusion they could never rally again.

In the English army there were some Cornish and Welsh men on foot, who had armed themselves with large knives; these advancing through the ranks of the men-at-arms and archers, who made way for them, came upon the French when they were in this danger, and falling upon earls, barons, knights, and squires, slew many, at which the king of England was exasperated. The valiant king of Bohemia was slain there; he was called Charles of Luxembourg, for he was the son of the gallant king and emperor, Henry of Luxembourg, and, having heard the order for the battle, he inquired where his son the Lord Charles was; his attendants answered that they did not know, but believed he was fighting. Upon this, he said to them, "Gentlemen, you are all my people, my friends, and brethren at arms this day; therefore, as I am blind, I request of you to lead me so far into the engagement that I may strike one stroke with my sword." The knights consented, and in order that they might not lose him in the crowd, fastened all the reins of their horses together, placing the king at their head that he might gratify his wish, and in this manner advanced toward the enemy. The Lord Charles of Bohemia, who already signed his name as king of Germany, and bore the arms, had come in good order to the engagement; but when he perceived that it was likely to turn out against the French he departed. The king, his father, rode in among the enemy, and he and his companions fought most valiantly; however, they advanced so far that they were all slain, and on the morrow they were found on the ground with all their horses tied together.

The earl of Alençon advanced in regular order upon the English, to fight with them, as did the earl of Flanders in another part. These two lords, with their detachments, coasting, as it were, the archers, came to the prince's battalion, where they fought valiantly for a length of time. The king of France was eager to march to the place where he saw their banners displayed, but there was a hedge of archers before him; he had that day made a present of a handsome black horse to Sir John of Hainault, who had mounted on it a knight of his, called Sir John de Fusselles, who bore his banner; the horse ran off with the knight and forced his way through the English army, and, when about to return, stumbled and fell into a ditch and severely wounded him; he did not, however, experience any other inconvenience than from his horse, for the English did not quit their ranks that day to make prisoners: his page alighted and raised him up, but the French knight did not return the way he came, as he would have found it difficult from the crowd. This battle, which was fought on Saturday, between La Broyes and Cressy, was murderous and cruel; and many gallant deeds of arms were performed that were never known; toward evening, many knights and squires of the French had lost their masters, and, wandering up and down the plain, attacked the English in small parties; but they were soon destroyed, for the English had determined that day to give no quarter, nor hear of ransom from anyone.

Early in the day some French, Germans, and Savoyards had broken through the archers of the prince's battalion, and had engaged with the men-at-arms; upon this the second battalion came to his aid, and it was time they did so, for otherwise he would have been hard pressed. The first division, seeing the danger they were in, sent a knight off in great haste to the king of England, who was posted upon an eminence near a windmill. On the knight's arrival, he said, "Sir, the earl of Warwick, the Lord Stafford, the Lord Reginald Cobham, and the others who are about your son, are vigorously attacked by the French, and they entreat that you will come to their assistance with your battalion, for, if numbers should increase against him, they fear he will have too much to do." The king replied, "Is my son dead, unhorsed, or so badly wounded that he cannot support himself?" "Nothing of the sort, thank God," rejoined the knight, "but he is in so hot an engagement that he has great need of your help." The king answered, "Now, Sir Thomas, return to those that sent you, and tell them from me not to send again for me this day, nor expect that I shall come, let what will happen, as long as my son has life; and say that I command them to let the boy win his spurs, for I am determined, if it please God, that all the glory of this day shall be given to him, and to those into whose care I have entrusted him." The knight returned to his lords and related the king's answer, which mightily encouraged them, and made them repent they had ever sent such a message.

It is a certain fact, that Sir Godfrey de Harcourt, who was in the prince's battalion, having been told by some of the English that they had seen the banner of his brother engaged in the battle against him, was exceedingly anxious to save him; but he was too late, for he was left dead on the field, and so was the earl of Aumarle, his nephew. On the other hand, the earls of Alençon and Flanders were fighting lustily under their banners with their own people; but they could not resist the force of the English, and were there slain, as well as many other knights and squires, who were attending on or accompanying them.

The earl of Blois, nephew to the king of France, and the duke of Lorraine, his brother-in-law, with their troops, made a gallant defense; but they were surrounded by a troop of English and Welsh, and slain in spite of their prowess. The earl of St. Pol and the earl of Auxerre were also killed, as well as many others. Late after vespers, the king of France had not more about him than sixty men, everyone included. Sir John of Hainault, who was of the number, had once remounted the king, for his horse had been killed under him by an arrow; and seeing the state he was in, he said, "Sir, retreat while you have an opportunity, and do not expose yourself so simply; if you have lost this battle, another time you will be the conqueror." After he had said this he took the bridle of the king's horse and led him off by force, for he had before entreated him to retire. The king rode on until he came to the castle of La Broyes, where he found the gates shut, for it was very dark; he ordered the governor of it to be summoned, who, after some delay, came upon the battlements, and asked who it was that called at such an hour. The king answered, "Open, open, governor, it is the fortune of France." The governor hearing the king's voice immediately descended, opened the gate, and let down the bridge; the king and his company entered the castle, but he had with him only five barons: Sir John of Hainault, the Lord Charles of Montmorency, the Lord of Beaujeu, the Lord of Aubigny, and the Lord of Montfort. It was not his intention, however, to bury himself in such a place as this, but having taken some refreshments, he set out again with his attendants about midnight, and rode on under the direction of guides who were well acquainted with the country, until about daybreak he came to Amiens, where he halted. This Saturday the English never quitted their ranks in pursuit of anyone, but remained on the field guarding their position and defending themselves against all who attacked them. The battle ended at the hour of vespers, when the king of England embraced his son and said to him, "Sweet son, God give you perseverance; you are my son; for most loyally have you acquitted yourself; you are worthy to be a sovereign." The prince bowed very low, giving all honor to the king, his father. The English during the night made frequent thanksgivings to the Lord for the happy issue of the day; and with them there was no rioting, for the king had expressly forbidden all riot or noise.

On the following day, which was Sunday, there were a few encounters with the French troops; however, they could not withstand the English, and soon either retreated or were put to the sword. When Edward was assured that there was no appearance of the French collecting another army, he sent to have the number and rank of the dead examined. This business was entrusted to Lord Reginald Cobham and Lord Stafford, assisted by three heralds to examine the arms, and two secretaries to write down the names. They passed the whole day upon the field of battle, and made a very circumstantial account of all they saw: according to their report it appeared that 80 banners, the bodies of 11 princes, 1200 knights, and about 30,000 common men were found dead on the field. After this very successful engagement, Edward marched with his victorious army to Wisant, and having halted there one whole day, arrived on the following Thursday before the strong town of Calais, which he had determined to besiege. When the governor of Calais saw the preparations of the king of England, he collected together all the poorer inhabitants and sent them out of the town, in order that the provisions of the place might last the longer; he resolved, moreover, to defend the town to the last.

⎍⎍⎍⎍⎍⎍⎍⎍⎍⎍⎍⎍⎍⎍⎍⎍⎍⎍⎍⎍⎍⎍⎍⎍⎍⎍

5. A sermon by Meister Eckhart

The following sermon by the Dominican Meister Eckhart (ca. 1260–1327) well illustrates the simplicity and directness of this first of the great German mystics of the late Middle Ages. These qualities helped win for Eckhart his wide popularity as a preacher, and assured him a lasting influence. The theme of the sermon, "Eternal Birth," also expresses a central idea in his system of mystical theology. He explains that God will always be born in the soul of one who has prepared himself for him.

The sermon is taken from Raymond Bernard Blakney, *Meister Eckhart, A Modern Translation* (New York: Harper and Row, 1941, Harper Torchbooks, 1957, TB/8), pp. 113–24, and is reprinted with the permission of the publishers.

External birth
Et cum factus esset Jesus annorum duodecim, etc. (Luke 2:42)

We read in the gospel that when our Lord was twelve years old he went to the temple at Jerusalem with Mary and Joseph and that, when they left, Jesus stayed behind in the temple without their knowledge. When they got home and missed him, they looked for him among acquaintances and strangers and relatives. They looked for him in the crowds and still they could not find him. Furthermore, they had lost him among the [temple] crowds and had to go back to where they came from. When they got back to their starting point, they found him.

Thus it is true that, if you are to experience this noble birth, you must depart from all crowds and go back to the starting point, the core [of the soul] out of which you came. The crowds are the agents of the soul and their activities: memory, understanding, and will, in all their diversifications. You must leave them all: sense perception, imagination, and all that you discover in self or intend to do. After that, you may experience this birth—but otherwise not—believe me! He was not found among friends, nor relatives, nor among acquaintances. No. He is lost among these altogether.

Thence we have a question to ask: Is it possible for man to experience this birth through certain things which, although they are divine, yet they come into the man through the senses from without? I refer to certain ideas of God, such as, for example, that God is good, wise, merciful, or whatever—ideas that are creatures of the reason, and yet divine. Can a man have the experience [of the divine birth] by means of these? No! Truly no. Even though [these ideas] are all good and divine, still he gets them all through his senses from without. If the divine birth is to shine with reality and purity, it must come flooding up and out of man from God within him, while all man's own efforts are suspended and all the soul's agents are at God's disposal.

This work [birth], when it is perfect, will be due solely to God's action while you have been passive. If you really forsake your own knowledge and will, then surely and gladly God will enter with his knowledge shining clearly. Where God achieves self-consciousness, your own knowledge is of no use, nor has it standing. Do not imagine that your own intelligence may rise to it, so that you may know God. Indeed, when God divinely enlightens you, no natural light is required to bring that about. This [natural light] must in fact be completely extinguished before God will shine in with his light, bringing back with him all that you have forsaken and a thousand times more, together with a new form to contain it all.

We have a parable for this in the gospel. When our Lord had held friendly conversation with the heathen woman at the well, she left her jug and ran to the city to tell the people that the true Messiah had come. The people, not believing her report, went out to see for themselves. Then they said to her: "Now we believe, not because of thy saying: for we have seen him ourselves." Thus it is true that you cannot know God by means of any creature science nor by means of your own wisdom. If you are to know God divinely, your own knowledge must become as pure ignorance, in which you forget yourself and every other creature.

But perhaps you will say: "Alas, sir, what is the point of my mind existing if it is to be quite empty and without function? Is it best for me to screw up my courage to this unknown knowledge which cannot really be anything at all? For if I know anything in any way, I shall not be ignorant, nor would I be either empty or innocent. Is it my place to be in darkness?"

Yes, truly. You could do not better than to go where it is dark, that is, unconsciousness.

"But, sir, must everything go and is there no turning back?"

Certainly not. By rights, there is no return.

"Then what is the darkness? What do you mean by it? What is its name?"

It has no name other than "potential sensitivity" and it neither lacks being nor does it want to be. It is that possible [degree of] sensitivity through which you may be made perfect. That is why there is no way back out of it. And yet, if you do return, it will not be for the sake of truth but rather on account of the world, the flesh, and the devil. If you persist in abandoning it, you necessarily fall [a victim to spiritual] malady and you may even persist so long that for you the fall will be eternal. Thus there can be no turning back but only pressing on to the attainment and achievement of this potentiality. There is no rest [in the process] short of complete fulfillment of Being. Just as matter can never rest until it is made complete by form, which represents its potential Being, so there is no rest for the mind until it has attained all that is possible to it.

On this point, a heathen master says: "Nature has nothing swifter than the heavens, which outrun everything else in their course." But surely the mind of man, in its course, outstrips them all. Provided it retains its active powers and keeps itself free from defilement and the disintegration of lesser and cruder things, it can outstrip high heaven and never slow down until it has reached the highest peak, and is fed and lodged by the highest good, which is God.

Therefore, how profitable it is to pursue this potentiality, until empty and innocent, a man is alone in that darkness of unselfconsciousness, tracking and tracing [every clue] and never retracing his steps! Thus you may win that [something] which is everything, and the more you make yourself like a desert, unconscious of everything, the nearer you come to that estate. Of this desert, Hosea writes: "I will allure her, and bring her into the wilderness, and speak to her heart." The genuine word of eternity is spoken only in that eternity of the man who is himself a wilderness, alienated from self and all multiplicity. The prophet longed for this desolated alienation from self, for he said: "Oh that I had wings like a dove! for then would I fly away, and be at rest." Where may one find peace and rest? Really only where he rejects all creatures, being alienated from them and desolate. So David said: "I would choose rather to sit at the threshold of the house of my God than to dwell with great honor and wealth in the tents of wickedness."

But you may say: "Alas, sir, does a man have to be alienated from creatures and always desolate, inwardly as well as outwardly, the soul's agents together with their functions—must all be done away? That would put one in a hard position—if then God should leave him without his support, and add to his misery, taking away his light and neither speaking to him nor acting in him, as you now seem to mean. If a person is to be in such a state of pure nothingness, would it not be better for him to be doing something to make the darkness and alienation supportable? Should he not pray, or read, or hear a sermon or do something else that is good to help himself through it?"

No! You may be sure that perfect quiet and idleness is the best you can do. For, see, you cannot turn from this condition to do anything, without harming it. This is certain: you would like in part to prepare yourself and in part to be prepared by God, but it cannot be so, for however quickly you desire or think of preparing, God gets there first. But suppose that the preparation could be shared between you and God for the [divine] work of ingress— which is impossible—then you should know that God must act and pour in as soon as he finds that you are ready. Do not imagine that God is like a carpenter who works or not, just as he pleases, suiting his own convenience. It is not so with God, for when he finds you ready he must act, and pour into you, just as when the air is clear and pure the sun must pour into it and may not hold back. Surely, it would be a very great defect in God if he did not do a great work, and anoint you with great good, once he found you empty and innocent.

The authorities, writing to the same point, assert that when the matter of which a child is made is ready in the mother's body, God at once pours in the living spirit which is the soul—the body's form. Readiness and the giving of form occur simultaneously. When nature reaches its highest point, God gives grace. When the [human] spirit is ready, God enters it without hesitation or waiting. It is written in the Revelation that our Lord told people: "I stand at the door and knock and wait. If any man let me in, I will sup with him." You need not look either here or there. He is no farther away than the door of the heart. He stands there, lingering, waiting for us to be ready and open the door and let him in. You need not call to him as if he were far away, for he waits more urgently than you for the door to be opened. You are a thousand times more necessary to him than he is to you. The opening [of the door] and his entry are simultaneous.

Still you may, ask: "How can that be? I do not sense his presence." But look! To sense his presence is not within your power, but his. When it suits him, he shows himself; and he conceals himself when he wants to. This is what Christ meant when he said to Nicodemus: "The wind [Spirit] bloweth where it listeth, and thou hearest the sound thereof but canst not tell whence it cometh and whither it goeth." There is an [apparent] contradiction in what he says: "You hear and yet do not know." When one hears, he knows. Christ meant: by hearing a man takes in or absorbs [the Spirit of God]. It was as if he wanted to say: You receive it without knowing it. But you should remember that God may not leave anything empty or void. That is not God's nature. He could not bear it. Therefore, however much it may seem that you do not sense his presence or that you are quite innocent of it, this is not the case. For if there were any void under heaven whatever, great or small, either the sky would have to draw it up to itself or bend down to fill it. God, the master of nature, will not tolerate any empty place. Therefore be quiet and do not waver lest, turning away from God for an hour, you never return to him.

Still you may say: "Alas, sir, you assume that this birth is going to happen and that the Son [of God] will be born in me. But by what sign shall I know that it has happened?"

Yes! Certainly! There may well be three trustworthy signs, but let me tell about one of them. I am often asked if it is possible, within time, that a person should not be hindered either by multiplicity or by matter. Indeed, it is. When this birth really happens, no creature in all the world will stand in your way and, what is more, they will all point you to God and to this birth. Take the analogy of the thunderbolt. When it strikes to kill, whether it is a tree or an animal or a person, at the coming of the blow, they all turn toward it and if a person's back were turned, he would instantly turn to face it. All the thousands of leaves of a tree at once turn the required sides to the stroke. And so it is with all who experience this birth. They, together with all around them, earthy as you please, are quickly turned toward it. Indeed, what was formerly a hindrance becomes now a help. Your face is turned so squarely toward it that, whatever you see or hear, you only get this birth out of it. Everything stands for God and you see only God in all the world. It is just as when one looks straight at the sun for a while: afterwards, everything he looks at has the image of the sun in it. If this is lacking, if you are not looking for God and expecting him everywhere, and in everything, you lack the birth.

Still you might ask: "While in this state, should one do penances? Isn't he missing something if he doesn't?"

The whole of a life of penitence is only one among a number of things such as fasting, watching, praying, kneeling, being disciplined, wearing hair shirts, lying on hard surfaces, and so on. These were all devised because of the constant opposition of the body and flesh to the spirit. The body is too strong for the spirit and so there is always a struggle between them—an eternal conflict. The body is bold and brave here, for it is at home and the world helps it. This earth is its fatherland and all its kindred are on its side: food, drink, and comforts are all against the spirit. Here the spirit is alien. Its race and kin are all in heaven. It has many friends there. To assist the spirit in its distress, to weaken the flesh for its part in this struggle so that it cannot conquer the spirit, penances are put upon the flesh, like a bridle, to curb it, so that the spirit may control it. This is done to bring it to subjection, but if you wish to make it a thousand times more subject, put the bridle of love on it. With love you may overcome it most quickly and load it most heavily.

That is why God lies in wait for us with nothing so much as love. Love is like a fisherman's hook. Without the hook he could never catch a fish, but once the hook is taken the fisherman is sure of the fish. Even though the fish twists hither and yon, still the fisherman is sure of him. And so, too, I speak of love: he who is caught by it is held by the strongest of bonds and yet the stress is pleasant. He who takes this sweet burden on himself gets further, and comes nearer to what he aims at than he would by means of any harsh ordinance ever devised by man. Moreover, he can sweetly bear all that happens to him; all that God inflicts he can take cheerfully. Nothing makes you God's own, or God yours, as much as this sweet bond. When one has found this way, he looks for no other. To hang on this hook is to be so [completely] captured that feet and hands, and mouth and eyes, the heart, and all a man is and has, become God's own.

Therefore there is no better way to overcome the enemy, so

that he may never hurt you, than by means of love. Thus it is
written: "Love is as strong as death and harder than hell." Death
separates the soul from the body but love separates everything from
the soul. It cannot endure anything anywhere that is not God or
God's. Whatever he does, who is caught in this net, or turned in
this direction, love does it, and love alone; and whether the man
does it or not, makes no difference.

The most trivial deed or function in such a person is more profitable and fruitful to himself and all men, and pleases God better,
than all other human practices put together, which, though done
without deadly sin, are characterized by a minimum of love. His
rest is more profitable than another's work.

Therefore wait only for this hook and you will be caught up
into blessing, and the more you are caught the more you will be
set free. That we all may be so caught and set free, may he help
us, who is love itself. Amen.

6. Chapters from the *Imitation of Christ*

The *Imitation of Christ*, written by Thomas à Kempis about 1425 and
revised in 1441, is probably the most attractive expression of the
devotio moderna, the new piety of the late Middle Ages which gained
extraordinary strength in Germany and the Low Countries. The Latin
of the original is at once simple, direct and appealing, and these
qualities have made it easy to translate into other languages. Next to
the Bible itself, it has remained through the centuries the most widely
read religious book among Christians of all denominations.

The *Imitation* derives its name from the title of the first chapter.
It stresses the cultivation of inner wisdom, to be achieved by shutting
out the temptations and distractions of the world and by inviting God
to speak directly to the soul. The *Imitation* is thoroughly orthodox,
but is openly critical of the scholastic theologians, who took such
great pride in fine dogmatic distinctions and subtle arguments. The
Christian will imitate Christ, Thomas believes, not by intellectual
speculation but by humbly welcoming God's presence within his
soul.

The following selection includes the first three chapters of book three. It is taken from Thomas à Kempis, *The Imitation of Christ*, trans. William Benham (New York: P. F. Collier and Son, 1909), pp. 268–71.

The Third Book
on Inward Consolation

Chapter I. Of the inward voice of Christ to the faithful soul
I will hearken what the Lord God shall say within me. Blessed is the soul which heareth the Lord speaking within it, and receiveth the word of consolation from his mouth. Blessed are the ears which receive the echoes of the soft whisper of God, and turn not aside to the whisperings of this world. Blessed truly are the ears which listen not to the voice that soundeth without, but to that which teacheth truth inwardly. Blessed are the eyes which are closed to things without, but are fixed upon things within. Blessed are they who search inward things and study to prepare themselves more and more by daily exercises for the receiving of heavenly mysteries. Blessed are they who long to have leisure for God, and free themselves from every hindrance of the world. Think on these things, O my soul, and shut the doors of thy carnal desires, so mayest thou hear what the Lord God will say within thee.

2. These things saith thy Beloved, "I am thy salvation, I am thy peace and thy life. Keep thee unto me, and thou shalt find peace." Put away then all transitory things, seek those things that are eternal. For what are all temporal things but deceits, and what shall all created things help thee if thou be forsaken by the Creator? Therefore put all things else away, and give thyself to the Creator, to be well pleasing and faithful to him, that thou mayest be able to attain true blessedness.

Chapter II. What the truth saith inwardly
without noise of words

Speak Lord, for thy servant heareth. I am thy servant; O give me understanding that I may know thy testimonies. Incline my heart unto the words of thy mouth. Let thy speech distill as the dew. The children of Israel spake in old time to Moses, *Speak thou unto us and we will hear, but let not the Lord speak unto us lest we die.* Not thus, O Lord, not thus do I pray, but rather with Samuel the prophet, I beseech thee humbly and earnestly, *Speak, Lord, for thy servant heareth.* Let not Moses speak to me, nor any prophet, but rather speak thou, O Lord, who didst inspire and illuminate all the prophets; for thou alone without them canst perfectly fill me with knowledge, whilst they without thee shall profit nothing. 2. They can indeed utter words, but they give not the spirit. They speak with exceeding beauty, but when thou art silent they kindle not the heart. They give us scriptures, but thou makest known the sense thereof. They bring us mysteries, but thou revealest the things which are signified. They utter commandments, but thou helpest to the fulfilling of them. They show the way, but thou givest strength for the journey. They act only outwardly, but thou dost instruct and enlighten the heart. They water, but thou givest the increase. They cry with words, but thou givest understanding to the hearer.

3. Therefore let not Moses speak to me, but thou, O Lord my God, Eternal Truth; lest I die and bring forth no fruit, being outwardly admonished, but not enkindled within; lest the word be heard but not followed, known but not loved, believed but not obeyed, rise up against me in the judgment. *Speak, Lord, for thy servant heareth; thou hast the words of eternal life.* Speak unto me for some consolation unto my soul, for the amendment of my whole life, and for the praise and glory and eternal honor of thy Name.

Chapter III. How all the words of God are to be heard with humility, and how many consider them not

"My Son, hear my words, for my words are most sweet, surpassing all the knowledge of the philosophers and wise men of this world. *My words are spirit, and they are life,* and are not to be weighed by man's understanding. They are not to be drawn forth for vain approbation, but to be heard in silence, and to be received with all humility and with deep love."

2. And I said, *"Blessed is the man whom thou teachest, O Lord, and instructest him in thy law, that thou mayest give him rest in time of adversity,* and that he be not desolate in the earth."

3. "I," saith the Lord, "taught the prophets from the beginning, and even now cease I not to speak unto all; but many are deaf and hardened against my voice; many love to listen to the world rather than to God, they follow after the desires of the flesh more readily than after the good pleasure of God. The world promiseth things that are temporal and small, and it is served with great eagerness. I promise things that are great and eternal, and the hearts of mortals

are slow to stir. Who serveth and obeyeth me in all things, with such carefulness as he serveth the world and its rulers?

> Be thou ashamed, O Sidon, saith the sea;
> And if thou reason seekest, hear thou me.

For a little reward men make a long journey; for eternal life many will scarce lift a foot once from the ground. Mean reward is sought after; for a single piece of money sometimes there is shameful striving; for a thing which is vain and for a trifling promise, men shrink not from toiling day and night."

4. "But, O shame! for an unchangeable good, for an inestimable reward, for the highest honor and for a glory that fadeth not away, it is irksome to them to toil even a little. Be thou ashamed therefore, slothful and discontented servant, for they are found readier unto perdition than thou unto life. They rejoice more heartily in vanity than thou in the truth. Sometimes, indeed, they are disappointed of their hope, but my promise faileth no man, nor sendeth away empty him who trusteth in me. What I have promised I will give; what I have said I will fulfill; if only a man remain faithful in my love unto the end. Therefore am I the rewarder of all good men, and a strong approver of all who are godly.

5. "Write my words in thy heart and consider them diligently, for they shall be very needful to thee in time of temptation. What thou understandest not when thou readest, thou shalt know in the time of thy visitation. I am wont to visit mine elect in twofold manner, even by temptation and by comfort, and I teach them two lessons day by day, the one in chiding their faults, the other in exhorting them to grow in grace. He who hath my words and rejecteth them, hath one who shall judge him at the last day."

A prayer for the spirit of devotion

6. O Lord my God, thou art all my good, and who am I that I should dare to speak unto thee? I am the very poorest of thy servants, an abject worm, much poorer and more despicable than I know or dare to say. Nevertheless remember, O Lord, that I am nothing, I have nothing, and can do nothing. Thou only art good, just and holy; thou canst do all things, art over all things, fillest all things, leaving empty only the sinner. Call to mind thy tender mercies, and fill my heart with thy grace, thou who wilt not that thy work should return to thee void.

7. How can I bear this miserable life unless thy mercy and grace strengthen me? Turn not away thy face from me, delay not thy visitation. Withdraw not thou thy comfort from me, lest my soul "gasp after thee as a thirsty land." Lord, teach me to do thy will, teach me to walk humbly and uprightly before thee, for thou art my wisdom, who knowest me in truth, and knewest me before the world was made and before I was born into the world.

7. A Lollard view of the world

The storm of heresies which disturbed ecclesiastical life in the late Middle Ages drew strength from a variety of sources: abuses in the Church and a crying need for reform, social dislocations and unrest, and national antagonisms. In England John Wycliffe and his followers, known as the Lollards, developed probably the most systematic attack upon the medieval Church. The following selection is from a Lollard tract called "The Lantern of Light." It was written about 1400 in English, perhaps by one John Grime. It contains a fierce condemnation of the evils of the day, and closes with a powerful and moving description of the Last Judgment. This passionate, even apocalyptic tract illustrates the emotional power which was stirring up the currents of religious upheaval in the world of the late Middle Ages.

The three churches which the author distinguishes are the invisible church of the predestined, the visible church of the present world embracing both good and evil, and the "church of the fiend," in which are placed all who do evil in this life.

The selection is taken from *Writings and Examinations of Brute Thorpe, Cobham, Hilton, Pecock, Bilney and Others, with the Lantern of Light written about A.D. 1400* (London: Religious Tract Society, 1831), pp. 182–88. The spelling has been modernized.

Chapter XIII. What is the Fiend's church, with its properties

I now speak of the third church, belonging to the devil, which is the number of those that are in bondage to serve him, according to his enticings, against God's commands.

First, we shall take our ground in the words of Ps. xxvi. "I have hated the church of malicious livers." These are they that stray away after their own desires, walking in the large way that leadeth them to hell. They will be governed neither by law nor by grace; neither will they for dread nor love cease and go from sin, because this world is full of lusts, and proffers its lovers a joy that soon passeth away; but they that seek after bliss suffer pain here. Therefore, fools without number joy with this world, as Christ saith, Matt. vii. "Enter ye by the strait gate; for large is the gate and broad is the way that leadeth to damnation, and many there are that enter by it. How painful is the gate and how strait is the way that leadeth to life, and few there are that find it." For St. John saith, I John ii. "All this world, that is, all those men and women that are overcome with this world, are set in malice; that is, burning in the fire of foul covetousness." For all that is in this world, either is the covetousness of the eye, or else the desire of the flesh, or else it is the pride of this life. And therefore this church is grounded upon the devil, in the gravel of false covetousness, as Paul saith, 1 Tim. vi. "For the root of all evils is covetousness, which some desiring, have erred from true belief, and have joined themselves to many sorrows."

The rearing up of this church is in gluttony and licentiousness, as the wise man saith in the book of Wisdom, (ii.) when rehearsing the words of those that shall be damned. And the raising of this church is pride and highness of life, as the prophet saith, (Ps. xxxvii.) "I have seen the unpiteous and the wicked raised and up-lifted as the cedar trees of Libanus, and they are the highest trees of this world. But as smoke rises suddenly, and soon vanishes to nought, so the proud are praised for a time, and presently they fall away, and we know not where they become."

The prophet speaks, (Ps. lv.) of the business and occupation of dwellers of this church. Night and day wickedness shall compass about this church upon her walls, and travail in the midst of it; and unrighteousness, deceit, and treachery have not ceased in her ways. Of this church, with this manner of building, Christ speaks in his gospel, Matt. vii. Luke vi. "Whoso heareth my words, and doeth them not, shall be like a foolish man, that hath built his house upon the gravel of covetousness and misbelief." And the rain of gluttony and lechery came down on this church, and the winds of pride blew upon this church; and these sins fell fiercely upon this church and drove it down, and her fall was great, for she fell from grace and glory to pain and mischief without end. As St. Augustine saith, "That is not the body of the Lord which shall not be with him without end; for hypocrites are not said to be with him, though they seem to be in his church."

Certainly the devil is head of all the wicked, which are in some manner his body, to go with him into the torment of everlasting fire. For when they took baptism they promised faith and truth to keep God's commands, as the prophet saith, speaking in the person of all the general church, Ps. cxix. "Lord, I have sworn and ordained to keep thy commandments." Upon this covenant Christ took them to his marriage; and with the ring of steadfast faith he solemnized his holy spousal. But now they leave this chaste love, our Lord Jesus Christ, in breaking this covenant, and have chosen the fiend, who is a spouse-breaker. For St. John Chrysostom saith, "Every soul either is Christ's spouse, or an adulteress of the devil." For Christ and the devil may in no wise rest together in man's soul; for they are so contrary, that whatever the one biddeth, the other forbiddeth. Christ seeketh salvation, the fiend damnation; Christ loveth virtue, the fiend loveth sin; Christ gathereth together, the fiend scattereth abroad. As Paul saith, 2 Cor. vi. "What participation of righteousness is there with wickedness? What fellowship is there of light to darkness? What communication of Christ with Belial? Or what part is there of a faithful man with an unfaithful man? Or what consent of the temple of God to idols?" Certainly none; for each of these gainsays the other according to its own working.

Now we shall tell what they are that dwell with the fiend, to serve him in his church, that is, in the temple of idols. Paul saith, 1 Cor. vi. These are vile speakers, liars, glossers, backbiters, murderers, swearers, and forswearers. As St. John saith, Rev. xxi. "To all liars, their part shall be in the pool burning with fire and brimstone, that is the second death." There are unchaste, robbers and extortioners, tyrants and oppressors. For the prophet saith, Zech. v. "There are untruth-tellers, unfaithful servants, reckless hired-men, rebellious disciples, and unprofitable laborers." For Christ saith, Matt. xxv. "Caste ye out the unprofitable servant into outward darknesses." There are all unclean men and women, as St. John saith, Rev. xxii, and as Christ saith, Matt. xxiv. "The Lord shall put his part with the hypocrites; there shall be weeping and gnashing of teeth." There are all that pray, serve or give gifts for church or spiritual benefices; all false possessioners, all mighty, willful oppressors, and all their sturdy maintainers. For St. Jude saith, "Woe to them that went the way of Cain, and were evil by the error of Balaam for reward, and perished in the gainsaying of Korah." There are the men that boose (push) out their breasts, pinch in their bodies, part their hose, crakowin (carve) their shoes, and all disguisers of their garments. There are those that nicely dress their faces, that bridle their heads with head-bands, that set above honeycombs, with much other attiring to make themselves keen to sin, and expose themselves to catch men with their lime-twigs. For God saith by the prophet Isaiah, "Because the daughters of Zion are become so proud, and come with stretched forth necks, and with vain, wanton eyes, seeing they come in tripping so nicely with their feet, I will make bald and smite the daughters of Zion." There are false law makers, God's law haters, finders of customs, destroyers of virtues, authors of sin. In this church are idolaters, heretics, enchanters, &c., and all those that believe that health may come of using God's word written, but only hanged on or carried about by man, or that so carried or borne about they are profitable to body or to soul.

There are merchants, chapmen, victuallers, vintners, changers, buyers, sellers, who use deceit in weight, number, or measure. In this church are usurers, false jurors, and all false witness bearers, as the prophet saith, Ps. xv. In this church are pleaders, lawyers, sequestrators, commissaries, officials, summoners, all such of them as sell truth or sin to take money, as is said, Ps. xxvi. In this church are auditors, receivers, treasurers, procurators, judges, all such as accept persons without a cause.

This church, when it is beaten, it waxes the harder; when it is blamed, it waxes the duller; when it is taught, it is the more ignorant; when it is done well to, it is the more opposed. And it falls down and comes to nought, when in man's eyes it seems most strongly to stand. St. Augustine saith, that Christ's church pursues evil-livers, in charity, by way of amendment. But the fiend's church pursues Christ's church in malice, by way of slander and slaying. And thus Cain, that false, envious, accursed man, slew his brother Abel, that blessed, simple, innocent man. As the expositors say, Cain was the beginning of Babylon, and Antichrist shall be the end. And Abel was the beginner of Jerusalem, and Christ shall be the ender. Ishmael persecuted Isaac, but Isaac did not so to Ishmael. Esau pursued his brother Jacob; but not so Jacob, by the counsel of his mother he fled into Mesopotamia from the wrath of his brother, till it was assuaged. Thus our mother, holy church, counsels her children to flee the malice of the fiend's church, till it be slaked, Matt. x. When the fiend's church shall pursue you in this city, flee ye to another. But this must be done with discretion, that we hurt not our brother's conscience. Christ pursued not the Jews, but the Jews pursued Jesus Christ. Heathen men slew the apostles, but the apostles slew not heathen men.

See new the frowardness of this world, that hath been from the beginning. When Isaiah, the holy prophet, prophesied and preached unto the people, they would not hear his words, nor suffer him to live. But people that rose after his death, read his books and said, "If we had lived in his days, he should not have been put to death." And yet, they slew Jeremiah, who by the Spirit of God told things that were to come, and taught them the truth. His successors took his books, and read them in their temples, and bewailed him for a holy man, that he was so slain amongst them; but they slew Ezekiel and many others more! Then the Jews, such as were scribes and Pharisees, made fair the tombs of these prophets, and said in hypocrisy, if they had been in their days, they should not have been slain. But they gave the counsel that Christ, who is the head of all saints, should be dead, with most despiteous death. The fiend's church in these days praise above the clouds Christ and his holy saints, with words and with signs; but they pursue to death the lovers of his law! And thus Christ saith in his gospel, Luke vi. "Right as ye do now, so did your fathers to their prophets in their days." And therefore, woe to you, for Christ saith, "In this world ye are rich, fat fed, laughing while pursuing others; weep ye, and make ye sorrow, for your pain shall be much in hell." Oh, these shall have a dreadful day when they are arraigned at the bar of judgment, when Christ shall rear up his cross, the banner of his sufferings!

Of the day of judgment speaketh the prophet, Zeph. i. "The great day of the Lord is nigh, and cometh fast, and wonders approach quickly; it shall not long tarry." In that day, he that is strong and mighty shall be troubled; for the voice of the Lord is bitter to the damned. That day is a day of wrath, a day of tribulation; that is a day of anger, of grief, of ruin, and of wretchedness. It is a day of darkness and of thick smoke, a day of clouds and of the raging whirlwind; it is a day of the trumpet and of hideous noise. For then they shall see their Judge above them, stirred to wrath. Then shall they see hell open beneath them, angels on their right side hastening them to hell, fiends on their left side drawing them to hell, saints approving God's doom, and all the world accusing; and then their own conscience open as a book, in which they shall read their own damnation! These wretches, beholding the great glory of those whom they despised in this world, then shall say, in the words of the wise man, (see the book of Wisdom v.) "These are they whom we sometime had in scorn and upbraiding; we foolish thought their life to be folly and madness, and we guessed their end should have been without honor. How now, for they are counted among the sons of God, and they take their lot among his saints? Therefore, we have erred from the way of truth, and the light of righteousness shone not to us: we are weary of the way of wickedness and damnation. What profit hath our pride done to us? or our great avaunt, or boast of riches? What hath it given to us? All those things are passed from us as the shadow!"

Then shall the Judge sternly say unto them, Matt. xxv. "Go away from me, ye accursed, into the fire of hell everlasting, which is ordained for the devil and his angels." Then may the soul say to the body these words, "Come, thou accursed carrion, come and go with me, for I am compelled to come again to thee, that we may go again to other shame, to take our reward, as we have deserved pain for evermore. That which we loved, now it is gone from us! and all that we hated is turned upon us! Now is our joy turned into sorrow, and our mirth into weeping. Now is our laughter turned into mourning, and all our pleasure into wailing. Nothing remaineth for us but fire, hot, burning horrors everlasting; fear intolerable, dread unspeakable, always discord without friendship, and full despair of any end!"

Strive in this life to leave the fiend's church, and to bring yourself, both body and soul, into the church of Jesus Christ while grace and mercy may be granted. Ask of him who offered himself willingly upon the cross, to save us all when we were lost. For thus it is written of the words of God, which he speaketh to a sinful soul. "Turn thee again, turn thee again, thou sinful soul; turn thee again, turn thee again, that we may behold thee," Cant. vi. 13. For God knoweth thy misgovernance, and will not forsake thee, if thou wilt turn again. As he saith in the prophet Jeremiah, iii. "Thou hast gone after many lovers, nevertheless turn thee to me, saith the Lord, and I shall receive thee, and take thee to grace."

Upon this saith St. Gregory, "Herein God showeth how much he loveth us; for when we forsake him, he forsaketh not us." St. Augustine saith, "O man, mistrust thou not the mercy of God, for more is his mercy than thy wretchedness." And thus Abner said of king David, 2 Sam. iii. "Ye that will have king David as a merciful lord to you, ye must bring with you this woman, Michal, if ye will see his gracious face." Here we consider David the king to bear the figure of Jesus Christ, and the name Michal, when it is declared, means the water, or sorrow, of all. Let us think it thus to mean—Ye that desire in all your might, to find and to have the mercy of God, and to see his gracious face in bliss, ye must have the sorrow of true repentance from your heart, with full contrition of will, never to turn to sin. And if ye will to be true, and no more to break this covenant, God will not that ye be dead, but that ye have everlasting life.